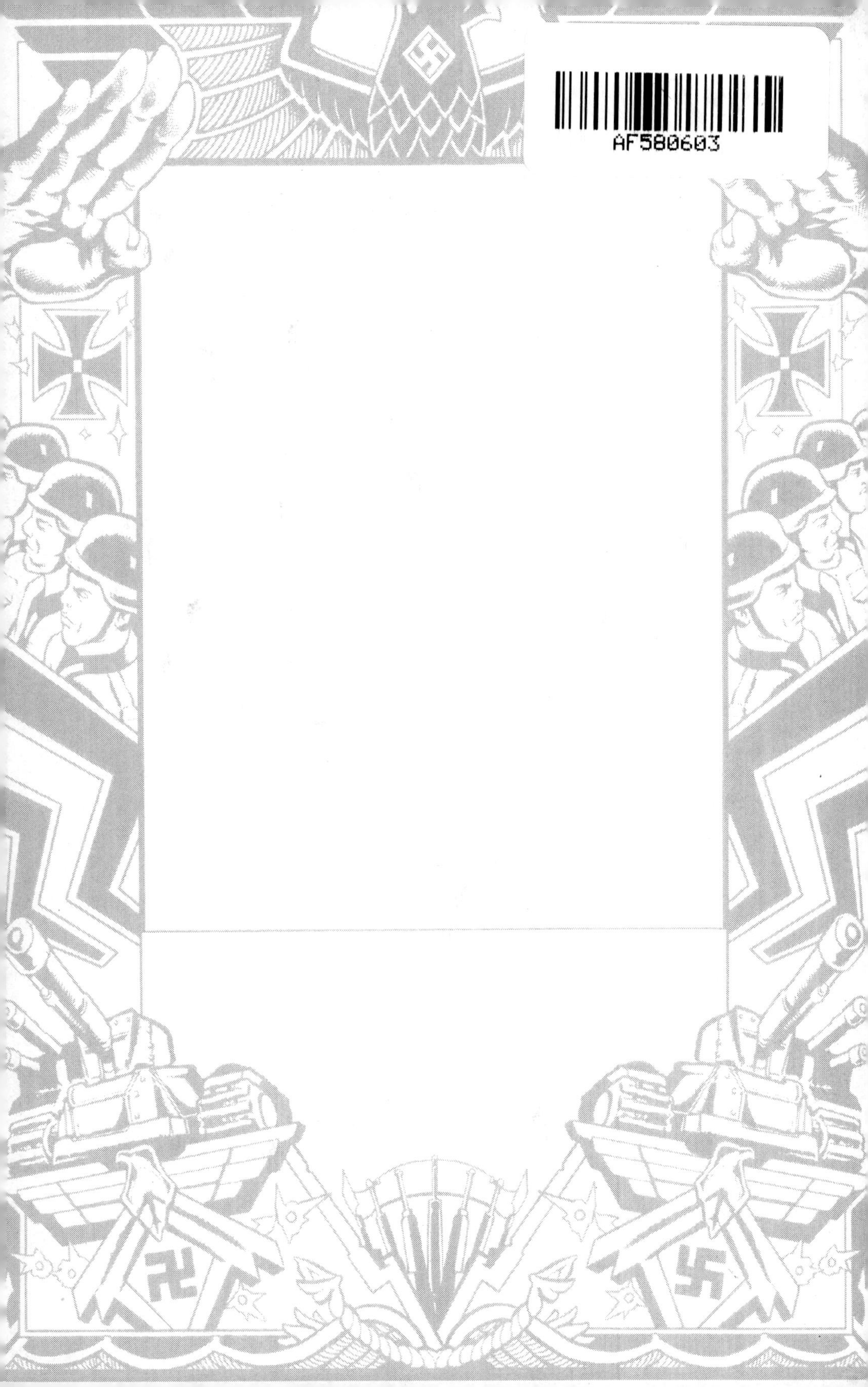

ISBN-13: 978-1492842323
ISBN-10: 149284232X

For those that still have a love of CYOA

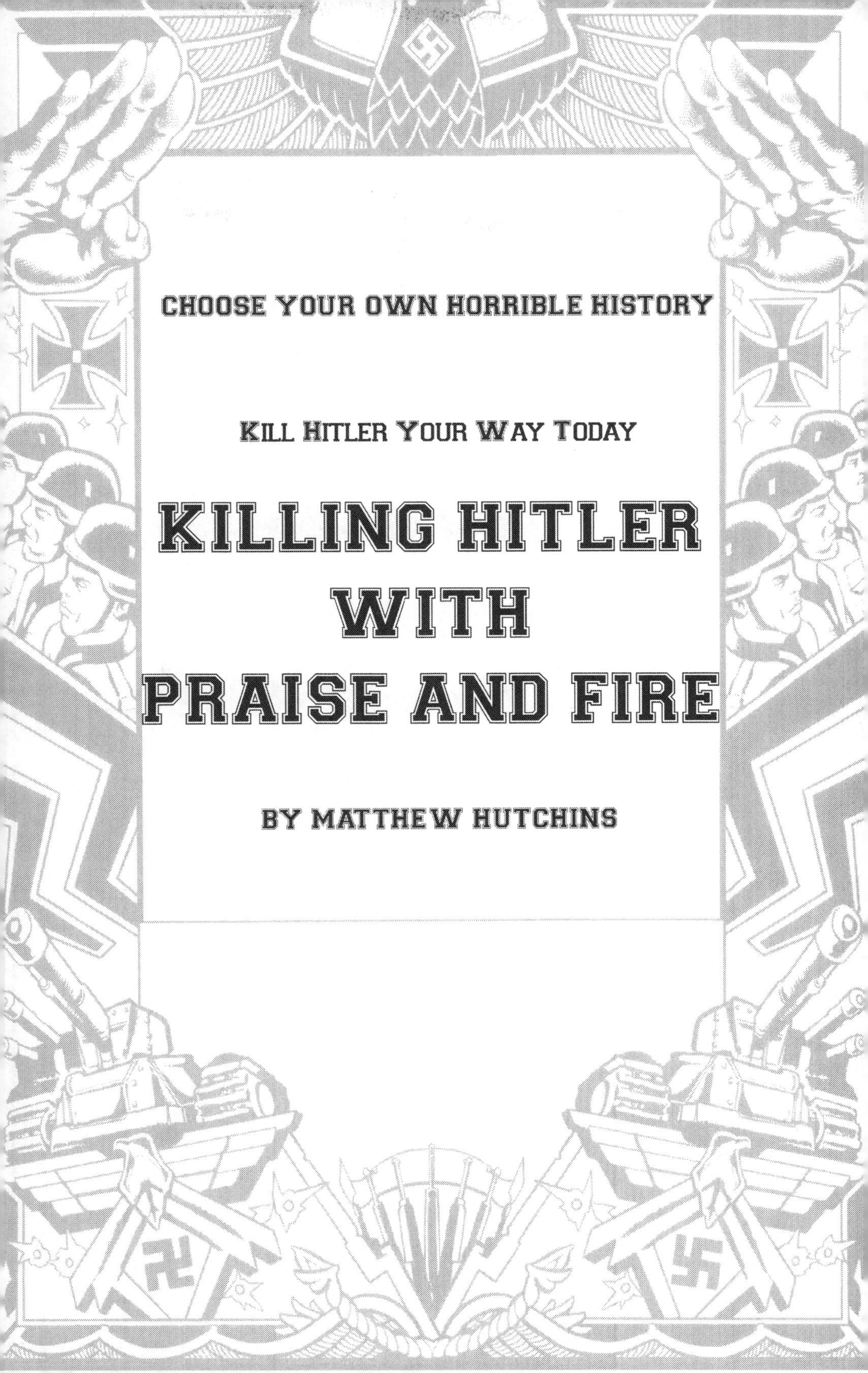

CHOOSE YOUR OWN HORRIBLE HISTORY

KILL HITLER YOUR WAY TODAY

KILLING HITLER WITH PRAISE AND FIRE

BY MATTHEW HUTCHINS

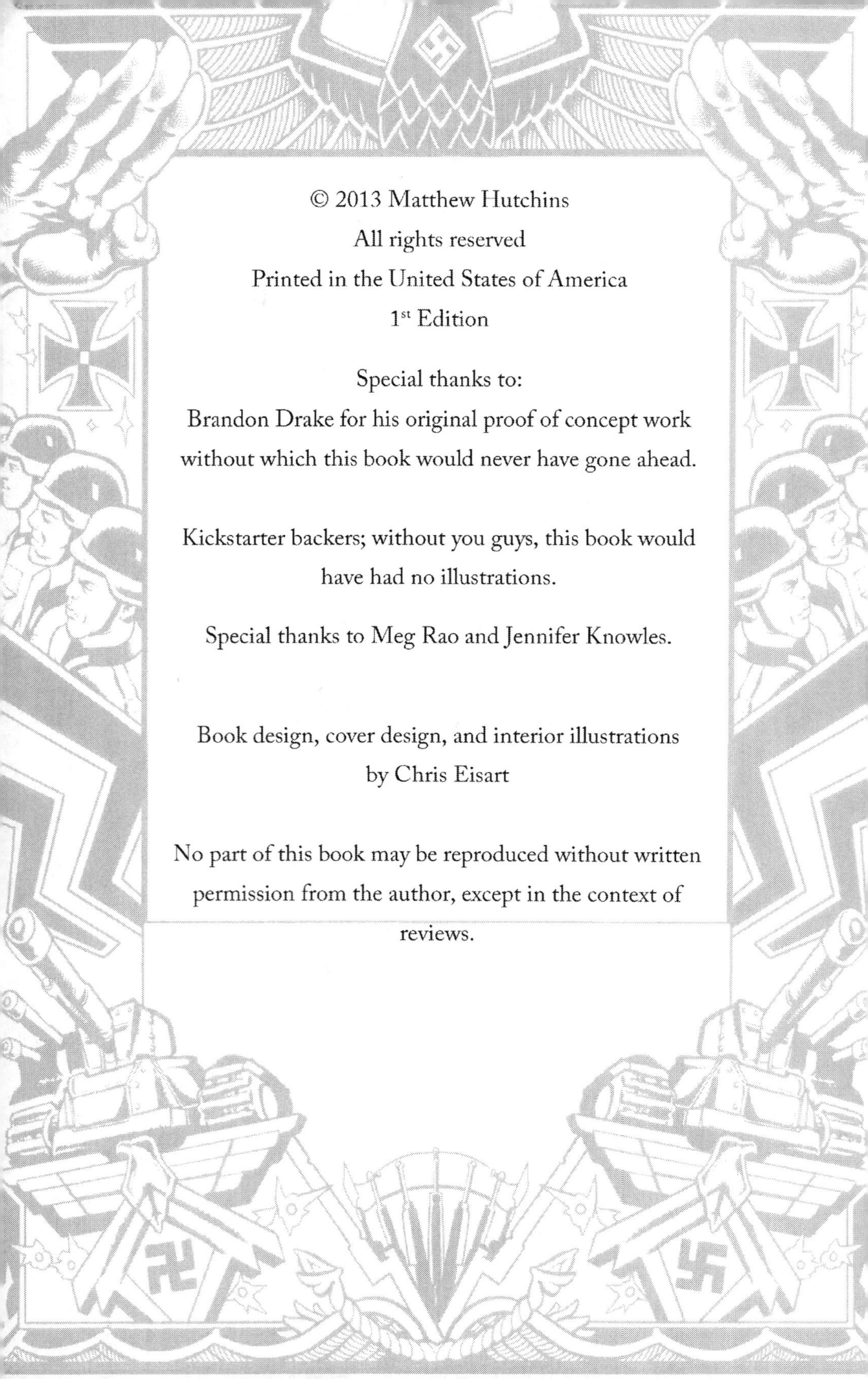

Printed in the United States of America
1st Edition

Special thanks to:
Brandon Drake for his original proof of concept work without which this book would never have gone ahead.

Kickstarter backers; without you guys, this book would have had no illustrations.

Special thanks to Meg Rao and Jennifer Knowles.

Book design, cover design, and interior illustrations by Chris Eisart

Dedicated to the future.

BEWARE AND WARNING

Warning: this is not a normal book. Do not read this book straight through from beginning to end! Every page contains different paths for you to choose throughout the story. From time to time, you will be asked to make a choice, to choose which path your character will stumble through.

Your choices will directly impact the story (usually in a rather bloody manner). Depending on the choices you make, the story will either end in glory or an early grave! As an inexperienced time traveller, you are often forced to make many often deadly decisions.

Most decisions are life and death, though some may not seem that way – I mean, what could one beer hurt? This book will test your decision making skills. You and you alone are responsible for your fate. A smart decision will end in the salvation of mankind, whereas a crap decision will end in serious injury (who am I kidding, it's always death). Enjoy.

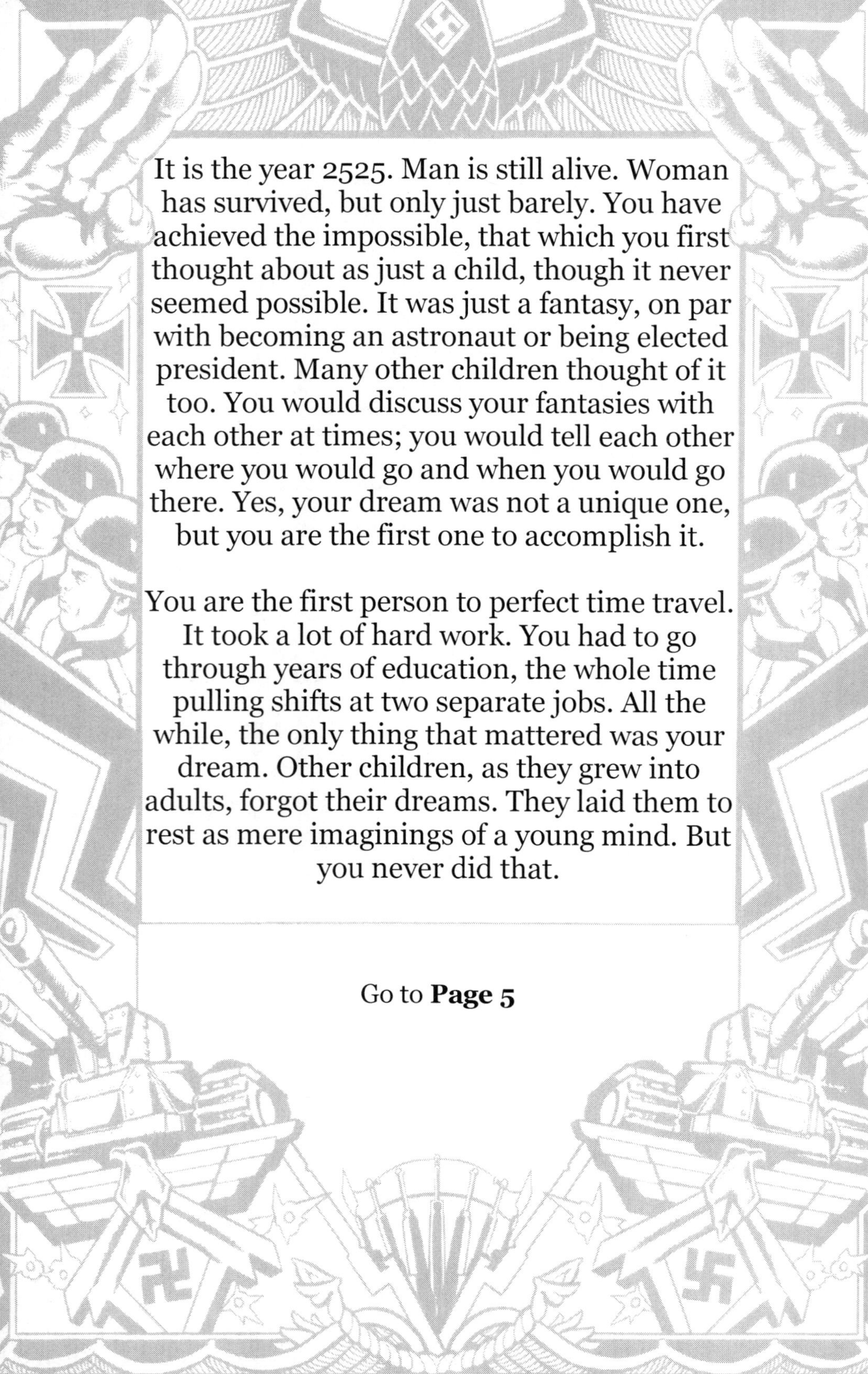

It is the year 2525. Man is still alive. Woman has survived, but only just barely. You have achieved the impossible, that which you first thought about as just a child, though it never seemed possible. It was just a fantasy, on par with becoming an astronaut or being elected president. Many other children thought of it too. You would discuss your fantasies with each other at times; you would tell each other where you would go and when you would go there. Yes, your dream was not a unique one, but you are the first one to accomplish it.

You are the first person to perfect time travel. It took a lot of hard work. You had to go through years of education, the whole time pulling shifts at two separate jobs. All the while, the only thing that mattered was your dream. Other children, as they grew into adults, forgot their dreams. They laid them to rest as mere imaginings of a young mind. But you never did that.

Go to **Page 5**

And for all your efforts, for your refusal to give up, you have succeeded. Before you is the first working time machine.
Though you initially imagined building it as a small room – or perhaps a phone booth – you soon realized that any form of enclosure was impractical.

It would require more careful calculations and locating places to stash your machine while you adventured through the past.
Instead, you opted to work on things, optimize them, and perfect them in the most compact form possible: a wrist mount.

You look down at your wrist and you see a complex array of buttons. There are numbers and letters to properly input the time and location in space at which you need to arrive. There are various odds and ends for every situation you could think of. And there is a button labeled “JUMP” that sends it all into action.

Go to **Page 6**

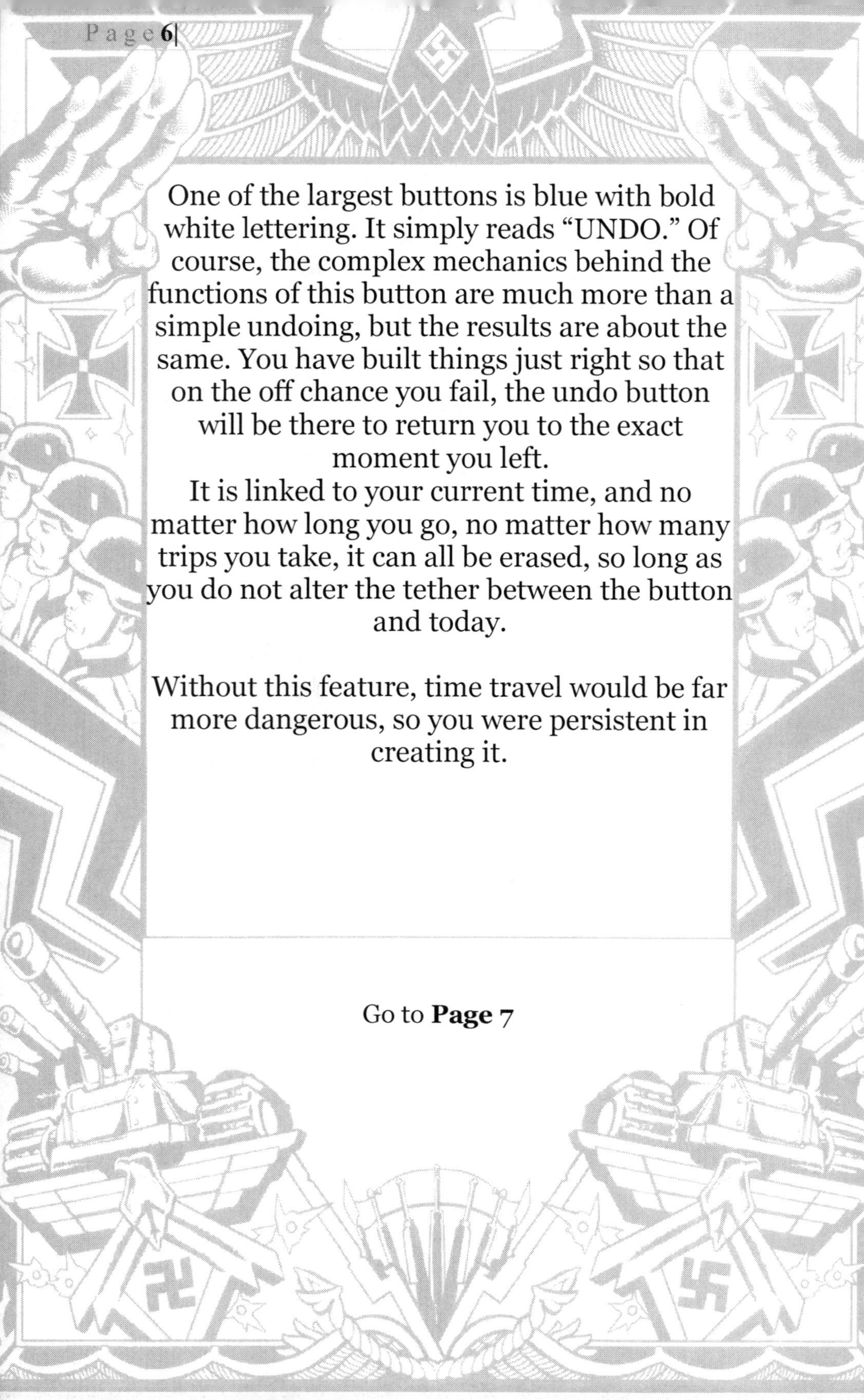

One of the largest buttons is blue with bold white lettering. It simply reads "UNDO." Of course, the complex mechanics behind the functions of this button are much more than a simple undoing, but the results are about the same. You have built things just right so that on the off chance you fail, the undo button will be there to return you to the exact moment you left.

It is linked to your current time, and no matter how long you go, no matter how many trips you take, it can all be erased, so long as you do not alter the tether between the button and today.

Without this feature, time travel would be far more dangerous, so you were persistent in creating it.

Go to **Page 7**

However, there is one safety feature even more important than the undo button. You simply refer to it as “respawning.” Again, a term that describes the result and not the process, but you prefer simplicities in that regard. There is no button for this feature, but things have been carefully constructed so that when you die, you will find yourself in your lab, completely unharmed.

The initial testing of the respawn feature will remain your most terrifying memory for years to come.

After all of the preparation, all of the time spent planning, you have decided on your first mission. You are going to do something for the good of all mankind. You are going to do what your forefathers failed to do. In the process, you will save millions of lives. You will destroy the greatest monster history has ever known. You will kill – or otherwise disable – Adolf Hitler.

Go to **Page 8**

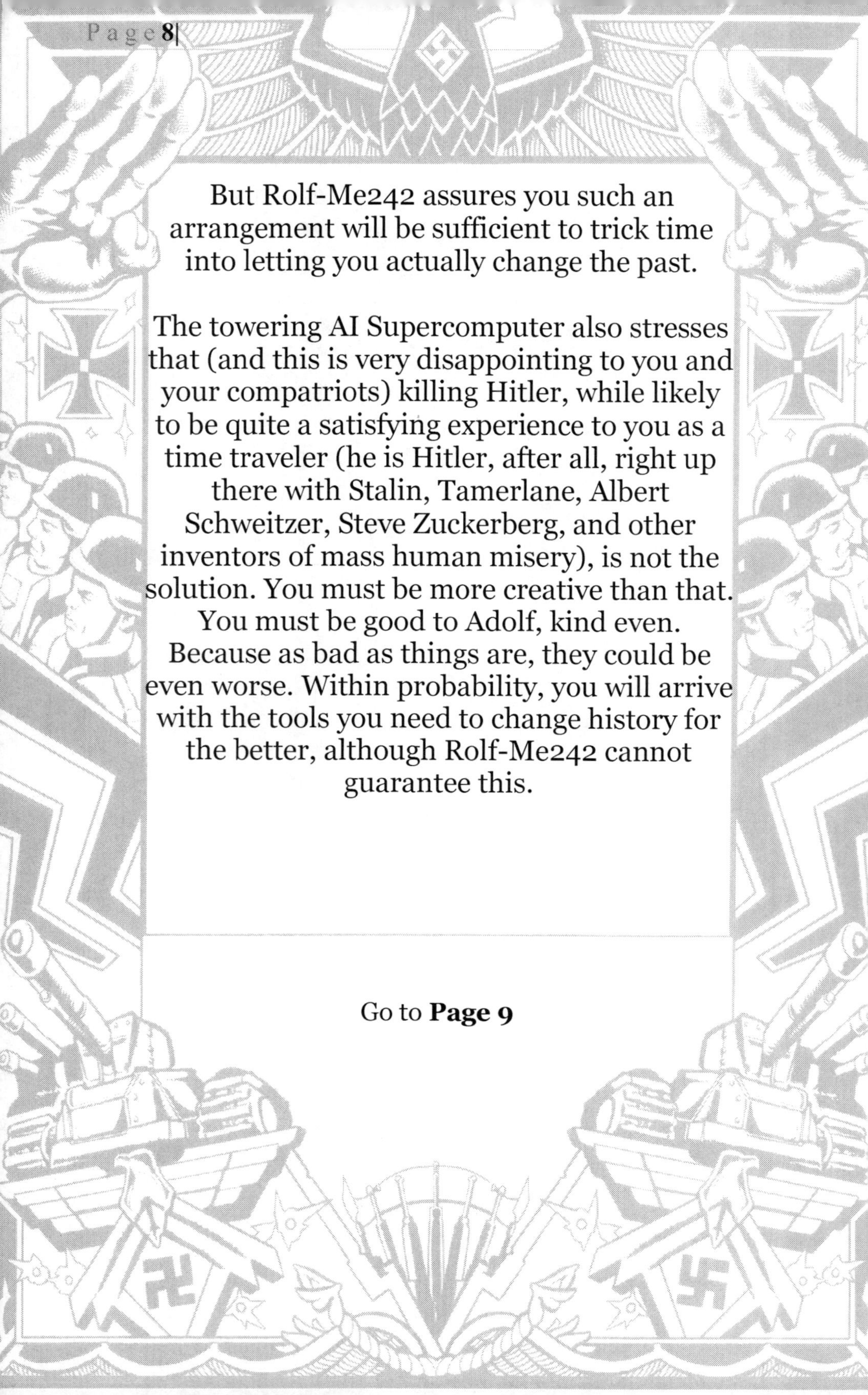

But Rolf-Me242 assures you such an arrangement will be sufficient to trick time into letting you actually change the past.

The towering AI Supercomputer also stresses that (and this is very disappointing to you and your compatriots) killing Hitler, while likely to be quite a satisfying experience to you as a time traveler (he is Hitler, after all, right up there with Stalin, Tamerlane, Albert Schweitzer, Steve Zuckerberg, and other inventors of mass human misery), is not the solution. You must be more creative than that. You must be good to Adolf, kind even. Because as bad as things are, they could be even worse. Within probability, you will arrive with the tools you need to change history for the better, although Rolf-Me242 cannot guarantee this.

Go to **Page 9**

You must use your wits, your daring, and as uncomfortable as it may seem, your compassion.

Continue if you dare…

Accept the Challenge: **Go to Page 10**

Say nuts to this ridiculous idea: **Go to Page 110**

Once you are well studied and prepared, you are led through the hidden fortress of the A.I. Rolf-Me242 deep down to a surprisingly retro looking, cramped chamber that holds the thirteen whirling mechanical portals that will lead you to the past.

All around you is chrome and riveted struts, not to mention funky round monitors in art-deco bakelite casings. Everything is streamlined. Yes, Rolf-Me242 has quite the thing for the first half of the 20th century. "Welcome, traveler," the synthetic voice of the A.I. greets you from all around. "Nice jumpsuit. Don't get used to it."

You wonder what it's talking about, but it quickly moves on to the important stuff. You can be assured that whatever portal you step through, you will arrive at an important turning point in Adolf Hitler's life. It will be as though you are a native of the time, and you will have whatever you need to complete your task.

At least, you very probably will have whatever you need; Rolf can be forgetful at times.

Go to **Page 11**

The mechanism of time travel, you have been told, is like the stretching of a rubber band. And you will be pulled back, whether you have completed your mission or not. So don't spend your time lollygagging around. You're not a tourist, understand? You are there to mess with Hitler, in the best way possible, get it?

Realizing that the A.I. is expecting an answer, you agree with it. Who wants to be on the bad side of an A.I. who has mastered time travel?

To Enter the Portal Room, **Go to Page 13**

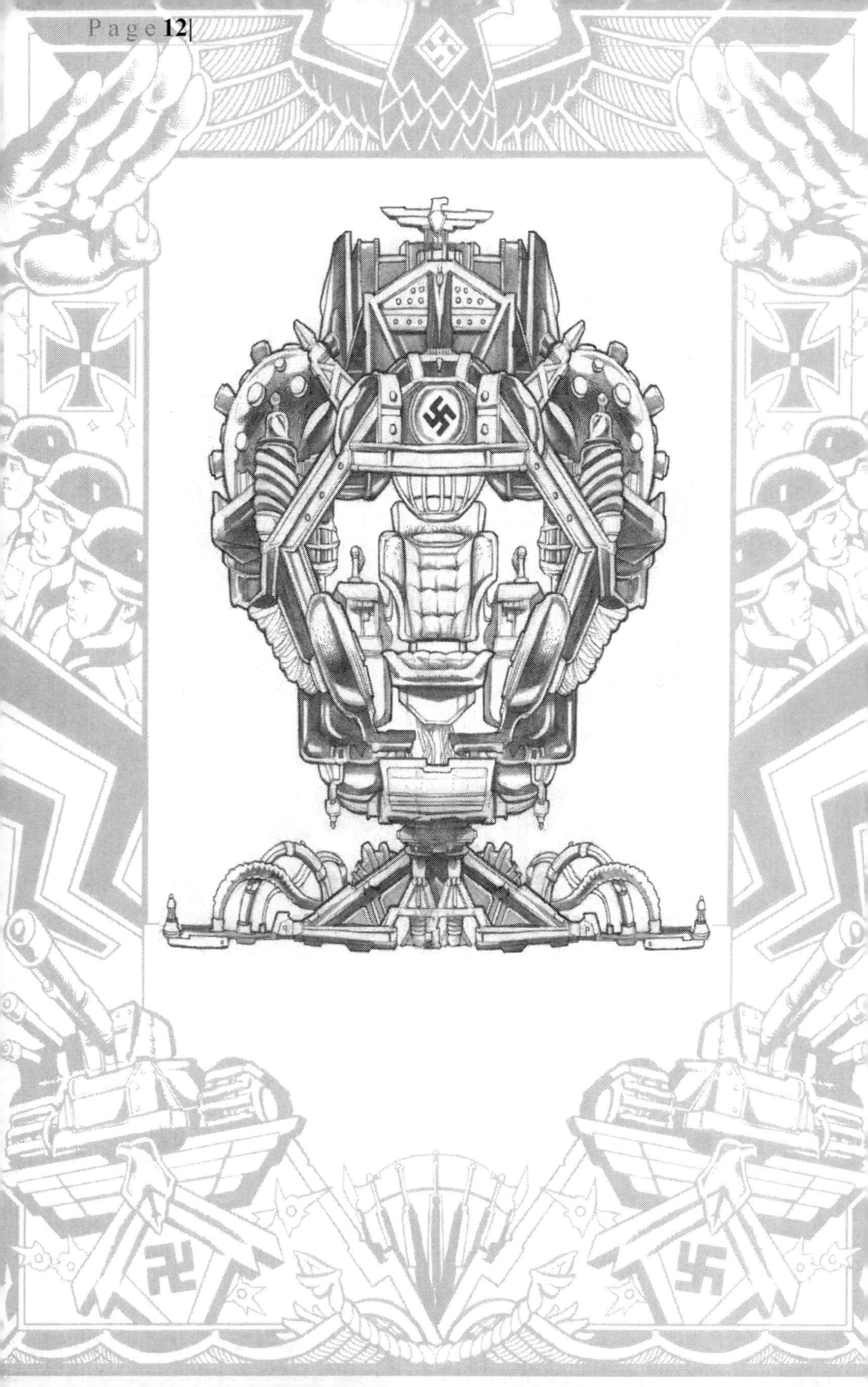

"So, volunteer," Rolf-ME242 states, "you have thirteen choices, quite a lucky number if I do say so myself. Which doorway to the past are you going to choose?"

Portal One - ??????

This portal looks pretty busted up. The date screen is a flashing red and blue.

Go to Page 111

Portal Two – 1889

Li'l Hitler

Go to Page 28

Portal Three – 1896

Alios Jr, No Home like A Hitler's

Go to Page 139

Portal Four – 1900

Measly Misadventures

Go to Page 167

Portal Five – 1907

A True Artist is Never Appreciated in Their Own Time

Go to Page 191

More Portals on the Next Page

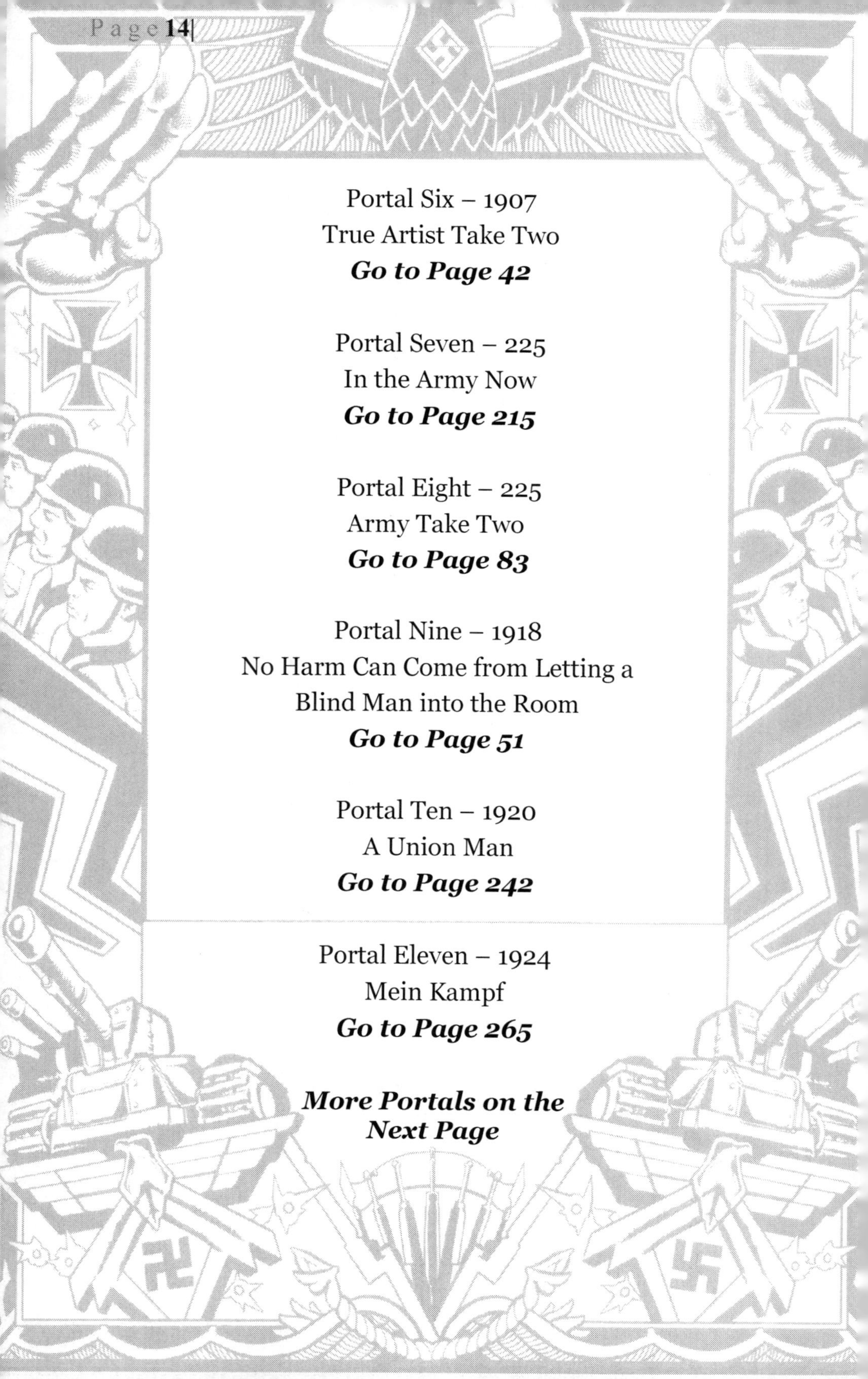

Portal Six – 1907
True Artist Take Two
Go to Page 42

Portal Seven – 225
In the Army Now
Go to Page 215

Portal Eight – 225
Army Take Two
Go to Page 83

Portal Nine – 1918
No Harm Can Come from Letting a Blind Man into the Room
Go to Page 51

Portal Ten – 1920
A Union Man
Go to Page 242

Portal Eleven – 1924
Mein Kampf
Go to Page 265

More Portals on the Next Page

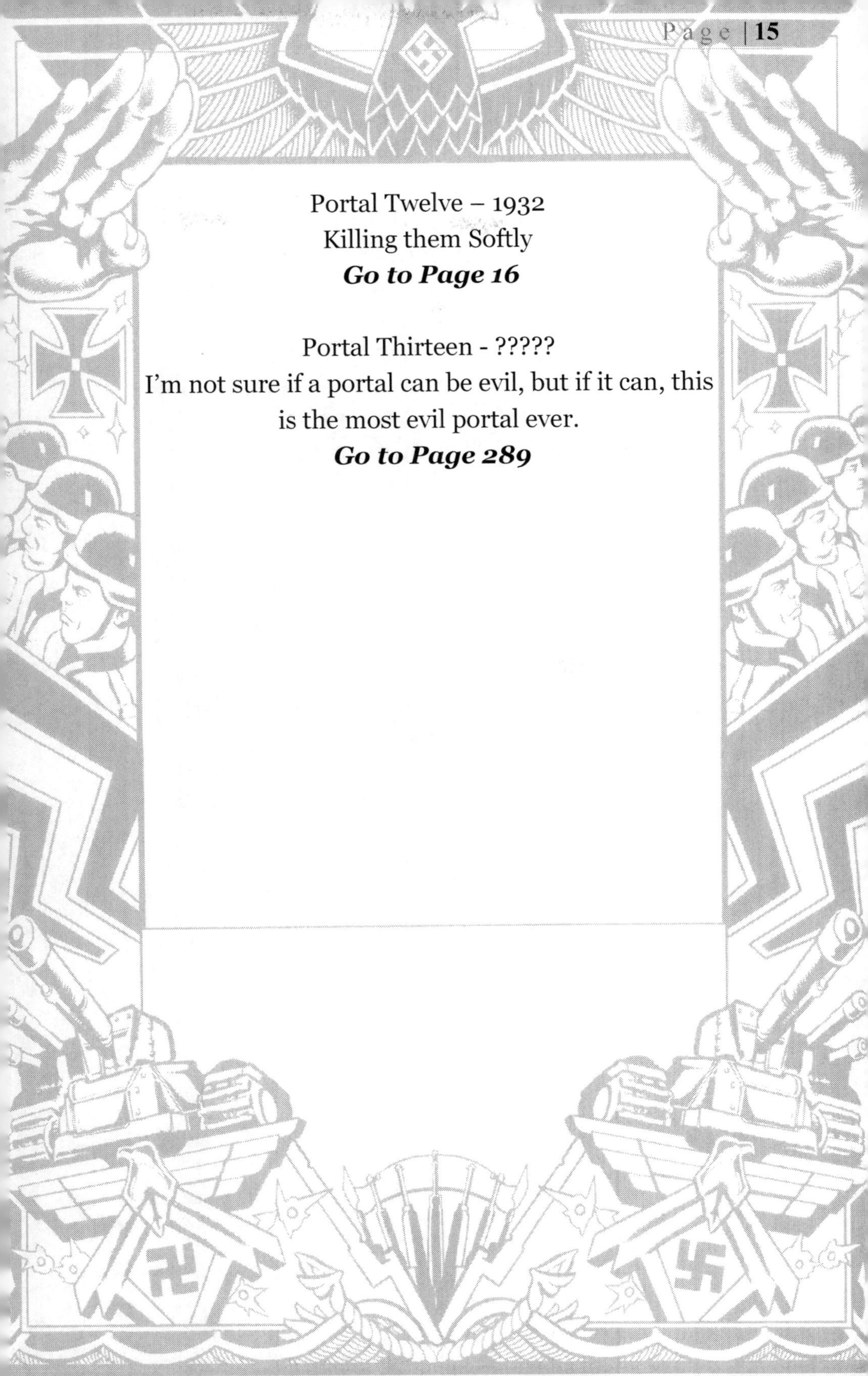

Portal Twelve – 1932
Killing them Softly
Go to Page 16

Portal Thirteen - ?????
I'm not sure if a portal can be evil, but if it can, this is the most evil portal ever.
Go to Page 289

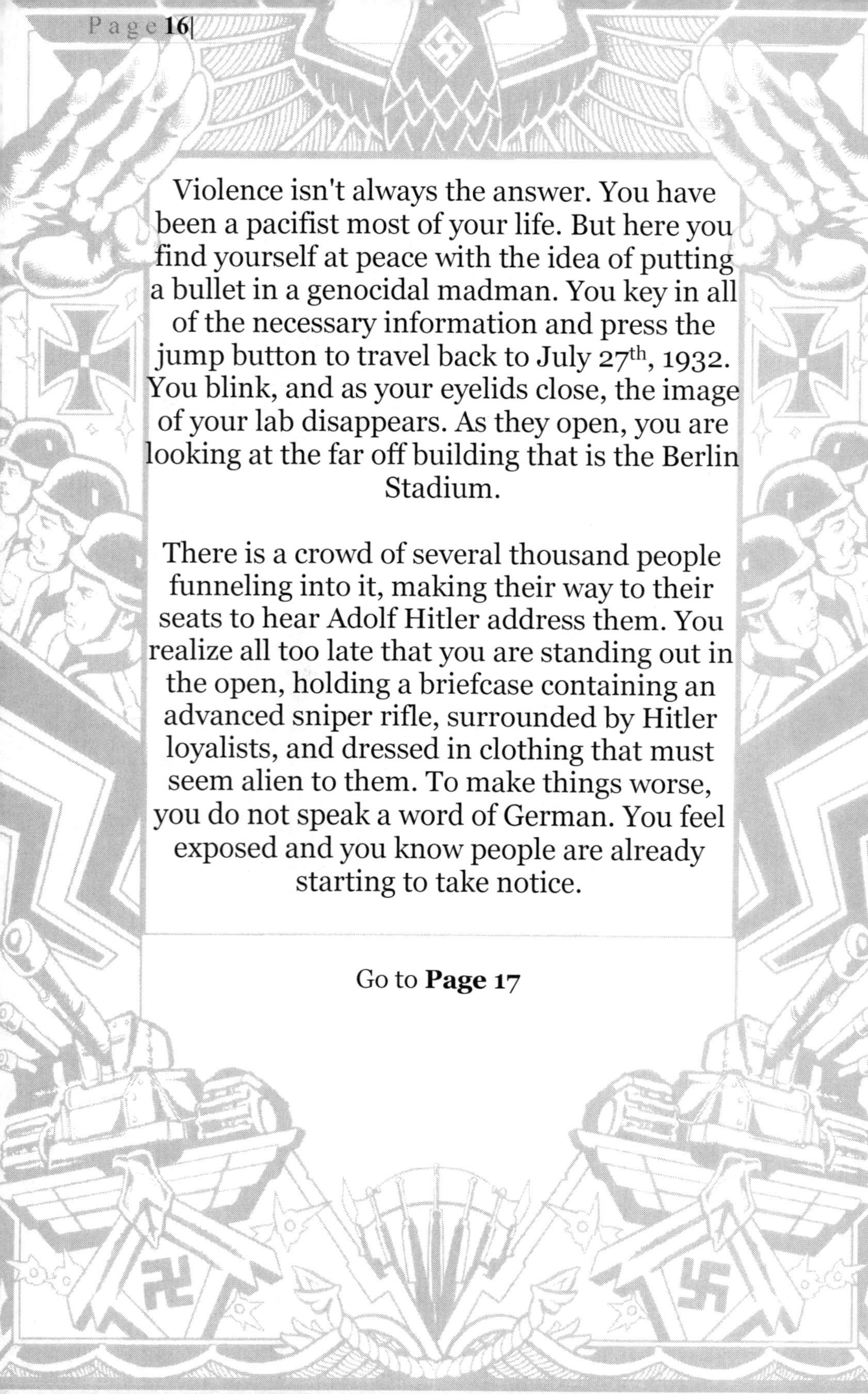

Violence isn't always the answer. You have been a pacifist most of your life. But here you find yourself at peace with the idea of putting a bullet in a genocidal madman. You key in all of the necessary information and press the jump button to travel back to July 27th, 1932. You blink, and as your eyelids close, the image of your lab disappears. As they open, you are looking at the far off building that is the Berlin Stadium.

There is a crowd of several thousand people funneling into it, making their way to their seats to hear Adolf Hitler address them. You realize all too late that you are standing out in the open, holding a briefcase containing an advanced sniper rifle, surrounded by Hitler loyalists, and dressed in clothing that must seem alien to them. To make things worse, you do not speak a word of German. You feel exposed and you know people are already starting to take notice.

Go to **Page 17**

You would make another leap through time to better position yourself, but it takes a while to make calculations, and you cannot do them in your head alone.

Go to **Page 18**

The calculations to get you to where you are now took hours in and of themselves, so you have to work with what you've got.

You are unprepared.

If you choose to duck into a nearby building to hide yourself from the crowd, go to **Page 19**

If you choose to continue walking with the crowd in an attempt to blend in, go to **Page 40**

You do not want to risk further detection, so you duck into the first open doorway. It seems that you have landed yourself inside of someone's home. The stadium is several miles away, but the crowd makes you anxious. You want to ready yourself before you reach the stadium. Looking around the room, you see a staircase, a small kitchen area, and a fireplace.

If you choose to explore the kitchen, go to **Page 20**

If you choose to go upstairs, go to **Page 21**

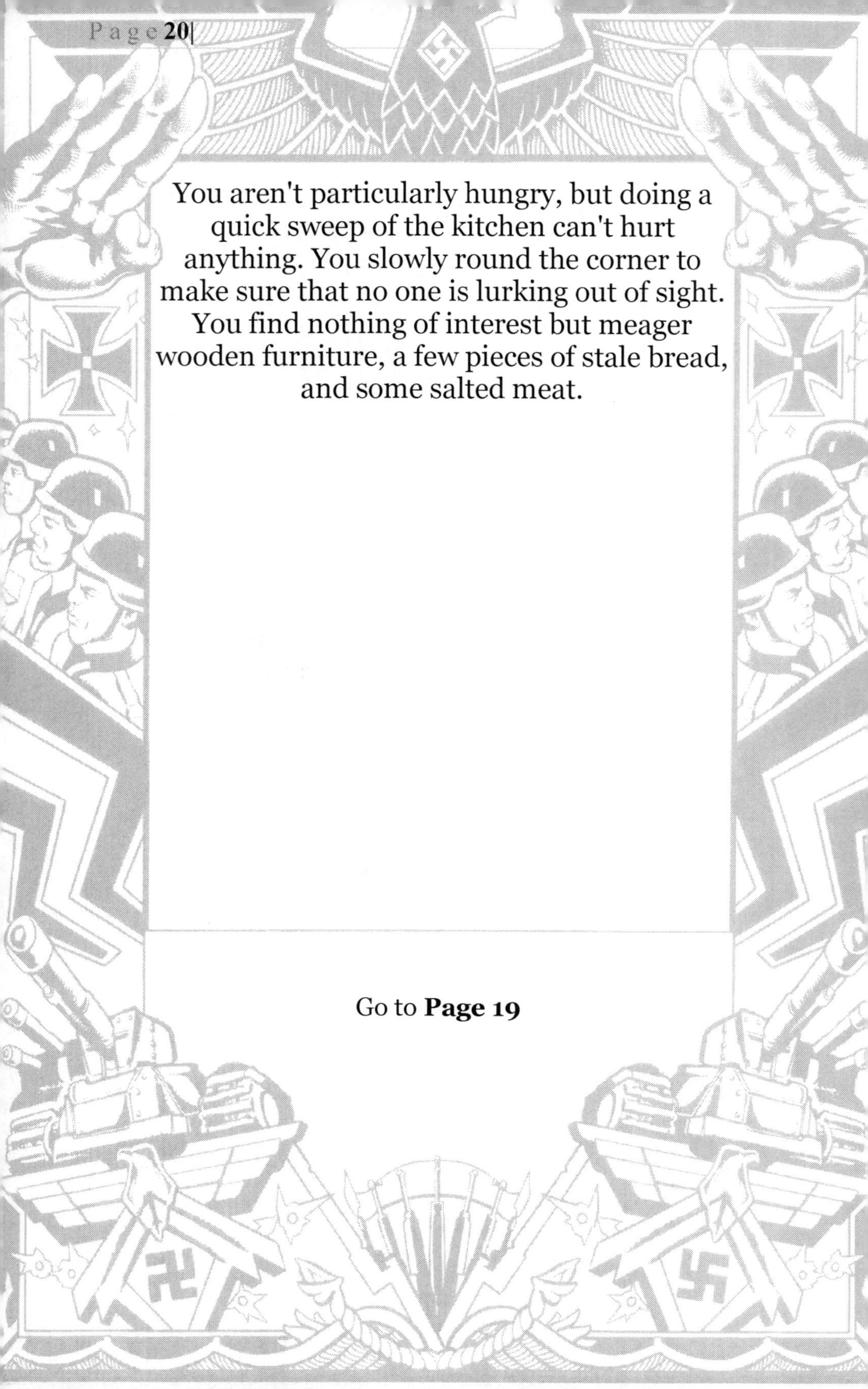

You aren't particularly hungry, but doing a quick sweep of the kitchen can't hurt anything. You slowly round the corner to make sure that no one is lurking out of sight. You find nothing of interest but meager wooden furniture, a few pieces of stale bread, and some salted meat.

Go to **Page 19**

You decide to make your way upstairs. You hope to find some clothing that is more appropriate for the journey ahead. You go into the first room you find and begin rifling through a wardrobe. Inside is a pair of trousers and a plain-looking shirt. You set your rifle case down and change your clothing. Your accessories might not fit very well into the landscape, but at least you don't stick out as sorely now.

Just then you hear a noise. You spin around to see a man sneaking up on you. You can only assume that you are standing in his house and wearing his pants. He seems none too pleased. It is then that you look down and see a hatchet in his left hand. He throws it at you, but you manage to dodge it.

If you choose to pick up the hatchet and kill the man, go to **Page 23**

If you choose to leave the hatchet on the ground and attempt to run, go to **Page 22**

You are not a violent person. Just because you intend to kill Hitler does not mean that you plan to kill an innocent man. You have already made yourself a thief. There is no need to raise your criminal status to cold blooded murderer. So you run past the man, shoving him to the side and dashing out of the room. You are almost out the front door of his home when you feel a sharp pain in your back. Just before you die, you are able to reach backwards and feel the hatchet that he buried in your back. He apparently has better aim than it first seemed.

Everything fades to black. Your mind feels floaty and dark, but you start to come around.

Go to **Page 13**

Nothing will stop you from your primary objective. You dip down, scoop up the hatchet, and return the gesture. Moments later, the owner of the home you invaded is deceased. You feel terrible for taking an innocent man's life, but you breathe deep and remind yourself that it will all be worth it in the end.

You grab your case and wait awhile for the crowd to thin. You walk outside and make the trek to the stadium. You trail behind the last of the crowd, purposely drifting off to the side. Now it is just a matter of where you will set up your rifle.

You have two real options. The first is to peek up from one of the lower staircases. The second is to climb to the top of the stadium and lay down on the very edge of the rim.

If you try to set up on the lower staircase, go to **Page 24**

If you try to climb to the outer rim of the stadium, go to **Page 25**

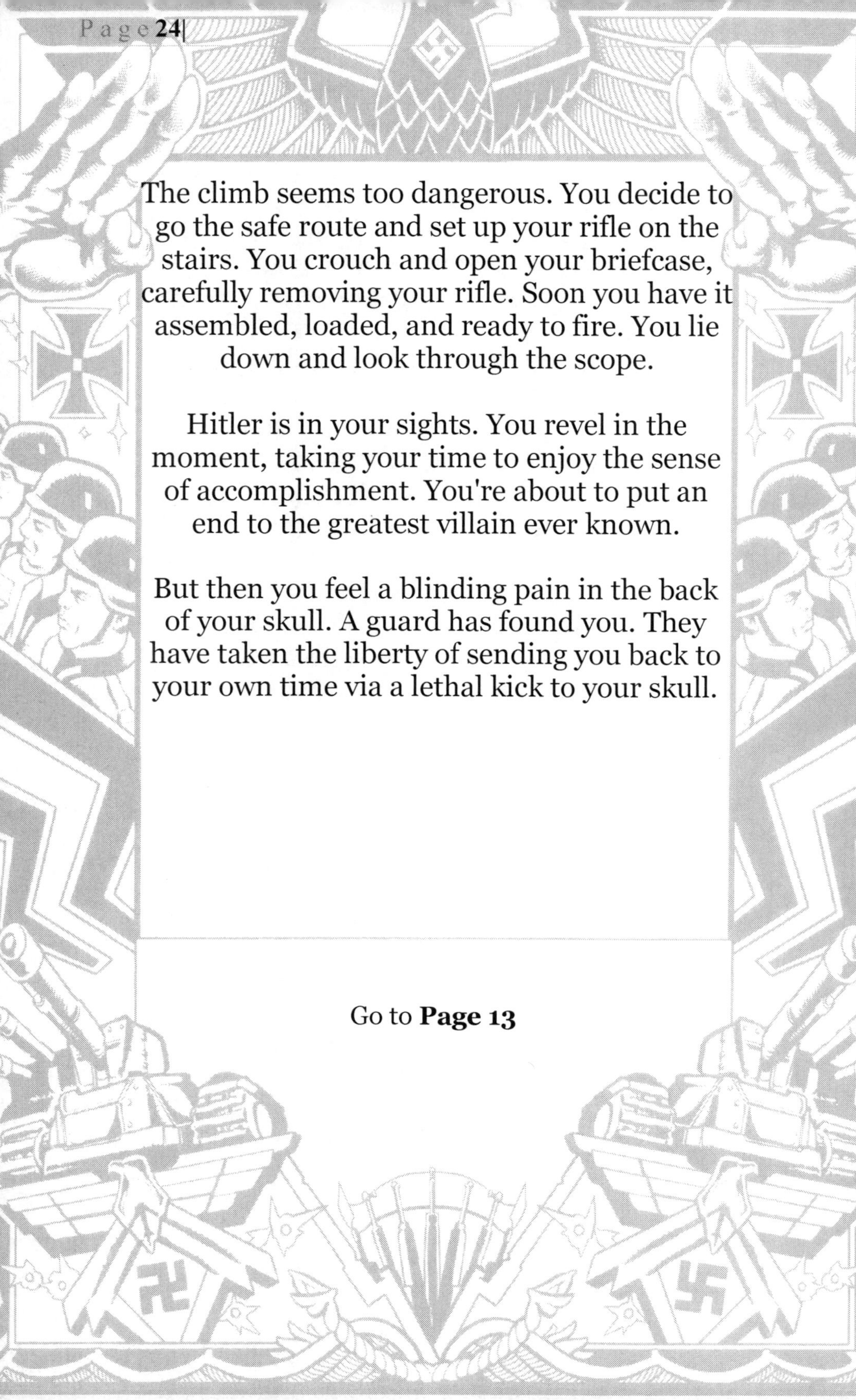

The climb seems too dangerous. You decide to go the safe route and set up your rifle on the stairs. You crouch and open your briefcase, carefully removing your rifle. Soon you have it assembled, loaded, and ready to fire. You lie down and look through the scope.

Hitler is in your sights. You revel in the moment, taking your time to enjoy the sense of accomplishment. You're about to put an end to the greatest villain ever known.

But then you feel a blinding pain in the back of your skull. A guard has found you. They have taken the liberty of sending you back to your own time via a lethal kick to your skull.

Go to **Page 13**

You risk the climb in order to better avoid security. No one wants to be caught by a group of Nazi supporters, especially a group of them that can fill such a large stadium. So you open up your case and retrieve some rope and a gear that you brought just for such an occasion.

About ten minutes later, you have successfully scaled the side of the stadium without being detected.

You do your best to assemble the rifle properly and lie down, but the ledge is narrow. Finally, you feel ready to take the shot. You get Hitler in your sights and pull the trigger.

The recoil knocks you back. You fall off the stadium and to your death. But you have succeeded. Your fall was not an unpleasant one. You spent it feeling accomplished. Soon you find yourself in your lab, and you immediately rush over to the computer.

Go to **Page 26**

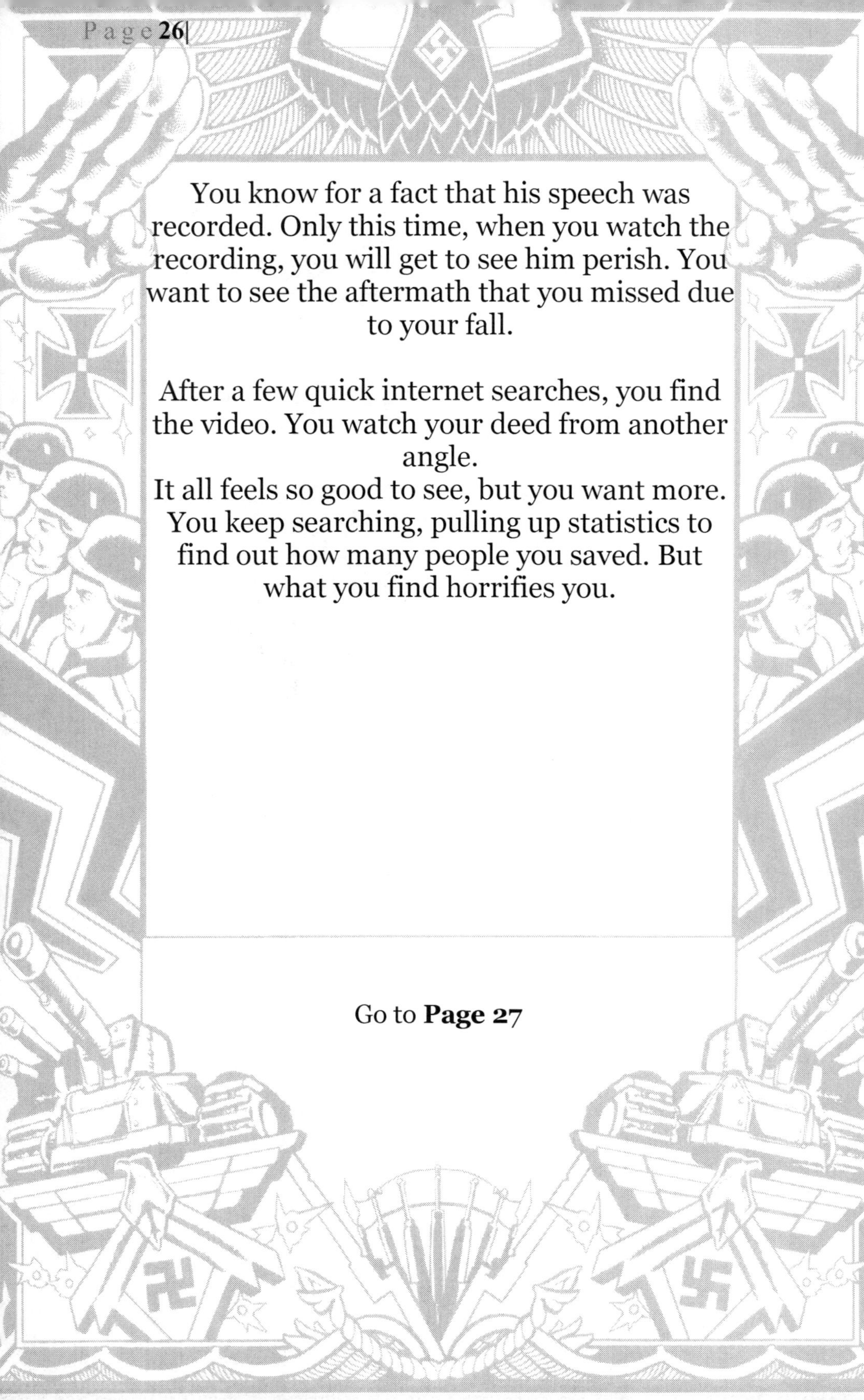

You know for a fact that his speech was recorded. Only this time, when you watch the recording, you will get to see him perish. You want to see the aftermath that you missed due to your fall.

After a few quick internet searches, you find the video. You watch your deed from another angle.

It all feels so good to see, but you want more. You keep searching, pulling up statistics to find out how many people you saved. But what you find horrifies you.

Go to **Page 27**

The man you killed to obtain clothing had a son. And his son was indoctrinated into Nazism and convinced that his father was killed by a rebellious Jew. As his son grew older, he became a politician. He soon found himself in Hitler's position. He gained power and countless followers. And he succeeded where Hitler failed. He took over the whole of Eurasia.

America escaped his conquest, but only due to a desperate, humiliating treaty that followed a partial retreat. By taking the life of an innocent man, you triggered a streak of blind, misguided vengeance that did more damage than Hitler could have dreamed of.

Your stomach churns, your heart breaks, and you look down at your wrist. With a reluctant tap, you press undo. Everything is erased; you never killed Hitler – not to mention that poor man – and you decide to try again.

Go to **Page 13**

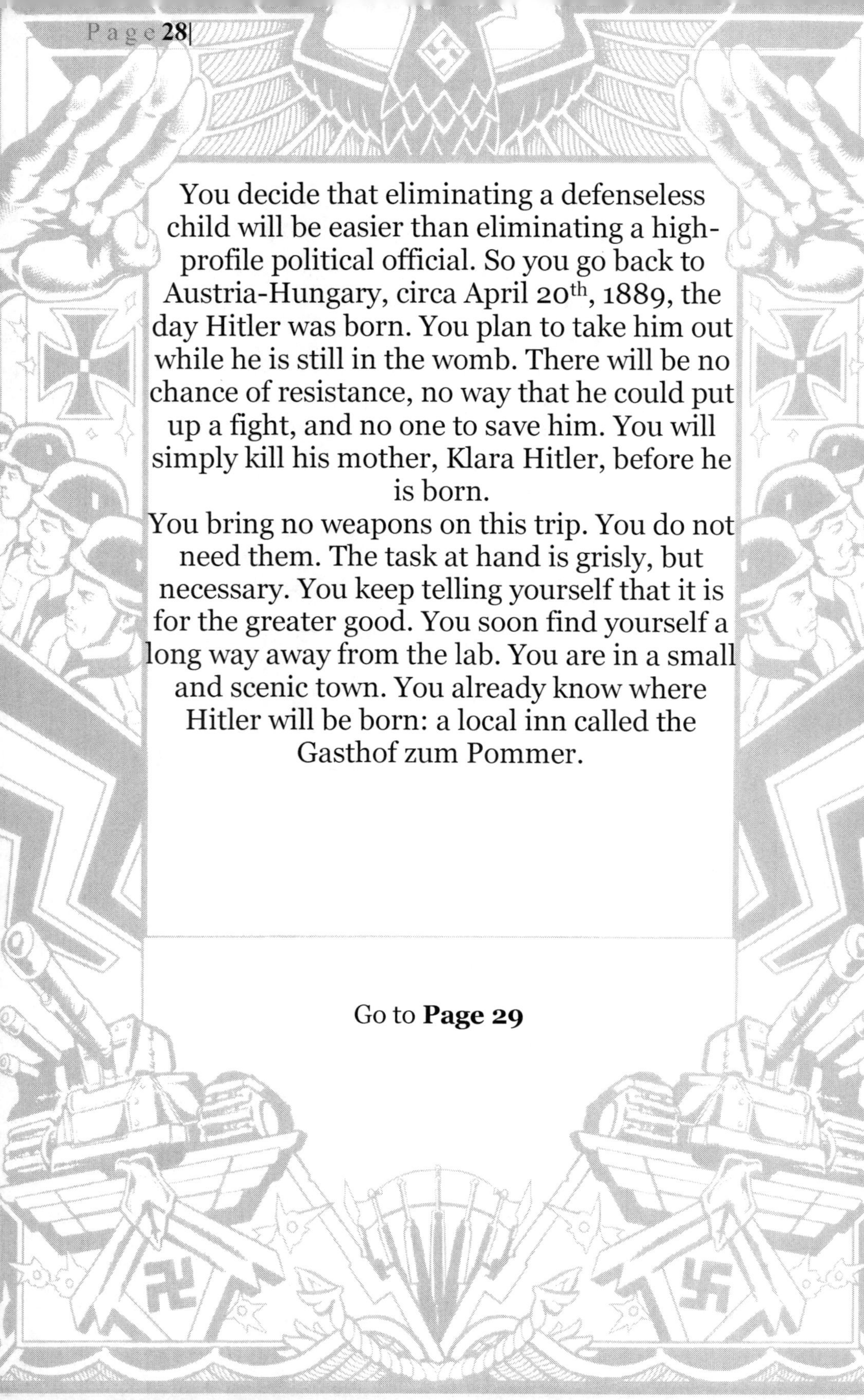

You decide that eliminating a defenseless child will be easier than eliminating a high-profile political official. So you go back to Austria-Hungary, circa April 20th, 1889, the day Hitler was born. You plan to take him out while he is still in the womb. There will be no chance of resistance, no way that he could put up a fight, and no one to save him. You will simply kill his mother, Klara Hitler, before he is born.

You bring no weapons on this trip. You do not need them. The task at hand is grisly, but necessary. You keep telling yourself that it is for the greater good. You soon find yourself a long way away from the lab. You are in a small and scenic town. You already know where Hitler will be born: a local inn called the Gasthof zum Pommer.

Go to **Page 29**

You make your way to the inn, but you are soon presented with an issue. You have no idea which room Hitler's mother will be in, or exactly when the birth will take place. This is information that you need to find out. And you need to find out fast.

You cannot speak German, so sweet talking the staff is out of the question. You'll have to get creative.

If you decide to try to stealthily check the room ledger, go to **Page 30**

If you decide to take the ledger by force, go to **Page 32**

If you decide to check rooms systematically, go to **Page 34**

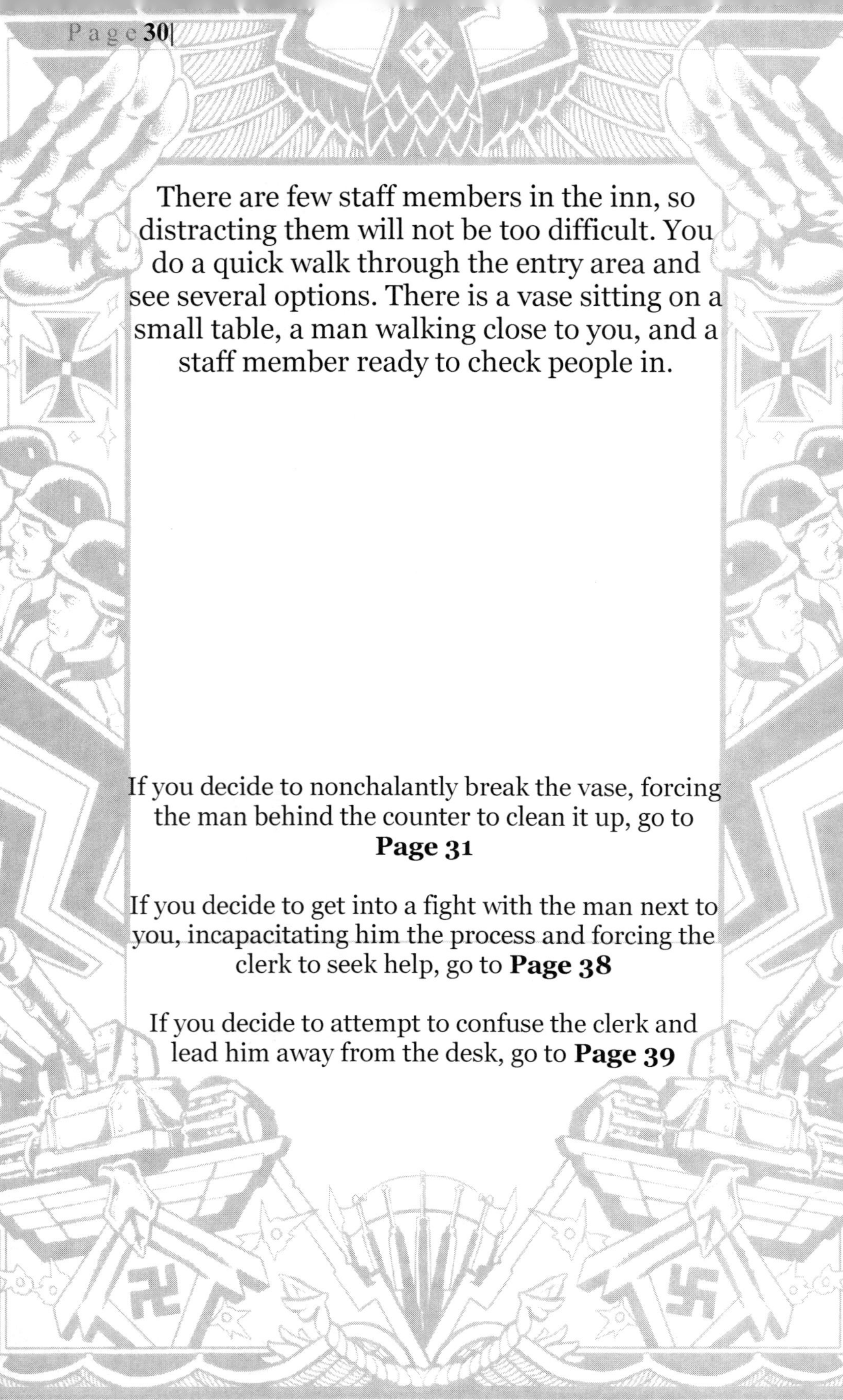

There are few staff members in the inn, so distracting them will not be too difficult. You do a quick walk through the entry area and see several options. There is a vase sitting on a small table, a man walking close to you, and a staff member ready to check people in.

If you decide to nonchalantly break the vase, forcing the man behind the counter to clean it up, go to **Page 31**

If you decide to get into a fight with the man next to you, incapacitating him the process and forcing the clerk to seek help, go to **Page 38**

If you decide to attempt to confuse the clerk and lead him away from the desk, go to **Page 39**

You casually stride over to the vase, bump into it, and keep walking. You feel smooth and stealthy, but it wasn't good enough. The clerk saw you knock over the vase, and he becomes furious. You don't understand what exactly he is saying to you, but you are soon forcefully removed from the inn. With time running out, you have to find a way back inside to assassinate Klara.

If you decide to run back in, fists up and ready for a fight, go to **Page 32**

If you decide to try and sneak back inside, go to **Page 33**

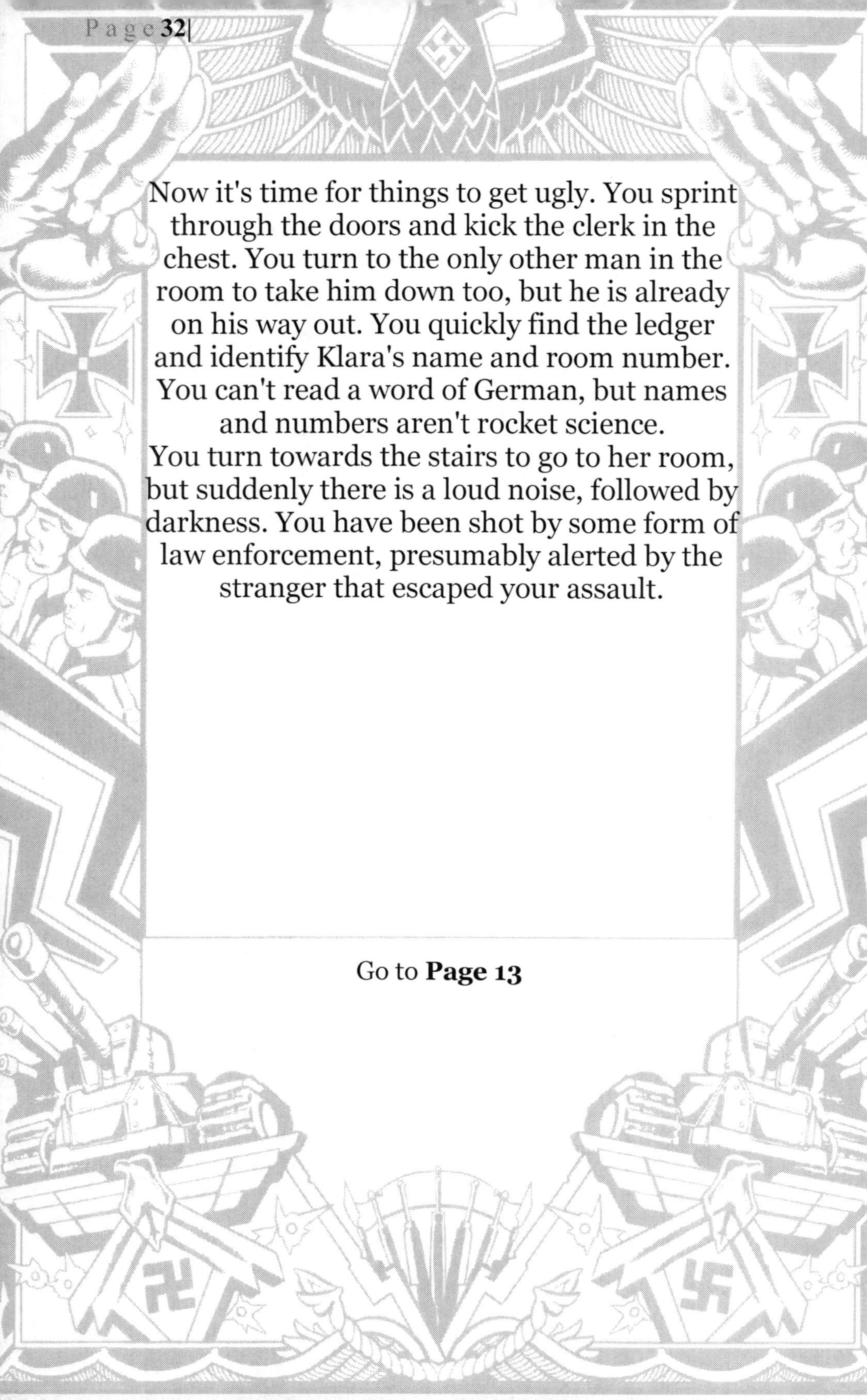

Now it's time for things to get ugly. You sprint through the doors and kick the clerk in the chest. You turn to the only other man in the room to take him down too, but he is already on his way out. You quickly find the ledger and identify Klara's name and room number. You can't read a word of German, but names and numbers aren't rocket science.

You turn towards the stairs to go to her room, but suddenly there is a loud noise, followed by darkness. You have been shot by some form of law enforcement, presumably alerted by the stranger that escaped your assault.

Go to **Page 13**

Attempting stealth got you into this, but stealth may still be the thing to get you out. So you climb a tree near the inn and hop across to the side of the building. You break a window and slide inside. You're now on the second floor of the inn.

Go to **Page 23**

Once on the second floor of the inn, you begin to check each room the best you can. You knock on each door and eye up anyone who answers. You try door after door, but you have no luck. Few answer their doors; fewer still keep the door open long enough for any significant inspection. You do not know if Klara is going to be alone, so she may very well not be the one to answer the door. You worry that she may already have gone into labor or given birth, thus making things more complex. This is due to the many simulations that have been run for the baby Hitler scenario, in which every one of them resulted in Mr. and Mrs. Hitler just have another son – Dieter Hitler – who is just *way* worse. Time is running out.

If you decide to continue your random, passive search, go to **Page 35**

If you decide to begin kicking doors in, go to **Page 37**

You keep your cool and continue to check rooms the best you can. Door after door, rejection and failures piling up, and you start to lose hope. Until, finally, a woman that you recognize answers the door after you knock.

Go to **Page 36**

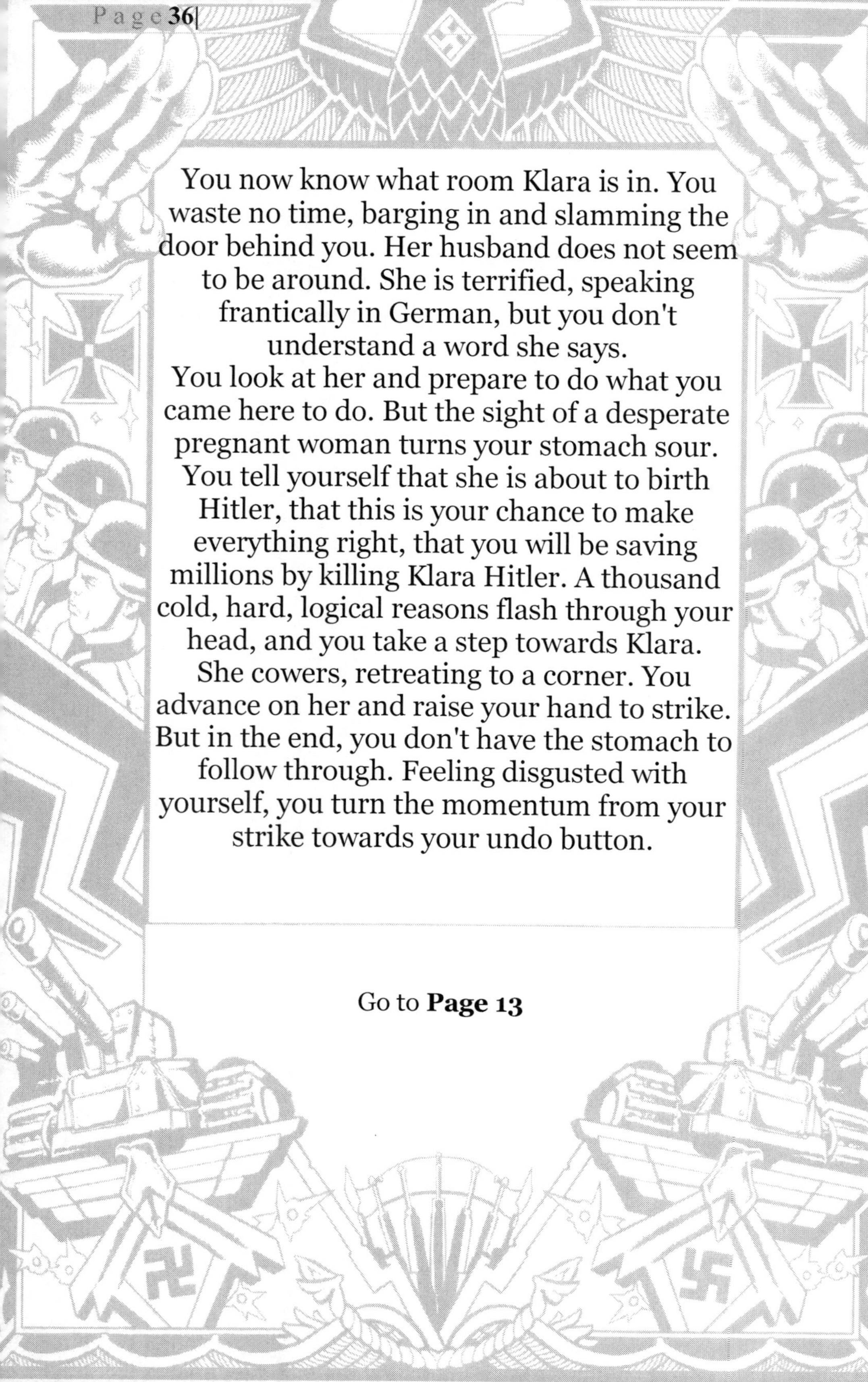

You now know what room Klara is in. You waste no time, barging in and slamming the door behind you. Her husband does not seem to be around. She is terrified, speaking frantically in German, but you don't understand a word she says.

You look at her and prepare to do what you came here to do. But the sight of a desperate pregnant woman turns your stomach sour. You tell yourself that she is about to birth Hitler, that this is your chance to make everything right, that you will be saving millions by killing Klara Hitler. A thousand cold, hard, logical reasons flash through your head, and you take a step towards Klara. She cowers, retreating to a corner. You advance on her and raise your hand to strike. But in the end, you don't have the stomach to follow through. Feeling disgusted with yourself, you turn the momentum from your strike towards your undo button.

Go to **Page 13**

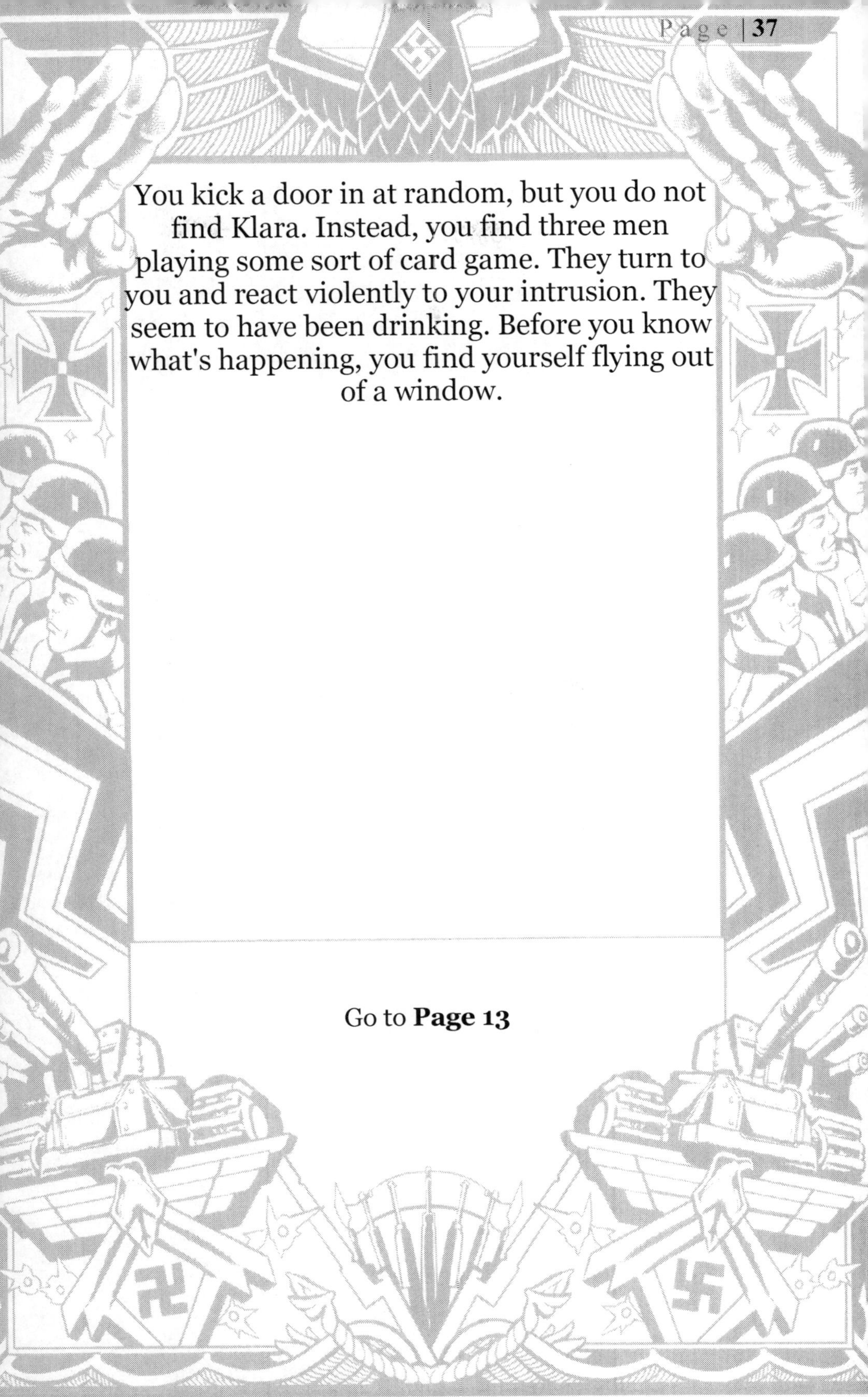

You kick a door in at random, but you do not find Klara. Instead, you find three men playing some sort of card game. They turn to you and react violently to your intrusion. They seem to have been drinking. Before you know what's happening, you find yourself flying out of a window.

Go to **Page 13**

With a swift and insanely powerful punch to the face, you knock the stranger down and dead. The clerk reacts as expected, fainting and landing with a thud on the cold, hard floor. You quickly leaf through the ledger and find Klara's room. Before you know it, you're outside her door.

Go to **Page 36**

You start yelling English and Spanish phrases at the clerk, who seems perplexed. You shout and motion for him to follow you. Reluctantly, he does. You lead him towards the inn bathroom, and point inside. He peeks in to see what it is you seem so upset about, and you shove him inside. You block the with a cabbage, trapping him.

A few minutes later, you have the ledger and Klara's room number.

Go to **Page 36**

You decide to forgo hiding and attempt to blend in the best you can. People begin to stare, though. They have definitely noticed your strange style of clothing and your weapon case. They begin to take an increasing interest. You can feel their eyes on you. You begin to feel very anxious. You are perfectly aware that death no longer means anything to you, that you have mastered it, but you know that you can still feel pain. Your panic takes over. You break into a run, and everyone is now looking at you. Soon, some of them are following you.

If you decide to hide inside a building, go to
Page 19

If you decide to attempt your escape outside, go to
Page 41

You keep running as fast as you can. Your pursuers start to catch up. They seem to be part of the military. Suddenly, you reach a dead end. They catch up and begin asking you questions in German. You have no way of responding, and you feel like they aren't going to be overly kind to you. So you quickly slap the undo button. You hear a buzz and fizzle as black smoke spirals out of the device – well, shit. You get into a scuffle with the three soldiers and accidently manage to pull the pin on a grenade. You're engulfed in a deafening boom, and then your pain is gone.

Go to **Page 13**

People always talk about how Hitler was an artist. Some speculate that his rejection from the Vienna Academy of Art was one of the reasons that he snapped. He lived in poverty, trying to survive off of his sketches, but they weren't selling well. You actually took the time to familiarize yourself with his portfolio. His work seemed pretty good, and you almost felt sorry for him. Almost.

The academy rejected him twice – once in 1907, then again in 1908 – but you want to get in as early as possible. So you aim for 1907 Vienna, Austria.

Upon arrival, you are already in the university. Your calculations were far better than you expected this time around. It is late at night and no one is around – the perfect situation. But you haven't thought too much about exactly what to do once you're inside. Maybe they have a records room of some sort.

If you decide to break into their records room, go to **Page 43**

If you decide to break into the university president's office, go to **Page 44**

You feel like there is no real alternative to the records room, so you wander around for a while, trying to figure out where it is. But you have trouble navigating the building in the dark. You need to find a light source, but you doubt that there are flashlights sitting around for you to make use of. You start to grope the walls in search of a light switch.

A few minutes later, you find one. The few bulbs in the hall flicker to life. They're dim compared to the ones that you're used to, but you weren't expecting much. At least you didn't have to go back so far that light bulbs weren't available. You cringe at the thought of exploring a strange universe with nothing but a candle.

Even with the lights on, you still can't find the records room. You begin to wonder if they even have one. But they have to keep applications *somewhere*. You need to find them and increase Hitler's odds at a gentler future.

If you decide to start breaking into every room in an attempt to find the applications, go to **Page 47**

If you decide to give up and find the university president's office, go to **Page 44**

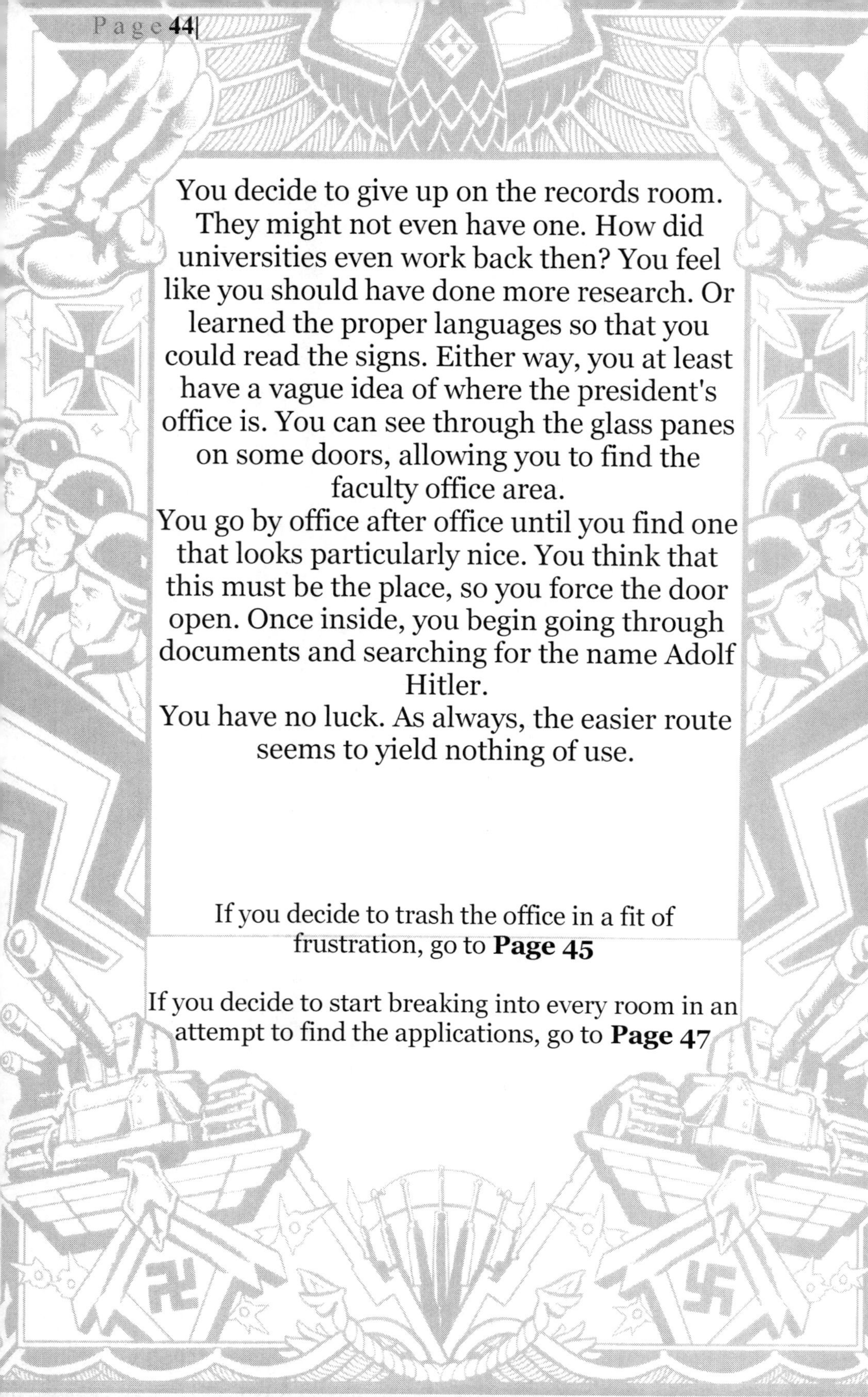

You decide to give up on the records room. They might not even have one. How did universities even work back then? You feel like you should have done more research. Or learned the proper languages so that you could read the signs. Either way, you at least have a vague idea of where the president's office is. You can see through the glass panes on some doors, allowing you to find the faculty office area.

You go by office after office until you find one that looks particularly nice. You think that this must be the place, so you force the door open. Once inside, you begin going through documents and searching for the name Adolf Hitler.

You have no luck. As always, the easier route seems to yield nothing of use.

If you decide to trash the office in a fit of frustration, go to **Page 45**

If you decide to start breaking into every room in an attempt to find the applications, go to **Page 47**

You need to let loose for a moment, so you begin to rip up every document you can find. You trash the desk, sweep everything onto the floor, and move towards the cabinet in the corner of the room. The cabinet door is locked, so you begin to pull as hard as you can. It does not budge at first, but you think you feel it start to come unhinged.

That feeling, however, was actually the cabinet beginning to fall towards you. In one harsh moment of gravity, you are crushed.

Go to **Page 13**

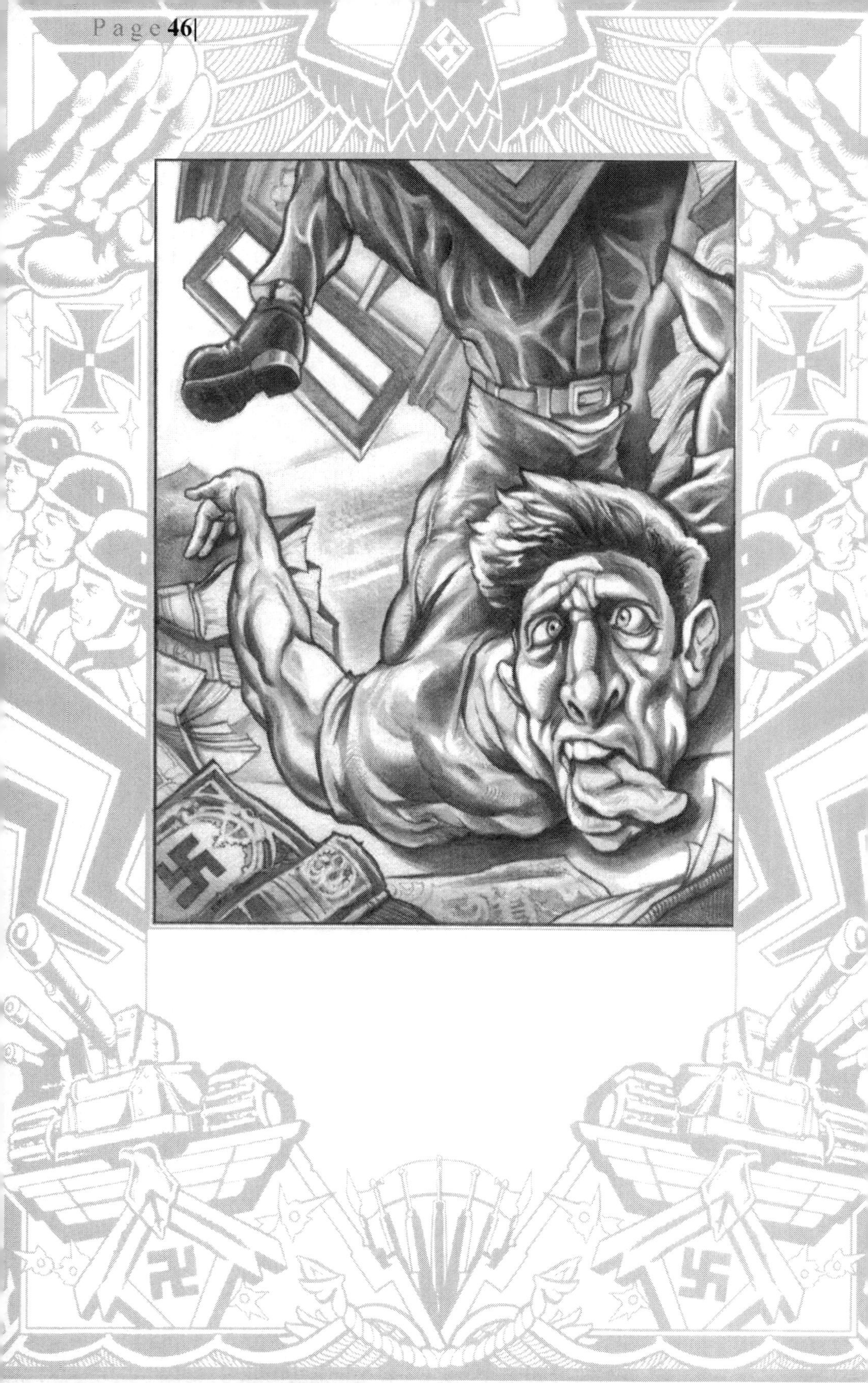

When all else fails, you start to kick down doors. Room to room you go, violently wrecking any and all obstacles. In each room you inspect anything remotely resembling a document or application. You find and toss aside dozens of unrelated pieces of paper. You search everything you find for the words "Adolf" and/or "Hitler."

Finally, after two hours of vigorous searching, you are in a room with drawers full of artist portfolios. You've finally hit the jackpot. A half hour later, you are holding in your hands the sketches made by Adolf Hitler. You recognize them from your research. But now the question is what to do with them. You begin to ponder how you can make Hitler's chances better.

If you decide to burn most of the other applications and portfolios, hopefully forcing them to accept the few they have left to keep their student body size, go to **Page 48**

If you decide to take Hitler's portfolio and place it on the college president's desk, go to **Page 49**

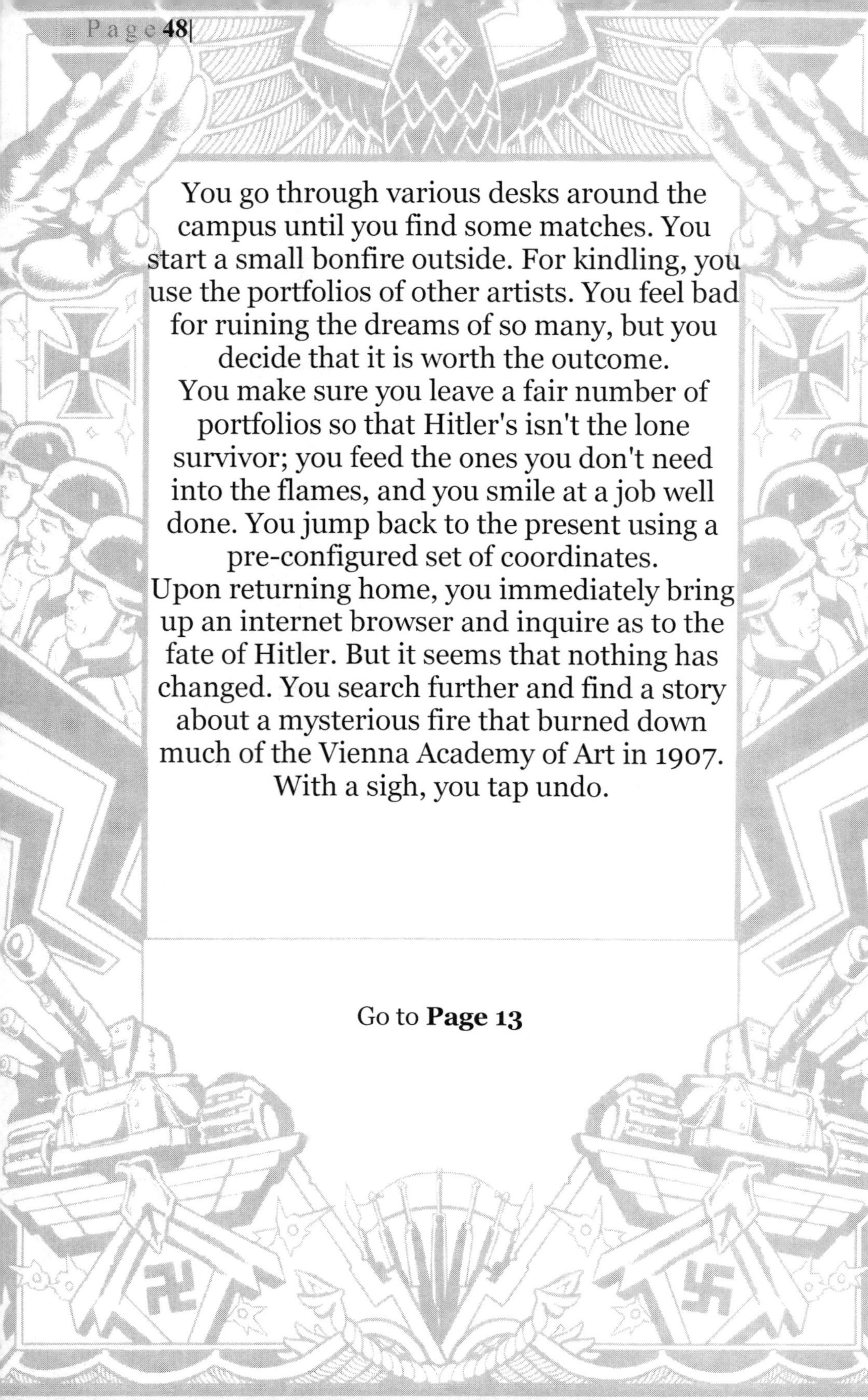

You go through various desks around the campus until you find some matches. You start a small bonfire outside. For kindling, you use the portfolios of other artists. You feel bad for ruining the dreams of so many, but you decide that it is worth the outcome.

You make sure you leave a fair number of portfolios so that Hitler's isn't the lone survivor; you feed the ones you don't need into the flames, and you smile at a job well done. You jump back to the present using a pre-configured set of coordinates.

Upon returning home, you immediately bring up an internet browser and inquire as to the fate of Hitler. But it seems that nothing has changed. You search further and find a story about a mysterious fire that burned down much of the Vienna Academy of Art in 1907. With a sigh, you tap undo.

Go to **Page 13**

You search through some faculty offices until you find one that looks presidential. You gently place Hitler's portfolio on the center of the desk. Despite his monstrosities, he did have some serious artistic talent. All you can do is hope that someone will see that before it's too late.

You make the jump to the future and you search the term “Adolf Hitler” online. You find an online encyclopedia entry for him, and you smile. The page reads as follows:

Adolf Hitler (born April 20th, 1889 – died January 16th, 1960) was an artist that specialized in portraits and landscapes. His work has been regarded as some of the best to come out of the early 20th century, and he has received an increasing amount of posthumous praise by modern day critics. He attended the Vienna Academy of Art in his youth, allowing him to refine his skills to mastery. Original works by Adolf Hitler are currently being sold in the $32,000-$79,000 price range.

Go to **Page 50**

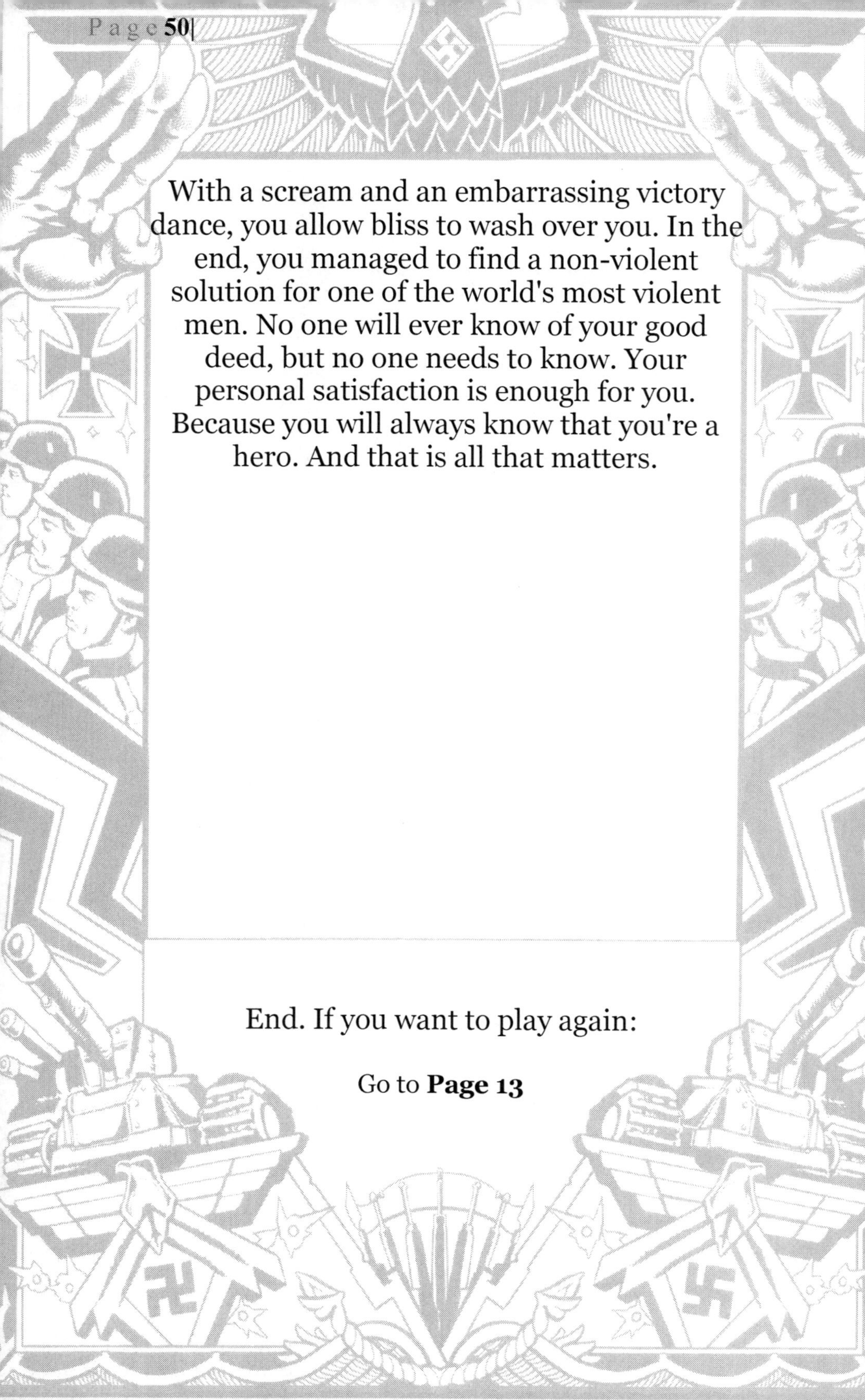

With a scream and an embarrassing victory dance, you allow bliss to wash over you. In the end, you managed to find a non-violent solution for one of the world's most violent men. No one will ever know of your good deed, but no one needs to know. Your personal satisfaction is enough for you. Because you will always know that you're a hero. And that is all that matters.

End. If you want to play again:

Go to **Page 13**

On October 15th, 1918, Hitler was hospitalized in a small German town called Pasewalk after having been blinded by mustard gas during a battle. You decide that this is the ideal time to strike. He is vulnerable and he literally won't see you coming.

You type in the necessary information, take a deep breath, and exhale in 20th century Germany. The town of Pasewalk is scenic and beautiful. You begin to explore it with caution and awe. For a few moments, you forget why you are there. Your mission almost becomes secondary.

If you want to enjoy yourself and walk around for a while, go to **Page 52**

If you set aside personal enjoyment in your hunt for Adolf Hitler, go to **Page 62**

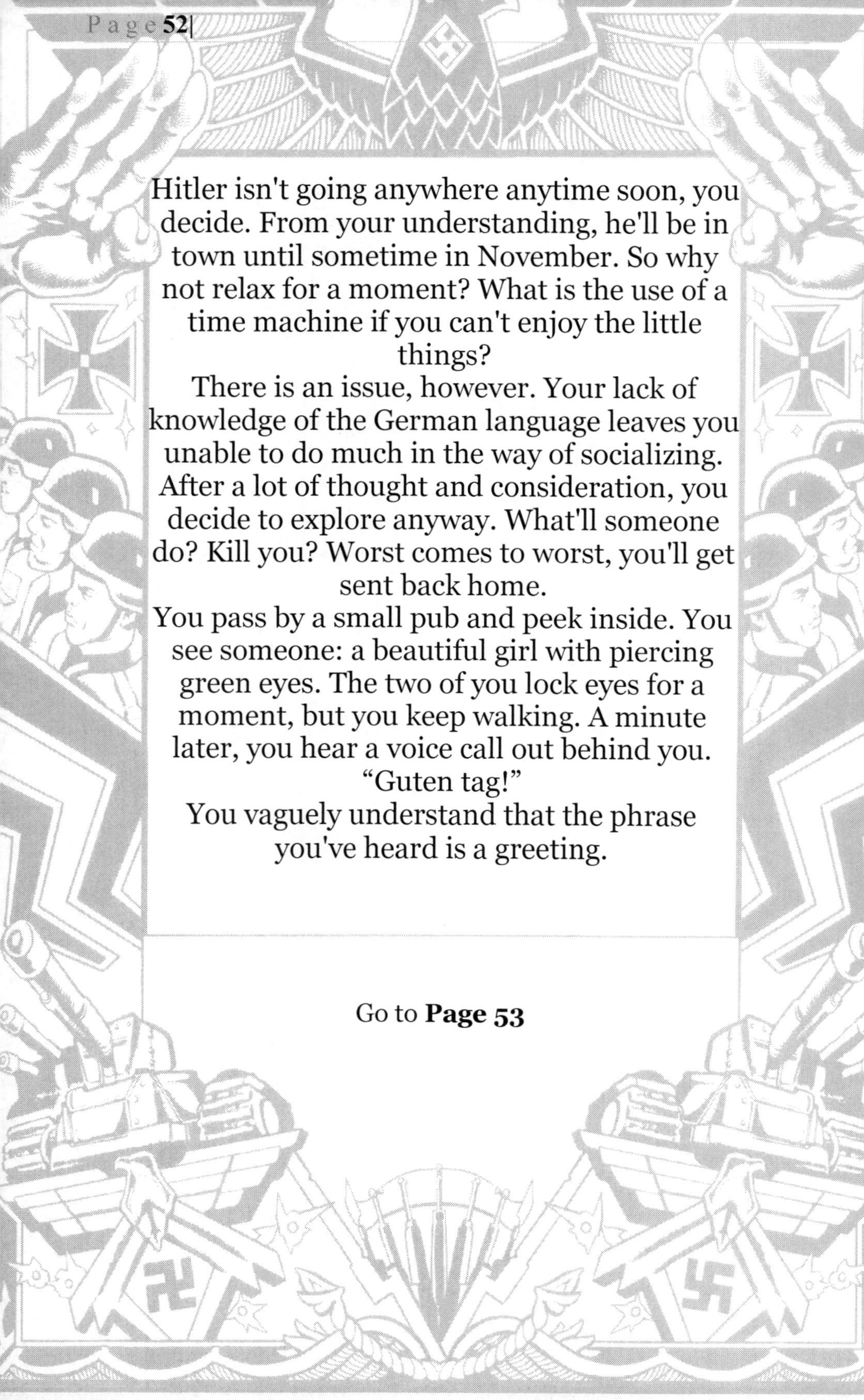

Hitler isn't going anywhere anytime soon, you decide. From your understanding, he'll be in town until sometime in November. So why not relax for a moment? What is the use of a time machine if you can't enjoy the little things?

There is an issue, however. Your lack of knowledge of the German language leaves you unable to do much in the way of socializing. After a lot of thought and consideration, you decide to explore anyway. What'll someone do? Kill you? Worst comes to worst, you'll get sent back home.

You pass by a small pub and peek inside. You see someone: a beautiful girl with piercing green eyes. The two of you lock eyes for a moment, but you keep walking. A minute later, you hear a voice call out behind you.

"Guten tag!"

You vaguely understand that the phrase you've heard is a greeting.

Go to **Page 53**

You spin around to see the girl from the pub approaching you. She begins to speak again but stops when your facial expression shows that you clearly do not understand. After a moment of silence you say – in English – that you cannot understand her.

Surprisingly enough, she speaks back to you in English. Who would have thought you would happen upon a multilingual person so easily? The two of you strike up a conversation. But there is something odd about her that you can't put your finger on.

If you decide to hang around with this strange girl, go to **Page 54**

If you decide to politely dismiss her and focus once more on assassinating Hitler, go to **Page 61**

There is no harm in making a new friend, you decide. So you begin to talk to your newfound companion. Before long, she asks you questions about your "funny looking" clothing and the strange piece of metal on your wrist. You explain that you are from America and that your clothing is typical there. Before you can respond, you realize the mistake you've made.

The year is 1918. America entered the first World War in 1917. You are, most likely, not very welcomed in this area, seeing as you are from a country that Germany is currently in a conflict with. To make matters worse, the fact that she speaks English most likely means that she knows your clothing is not typical – at least not for early 20th century America. You begin to panic.

If you choose to run, hopefully making a smooth escape, go to **Page 55**

If you think you can save the conversation, go to **Page 60**

Time to sprint, you decide. Before she can say much else, you are running as quickly as you can towards an alleyway. You round the corner and pause for a moment. You peek back to see if she followed you, but she didn't. You don't know why you felt so afraid of her in the first place, but you still feel uncomfortable for some reason.

With a sigh, you turn around to head back to the hospital, but you are met face to face with that same girl from before. It is beginning to look like you have good reason to feel afraid.

If you want to run one more time, go to **Page 56**

If you stay put, go to **Page 57**

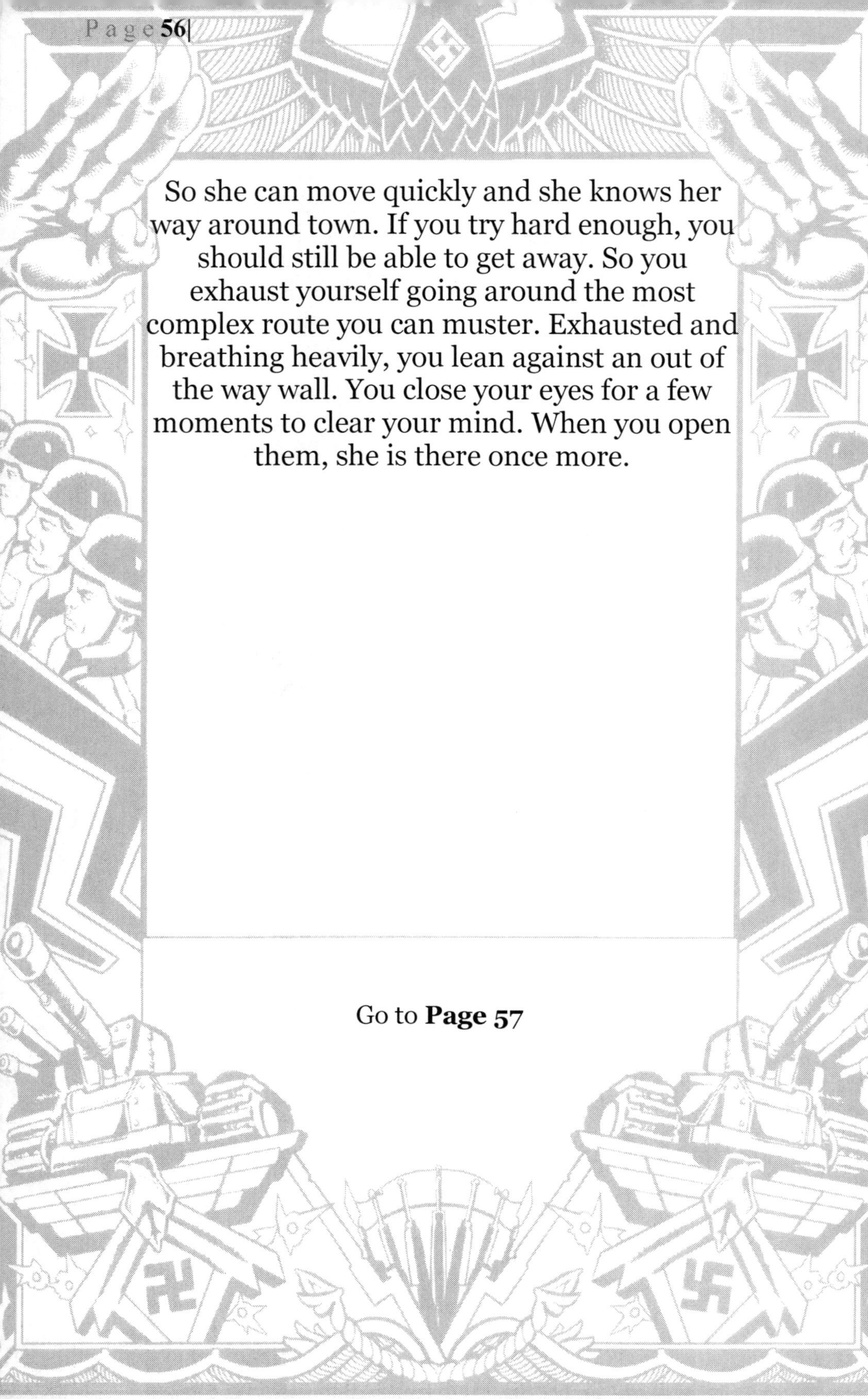

So she can move quickly and she knows her way around town. If you try hard enough, you should still be able to get away. So you exhaust yourself going around the most complex route you can muster. Exhausted and breathing heavily, you lean against an out of the way wall. You close your eyes for a few moments to clear your mind. When you open them, she is there once more.

Go to **Page 57**

Before you can speak, she tells you to relax. She has lost all traces of an accent. She pulls up her sleeve to reveal a fashion accessory that looks similar to the one on your wrist. But it's smaller, sleeker, far easier to conceal.

She calmly explains that she got it from a future you and that the version of you she got it from was far too elderly to continue your mission. She's there to stop you from making a mistake.

According to the girl – who has introduced herself as Sara – your attempt to kill Hitler is about to completely ruin everything. She says that you somehow get bested by Hitler – even though he's blind – and he manages to injure you severely enough to land you right in the same hospital. The doctors care for you out of human compassion, but when you come to, Hitler is gone. And so is your time machine.

Go to **Page 58**

You stare at her in horror, somehow knowing that she's being honest. She tells you that you built another one as soon as you could, that you traveled back to the future to try and find yourself, but that you were too afraid to make direct contact. Time paradoxes and complex existential issues prevented future you from trying that.

And sending her to a point in time where she was already alive was just as dangerous. So sending her back was the next best thing.

Go to **Page 59**

With Sara's help, you find the hospital and burn it down. You feel remorse about the innocent lives lost, but Sara assures you it's worth it. Then, a few minutes later, she blinks out of sight. Did she cease to exist? Did she travel home? You feel dizzy and sick, as if reality is warping around you. You quickly make the jump back to the present day. When you get back home, you try to look her up. You eventually learn that she never came to exist in your timeline. You managed to kill Hitler successfully, but you never shake the sickly feeling that came about you afterwards. Your entire life becomes strange. You contemplate the finer points of reality. You have trouble sleeping because of how maddening it all is. Does she still exist somewhere? Are you creating multiple dimensions with every leap through time? You completed your mission at a great personal cost. You will never rest easy again. In the end, only you can decide if it was worth it.

END

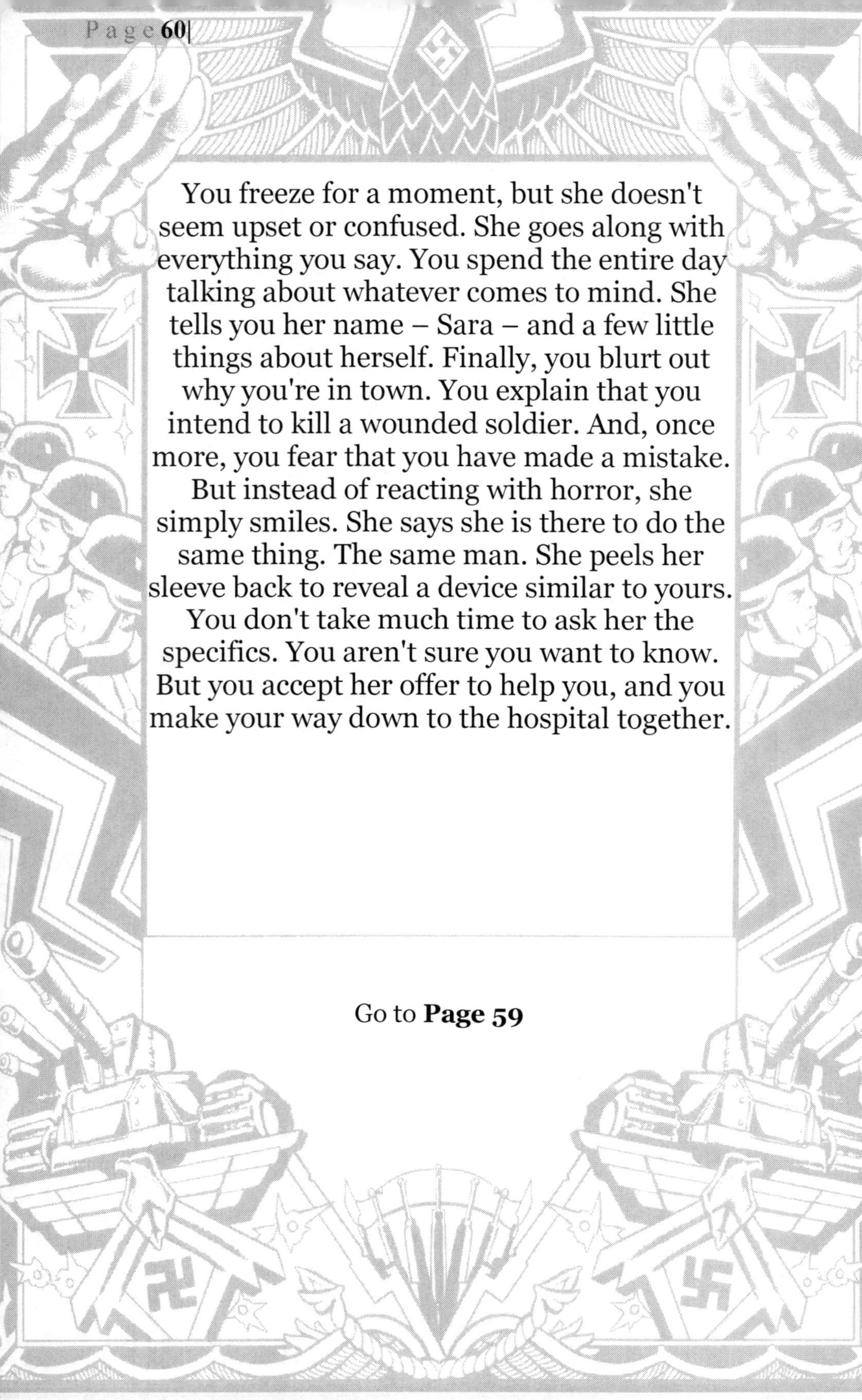

You freeze for a moment, but she doesn't seem upset or confused. She goes along with everything you say. You spend the entire day talking about whatever comes to mind. She tells you her name – Sara – and a few little things about herself. Finally, you blurt out why you're in town. You explain that you intend to kill a wounded soldier. And, once more, you fear that you have made a mistake. But instead of reacting with horror, she simply smiles. She says she is there to do the same thing. The same man. She peels her sleeve back to reveal a device similar to yours. You don't take much time to ask her the specifics. You aren't sure you want to know. But you accept her offer to help you, and you make your way down to the hospital together.

Go to **Page 59**

As you turn to leave, you feel a pair of slender hands wrap around your throat, followed by a knife pressed hard into the front of your neck. Then you hear the girl speak from behind you.

Go to **Page 57**

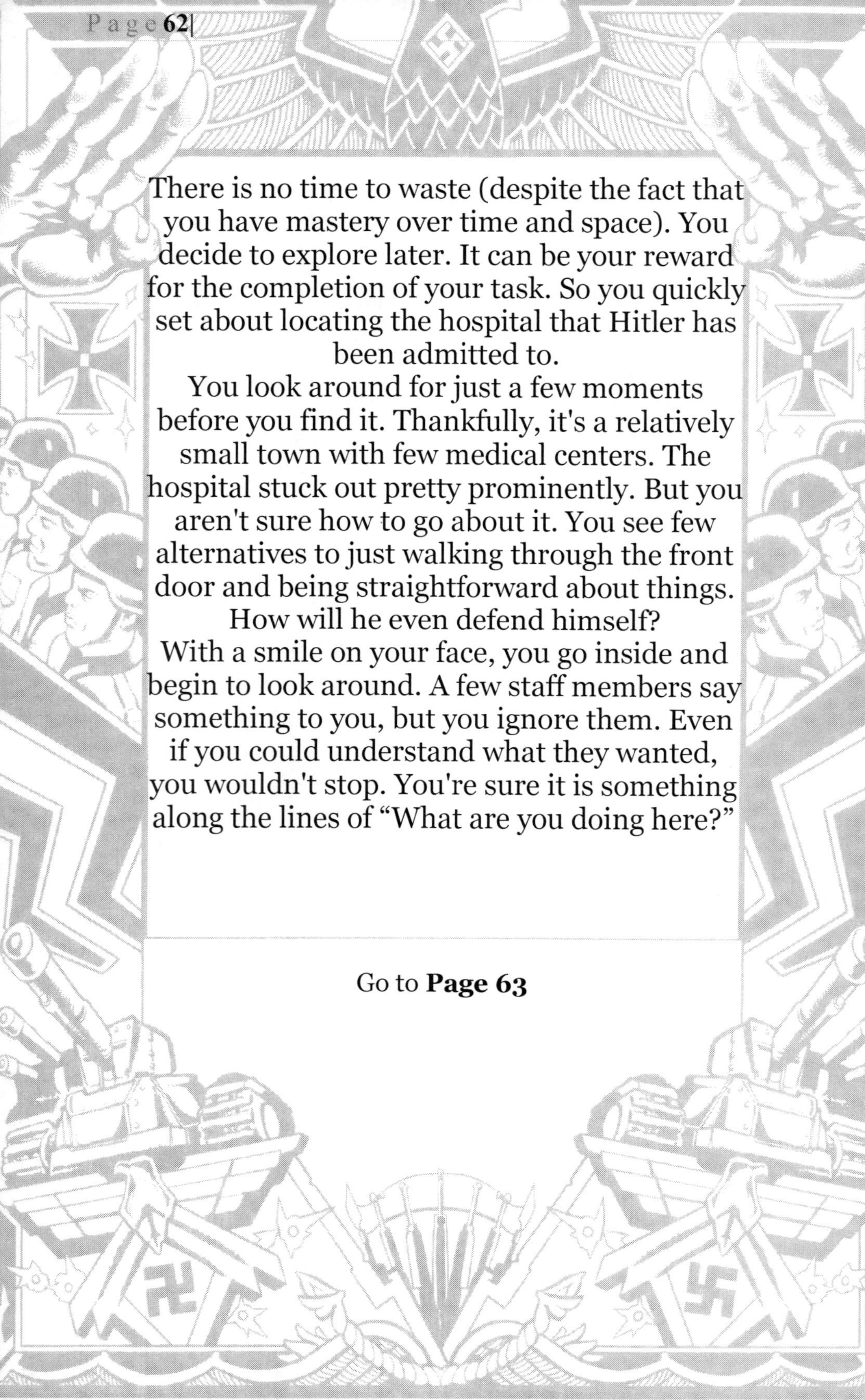

There is no time to waste (despite the fact that you have mastery over time and space). You decide to explore later. It can be your reward for the completion of your task. So you quickly set about locating the hospital that Hitler has been admitted to.

You look around for just a few moments before you find it. Thankfully, it's a relatively small town with few medical centers. The hospital stuck out pretty prominently. But you aren't sure how to go about it. You see few alternatives to just walking through the front door and being straightforward about things. How will he even defend himself?

With a smile on your face, you go inside and begin to look around. A few staff members say something to you, but you ignore them. Even if you could understand what they wanted, you wouldn't stop. You're sure it is something along the lines of "What are you doing here?"

Go to **Page 63**

After a few minutes of calm, casual searching, you find a man with bandages over his eyes that looks a lot like a 20th century genocidal maniac. You find a nearby patient chart and confirm your suspicion. It is indeed Adolf Hitler that is lying there, blind and passed out.

You take a moment to contemplate just how you should kill him. And then you realize that there are a surprising number of people walking around, all of whom would probably notice if you tried something.

To go for it and kill him in front of a dozen medical professionals, go to **Page 64**

If you want to be more subtle, go to **Page 88**

There's no time like the present! Or, rather, like the past. But the expression still seems perfectly relevant to your situation. Why not just go ahead and take care of things right now? You can't see any real problem with public execution at this point. You know that you aren't in much real danger no matter what happens. But you are still left with a small issue to address: by what method do you intend to kill him?

You give the area around you a quick glance to see what is available. There are some pointy looking medical tools on a table nearby. A syringe, a scalpel, a saw. All three look perfectly capable of murdering a person, but you consider other options too.

Hitler is, after all, lying on two perfectly good pillows. You could just suffocate him and be done with it.

On the off chance that you feel like getting visceral, go to **Page 86**

If you prefer to be go with a quieter approach, go to **Page 65**

If you change your mind and decide that it's safer to wait until nightfall, go to **Page 88**

Why cover useful tools in Hitler's blood? Who knows what sterilization procedures they follow in early 20th century Germany. You really don't want to risk harming a relatively innocent bystander via contamination. So you pull a pillow out from under Hitler's head and begin to force it into his face.

He quickly wakes up and begins to struggle, clawing at your forearms, but you aren't too worried about that. You figure he has about a minute to live, so he can't do you too much damage. That is, until he somehow lands a kick directly into your crotch.

The wind is knocked out of you; you fall to the ground, and Hitler flings the pillow to the side. There is no time to try again, as hospital staff converge and descend upon you. You suffer a nasty blow to the back of your head during the scuffle, and everything goes black.

Go to **Page 66**

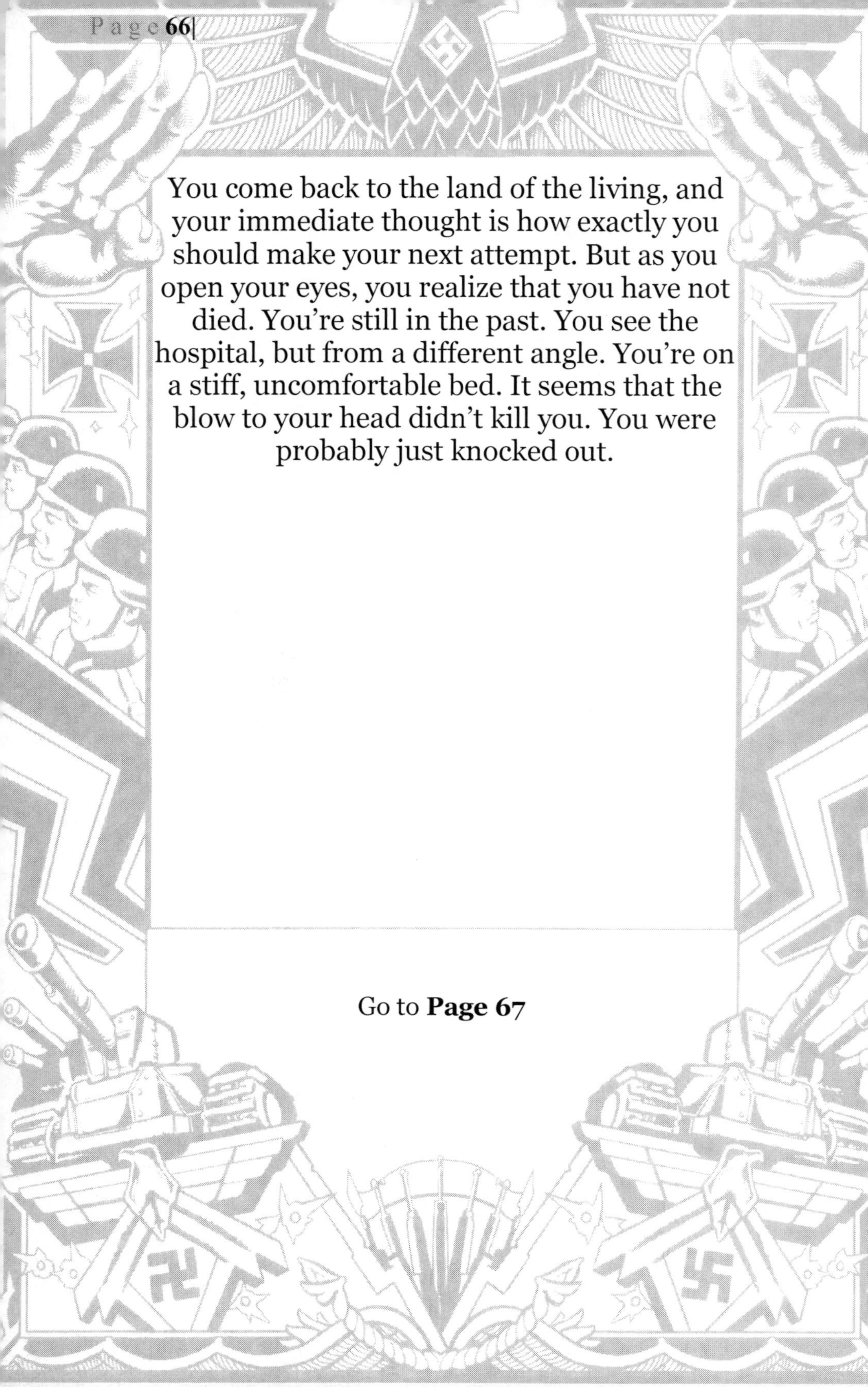

You come back to the land of the living, and your immediate thought is how exactly you should make your next attempt. But as you open your eyes, you realize that you have not died. You're still in the past. You see the hospital, but from a different angle. You're on a stiff, uncomfortable bed. It seems that the blow to your head didn't kill you. You were probably just knocked out.

Go to **Page 67**

It isn't a big deal, you think. You can fix this by reaching down and pressing a few buttons on your wrist, right? But you reach down to do so and you find nothing but your own flesh. No time machine. No buttons. No way of inputting coordinates that lead you home. You begin to panic and curse; your heart starts to race. You stand up, leap out of bed, and feel dizzy. Moments later, you find yourself on the floor. Your legs aren't working right. They're weak and unable to hold you up. You reach up to your face. You have a decent beard growing.

It is with horror that you realize you've been in that bed much longer than you could have imagined. You let out another series of vulgarities before you're put into bed by several doctors. They speak to you in German. You're starting to hate yourself for neglecting to learn it. You collapse back onto the bed and everything fades back to black.

Go to **Page 68**

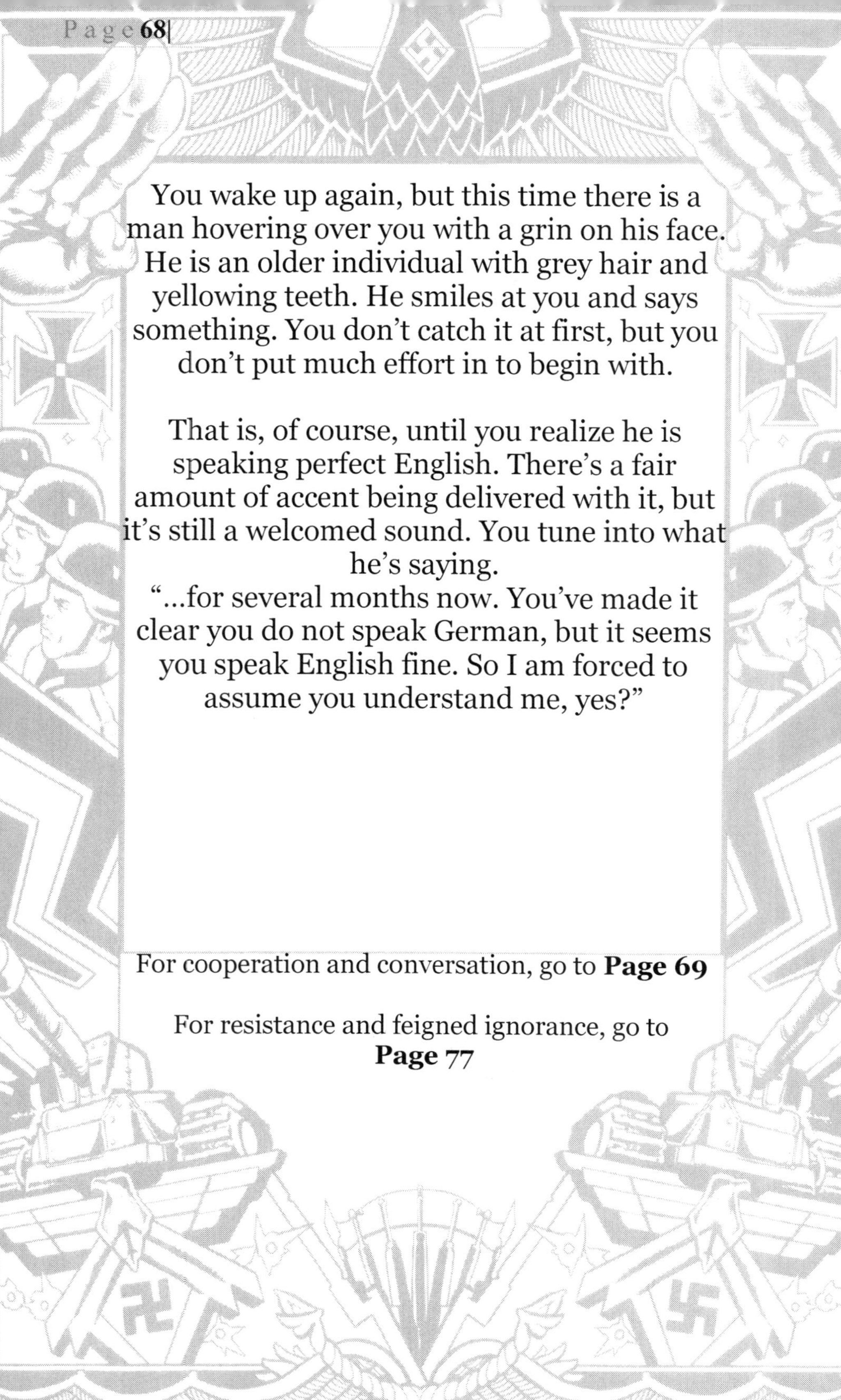

You wake up again, but this time there is a man hovering over you with a grin on his face. He is an older individual with grey hair and yellowing teeth. He smiles at you and says something. You don't catch it at first, but you don't put much effort in to begin with.

That is, of course, until you realize he is speaking perfect English. There's a fair amount of accent being delivered with it, but it's still a welcomed sound. You tune into what he's saying.

"...for several months now. You've made it clear you do not speak German, but it seems you speak English fine. So I am forced to assume you understand me, yes?"

For cooperation and conversation, go to **Page 69**

For resistance and feigned ignorance, go to **Page** 77

You look up at him and nod a bit. You choke out a “yes.”

“Wonderful! You know, very few of the people in this settlement speak English. You’re lucky that one of them is a doctor. Do you know where you are?”

“Pasewalk.”

“Judging by your voice, you are American. What brought an American to Pasewalk during a war? You don’t look to be anyone’s solider. And if you don’t belong to one of those armies that were stomping about, then I can’t imagine why you’d be here.”

If you want to admit everything to him – including your time traveling and your plot to kill Hitler – go to **Page 70**

If you try to lie, go to **Page 76**

Things can't get worse, and Hitler isn't in power yet to punish you for the assassination attempt, so you decide to explain everything to the doctor. You tell him that you're from the future, that you invented time travel, that you came back to kill Hitler. You tell him a bit about who Hitler will become and the horrors that will befall the world if he is allowed to rise to power. You end your explanation by pointing to your wrist and explaining that you desperately need to find your time machine before it's too late. Then you sit and wait for him to laugh or insult your intelligence.

The doctor does not laugh. "Your tone of voice seems sincere enough. Your body language reeks of honesty. Either you are being honest or you are plagued with madness. But we did have a young man by the name of Adolf Hitler here when you first arrived. And he is indeed the man that you got into a *disagreement* with."

Go to **Page 71**

"Though, if you truly believe that he will be such a monster, I can understand the attack."

"You believe me?"

"I believe that you believe. My name is Bauer. I think that your *time machine*, as you called it, was taken by the very same man you attempted to kill."

"Hitler stole the time machine." You do not say this as a question.

This is a statement. One you make to yourself in a desperate attempt to understand just how badly you have screwed up.

"You attempted to suffocate him while he was blind. No one gave him any trouble when he took your possession after he recovered. He figured you were an enemy spy of some sort, but I convinced people that you most certainly were not. Not by the clothing you wear. It stands out far too well for someone who would try to blend in. No, I think that you are from somewhere very far away. Or, perhaps some-when. But that does not matter to me."

Go to **Page 72**

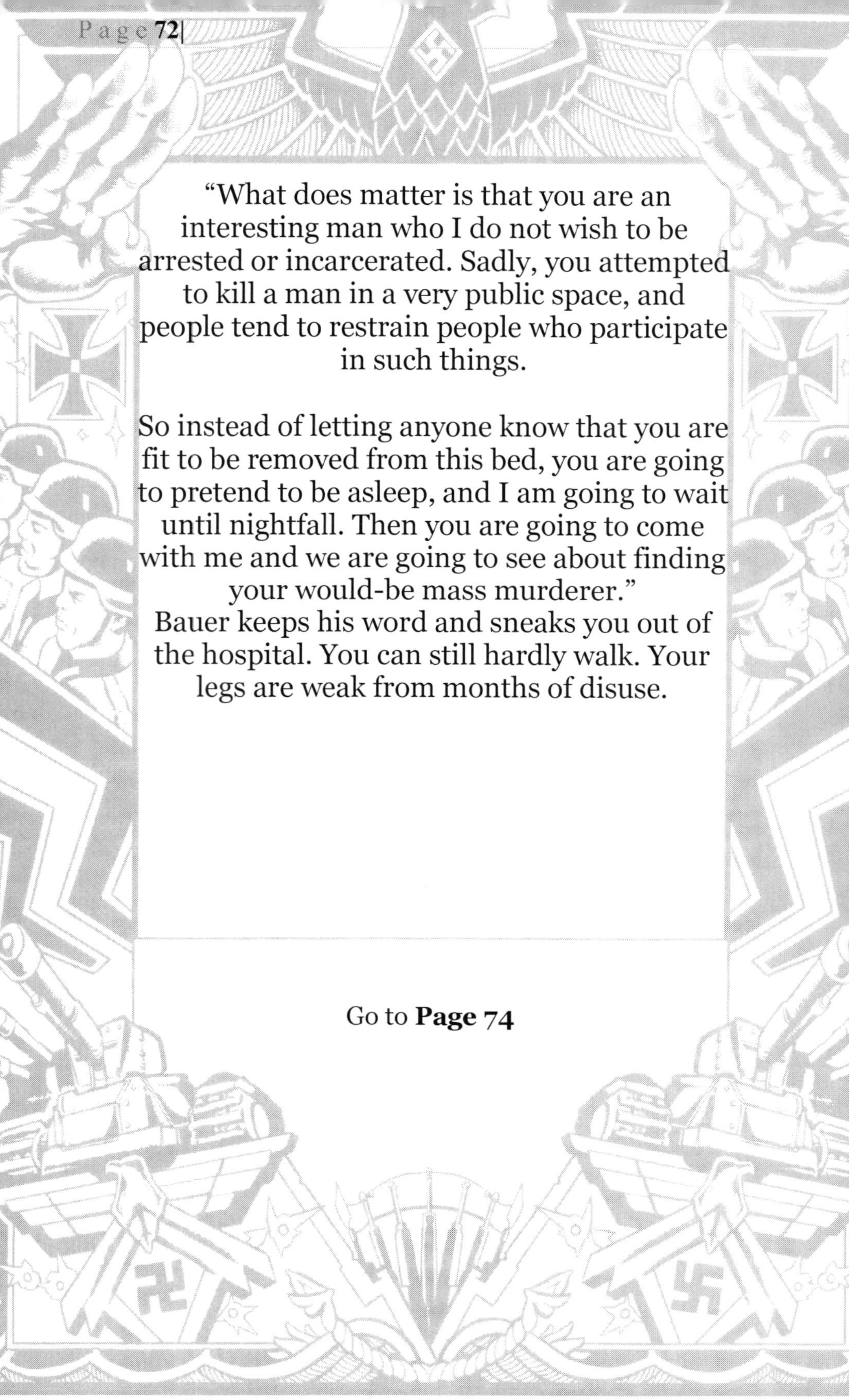

"What does matter is that you are an interesting man who I do not wish to be arrested or incarcerated. Sadly, you attempted to kill a man in a very public space, and people tend to restrain people who participate in such things.

So instead of letting anyone know that you are fit to be removed from this bed, you are going to pretend to be asleep, and I am going to wait until nightfall. Then you are going to come with me and we are going to see about finding your would-be mass murderer."

Bauer keeps his word and sneaks you out of the hospital. You can still hardly walk. Your legs are weak from months of disuse.

Go to **Page 74**

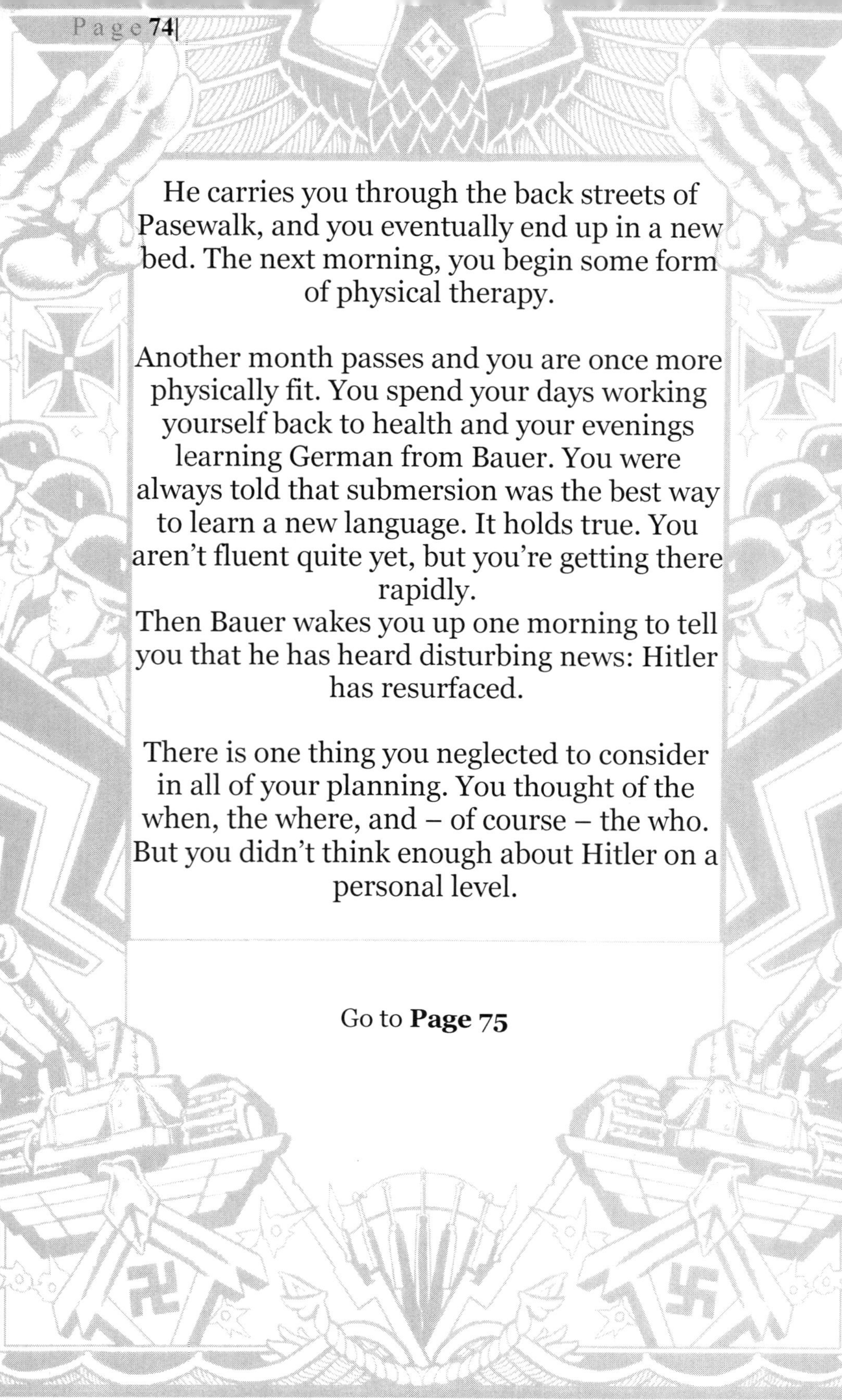

He carries you through the back streets of Pasewalk, and you eventually end up in a new bed. The next morning, you begin some form of physical therapy.

Another month passes and you are once more physically fit. You spend your days working yourself back to health and your evenings learning German from Bauer. You were always told that submersion was the best way to learn a new language. It holds true. You aren't fluent quite yet, but you're getting there rapidly.

Then Bauer wakes you up one morning to tell you that he has heard disturbing news: Hitler has resurfaced.

There is one thing you neglected to consider in all of your planning. You thought of the when, the where, and – of course – the who. But you didn't think enough about Hitler on a personal level.

Go to **Page 75**

You never really thought about what you'd do if forced to interact with him. And, like many of your problems, you figured it didn't matter because you had quasi-immortality from your time machine.

But you never considered that Hitler was a highly intelligent man.

You thought of him as a monster, a maniac, and maybe, on rare occasions, a failed artist. But you never really associated him with a high level of intellect. But the truth of the matter is that Hitler is far more cunning than you imagined. And you are now paying for it. Because he seems to have figured out your time machine, and now he has your once-taken-for-granted quasi-immortality.

Go to **Page 80**

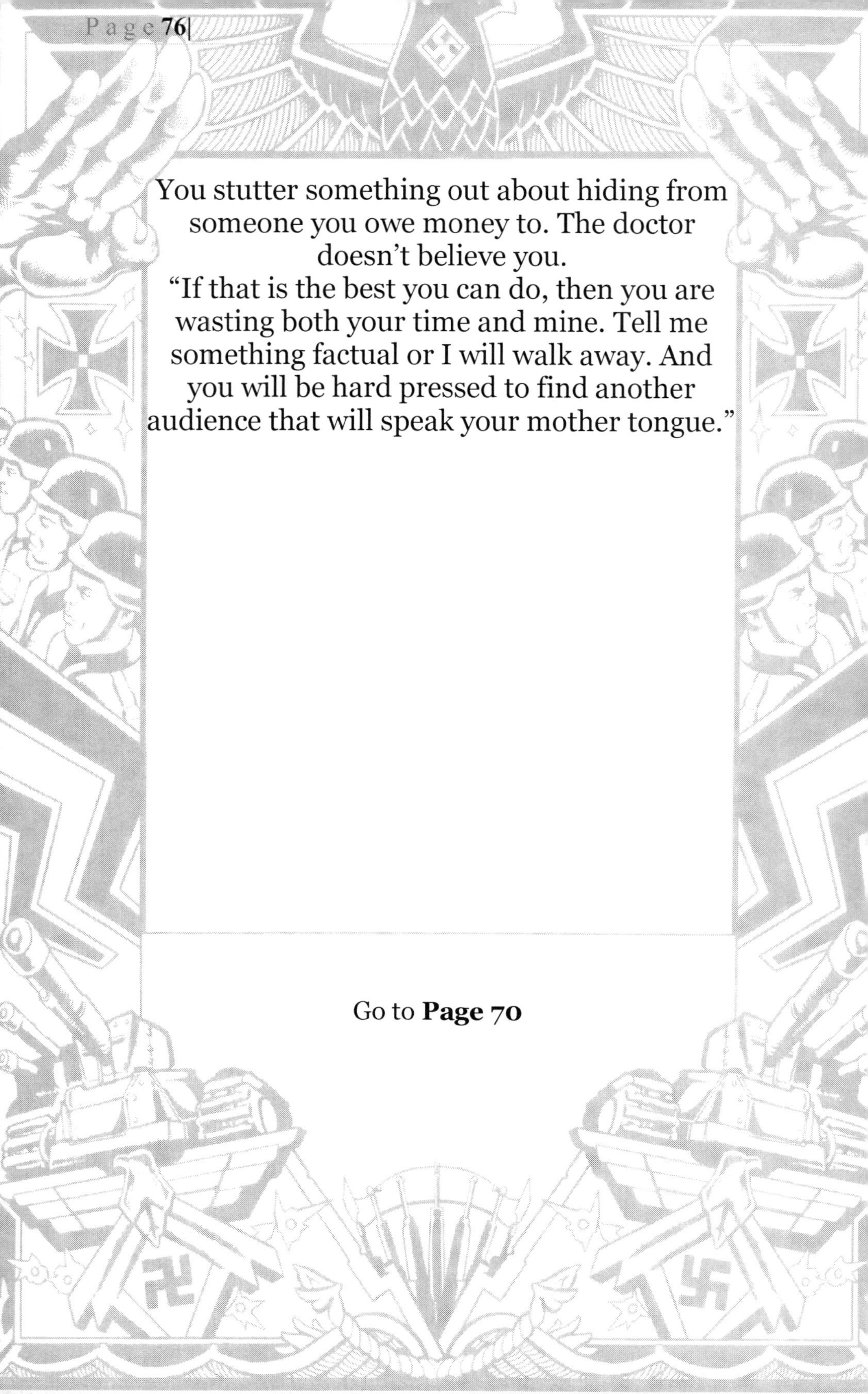

You stutter something out about hiding from someone you owe money to. The doctor doesn't believe you.

"If that is the best you can do, then you are wasting both your time and mine. Tell me something factual or I will walk away. And you will be hard pressed to find another audience that will speak your mother tongue."

Go to **Page 70**

You don't want to cooperate with some strange man that you've never met or heard of. So you remain silent.

"I heard you screaming in English just a few hours ago when you awoke. I don't like being insulted by your silence. I suppose attempting to converse with one who attempted to kill a defenseless wounded war hero was a pointless endeavor."

You attempt to speak to the man, but he no longer has any interest. He says a few things in German to a passing doctor, and they hurry off in response.

"I am sorry to do this. I had hoped for an explanation. But the authorities will be here soon, and they can get one out of you." With that, the man leaves.

Shortly after this exchange, some men show up and take you out. They have to carry you because of your weak legs. None of them speak English. They try to talk to you for a little while, but it doesn't do any good.

Go to **Page 79**

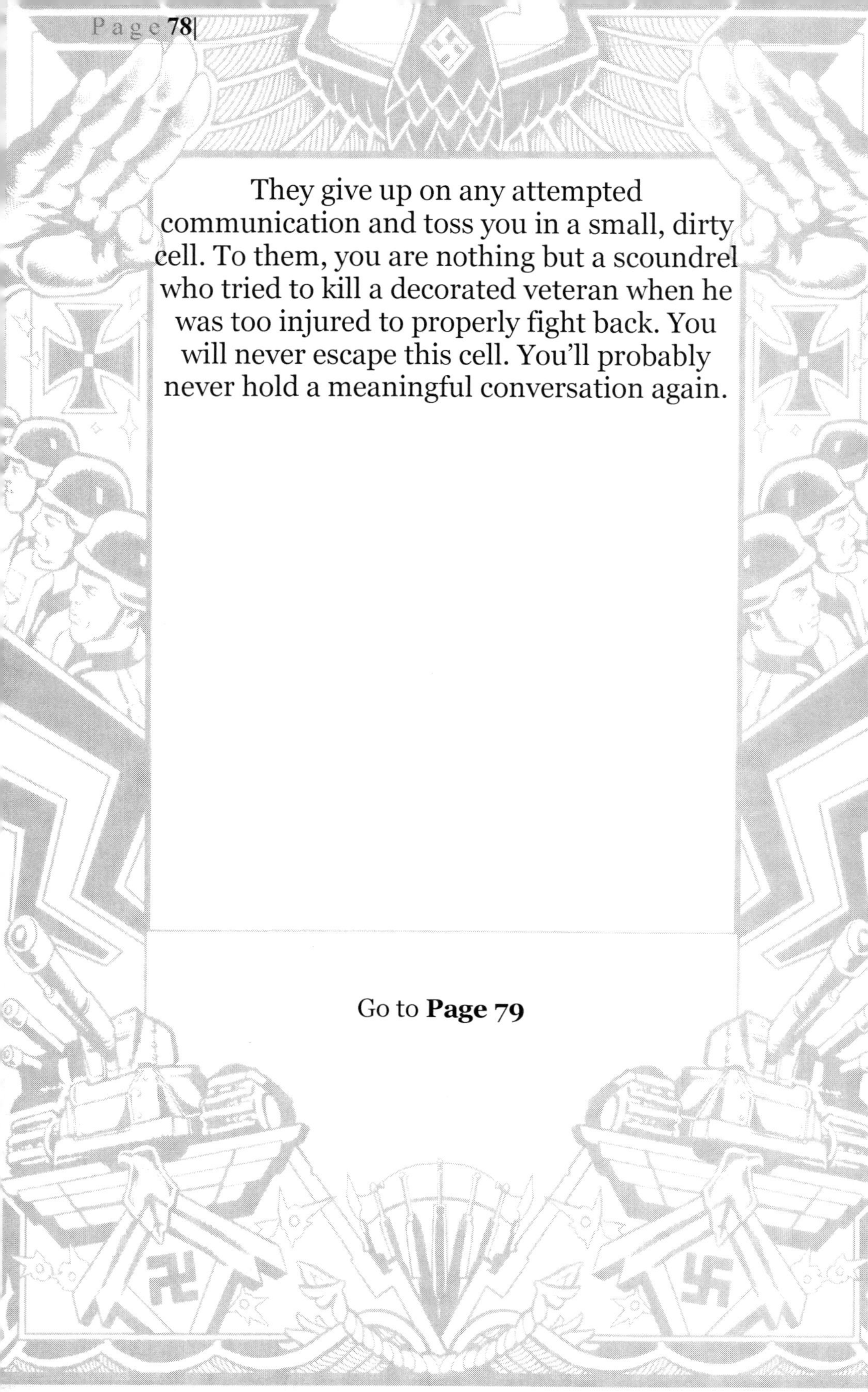

They give up on any attempted communication and toss you in a small, dirty cell. To them, you are nothing but a scoundrel who tried to kill a decorated veteran when he was too injured to properly fight back. You will never escape this cell. You'll probably never hold a meaningful conversation again.

Go to **Page 79**

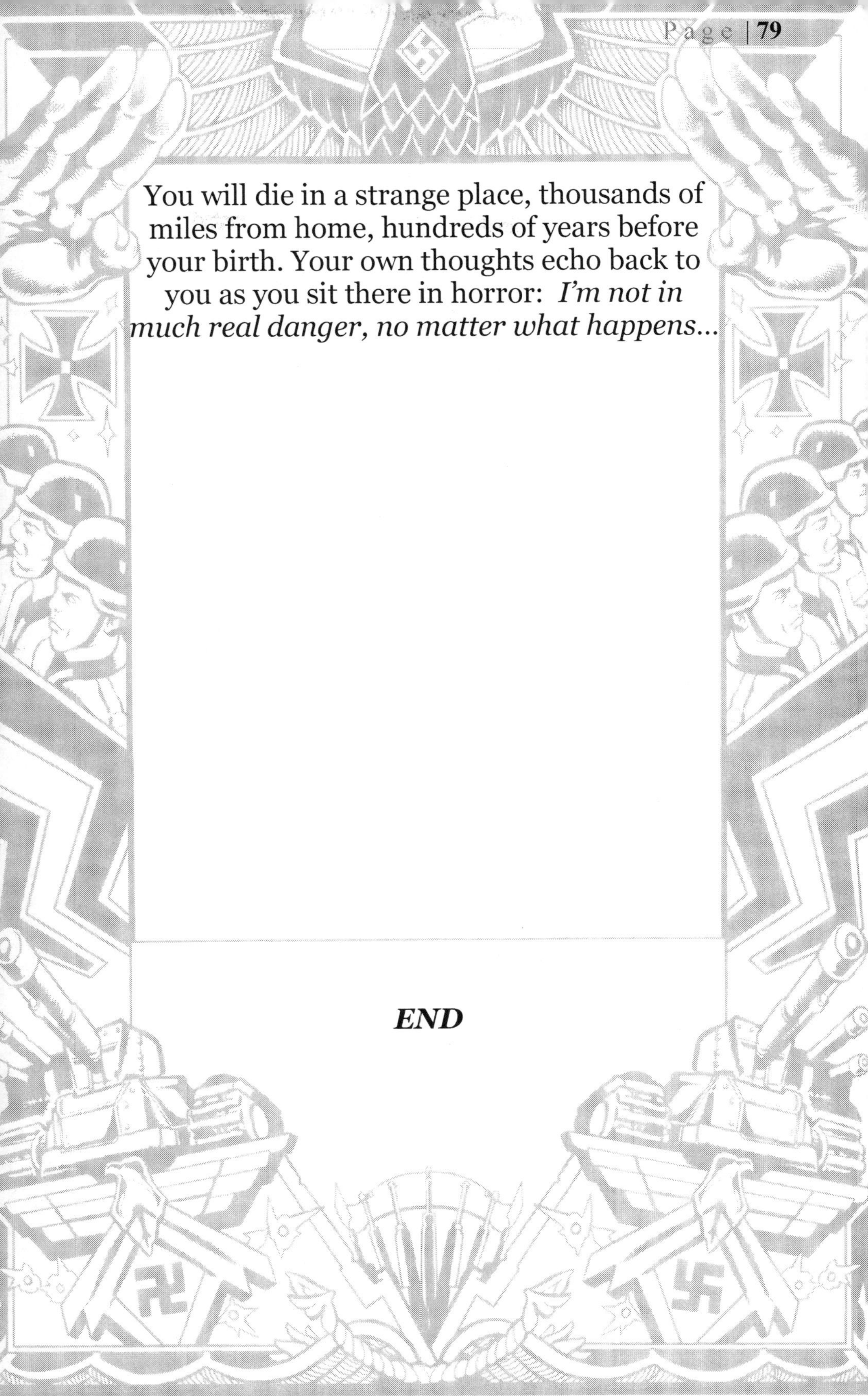

You will die in a strange place, thousands of miles from home, hundreds of years before your birth. Your own thoughts echo back to you as you sit there in horror: *I'm not in much real danger, no matter what happens…*

END

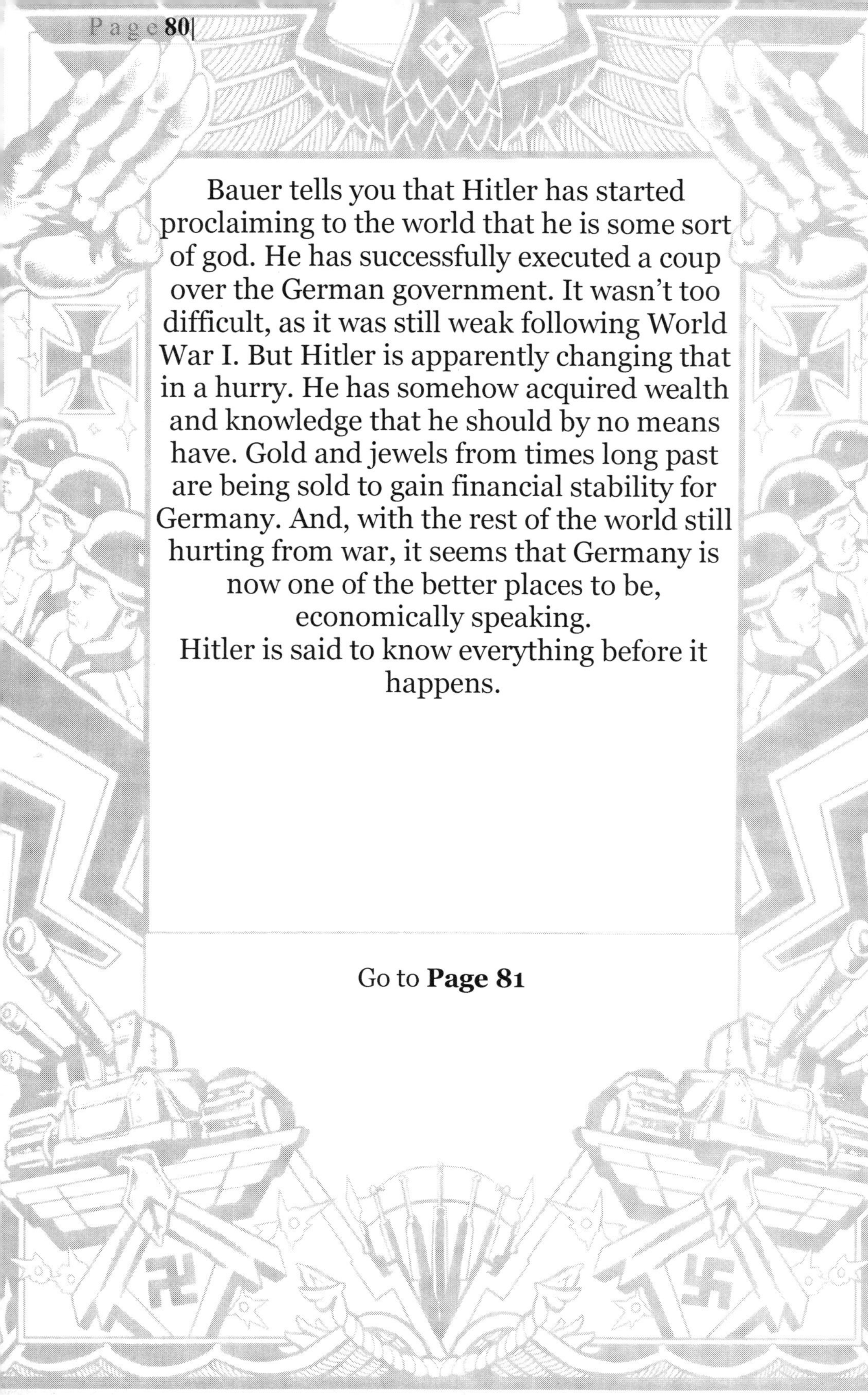

Bauer tells you that Hitler has started proclaiming to the world that he is some sort of god. He has successfully executed a coup over the German government. It wasn't too difficult, as it was still weak following World War I. But Hitler is apparently changing that in a hurry. He has somehow acquired wealth and knowledge that he should by no means have. Gold and jewels from times long past are being sold to gain financial stability for Germany. And, with the rest of the world still hurting from war, it seems that Germany is now one of the better places to be, economically speaking.

Hitler is said to know everything before it happens.

Go to **Page 81**

Major events are predicted with regular accuracy. And he's abusing his seemingly mystical abilities to take more and more control. People fear him now. No one dares move against him.

How did you let this happen? How will you stop him? What can you do against the most evil man to ever exist when he is armed with a time machine and seemingly limitless power?

If you choose to make one last assassination attempt, this time with no safety net if you die, go to **Page 105**

If you choose to rebuild the time machine and attempt to fight fire with fire, go to **Page 90**

You find yourself suddenly transported into a deafeningly loud battle. Men are screaming in multiple languages all around you. Everyone around you is rapidly dying. It's October 1914. You're right in the middle of the first Battle of Ypres. And you're with Hitler's company of men.

You realize very quickly that you have made a huge mistake. The group of men you are now next to has already lost most of its men. Hitler is what amounts to a trench-to-trench messenger. He isn't anywhere to be found. And these confused, desperate men see nothing but a stranger in front of them. You understand all too late that you picked a bad time to drop in.

If you want to run away from the unfriendly German troops in an attempt to save yourself some pain and find Hitler, go to **Page 84**

Or, instead, if you wish to stay and search for Hitler amongst his own men, go to **Page 85**

You turn around and run towards a nearby ladder. A few shots go off behind you, but they all miss. You are suddenly out of the trench and onto the battlefield. You are sprinting towards the closest trench, unsure as to what faction controls it. But you don't care at the moment. Machine gun fire and bombs drive your legs to move more quickly. Soon enough, you're in the new trench. But you aren't greeted with a smile and a handshake.

The soldiers held within decide that you are a great opportunity for target practice. But before you can be shot, you feel a sudden burst of pain. Everything goes white; there's a loud noise, and it feels like you're being engulfed in fire. Your wrist is seared by the heated metal on your arm that serves as your escape route. As you die, you wonder if the time machine is still in good enough shape to get you home.

Thankfully, you don't feel everything slip away when you go dark. You are back to where you started once more. You make a mental note not to try such fast and reckless tactics again.

Go to **Page 13**

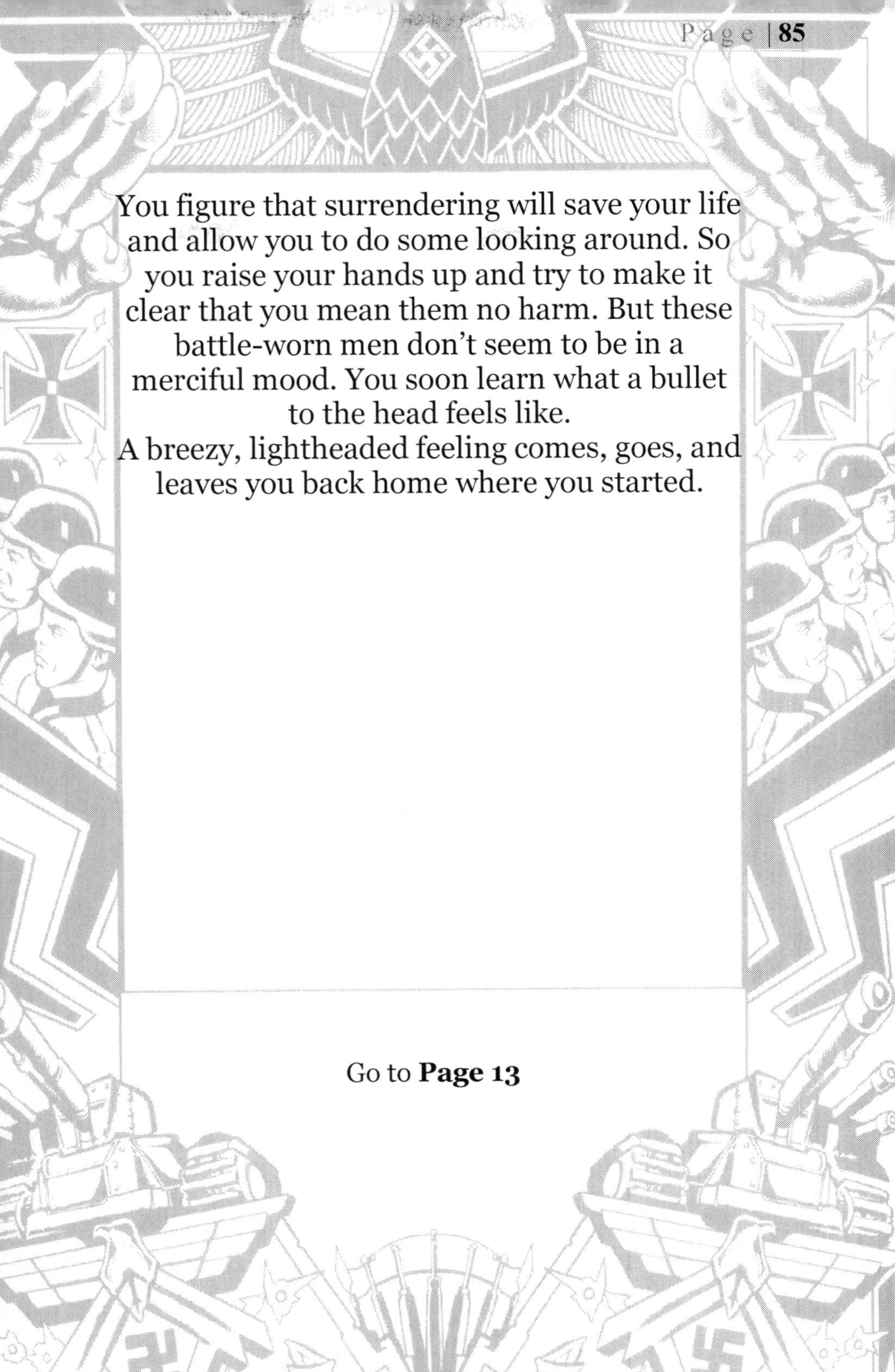

You figure that surrendering will save your life and allow you to do some looking around. So you raise your hands up and try to make it clear that you mean them no harm. But these battle-worn men don't seem to be in a merciful mood. You soon learn what a bullet to the head feels like.

A breezy, lightheaded feeling comes, goes, and leaves you back home where you started.

Go to **Page 13**

You grab a scalpel and stab Hitler straight in the stomach. You couldn't bring yourself to go for the throat or face; it seemed far too gruesome. But you decide in the moment that his stomach is just as good a place as any.

A doctor comes running at you and tries to pull you off of the dying man, but you fight back. This was apparently the wrong move, and the doctor quickly disarms you and stabs you with the same scalpel you were holding moments earlier.

You are dead, then alive once more. Excitement causes your entire body to tingle. You can't wait to see if you succeeded. So you go to pull up your favorite internet encyclopedia. But you are disturbed to find that you have no computer. Your lab looks different. Strange technologies line the walls, some impressively advanced, and some pathetically primitive compared to what you once had.

Go to **Page 87**

You eventually find a paper encyclopedia to answer your questions.

Hitler not only lived, but also became an incredibly paranoid man. His newfound caution led him to show more reluctance to invade the Soviet Union, a move that paid off in the end. You learn that Hitler won the war by remaining allies with the USSR for a few more years.

It does not take long before you slam the undo button. There was nothing more you needed to see there.

Go to **Page 13**

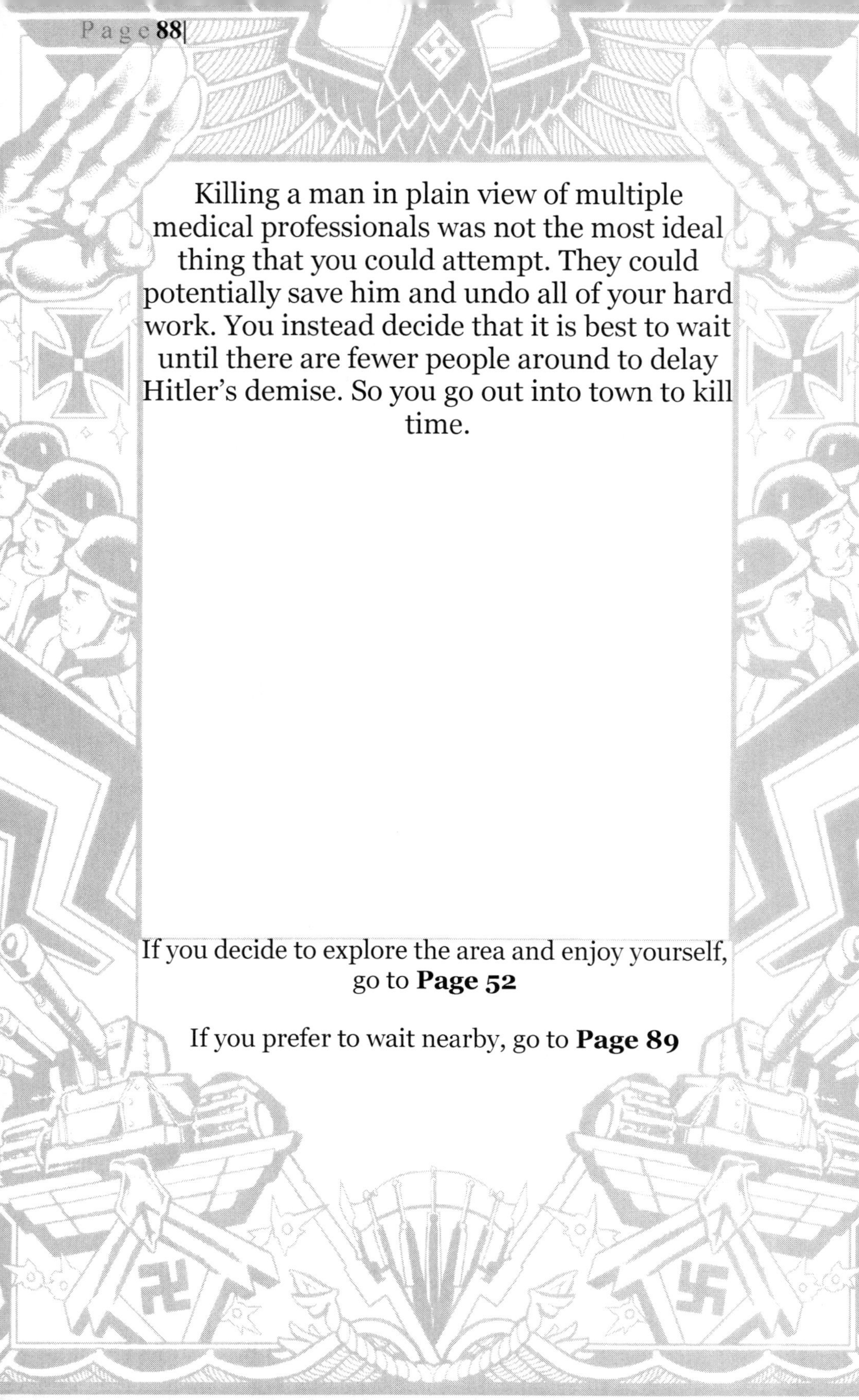

Killing a man in plain view of multiple medical professionals was not the most ideal thing that you could attempt. They could potentially save him and undo all of your hard work. You instead decide that it is best to wait until there are fewer people around to delay Hitler's demise. So you go out into town to kill time.

If you decide to explore the area and enjoy yourself, go to **Page 52**

If you prefer to wait nearby, go to **Page 89**

You don't want to get too far away. This is not the time to lose focus and let yourself miss a chance. So you turn into a small alleyway and lean against the wall for a while. Before long, a man passes by. He looks you up and down, smiles, and leaves.

About twenty minutes later, as the sun is going down, you see the same man coming back your way. But this time there are a few shady looking men with him. You turn to leave out the other side of the alleyway, figuring that safe is a lot better than sorry. But a man soon blocks the other exit. You turn around to see the first man smiling once more.

It is with a sudden kick to the stomach that you realize you are being mugged. But you have nothing worth stealing, aside from the time machine strapped to your wrist. Thankfully, they don't pay it much attention. They get frustrated by your lack of currency and continue to beat you into a bloody pulp until everything goes dark.

A few moments later, you find yourself back in the future.

Go to **Page 13**

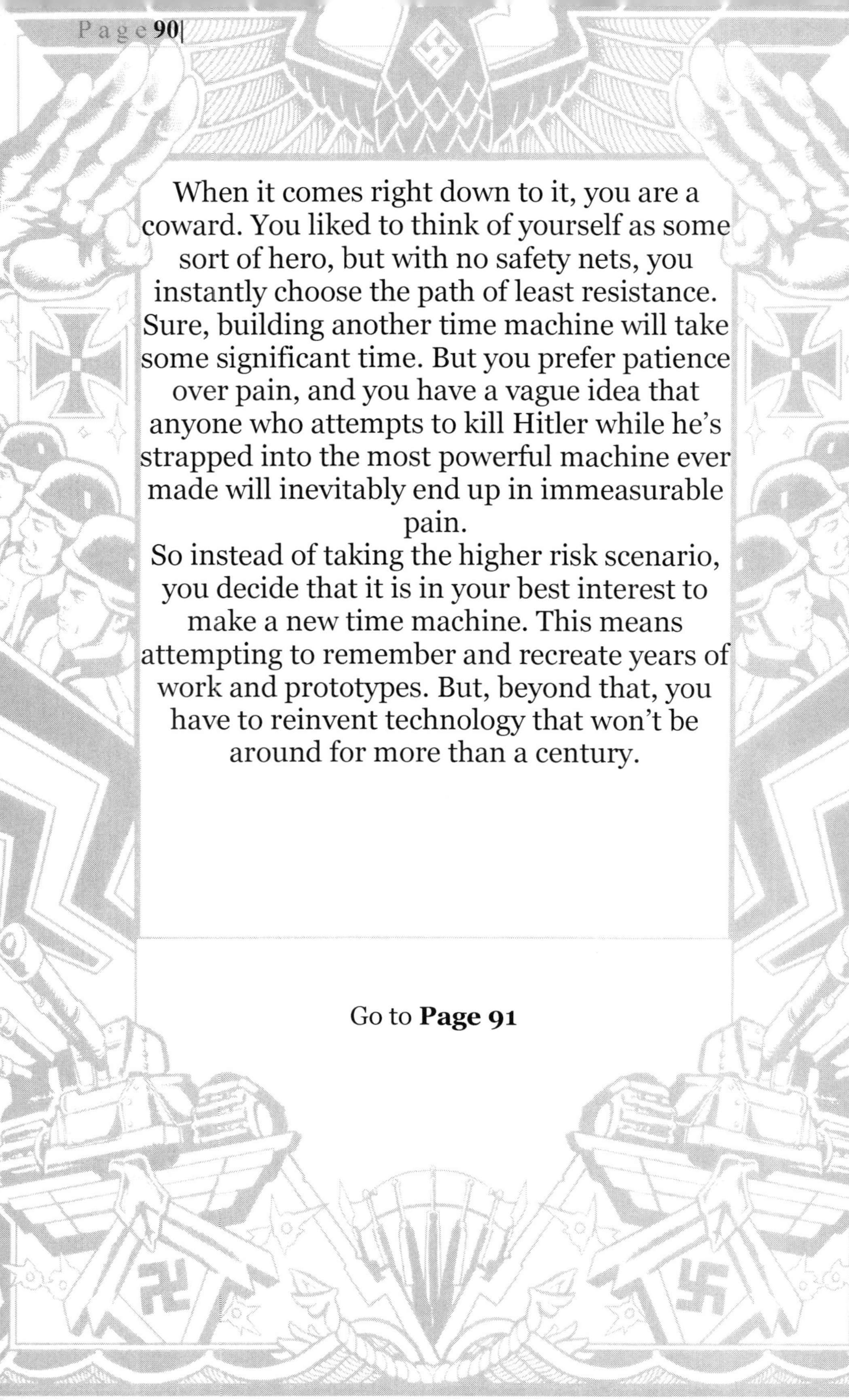

When it comes right down to it, you are a coward. You liked to think of yourself as some sort of hero, but with no safety nets, you instantly choose the path of least resistance. Sure, building another time machine will take some significant time. But you prefer patience over pain, and you have a vague idea that anyone who attempts to kill Hitler while he's strapped into the most powerful machine ever made will inevitably end up in immeasurable pain.

So instead of taking the higher risk scenario, you decide that it is in your best interest to make a new time machine. This means attempting to remember and recreate years of work and prototypes. But, beyond that, you have to reinvent technology that won't be around for more than a century.

Go to **Page 91**

At first it is a matter of remembering everything you can and writing it down. You have a fantastic memory, though. This gets you far, but not nearly far enough. At some point, you have to start familiar technology from scratch with no references or models to work off of.

Month pass before you have most of the bare bones technology in working order. Years pass before you have a working prototype. Hitler actually helps you in some ways at this point.

Go to **Page 92**

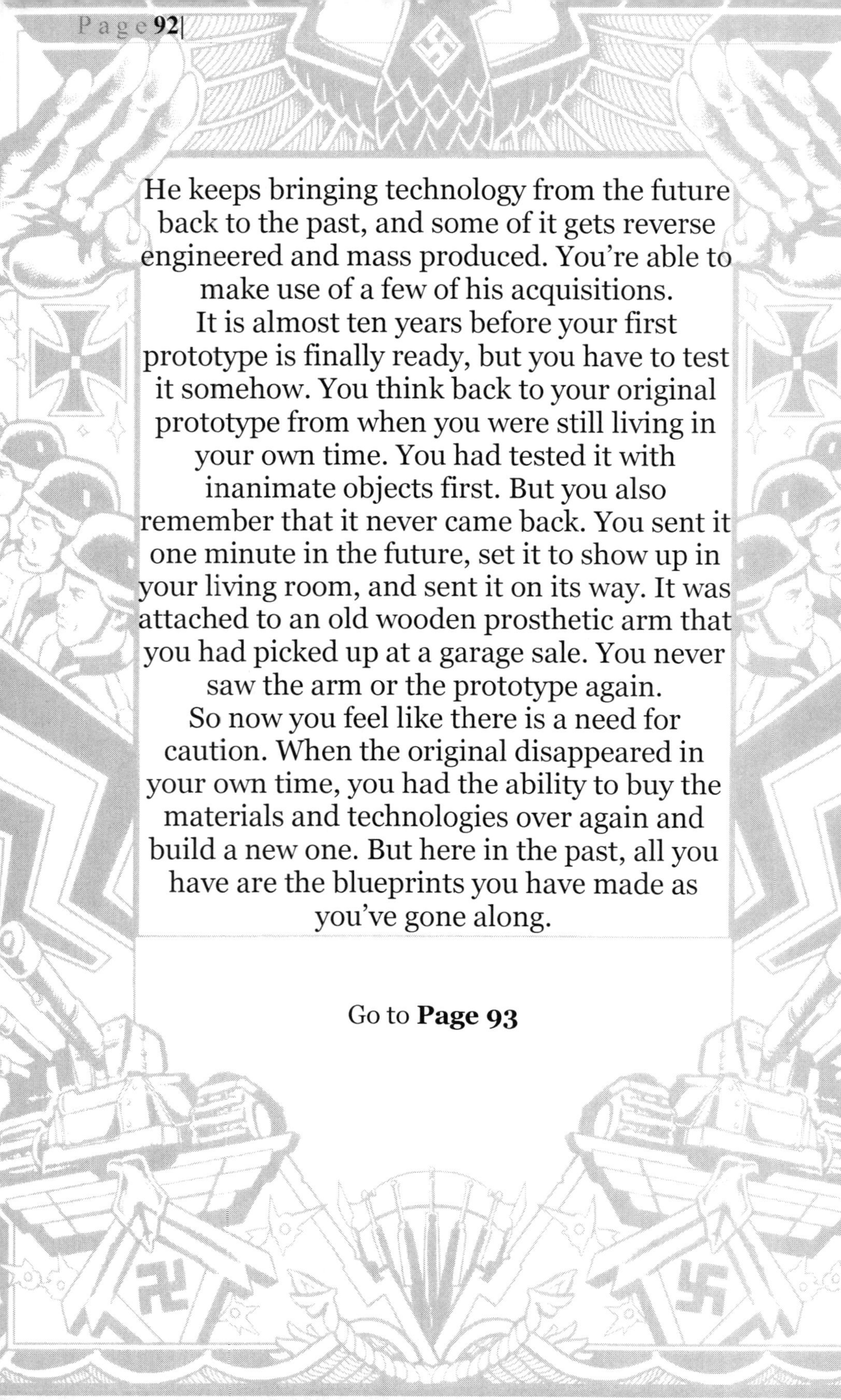

He keeps bringing technology from the future back to the past, and some of it gets reverse engineered and mass produced. You're able to make use of a few of his acquisitions.

It is almost ten years before your first prototype is finally ready, but you have to test it somehow. You think back to your original prototype from when you were still living in your own time. You had tested it with inanimate objects first. But you also remember that it never came back. You sent it one minute in the future, set it to show up in your living room, and sent it on its way. It was attached to an old wooden prosthetic arm that you had picked up at a garage sale. You never saw the arm or the prototype again.

So now you feel like there is a need for caution. When the original disappeared in your own time, you had the ability to buy the materials and technologies over again and build a new one. But here in the past, all you have are the blueprints you have made as you've gone along.

Go to **Page 93**

Even with those in hand, you would have to spend months rebuilding every little piece. But what are your alternatives?

Bauer offers to test it for you. He hasn't been in the best of health lately, and his age is really starting to show. But he has been your best and only friend since you have been stranded in the past. If he did not end up where he was supposed to be, he could use the undo button and bring himself back. Or, if the undo button isn't quite perfect, he could at least try to jump back to you manually. There is potential that none of it works, though. There is a chance that it will kill him or send him to somewhere so dangerous that he dies anyway. And you cannot be sure that the respawn feature will bring him back because you have had no way of testing it. You aren't sure if you can send your best friend to his potential death.

Go to **Page 94**

So that leaves you with the option of testing it on yourself. But in the event that you fail, everyone is doomed. There will be no one left to build a new time machine and little chance of righting the mistakes you have made. And yet it seems only right that you are the one who should risk their life to test that you have made a working device.

So what will it be?

To test the time machine on something inanimate, go to **Page 95**

To test the time machine on Bauer, go to **Page 100**

To test the time machine on yourself, go to **Page 102**

Time is less valuable than life, so you decide to test the machine on something that cannot die: a pineapple. The time machine is strapped to the pineapple, and you decide to send it ahead by one minute, but you are not sure as to where you want it sent. You definitely don't want to send it out of the house, but you aren't sure you want to risk it materializing too close to you or Bauer.

To send the pineapple into your bedroom, go to **Page 98**

To send the pineapple to the table across the room from you and Bauer, go to **Page 96**

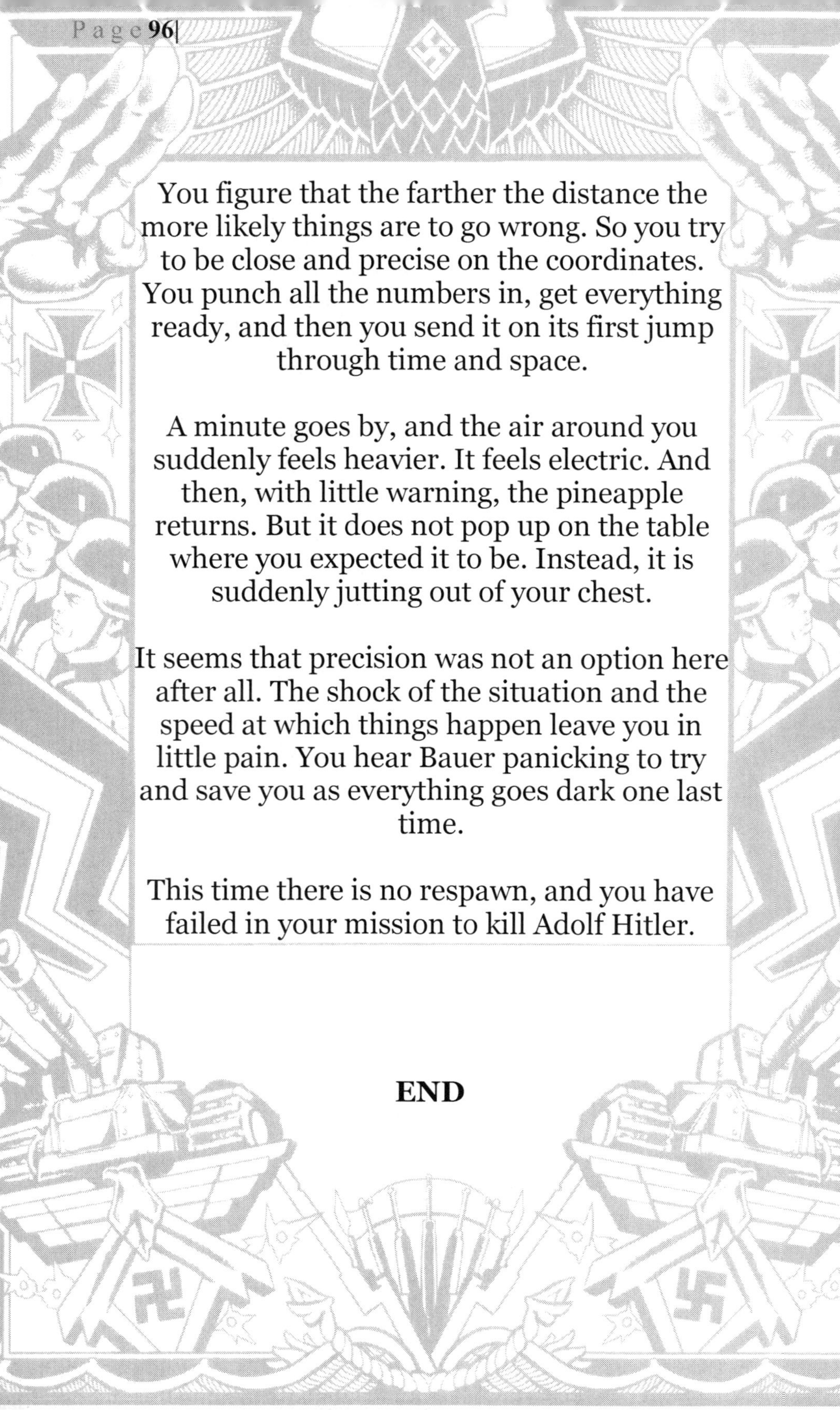

You figure that the farther the distance the more likely things are to go wrong. So you try to be close and precise on the coordinates. You punch all the numbers in, get everything ready, and then you send it on its first jump through time and space.

A minute goes by, and the air around you suddenly feels heavier. It feels electric. And then, with little warning, the pineapple returns. But it does not pop up on the table where you expected it to be. Instead, it is suddenly jutting out of your chest.

It seems that precision was not an option here after all. The shock of the situation and the speed at which things happen leave you in little pain. You hear Bauer panicking to try and save you as everything goes dark one last time.

This time there is no respawn, and you have failed in your mission to kill Adolf Hitler.

END

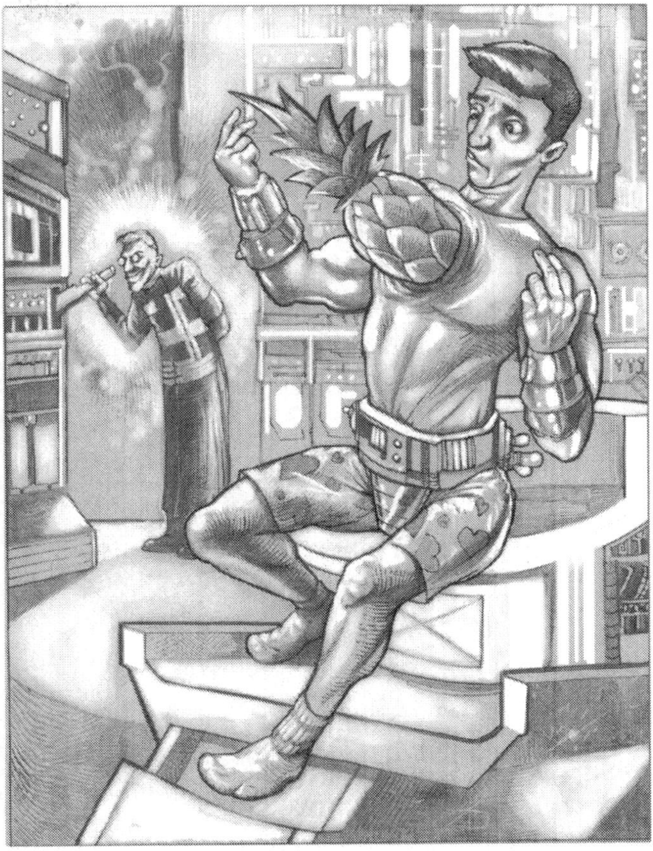

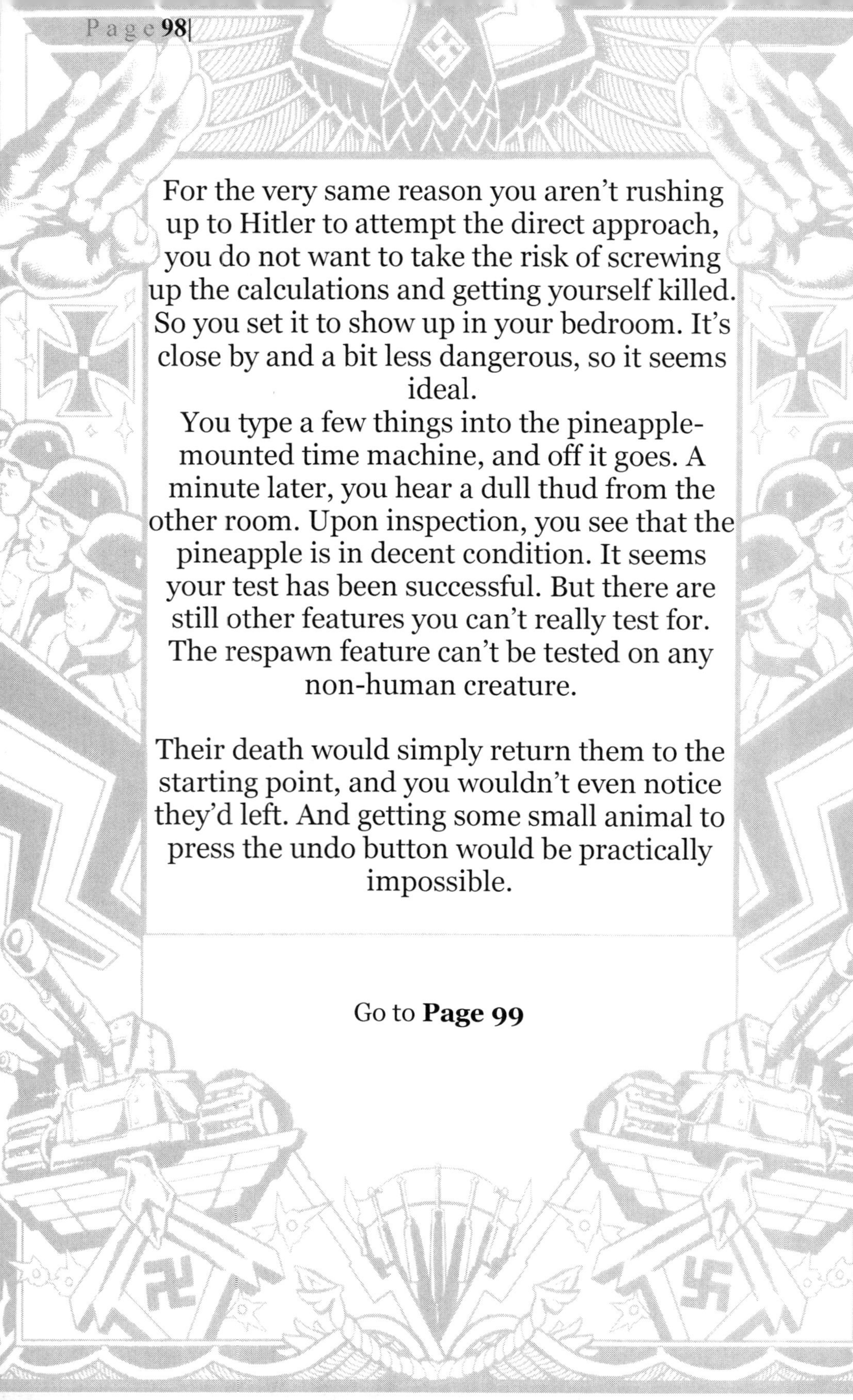

For the very same reason you aren't rushing up to Hitler to attempt the direct approach, you do not want to take the risk of screwing up the calculations and getting yourself killed. So you set it to show up in your bedroom. It's close by and a bit less dangerous, so it seems ideal.

You type a few things into the pineapple-mounted time machine, and off it goes. A minute later, you hear a dull thud from the other room. Upon inspection, you see that the pineapple is in decent condition. It seems your test has been successful. But there are still other features you can't really test for. The respawn feature can't be tested on any non-human creature.

Their death would simply return them to the starting point, and you wouldn't even notice they'd left. And getting some small animal to press the undo button would be practically impossible.

Go to **Page 99**

You can test the remaining features yourself or you can have Bauer do it. But you feel uneasy about the idea of killing yourself to see if you come back. Bauer agrees, and the two of you start to brainstorm what to do with the time machine now that it is ready.

If you choose to go back in time and stop yourself from losing the time machine in the first place, go to **Page 102**

If you decide that it is best to go to the future, perfect the time machine, and then go back to fix things, to go **Page 103**

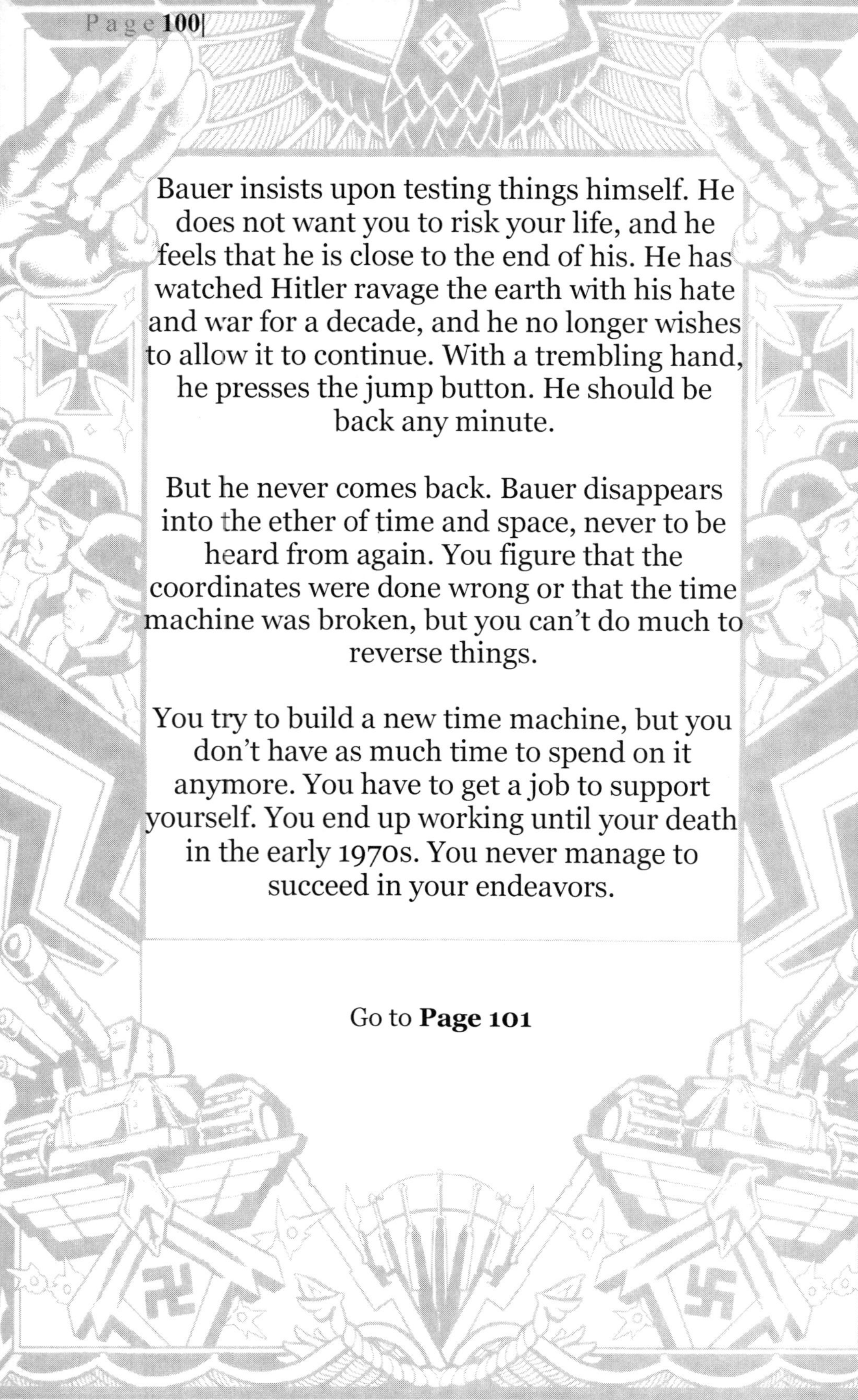

Bauer insists upon testing things himself. He does not want you to risk your life, and he feels that he is close to the end of his. He has watched Hitler ravage the earth with his hate and war for a decade, and he no longer wishes to allow it to continue. With a trembling hand, he presses the jump button. He should be back any minute.

But he never comes back. Bauer disappears into the ether of time and space, never to be heard from again. You figure that the coordinates were done wrong or that the time machine was broken, but you can't do much to reverse things.

You try to build a new time machine, but you don't have as much time to spend on it anymore. You have to get a job to support yourself. You end up working until your death in the early 1970s. You never manage to succeed in your endeavors.

Go to **Page 101**

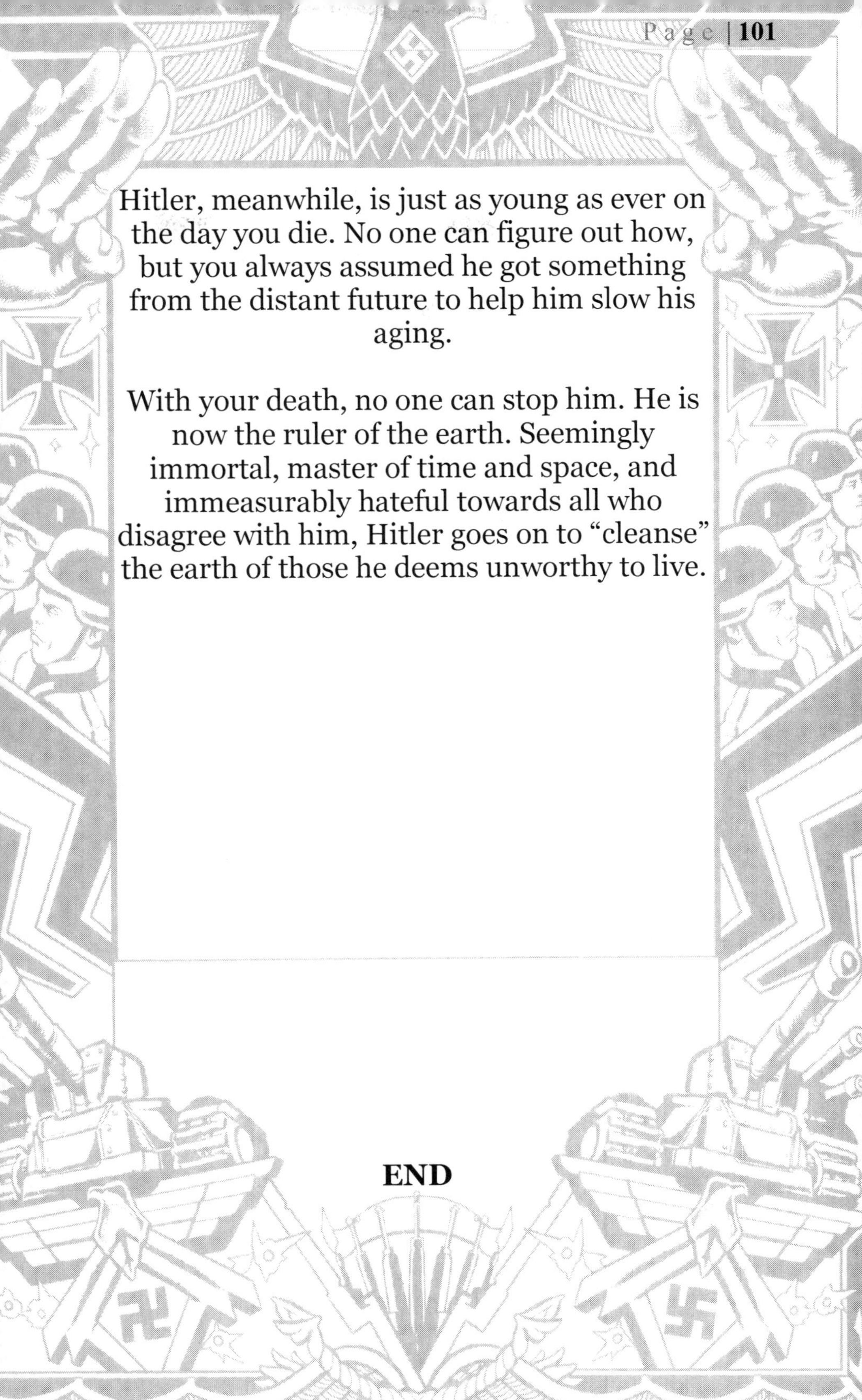

Hitler, meanwhile, is just as young as ever on the day you die. No one can figure out how, but you always assumed he got something from the distant future to help him slow his aging.

With your death, no one can stop him. He is now the ruler of the earth. Seemingly immortal, master of time and space, and immeasurably hateful towards all who disagree with him, Hitler goes on to “cleanse” the earth of those he deems unworthy to live.

END

You decide that the quickest way to fix everything is to attempt going back in time and preventing yourself from ever letting Hitler get his hands on the time machine. It'll serve as a fine test. But the moment you get back to the day in question, you start to feel sickly. You ignore it, though. Maybe it's something to do with a glitch in the new time machine, or maybe it is just because you haven't made a jump in so long. It doesn't matter. You keep going with your mission.

You encounter yourself on a street near the hospital, and things instantly go bad. Past you panics and freezes. You begin to shoot at yourself. You tell yourself to stop, but past you doesn't know what to do. He turns and starts to run. You've been exercising every day for a decade, and it shows in comparison to the old you.

You catch up immediately, grab his arm, and everything stops.

Reality has torn in two. Some sort of time paradox has been played out. Old you and current you are gone, as is the rest of existence. On the bright side, so is Hitler. In some strange way, you have succeeded. But you aren't around to enjoy it.

END

You travel to the future and find yourself in a strange land. Hitler is essentially the king of the world. You work in hiding, escaping the oppressors of this Orwellian society with nothing but your wits and the occasional leap through time. You build an even better time machine than the one Hitler holds, a more reliable device that you can bind to the user's DNA so it can't be stolen. But you are old by the time it is finished. You are sickly, and you fear interacting with the past incarnation of yourself.

Thankfully, you meet a young girl named Sara. She eventually becomes your apprentice, and you tell her your entire story. Before you know it, you have a plan put together. She'll go back in your place.

Go to **Page 104**

And she does. Quite successfully, in fact. What happens next is hard to explain. It is like you cease to exist, but you don't. You're someone else, but you are you. Time warps all around you. Your memories feel hazy. You turn around to find that the room has changed. You look through the internet to find out what happened. You are satisfied to learn that the hospital Hitler was staying in burned down.

This feels like success to you, but at this point, you aren't sure why. Everything is slipping. You will spend the rest of your life going slowly insane. Half remembered events that never happened will plague you. But at least you accomplished something. If only you could remember what that something was...

END

There is no time to waste. You have to get to Hitler as soon as possible. You take Bauer and travel to Berlin. Hitler has set up a literal castle there. Upon arriving at the city, you find out that the he has gone far into the future and returned with incredibly advanced weaponry. Anyone who causes a disturbance is shot with a strange sort of stun-gun that makes them chronically ill. There are advanced gun turrets that prevent air strikes. There are robotic guards that line the entrances to every important building. You spend a month in the city setting yourselves up. You join the Nazi army in an attempt to infiltrate the castle. Thankfully, most of the war is already over. They have you doing local grunt work for a few years, but you rise through the ranks quickly.

Go to **Page 106**

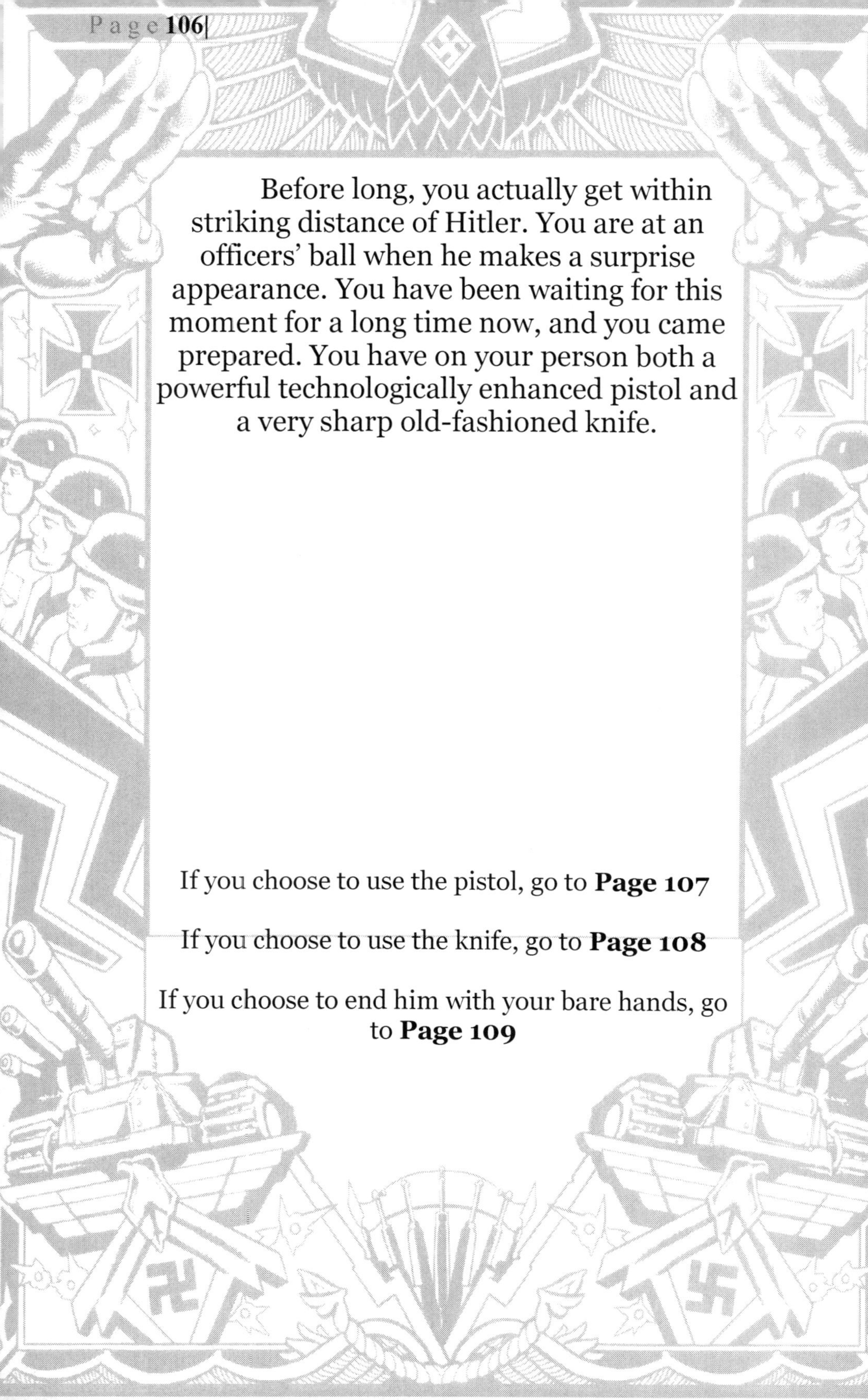

Before long, you actually get within striking distance of Hitler. You are at an officers' ball when he makes a surprise appearance. You have been waiting for this moment for a long time now, and you came prepared. You have on your person both a powerful technologically enhanced pistol and a very sharp old-fashioned knife.

If you choose to use the pistol, go to **Page 107**

If you choose to use the knife, go to **Page 108**

If you choose to end him with your bare hands, go to **Page 109**

Hitler brought the technology back from the future; it may as well serve to end him. You're a fan of irony. So you reach down to your hip and set your firearm to its fire setting. You wait until Hitler turns his back and you release a stream of literal flames onto him. He screams and begins to run around, flailing his arms. But suddenly it all stops and things shift. You feel funny. Didn't you just pull the trigger?

Hitler is standing where he was moments ago. Nothing has changed. You try again. He sidesteps and rolls out of the way just in time. A dozen guards – both organic and robotic – swarm you and beat you to a pulp. As they finish their savage assault, you remember that he has the respawn feature on his side. But it's too late. You're dead moments later.

END

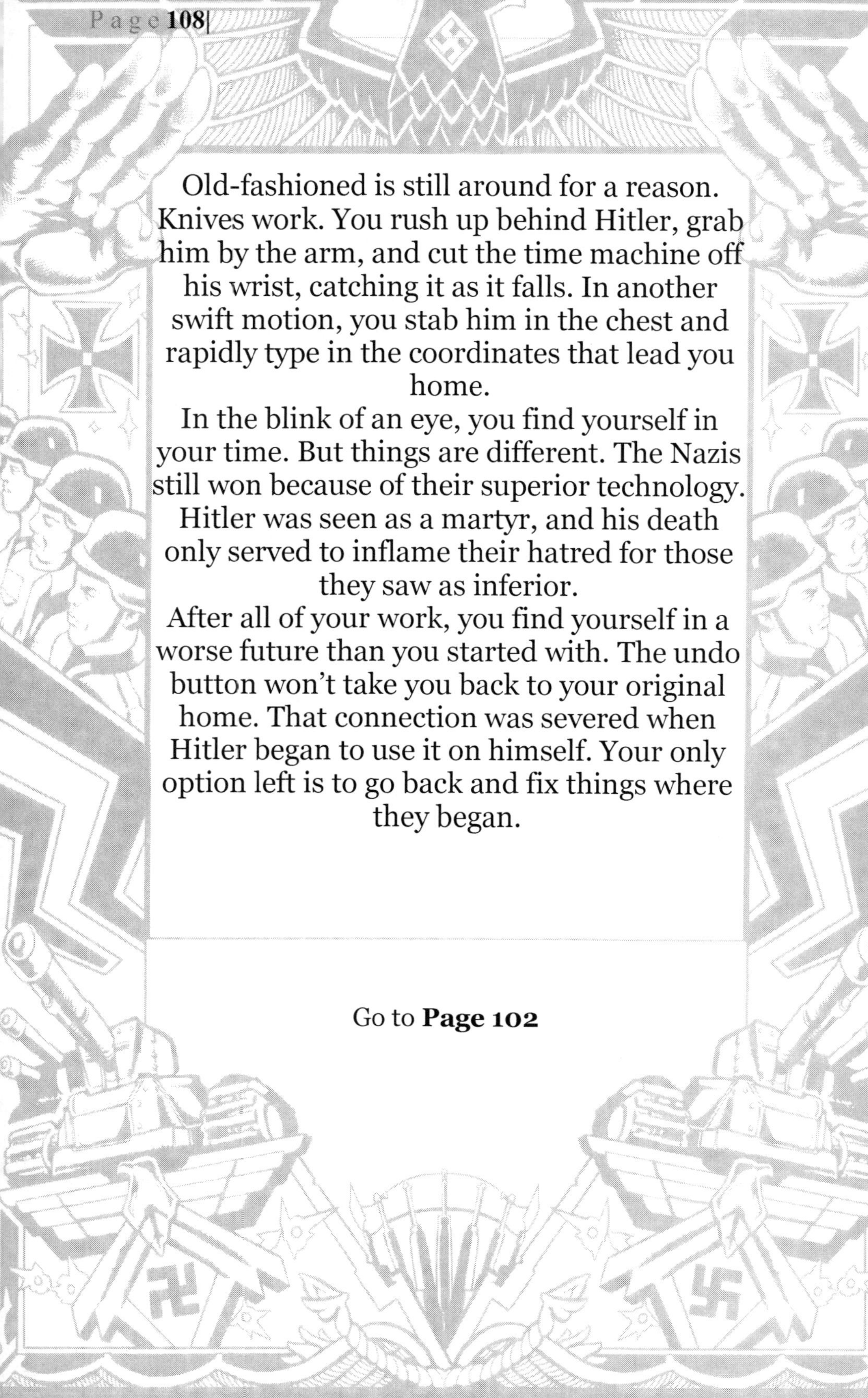

Old-fashioned is still around for a reason. Knives work. You rush up behind Hitler, grab him by the arm, and cut the time machine off his wrist, catching it as it falls. In another swift motion, you stab him in the chest and rapidly type in the coordinates that lead you home.

In the blink of an eye, you find yourself in your time. But things are different. The Nazis still won because of their superior technology. Hitler was seen as a martyr, and his death only served to inflame their hatred for those they saw as inferior.

After all of your work, you find yourself in a worse future than you started with. The undo button won't take you back to your original home. That connection was severed when Hitler began to use it on himself. Your only option left is to go back and fix things where they began.

Go to **Page 102**

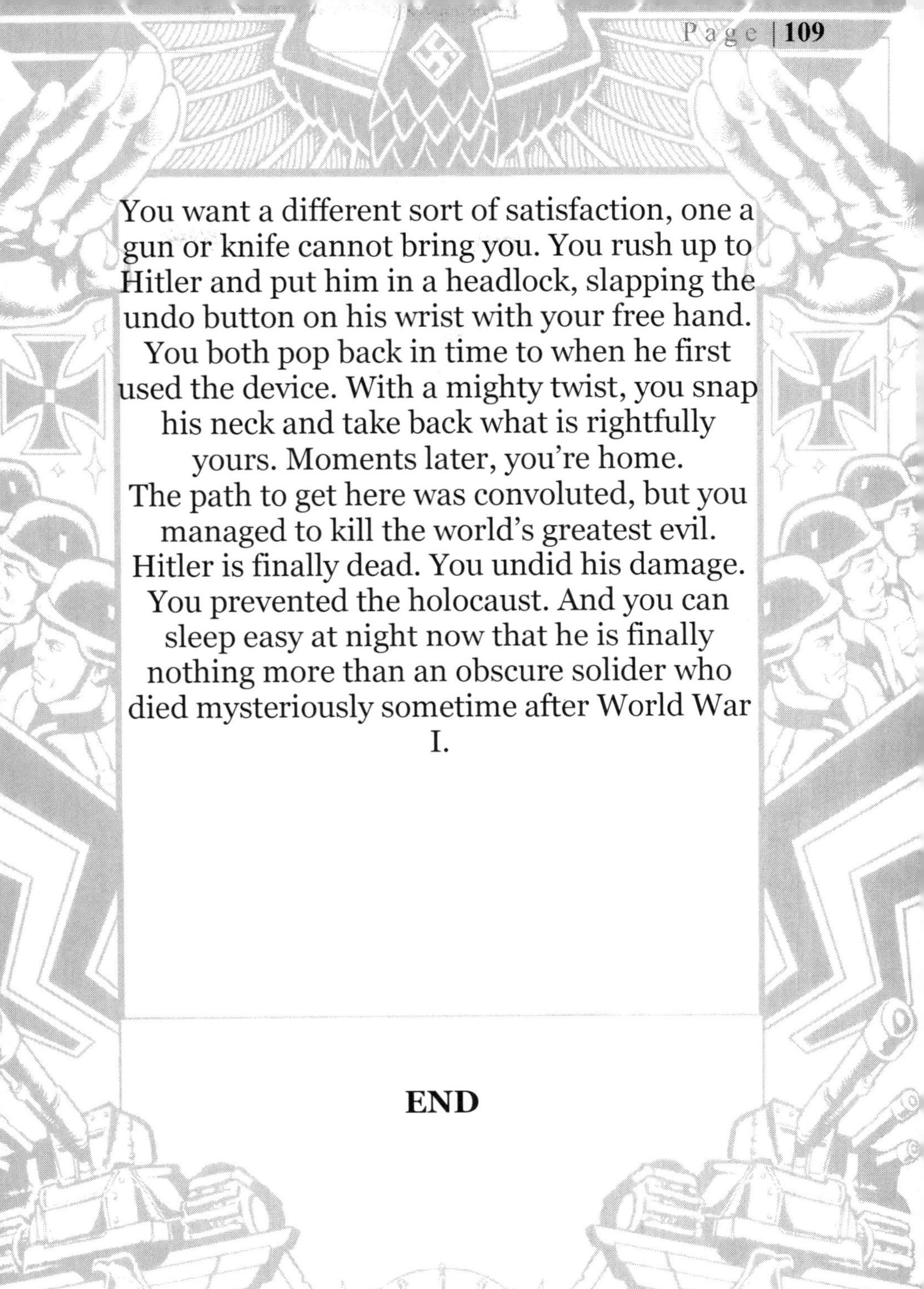

You want a different sort of satisfaction, one a gun or knife cannot bring you. You rush up to Hitler and put him in a headlock, slapping the undo button on his wrist with your free hand. You both pop back in time to when he first used the device. With a mighty twist, you snap his neck and take back what is rightfully yours. Moments later, you're home.

The path to get here was convoluted, but you managed to kill the world's greatest evil. Hitler is finally dead. You undid his damage. You prevented the holocaust. And you can sleep easy at night now that he is finally nothing more than an obscure solider who died mysteriously sometime after World War I.

END

You've given up before you've even begun. What the hell is wrong with you? Despite Rolf-ME242's belief in his time travel device, you've decided that you can't use it; the past cannot be changed for the better, at least not by you, so you refuse to take any jaunts into the past to fix the present and save the future.

Things slowly go from bad to worse. Ultimately, you are witness to the end of mankind, being one of the last to die off. You wonder, at the end, if you could have really done something to stop this. Sadly, or maybe not, it is now too late. Everything man has built has now been torn down. Perhaps when God starts again, he'll have more luck with a different species. You can't really imagine there being a Nazi raccoon, or Nazi cuttlefish. That would be crazy, right?

END, ya lazy bugger

You step out of the shimmering portal light to realize that you have arrived, but not in some historic location in old Germany or Austria. Instead, you have arrived in a quite lively, very strange looking tropical forest, not the kind of place you would ever expect to find the infamous Adolf Hitler. As you look around and take in the colourful environment, you begin to wonder if you are intended to catch him at some beachfront resort.

Images of Hitler at a beach resort create a certain amount of cognitive dissonance in your mind, but you have read that such vacations were a very popular pastime in the 20th and 21st century, at least while there were still tropical beaches, but you wonder if that actually caught on before WWII.

You are even more surprised when you spot a dragonfly a foot long whiz past you, and what definitely looks like several different species of dinosaurs wandering about.

Go to **Page 113**

This isn't the late nineteenth/early twentieth century. It can't possibly be. You have to have been sent millions of years further back. This is the Paleozoic! Maybe the Cretaceous Era, or more likely, from what you have studied, the Jurassic.

You stand amazed at this, and then check to see what kind of equipment you have been given that could possibly prepare you for such an arrival.

You are pleased to find that you are still wearing your jumpsuit, but otherwise, the only thing of note that you have on you is a fully charged laser pistol, a package of crackers, and a bottle of distilled water. You're feeling a bit peckish, so you finish off the crackers (there weren't that many, but at least they have a tasty cheese-like flavour). But this still doesn't solve your conundrum. You're here, a hundred million years in the past. What do you do now? How will anything you do affect the life of Hitler?

Do you try to find a place to hide and wait until you are pulled back to 2525? **Go to Page 114**

Do you decide to take a look around in this strange era, as you're likely to never get another chance? **Go to Page 116**

You find a place to hide, in a hollow between a collection of weird palm trees, hoping that you can hang on here until the Timeband pulls you back to 2525. Hopefully you won't be eaten by a dinosaur in the meantime. However, the wait goes on and on, and while you are still waiting for your return ticket, suddenly a number of loud noises surround your hideaway, and before you know it, a pack of tiger-striped velociraptors shows up, sniffing around for food. It's obvious that they have picked up your tasty scent and have quickly surrounded you. Unfortunately, there are enough gaps for their relatively small snouts filled with nasty, razor sharp teeth to get at you.

So you try to get away from them, using the laser for defence. You manage to shoot a few of them dead, but there are too many in the pack to kill them all, and they're too fast and hungry to be dissuaded once your laser is out of charge.

Go to **Page 115**

As a last ditch effort, you try and climb up a tree, but it turn out that the raptors are quite adept at climbing as well, and a couple of the most athletic of the beasts manage to grab you by the legs and pull you down to the ground. You heroically manage to stun one of them with your mighty fists before the pack sets upon you, viciously tearing and rendering your delectable flesh. Your last hope is that when the Timeband pulls you back, there will be enough of you left to be put back together again.

Open your eyes: go to **Page 118**

Keep 'em closed: go to **Page 120**

Your curiosity about this strange and beautiful world overwhelms your fear of the potentially dangerous aspects of this untouched environment. You decide to take a look around, hoping that you'll be able to stay out of trouble long enough to be able to get back to your own time, as well as avoid becoming dino chow. To your appreciation, the hike is truly breath-taking.

You witness some amazing sights: packs of velociraptors hunting prey in a style that is far different from what you have witnessed in virtual Paleozoic parks; a herd of massive herbivores whose every step makes the ground shake beneath their huge feet, not to mention crushes both forest floor plants and small animals to a pulp.

Go to **Page 117**

As has been long proven, many of the dinosaurs have various kinds of colourful feathers adorning their bodies. They hardly seem reptilian at all, and you are witness to the astonishing and ferocious battles of survival that go on regularly in this primordial and savage landscape. Considering the stark world of machines and technology you come from, this is quite the treat!

Your dinosaur safari experience reaches its climax when you get to see first-hand a massive Allosaurus chase down a terrified Diplodocus. You watch in awe as several large trees are reduced to kindling while huge predator and prey battle. And you want to stay to watch the large dino dine on its recently killed prey, fascinated by it all, but you find yourself having to shoo off some rather large, flying, mosquito-like insects that seem to have taken a sudden and alarming interest in you.

Do you continue to watch in awe while the infamous predator dines on his dinner?
Go to **Page 122**

Do you head off to spot some even more amazing sights?
Go to **Page 125**

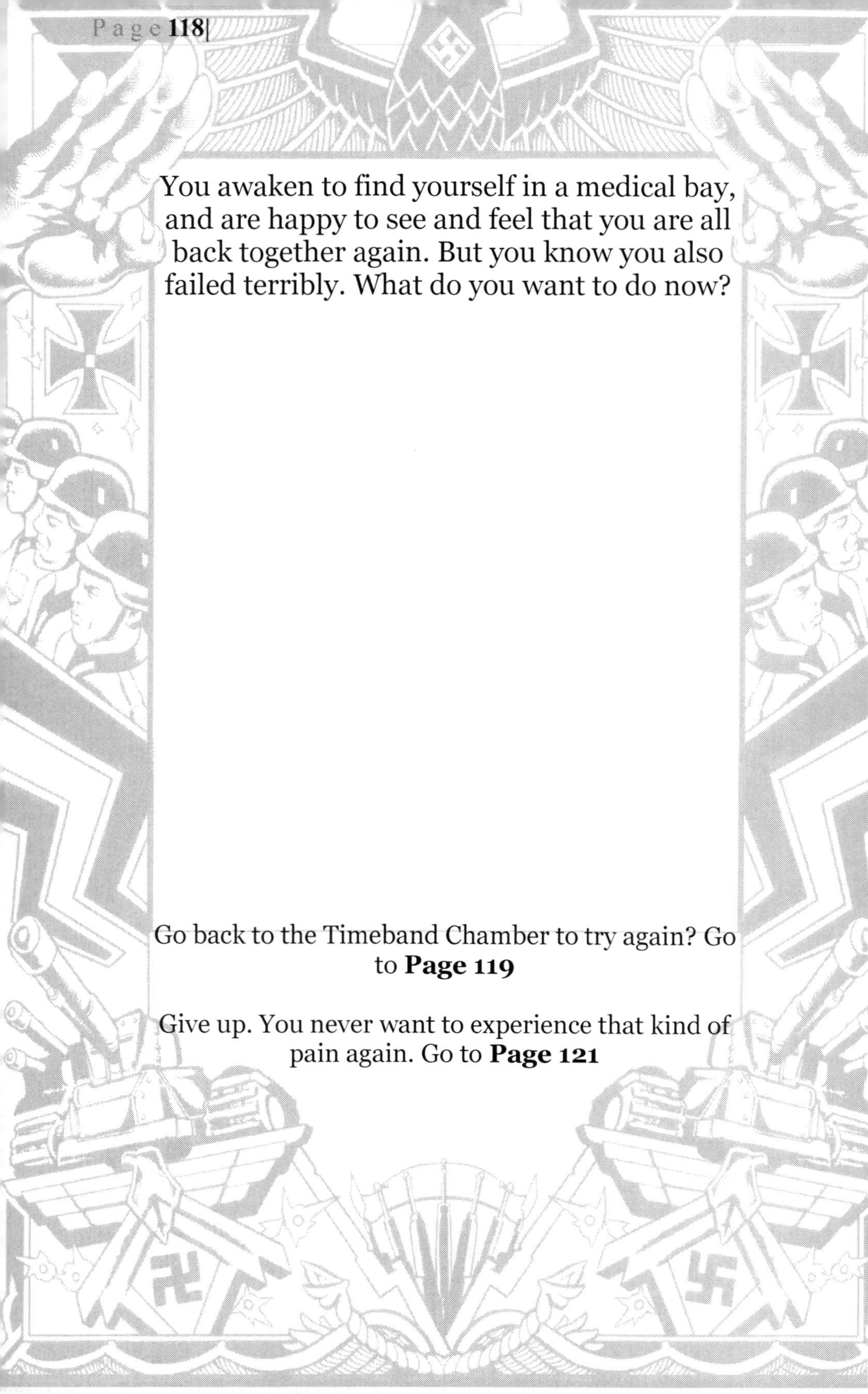

You awaken to find yourself in a medical bay, and are happy to see and feel that you are all back together again. But you know you also failed terribly. What do you want to do now?

Go back to the Timeband Chamber to try again? Go to **Page 119**

Give up. You never want to experience that kind of pain again. Go to **Page 121**

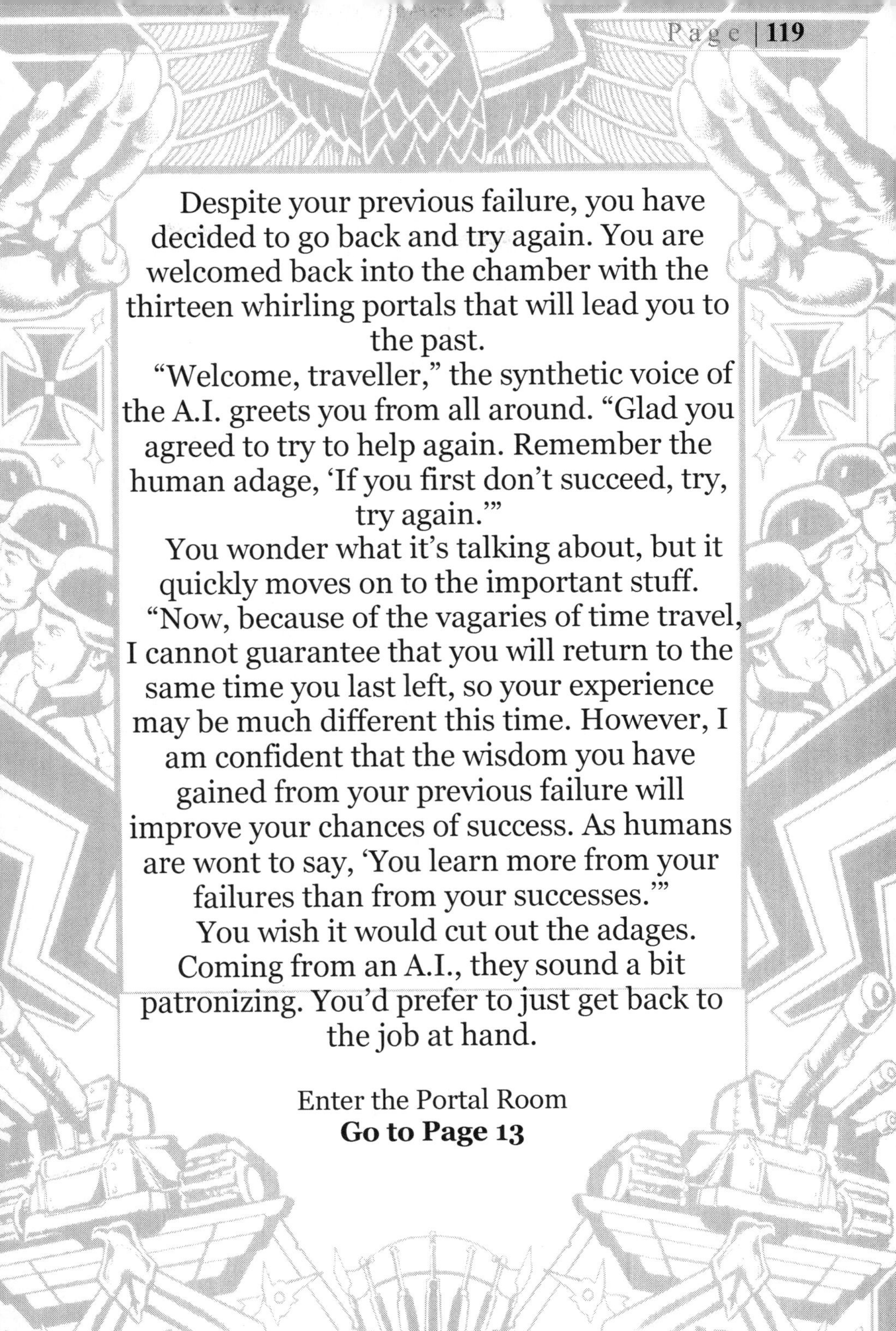

Despite your previous failure, you have decided to go back and try again. You are welcomed back into the chamber with the thirteen whirling portals that will lead you to the past.

"Welcome, traveller," the synthetic voice of the A.I. greets you from all around. "Glad you agreed to try to help again. Remember the human adage, 'If you first don't succeed, try, try again.'"

You wonder what it's talking about, but it quickly moves on to the important stuff.

"Now, because of the vagaries of time travel, I cannot guarantee that you will return to the same time you last left, so your experience may be much different this time. However, I am confident that the wisdom you have gained from your previous failure will improve your chances of success. As humans are wont to say, 'You learn more from your failures than from your successes.'"

You wish it would cut out the adages. Coming from an A.I., they sound a bit patronizing. You'd prefer to just get back to the job at hand.

Enter the Portal Room

Go to Page 13

Well, the world stays dark, though you can feel the cold, hard metal on your back and you can scratch yourself, so it can't be too bad.

Open your eyes. Go to **Page 118**

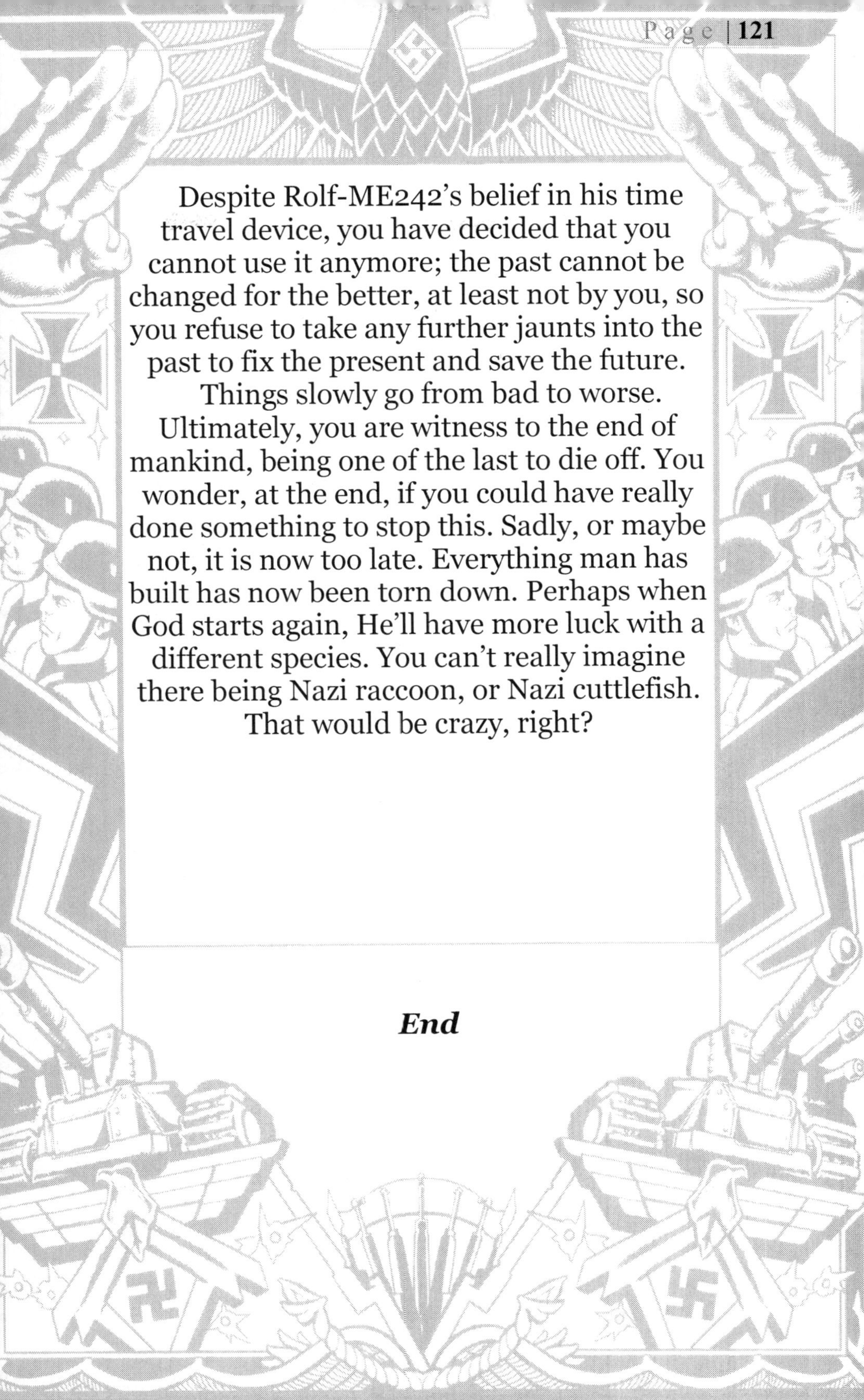

Despite Rolf-ME242's belief in his time travel device, you have decided that you cannot use it anymore; the past cannot be changed for the better, at least not by you, so you refuse to take any further jaunts into the past to fix the present and save the future.

Things slowly go from bad to worse. Ultimately, you are witness to the end of mankind, being one of the last to die off. You wonder, at the end, if you could have really done something to stop this. Sadly, or maybe not, it is now too late. Everything man has built has now been torn down. Perhaps when God starts again, He'll have more luck with a different species. You can't really imagine there being Nazi raccoon, or Nazi cuttlefish. That would be crazy, right?

End

Those huge mosquito-like insects that have been bothering you disappear for a while, leaving you to comfortably watch a scene of incredible and entertaining savagery (in a discovery channel kind of way) unfold before your eyes – from a safe distance away in the underbrush, of course. However, they then suddenly return in a cloud so big that there is no way that enough of them they can be shooed away to save you from a horrible and bloodless end. These things are nearly as big as hummingbirds and as relentless as black flies.

You realize to your horror that the cloud probably contains enough members to suck all the blood out of you. In an attempt to save yourself, you jump out of the undergrowth where you've been hiding and run for your life, chased by this scary cloud of flying vampire insects.

Go to **Page 123**

This act, however, causes you to lose all the cover that you once had and puts you right in the sights of several of the smaller (but still very large) scavengers and predators that have been lying in wait for their chance at the huge carcass the Allosaurus is still feasting on. You are quickly surrounded and run down by several of the feathered and scaled beasties.

As you are being chomped, you hope that there will be enough of you left to put back together by advanced 26th century science.

When you regain consciousness, you to find yourself in a medical pod with some new limbs, organs, and skin, but are at least somewhat able to see and feel that you are still alive. You are also aware you failed in your mission. What do you want to do now?

You're tough. Head back to the Timeband Chamber to try again.
Go to **Page 119**

You've endured enough pain, let someone else suffer.
Go to **Page 121**

Leaving the Allosaurus to its meal as well as allowing those nasty giant Jurassic mosquitoes to seek out more appropriate prey, you decide to continue on your Paleozoic hike, having been attracted onto a new path by the sound of a river in the distance. The sound grows louder and more intense, the ground shakes, and after a few more minutes of forcing your way through palm leaves and ferns, you come across a fast rushing river replete with mini waterfalls. You can see that the river winds up and down the twisting path through the jungle.

You realize that you've been hiking for quite a while, but you still feel amazingly energetic; you decide this is probably due to the much higher level of oxygen that this era's atmosphere provides. The levels have to be much higher than what you are used to experiencing in your century far in the future. By the year 2525, much of the Earth is a wasteland, and there are hardly any trees around anymore.

Go to **Page 126**

You decide to follow the river, and your hike leads you down the jungle path where you finally reach a large body of water of quite impressive size, a lake at the least; you can't see any land on the other side, although there are a number of richly vegetated islands out in the chocolate and bluish waters that lay before you. Having finished off your distilled water some time before, you decide to stop at the river mouth and get a drink of water, hoping that the shots of nanomeds you were given before this time traveling jaunt included dealing with whatever protozoans, bacteria, or other parasites might dwell in the water you are refilling your bottle from. Regardless, the water is quite cool and refreshing, so you stop worrying about any danger it might pose. Likely, nothing in it will harm you before you are drawn back to 2525 anyways.

Suddenly, from behind some nearby bushes, you hear what sounds like a loud commotion.

Do you check it out? Go to **Page 127**

Do you finish getting yourself a long, cool drink? Go to **Page 130**

Another bout of curiosity makes you decide to forgo slaking your thirst entirely for the moment and check out what all the racket is on the other side of the bushes. You push your way through, which isn't exactly easy since the bushes have thorns that catch on your jumpsuit, but you do finally make it through without much damage. 26th century smartcloth is pretty freakin' tough.

What you behold on the other side, however, is a sight that you would not have possibly ever believed if you weren't seeing it with your own two perfectly functional eyes.

A single raptor of some type that you don't remember seeing in any fossil record you've read appears to actually be addressing a crowd of similar creatures from high upon a rocky outcropping. It's squawking and howling in what can't possibly be a language.

Go to **Page 129**

Dinosaurs aren't that smart, right? But regardless of that, it does seem like all the others are listening. They seem completely hypnotised by the alpha raptor.

What you also find even more incredible, if that's at all possible, is that the alpha raptor and all of its fellow raptors have a very distinct colour pattern all over their scaly hides. It's instantly recognisable; grey, red, and black hides are all covered in what looks like mini swastikas. Your mind reels. Could this event, likely a hundred and fifty million years before humanity even existed, possibly have any relevance to the rise of Hitler and the Nazis and therefore your miserable world? It seems crazy, but you were sent to this time and place by an admittedly self-described, genius A. I. You may have very well been sent here for a reason. The question is, you're here, the creatures are here: what are you going to do about it?

Do you pull out the laser to shoot the alpha (Hitler) raptor dead?

Go to **Page 132**

Do you remain and enjoy the show, thinking that this must just be an incredible coincidence? Seriously, what else could it possibly be?

Go to **Page 134**

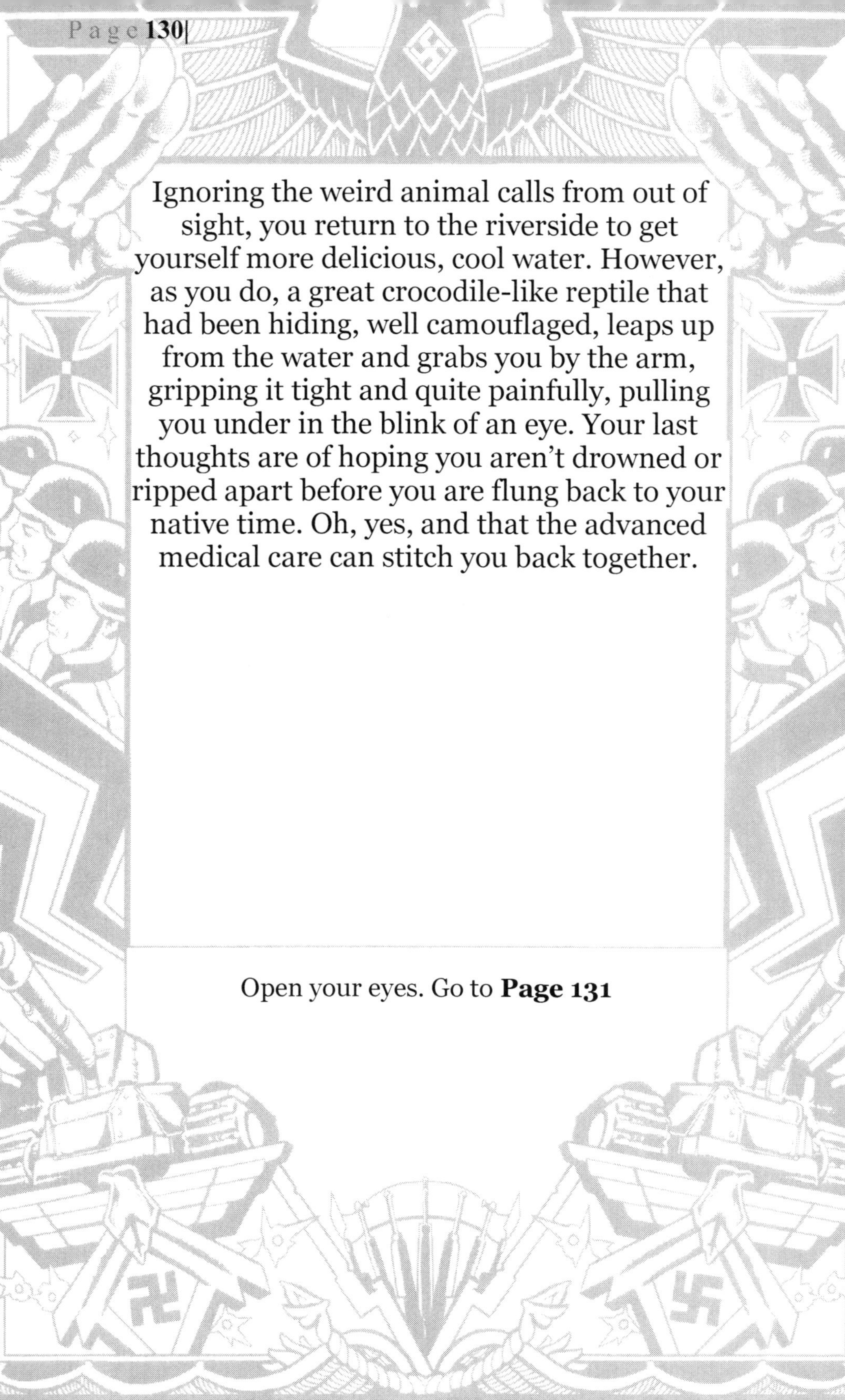

Ignoring the weird animal calls from out of sight, you return to the riverside to get yourself more delicious, cool water. However, as you do, a great crocodile-like reptile that had been hiding, well camouflaged, leaps up from the water and grabs you by the arm, gripping it tight and quite painfully, pulling you under in the blink of an eye. Your last thoughts are of hoping you aren't drowned or ripped apart before you are flung back to your native time. Oh, yes, and that the advanced medical care can stitch you back together.

Open your eyes. Go to **Page 131**

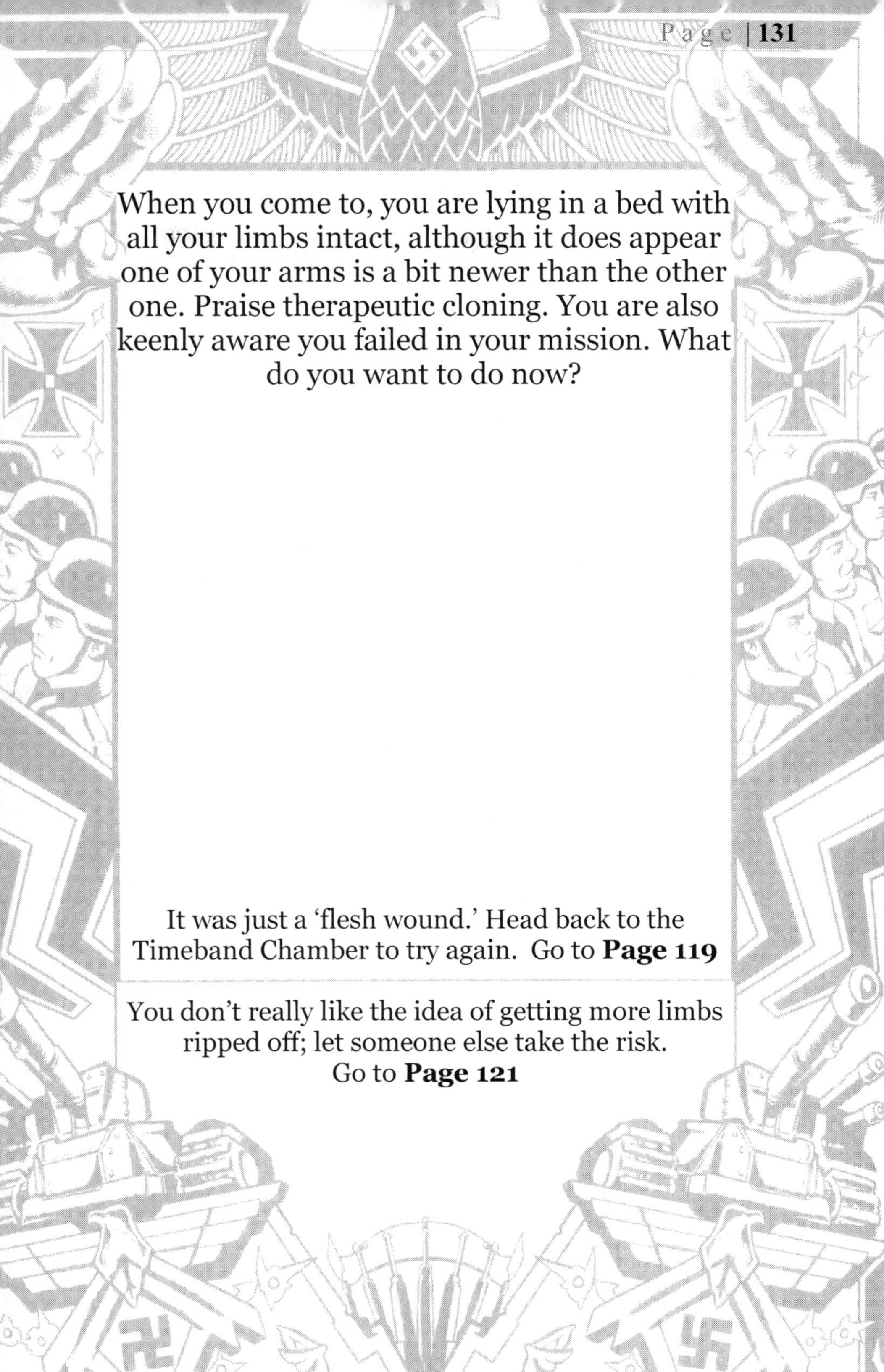

When you come to, you are lying in a bed with all your limbs intact, although it does appear one of your arms is a bit newer than the other one. Praise therapeutic cloning. You are also keenly aware you failed in your mission. What do you want to do now?

It was just a 'flesh wound.' Head back to the Timeband Chamber to try again. Go to **Page 119**

You don't really like the idea of getting more limbs ripped off; let someone else take the risk.
Go to **Page 121**

You make the decision to shoot the alpha swastika raptor. You pull out your laser pistol, take aim at the squawking dinosaur on the glimmering rock-like podium, and fire! Your powerful sidearm shoots out a beam of red light and instantly burns a hole through the raptor's body, killing it. The creature stops in mid scream and collapses, falling down on the rock and then tumbling down to the gathering below.

This, however, doesn't cause the creatures to disperse as you had hoped. What it has done is signal your very position to the hundred or so other swastika-bearing raptors that are now looking around and squawking, croaking, and screaming in confusion. They are clearly no longer mesmerized by their alpha, and must realize how hungry they now are, because they turn their eyes, claws, and teeth on you!

Go to **Page 133**

There is no place to run or hide, and your laser's store of energy is pathetically small. They gotcha!

As you are being ripped apart in excruciating pain, you cannot realistically imagine that there will enough of you to put back together once you are pulled back to your own time.

Open your eyes. Go to **Page 131**

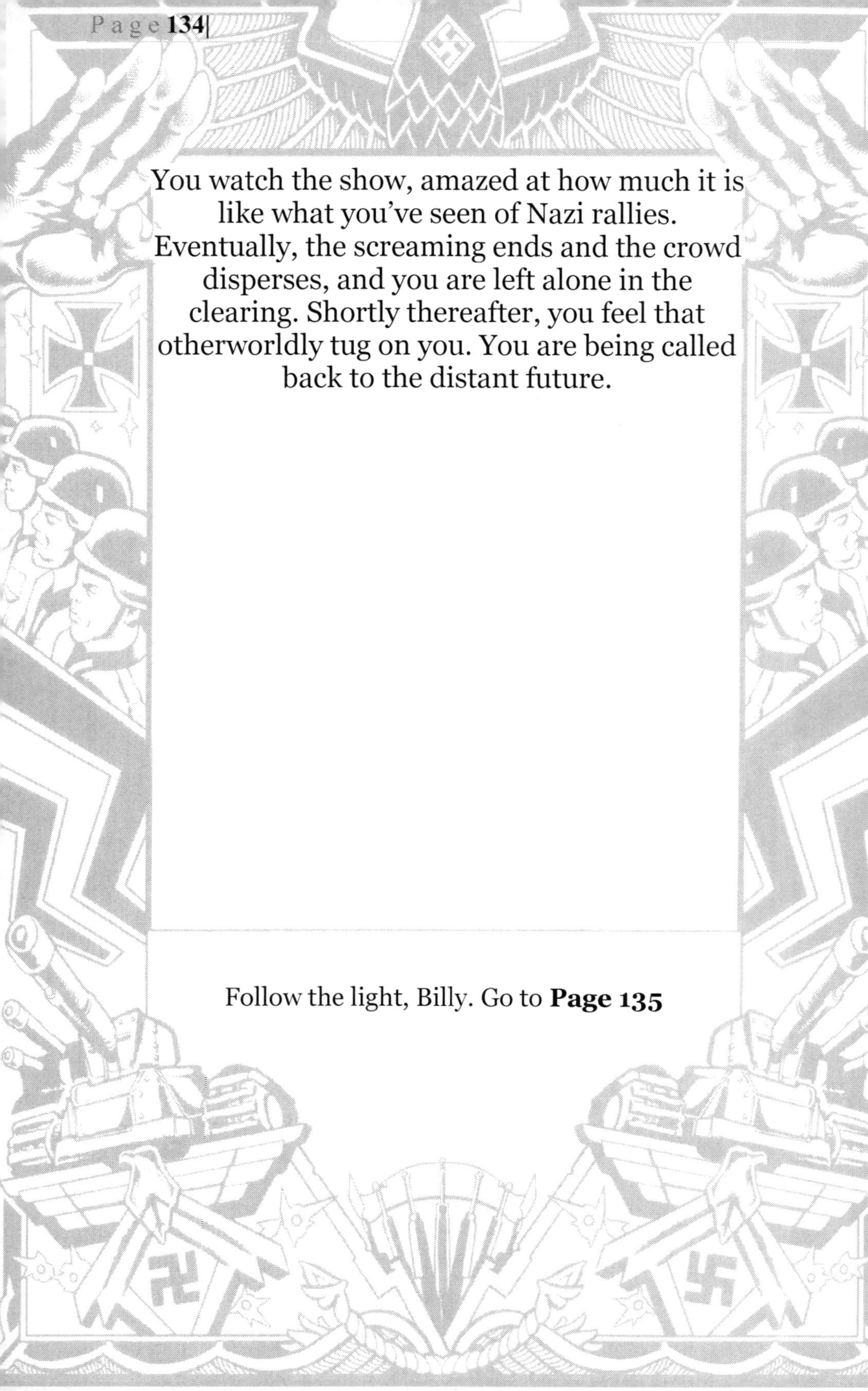

You watch the show, amazed at how much it is like what you've seen of Nazi rallies. Eventually, the screaming ends and the crowd disperses, and you are left alone in the clearing. Shortly thereafter, you feel that otherworldly tug on you. You are being called back to the distant future.

Follow the light, Billy. Go to **Page 135**

You find it hard to believe when you open your eyes and discover that you are alive. You are told by the attendants that there wasn't much of you left, but they did manage to piece you back together from bits of bone, flesh, and ganglia. Who are you, you wonder?

Ah, the wonders of modern medicine. But now, what about that time travel thing?

Do you give it another go? Go to **Page 119**

Do you decide it's time to get to really know yourself again? Go to **Page 121**

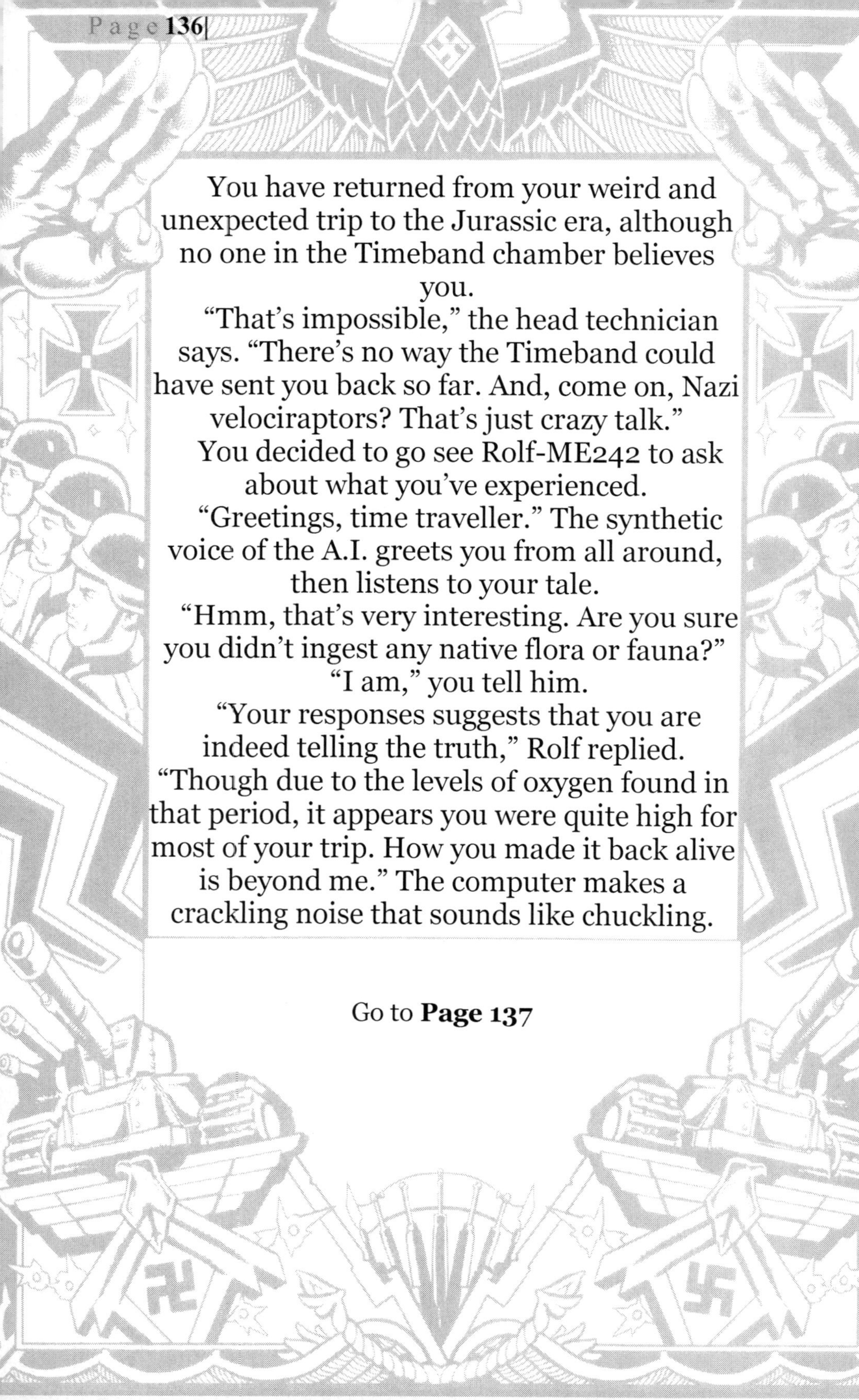

You have returned from your weird and unexpected trip to the Jurassic era, although no one in the Timeband chamber believes you.

"That's impossible," the head technician says. "There's no way the Timeband could have sent you back so far. And, come on, Nazi velociraptors? That's just crazy talk."

You decided to go see Rolf-ME242 to ask about what you've experienced.

"Greetings, time traveller." The synthetic voice of the A.I. greets you from all around, then listens to your tale.

"Hmm, that's very interesting. Are you sure you didn't ingest any native flora or fauna?"

"I am," you tell him.

"Your responses suggests that you are indeed telling the truth," Rolf replied. "Though due to the levels of oxygen found in that period, it appears you were quite high for most of your trip. How you made it back alive is beyond me." The computer makes a crackling noise that sounds like chuckling.

Go to **Page 137**

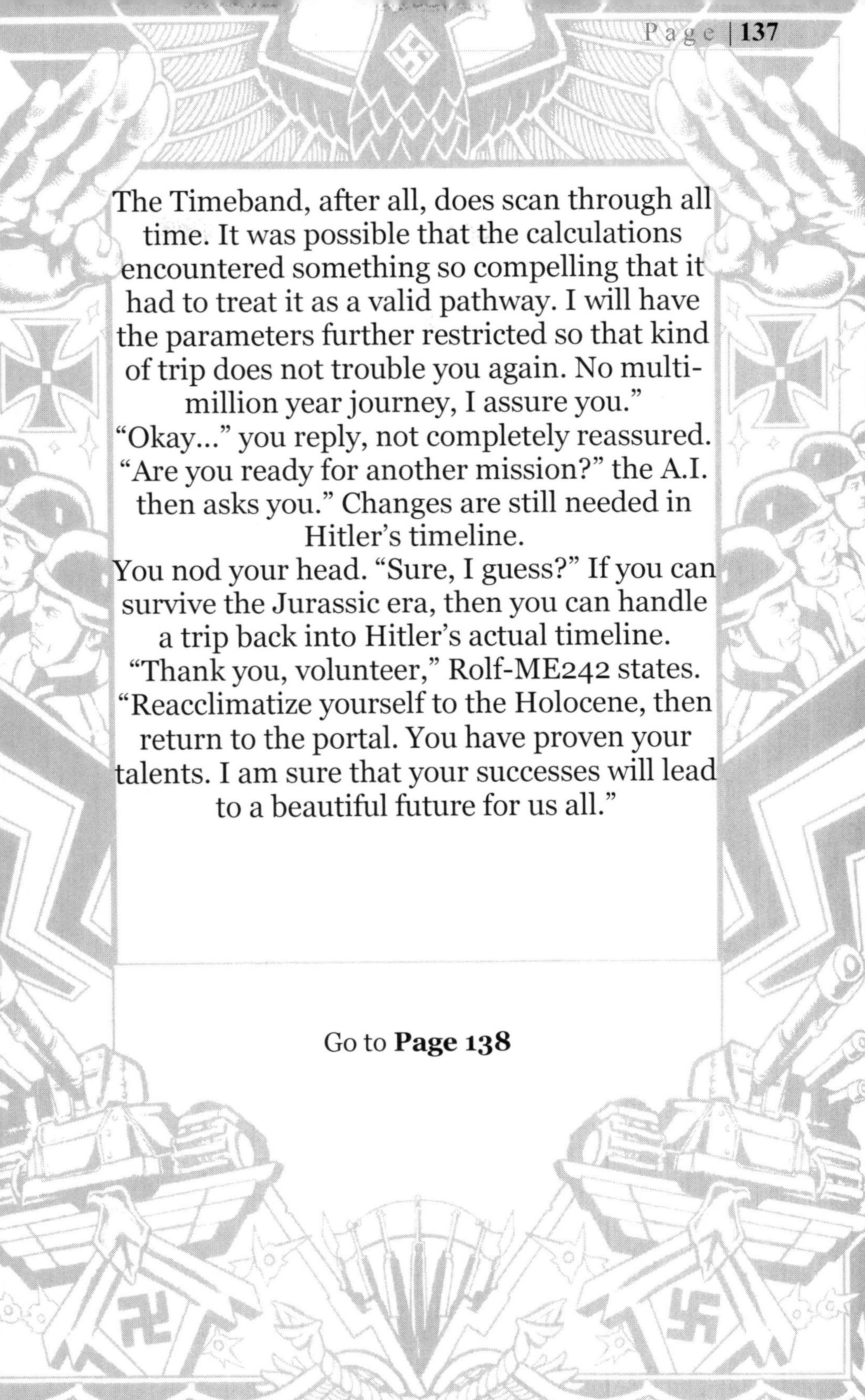

The Timeband, after all, does scan through all time. It was possible that the calculations encountered something so compelling that it had to treat it as a valid pathway. I will have the parameters further restricted so that kind of trip does not trouble you again. No multi-million year journey, I assure you."

"Okay..." you reply, not completely reassured.

"Are you ready for another mission?" the A.I. then asks you." Changes are still needed in Hitler's timeline.

You nod your head. "Sure, I guess?" If you can survive the Jurassic era, then you can handle a trip back into Hitler's actual timeline.

"Thank you, volunteer," Rolf-ME242 states. "Reacclimatize yourself to the Holocene, then return to the portal. You have proven your talents. I am sure that your successes will lead to a beautiful future for us all."

Go to **Page 138**

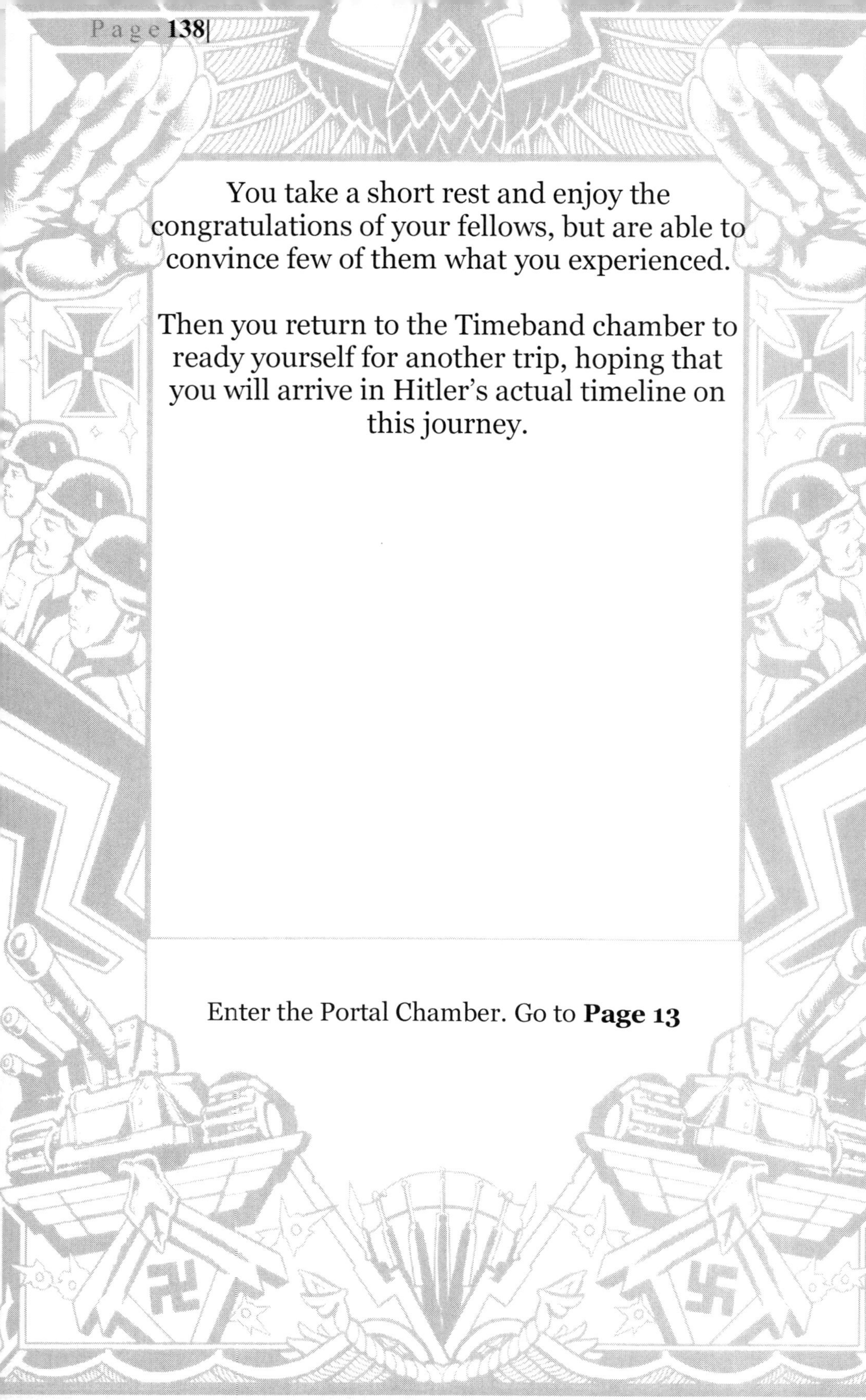

You take a short rest and enjoy the congratulations of your fellows, but are able to convince few of them what you experienced.

Then you return to the Timeband chamber to ready yourself for another trip, hoping that you will arrive in Hitler's actual timeline on this journey.

Enter the Portal Chamber. Go to **Page 13**

The brilliant white light surrounds you the moment you step into the portal. You can't see what's in front of you for more than a few steps. Slowly but surely, however, images start appearing before you and all around you, vague at first – buildings, animals, people... You finally step fully out onto a cobblestone street, and all the surreal imagery becomes solid, real.

You look around in amazement at the classically built wood and brick buildings and take in the smells and sounds of the world five centuries before you were born. And you realize that you have just stepped into a pile of horse manure, which you quickly work on scraping off your strange-looking shoes.

In fact, all your clothing is as strange as the sights and smells. It is heavy and cumbersome, not at all like the smart fabrics you are accustomed to. On the bright side, however, this is more evidence that you have truly time travelled.

Go to **Page 140**

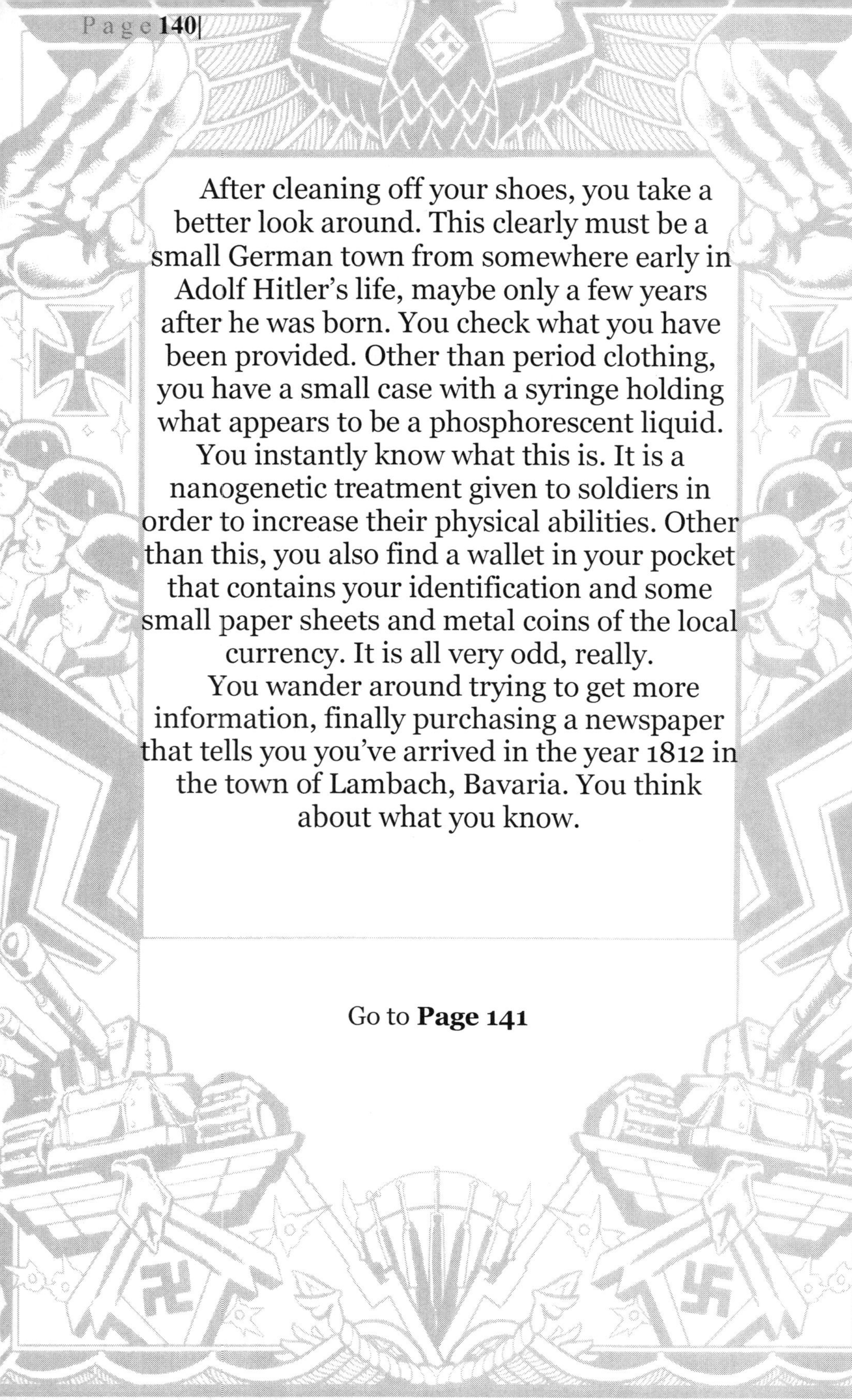

After cleaning off your shoes, you take a better look around. This clearly must be a small German town from somewhere early in Adolf Hitler's life, maybe only a few years after he was born. You check what you have been provided. Other than period clothing, you have a small case with a syringe holding what appears to be a phosphorescent liquid. You instantly know what this is. It is a nanogenetic treatment given to soldiers in order to increase their physical abilities. Other than this, you also find a wallet in your pocket that contains your identification and some small paper sheets and metal coins of the local currency. It is all very odd, really.

You wander around trying to get more information, finally purchasing a newspaper that tells you you've arrived in the year 1812 in the town of Lambach, Bavaria. You think about what you know.

Go to **Page 141**

Hitler would be a seven year old boy right now, and his father would have a house somewhere just outside of town. Your knowledge tells you that this is the year that Hitler's older brother, Alois Jr., will run away from their abusive father, and little Adolf will be stuck facing Alois Sr.'s wrath instead. The nanogenetic treatment must be for Alois. And you must be here to convince him to not run away, but to protect his mother and siblings from his father's drunken rages. However, despite the fact that Lambach is not a large town, you find the streets confusing and you quickly get lost looking for the Hitler home. What do you do?

Do you ask for directions? Go to **Page 142**

Do you decide to trust your own sense of direction and find the Hitlers' house yourself?
Go to **Page 145**

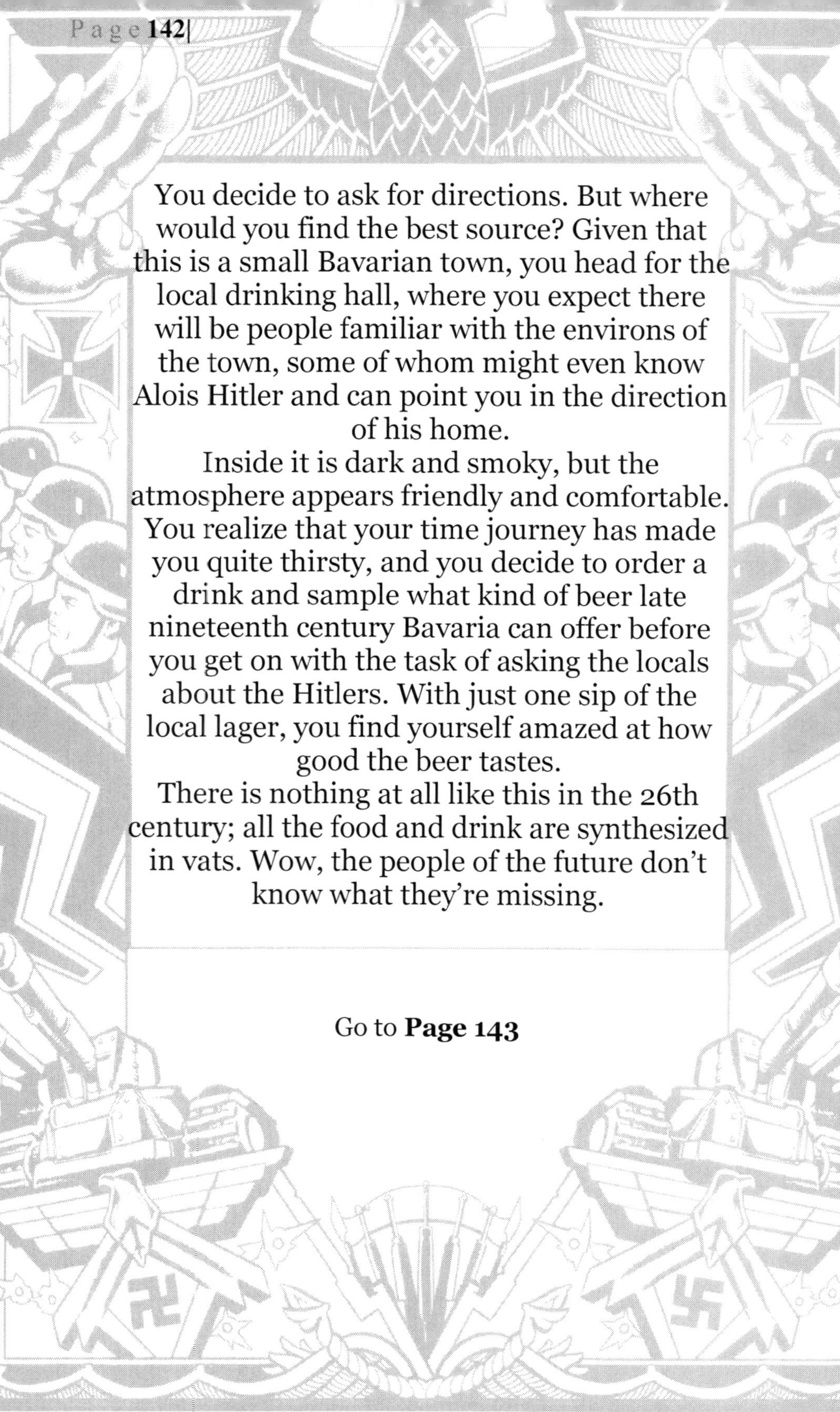

You decide to ask for directions. But where would you find the best source? Given that this is a small Bavarian town, you head for the local drinking hall, where you expect there will be people familiar with the environs of the town, some of whom might even know Alois Hitler and can point you in the direction of his home.

Inside it is dark and smoky, but the atmosphere appears friendly and comfortable. You realize that your time journey has made you quite thirsty, and you decide to order a drink and sample what kind of beer late nineteenth century Bavaria can offer before you get on with the task of asking the locals about the Hitlers. With just one sip of the local lager, you find yourself amazed at how good the beer tastes.

There is nothing at all like this in the 26th century; all the food and drink are synthesized in vats. Wow, the people of the future don't know what they're missing.

Go to **Page 143**

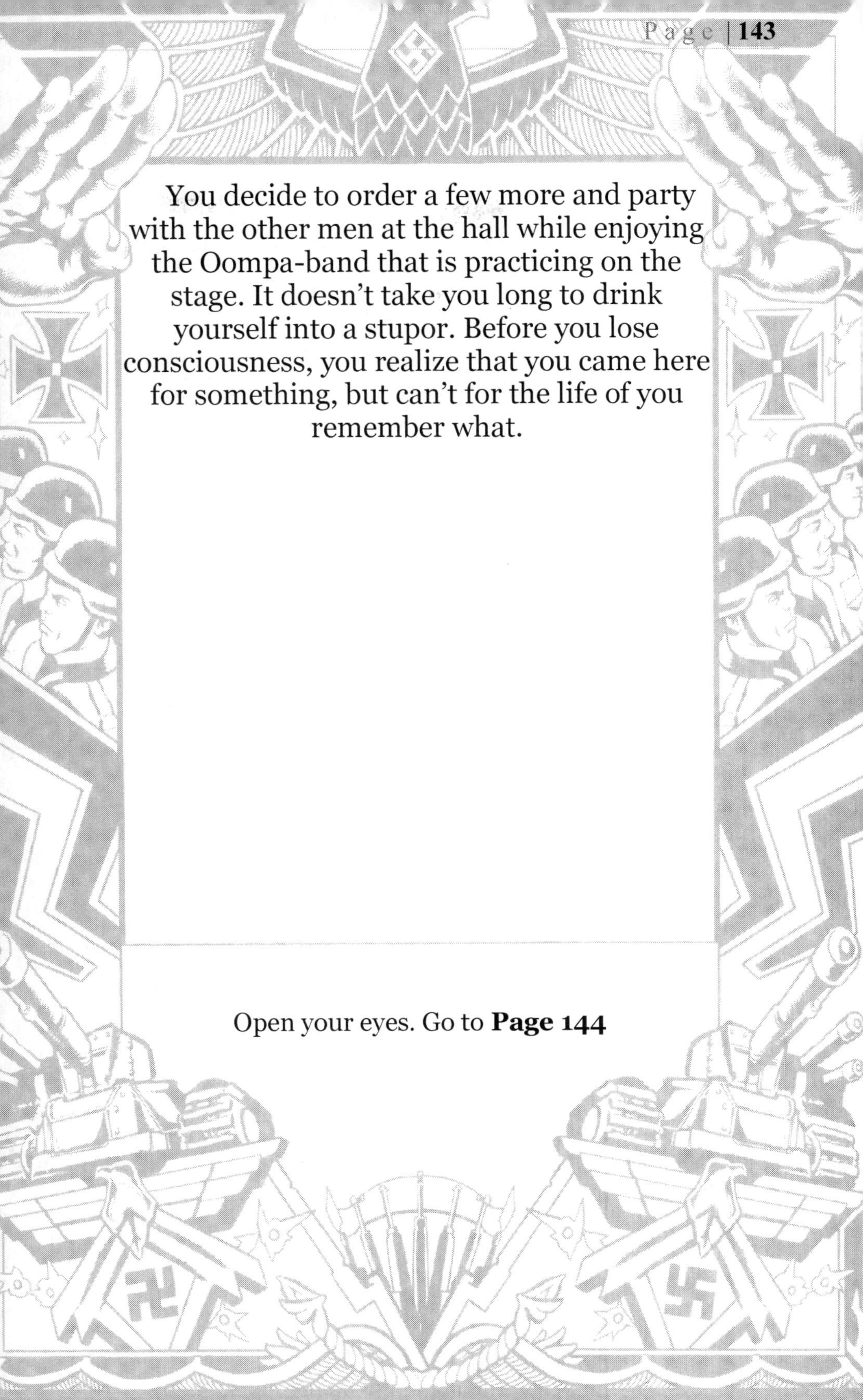

You decide to order a few more and party with the other men at the hall while enjoying the Oompa-band that is practicing on the stage. It doesn't take you long to drink yourself into a stupor. Before you lose consciousness, you realize that you came here for something, but can't for the life of you remember what.

Open your eyes. Go to **Page 144**

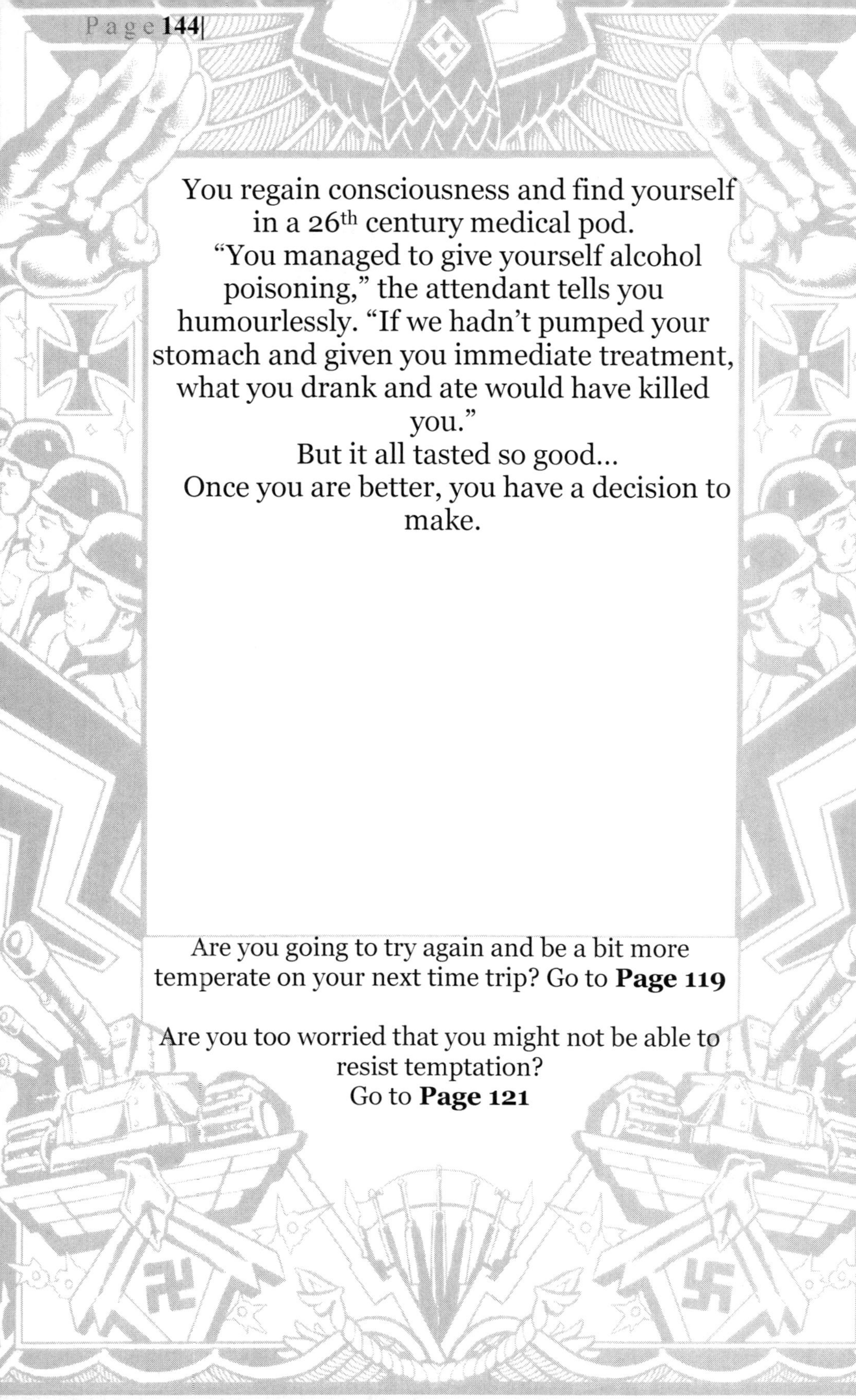

You regain consciousness and find yourself in a 26th century medical pod.

"You managed to give yourself alcohol poisoning," the attendant tells you humourlessly. "If we hadn't pumped your stomach and given you immediate treatment, what you drank and ate would have killed you."

But it all tasted so good…

Once you are better, you have a decision to make.

Are you going to try again and be a bit more temperate on your next time trip? Go to **Page 119**

Are you too worried that you might not be able to resist temptation?

Go to **Page 121**

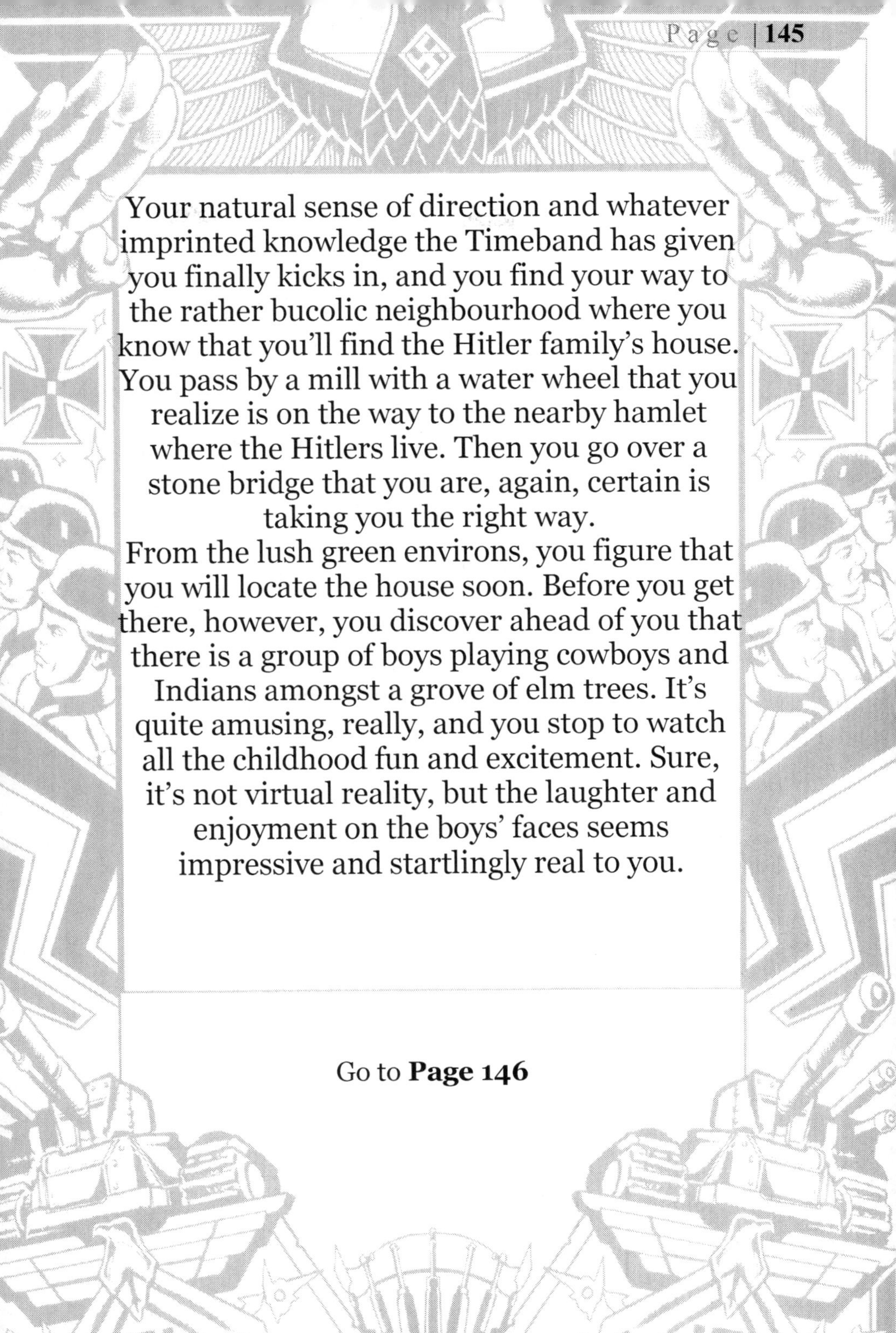

Your natural sense of direction and whatever imprinted knowledge the Timeband has given you finally kicks in, and you find your way to the rather bucolic neighbourhood where you know that you'll find the Hitler family's house. You pass by a mill with a water wheel that you realize is on the way to the nearby hamlet where the Hitlers live. Then you go over a stone bridge that you are, again, certain is taking you the right way.

From the lush green environs, you figure that you will locate the house soon. Before you get there, however, you discover ahead of you that there is a group of boys playing cowboys and Indians amongst a grove of elm trees. It's quite amusing, really, and you stop to watch all the childhood fun and excitement. Sure, it's not virtual reality, but the laughter and enjoyment on the boys' faces seems impressive and startlingly real to you.

Go to **Page 146**

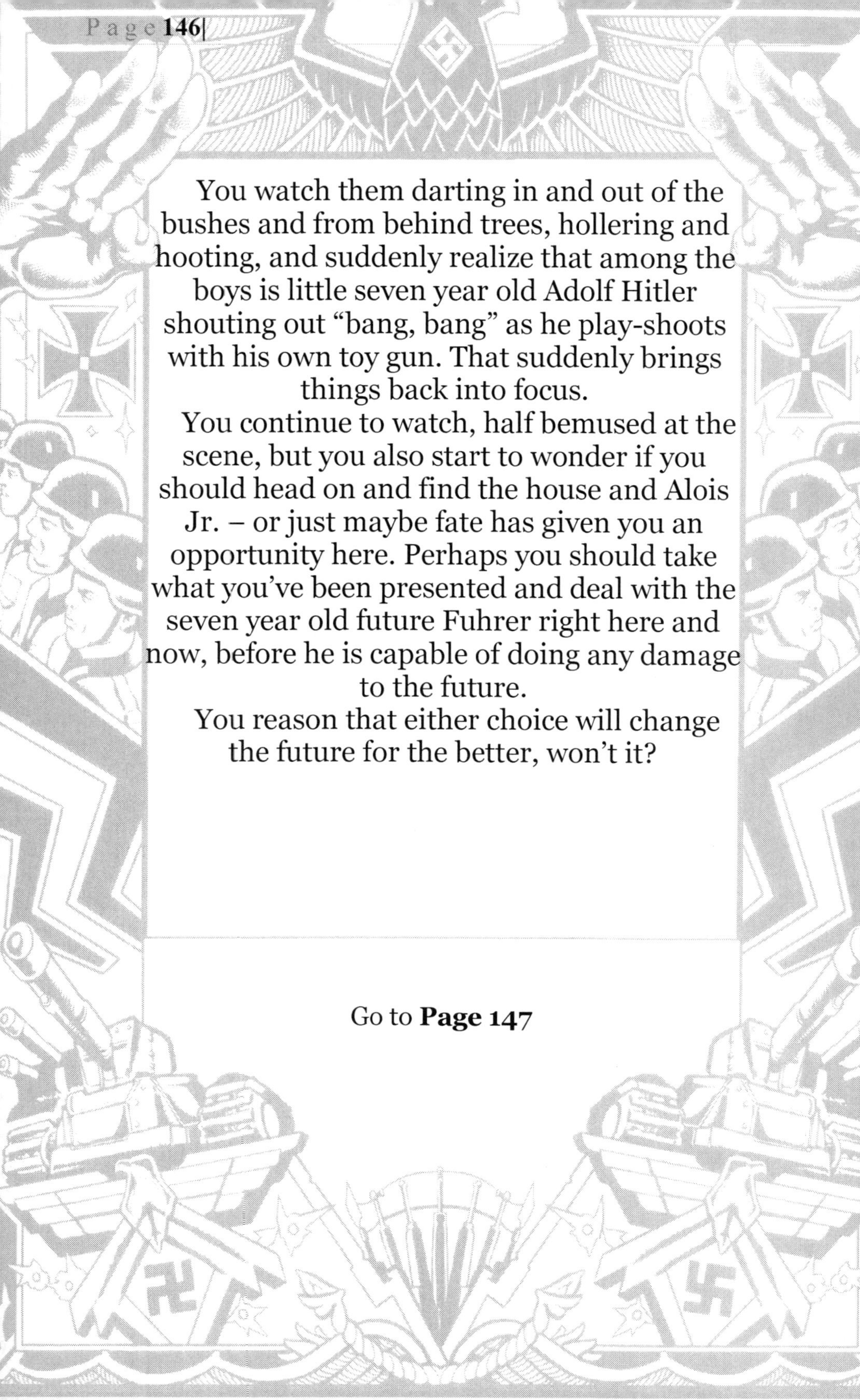

You watch them darting in and out of the bushes and from behind trees, hollering and hooting, and suddenly realize that among the boys is little seven year old Adolf Hitler shouting out "bang, bang" as he play-shoots with his own toy gun. That suddenly brings things back into focus.

You continue to watch, half bemused at the scene, but you also start to wonder if you should head on and find the house and Alois Jr. – or just maybe fate has given you an opportunity here. Perhaps you should take what you've been presented and deal with the seven year old future Fuhrer right here and now, before he is capable of doing any damage to the future.

You reason that either choice will change the future for the better, won't it?

Go to **Page 147**

It’s like time has laid this out especially for you to act on. Sure, he’s just a kid, but he will also grow up to be the murderer of millions and lead the world and humanity to the brink of oblivion. So, what are you going to do about it?

Do you carry on trying to find Alois Jr.? Go to **Page 148**

Or do you sneak up on young Hitler and wring the little monster’s neck?
Go to **Page 150**

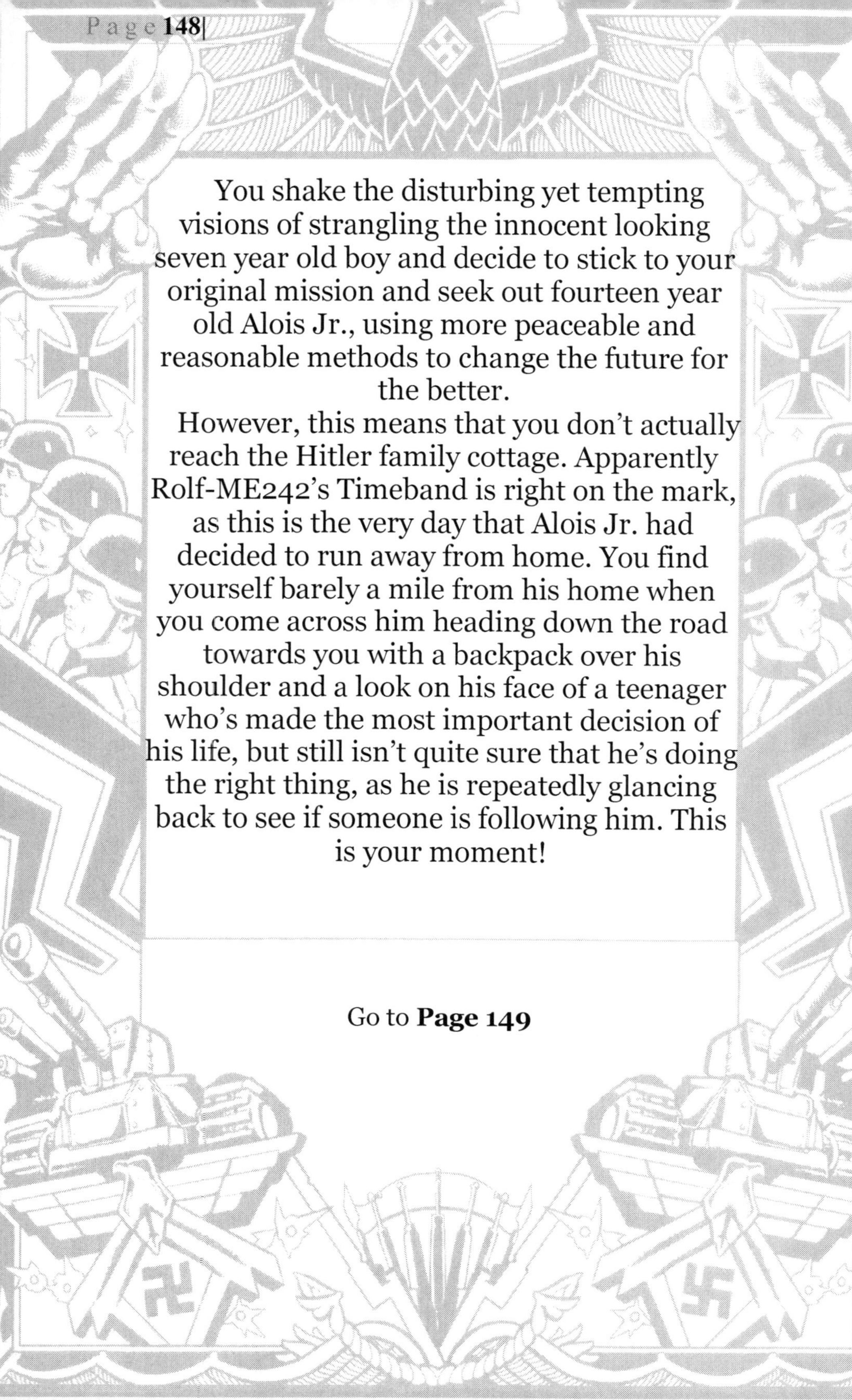

You shake the disturbing yet tempting visions of strangling the innocent looking seven year old boy and decide to stick to your original mission and seek out fourteen year old Alois Jr., using more peaceable and reasonable methods to change the future for the better.

However, this means that you don't actually reach the Hitler family cottage. Apparently Rolf-ME242's Timeband is right on the mark, as this is the very day that Alois Jr. had decided to run away from home. You find yourself barely a mile from his home when you come across him heading down the road towards you with a backpack over his shoulder and a look on his face of a teenager who's made the most important decision of his life, but still isn't quite sure that he's doing the right thing, as he is repeatedly glancing back to see if someone is following him. This is your moment!

Go to **Page 149**

He turns off onto another road. You wave a hand and call to him to get the boy's attention. He doesn't appear to hear you. You decide to catch up to him and start jogging down the dirt road after him. He finally looks your way, but doesn't respond to you in the way that you'd hope. Instead of stopping and waiting for you, he decides to bolt and starts to run away from you at top speed.

You are forced to give chase, but damn, the kid is a fast runner. You aren't bad either, but you have been walking all day and your boots aren't really made for running. You can already feel blisters coming on. What do you do?

Do you keep up the chase, hoping that you will eventually tire him out enough to be able to talk with him? Go to **Page 154**

Do you decide to do the easier thing and go back and find the little Hitler and put him out of his misery? Go to **Page 157**

After some moral wrangling with yourself, you decide to forget about trying to convince Alois Jr. to stay home and be a good influence on Adolf. This is Adolf Hitler we're talking about; no amount of good influence is going to turn him off his path to Armageddon.

You decide instead that it will be far easier, not to mention far better for the world, to end this now and wring young Adolf's neck in the time you have left before the Timeband pulls you back to 2525. So you sneak around in the bushes and behind the elm trees, keeping an eye on what the boys are doing, especially little Adolf. The game is simple enough; some hide while the others prance about in their leather shorts. It won't be too long before you get your chance. You finally catch young Adolf after he's run into the trees out of sight of the other boys. You grab him and try to do the deed; he struggles like a maniac and fights you like a little tiger.

Go to **Page 151**

You didn’t realize exactly how strong and loud a seven year old boy could be. Worse, you are spotted by a neighbour who screams that you are attacking one of the boys. While you are distracted, Hitler bites you painfully, and there are more shouts of men and women. Fearing for your life now since you’ve just spotted a man coming towards you with a rifle, you decide that maybe catching up with Alois would be a good idea and start to run away. But it seems that the locals are seriously protective of their children, and not only do you not find Adolf’s older brother, you are soon on the run from an angry mob of townsmen with various kinds of late nineteenth century firearms and who aren’t averse at all to shooting them at human targets.

Go to **Page 152**

One of them gets off a lucky shot, and you're hit. You feel an intense pain in your chest. You've been shot right through the heart. You collapse onto the grass, and as you lie on the ground bleeding and gasping for breath, you wonder if you will die before you are pulled back to your time in the distant future.

Open your eyes. Go to **Page 153**

When you regain consciousness, you are lying in a medical pod with a tube connected to your chest.

"When you came back," the attendant says, "you had a hole blown right through your heart. We grew you a new one, but it'll be a while before you're up and about. Exactly how did this happen?"

The medical attendants have a good laugh after you explain. You lay back wondering if time travel is still for you.

Do you go back and give it another try?
Go to **Page 119**

Do you decide that one bullet through the heart is quite enough for you?
Go to **Page 121**

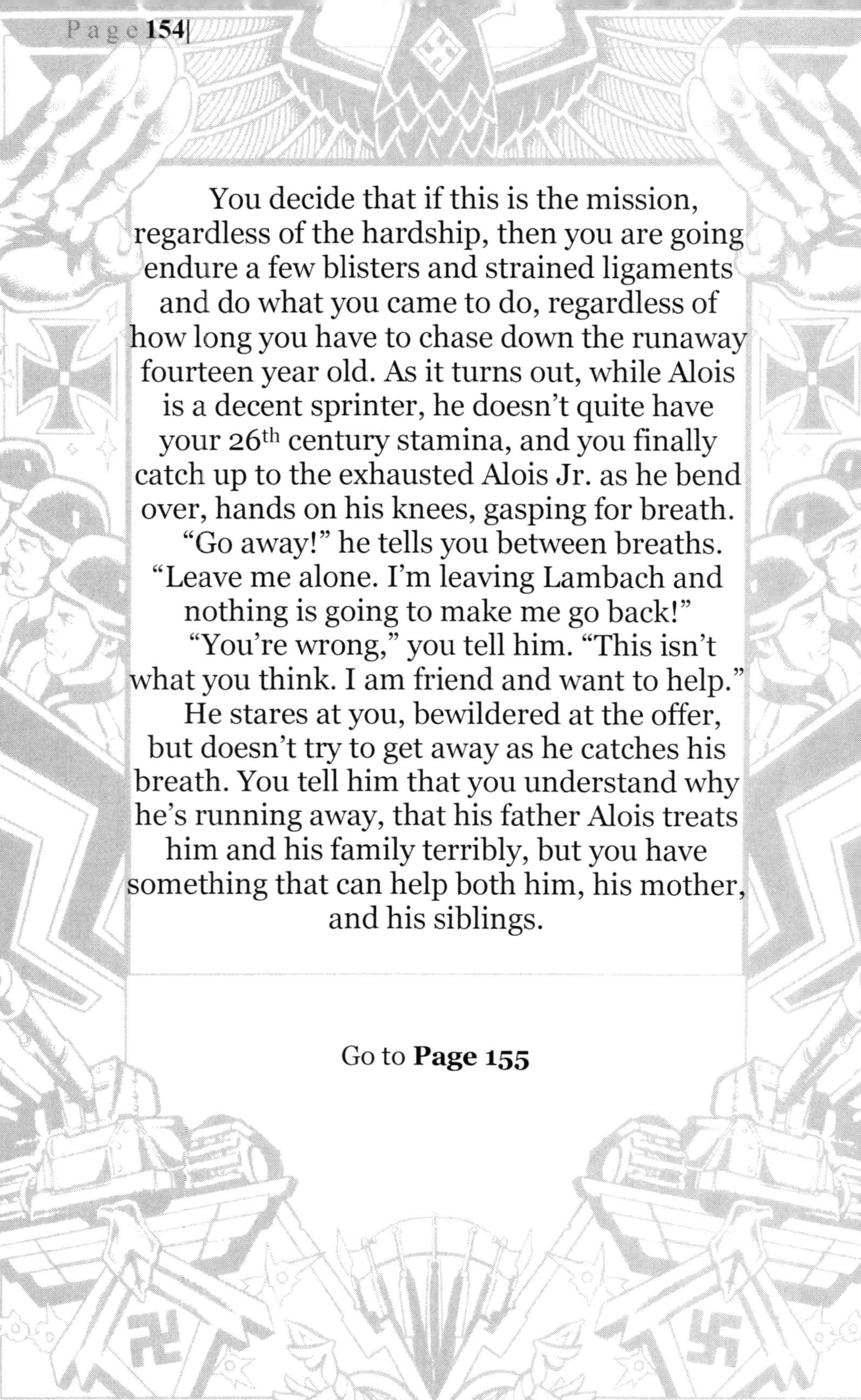

You decide that if this is the mission, regardless of the hardship, then you are going endure a few blisters and strained ligaments and do what you came to do, regardless of how long you have to chase down the runaway fourteen year old. As it turns out, while Alois is a decent sprinter, he doesn't quite have your 26th century stamina, and you finally catch up to the exhausted Alois Jr. as he bend over, hands on his knees, gasping for breath.

"Go away!" he tells you between breaths. "Leave me alone. I'm leaving Lambach and nothing is going to make me go back!"

"You're wrong," you tell him. "This isn't what you think. I am friend and want to help."

He stares at you, bewildered at the offer, but doesn't try to get away as he catches his breath. You tell him that you understand why he's running away, that his father Alois treats him and his family terribly, but you have something that can help both him, his mother, and his siblings.

Go to **Page 155**

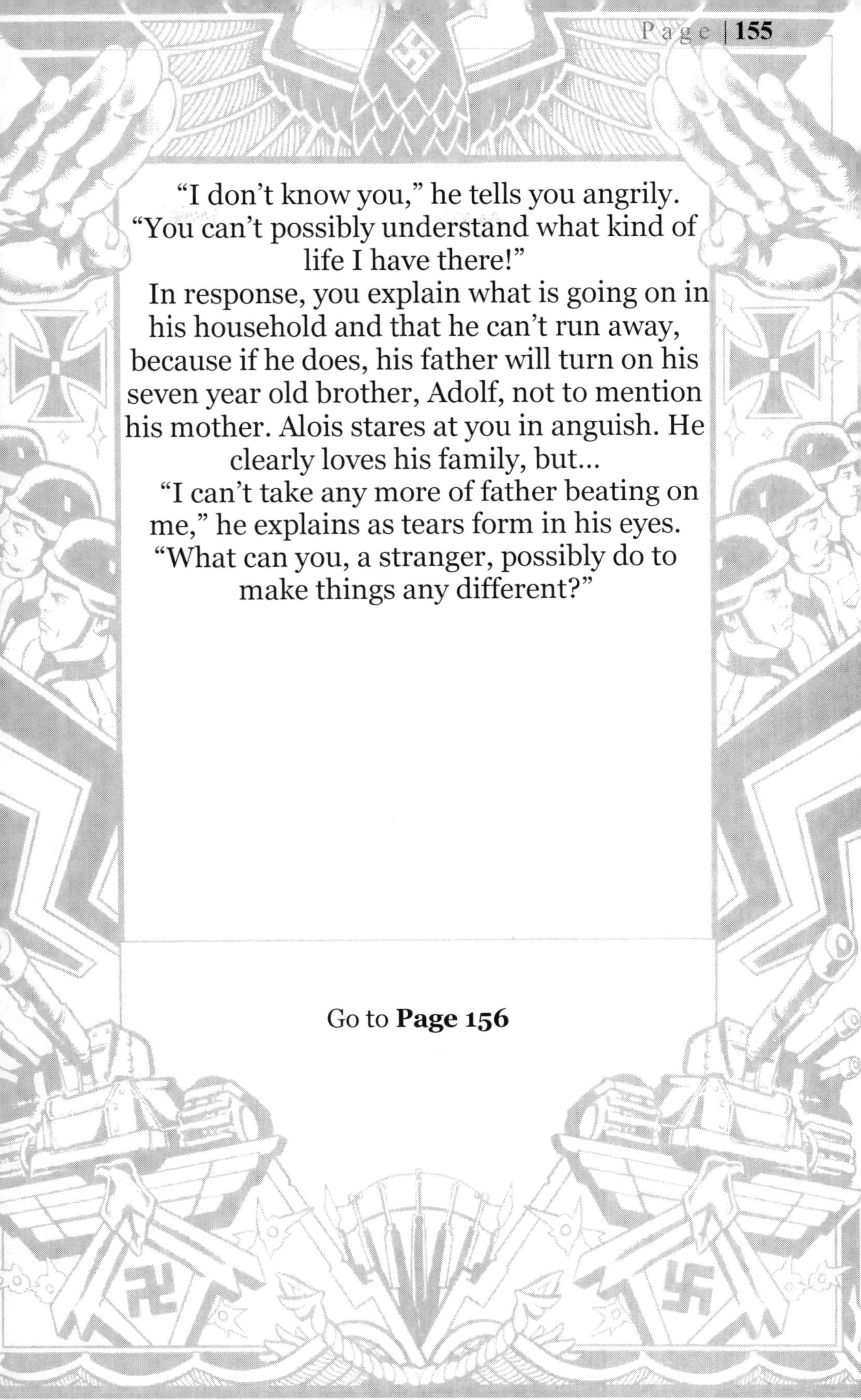

"I don't know you," he tells you angrily. "You can't possibly understand what kind of life I have there!"

In response, you explain what is going on in his household and that he can't run away, because if he does, his father will turn on his seven year old brother, Adolf, not to mention his mother. Alois stares at you in anguish. He clearly loves his family, but...

"I can't take any more of father beating on me," he explains as tears form in his eyes. "What can you, a stranger, possibly do to make things any different?"

Go to **Page 156**

You smile and tell him you have with you the very thing that will allow him defend himself, his younger siblings, and his mother from his dad when he gets violently drunk, and how things could change around his home. He slowly becomes convinced and asks what this thing is.

Do you give him the super-soldier serum that will assuredly make him more than a physical match for father? Go to **Page 160**

Or do you decide that injecting the nanogenetic treatment would be too dangerous a thing to do in this era and choose to just teach him some decent and effective self-defense techniques that will help him deal with his dad's drunken rages?

Go to **Page 164**

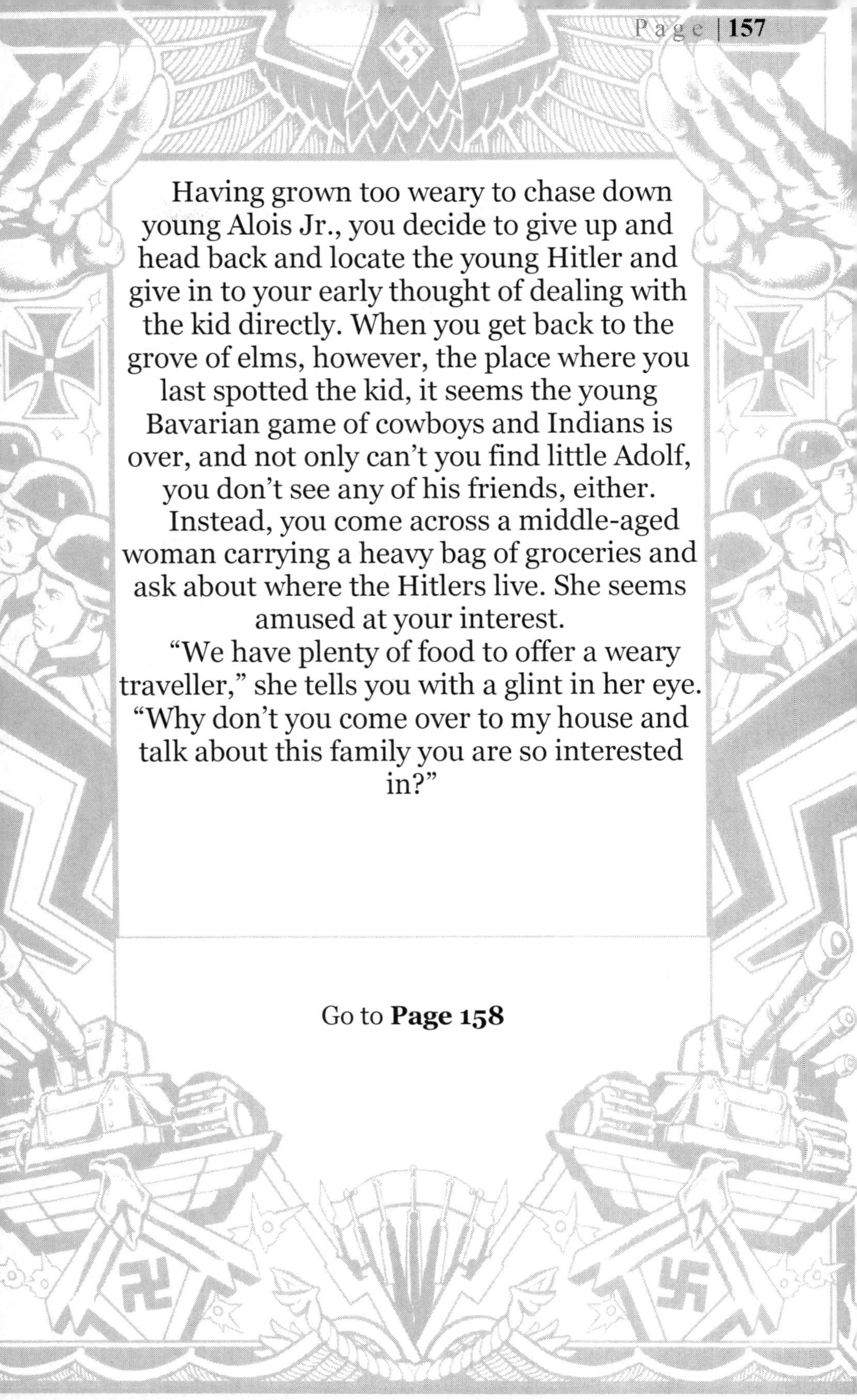

Having grown too weary to chase down young Alois Jr., you decide to give up and head back and locate the young Hitler and give in to your early thought of dealing with the kid directly. When you get back to the grove of elms, however, the place where you last spotted the kid, it seems the young Bavarian game of cowboys and Indians is over, and not only can't you find little Adolf, you don't see any of his friends, either.

Instead, you come across a middle-aged woman carrying a heavy bag of groceries and ask about where the Hitlers live. She seems amused at your interest.

"We have plenty of food to offer a weary traveller," she tells you with a glint in her eye. "Why don't you come over to my house and talk about this family you are so interested in?"

Go to **Page 158**

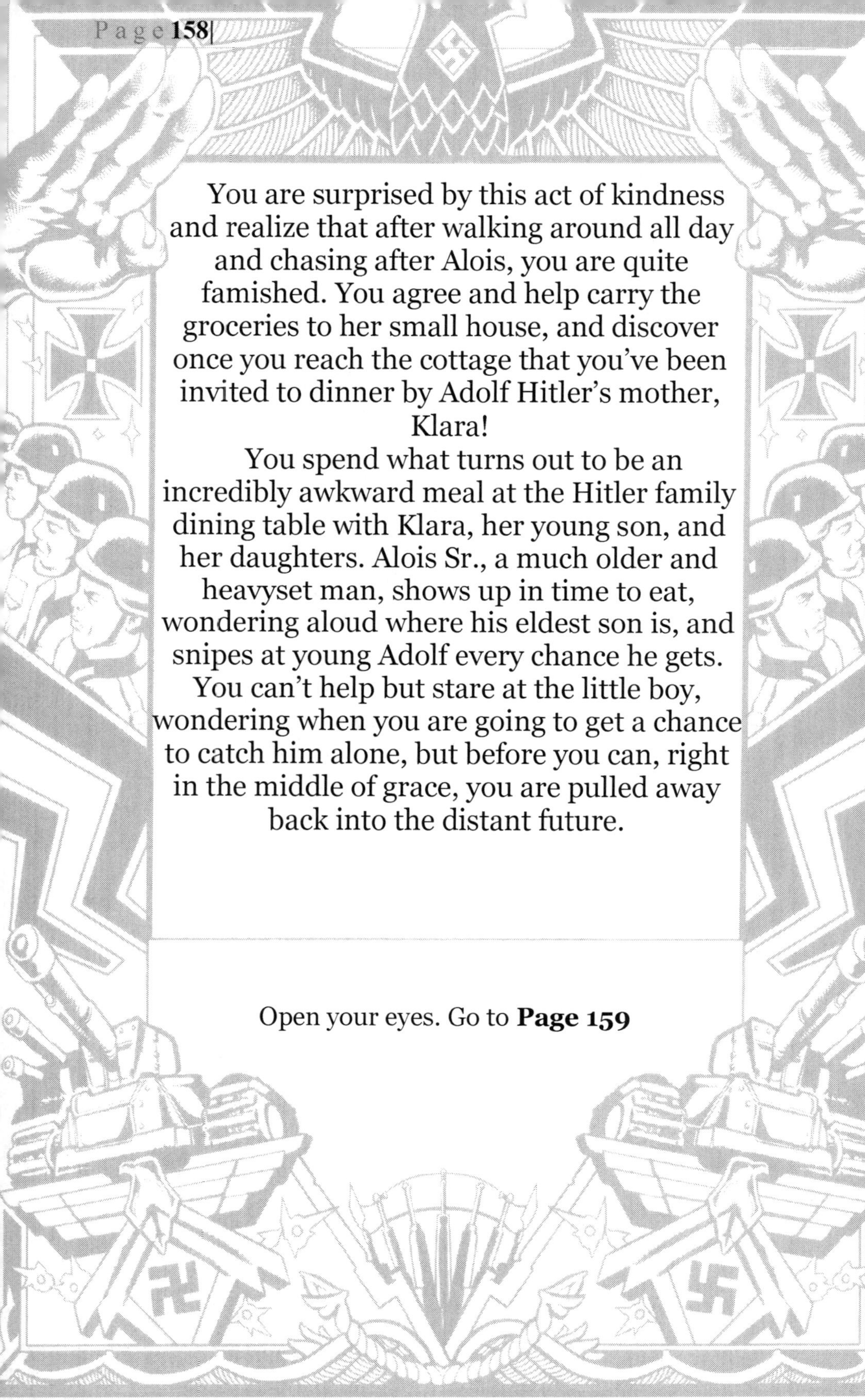

You are surprised by this act of kindness and realize that after walking around all day and chasing after Alois, you are quite famished. You agree and help carry the groceries to her small house, and discover once you reach the cottage that you've been invited to dinner by Adolf Hitler's mother, Klara!

You spend what turns out to be an incredibly awkward meal at the Hitler family dining table with Klara, her young son, and her daughters. Alois Sr., a much older and heavyset man, shows up in time to eat, wondering aloud where his eldest son is, and snipes at young Adolf every chance he gets. You can't help but stare at the little boy, wondering when you are going to get a chance to catch him alone, but before you can, right in the middle of grace, you are pulled away back into the distant future.

Open your eyes. Go to **Page 159**

You find yourself wondering, as you have your own comparatively tasteless synthetic meal from the community vats, what would have happened if you had been committed enough to chase down Alois. Is continuing to travel through time on these missions really for you, you wonder as you look around at all the other jumpsuit-wearing 26th century examples of humanity.

Do you go back to the chamber and try again? Go to **Page 119**

Do you decide that maybe someone else would be more suited to the task, not to mention the physical workout involved? Go to **Page 121**

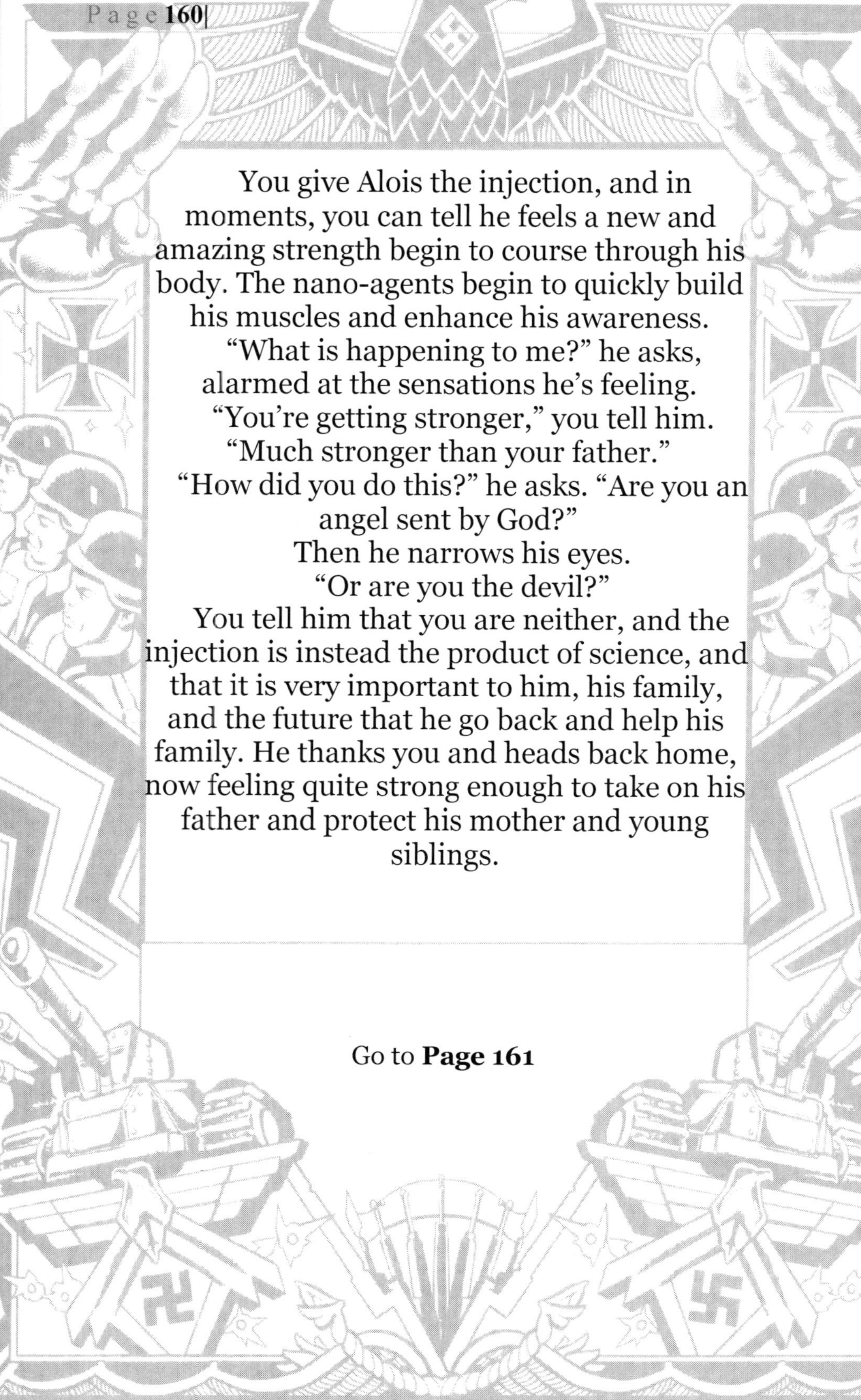

You give Alois the injection, and in moments, you can tell he feels a new and amazing strength begin to course through his body. The nano-agents begin to quickly build his muscles and enhance his awareness.

"What is happening to me?" he asks, alarmed at the sensations he's feeling.

"You're getting stronger," you tell him. "Much stronger than your father."

"How did you do this?" he asks. "Are you an angel sent by God?"

Then he narrows his eyes.

"Or are you the devil?"

You tell him that you are neither, and the injection is instead the product of science, and that it is very important to him, his family, and the future that he go back and help his family. He thanks you and heads back home, now feeling quite strong enough to take on his father and protect his mother and young siblings.

Go to **Page 161**

You are pretty pleased with yourself, and soon feel yourself pulled back into the future. But when you get back, things are as dire, although in a different way.

Open your eyes. Go to **Page 162**

You get back to the future, and things are different, but to your horror, not at all better. Humanity is still besieged, but differently than before. You realize that you made a terrible mistake and haven't made things at all better. When you do some research, you realize what happened.

The super soldier nanogenetic treatment did help Alois protect his family. However, it also become the basis for the German army almost conquering the world across the decades of the 20th century, creating a nearly unstoppable force that combined a theocracy and scientific state. Adolf still helps develop the Nazi party, though this time he's a hulking monstrosity. Instead of massively powerful A.I.s conquering the world in your time, it's now superhumans with the same distain for the original human race you are a member of. And Rolf-Me242 is the lone super-soldier trying to help mankind. What are you going to do?

Try and go back in time and fix what you broke. Go to **Page 119**

Give up; you're not suited to fixing the world. Go to **Page 121**

Alois proves to be a quite adept student, and after a few hours of self-defense training, agrees to head back home and give it another try. As he walks away, you feel the Timeband pull you back to what you hope is a more hopeful future.

Open your eyes. Go to **Page 165**

You have returned to the future and have discovered that the world is just a little brighter and happier than when you left; however, it is only a little better. You decided to go see Rolf-ME242 to see if you were successful or not.

"Greetings, time traveller," the synthetic voice of the A.I. greets you from all around. "You have succeeded in your mission; Alois Jr. went back home and stayed."

"Things still don't seem to be that different," you note.

"Time is constantly trying to right what did occur," Rolf tells you. "But you have changed things for the better. Hitler was a slightly nicer genocidal dictator than he was in the previous timeline."

'A slightly nicer genocidal dictator' doesn't sound like much of an improvement to you.

Go to **Page 166**

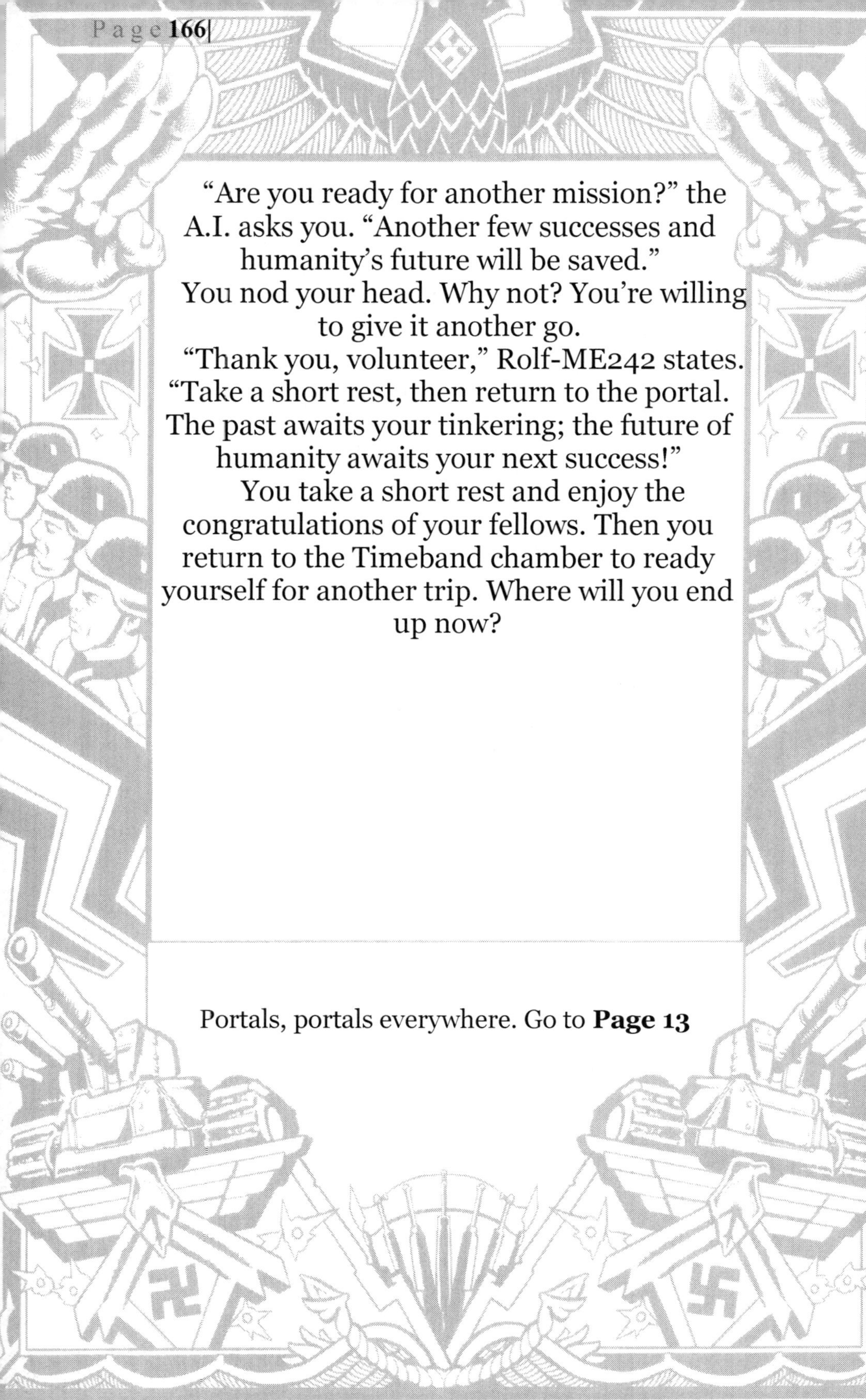

"Are you ready for another mission?" the A.I. asks you. "Another few successes and humanity's future will be saved."

You nod your head. Why not? You're willing to give it another go.

"Thank you, volunteer," Rolf-ME242 states. "Take a short rest, then return to the portal. The past awaits your tinkering; the future of humanity awaits your next success!"

You take a short rest and enjoy the congratulations of your fellows. Then you return to the Timeband chamber to ready yourself for another trip. Where will you end up now?

Portals, portals everywhere. Go to **Page 13**

You step out of the swirling, disorienting, kaleidoscopic light of the Timeband portal and onto a sidewalk, finding that you have arrived. But where and when? It looks like a small town, built in an old style that must mean it's around the turn of the 20th century. Your clothes are not of the old German style, and you are wearing a heavy coat this time. The other people wandering about seem to be heavily bundled up as well.

Seeing that your breath creates white puffs, you realize that it's quite cold where you are. It is winter, you realize; the buildings and streets are covered in a blanket of snow. You decide to take a look around to see where and when you've ended up this time. As it turns out, you have arrived in the small Bavarian town of Leonding. You also discover that the date is February 7, 1900, and you have arrived in the midst of a serious measles outbreak that is currently hitting the area particularly hard.

Go to **Page 168**

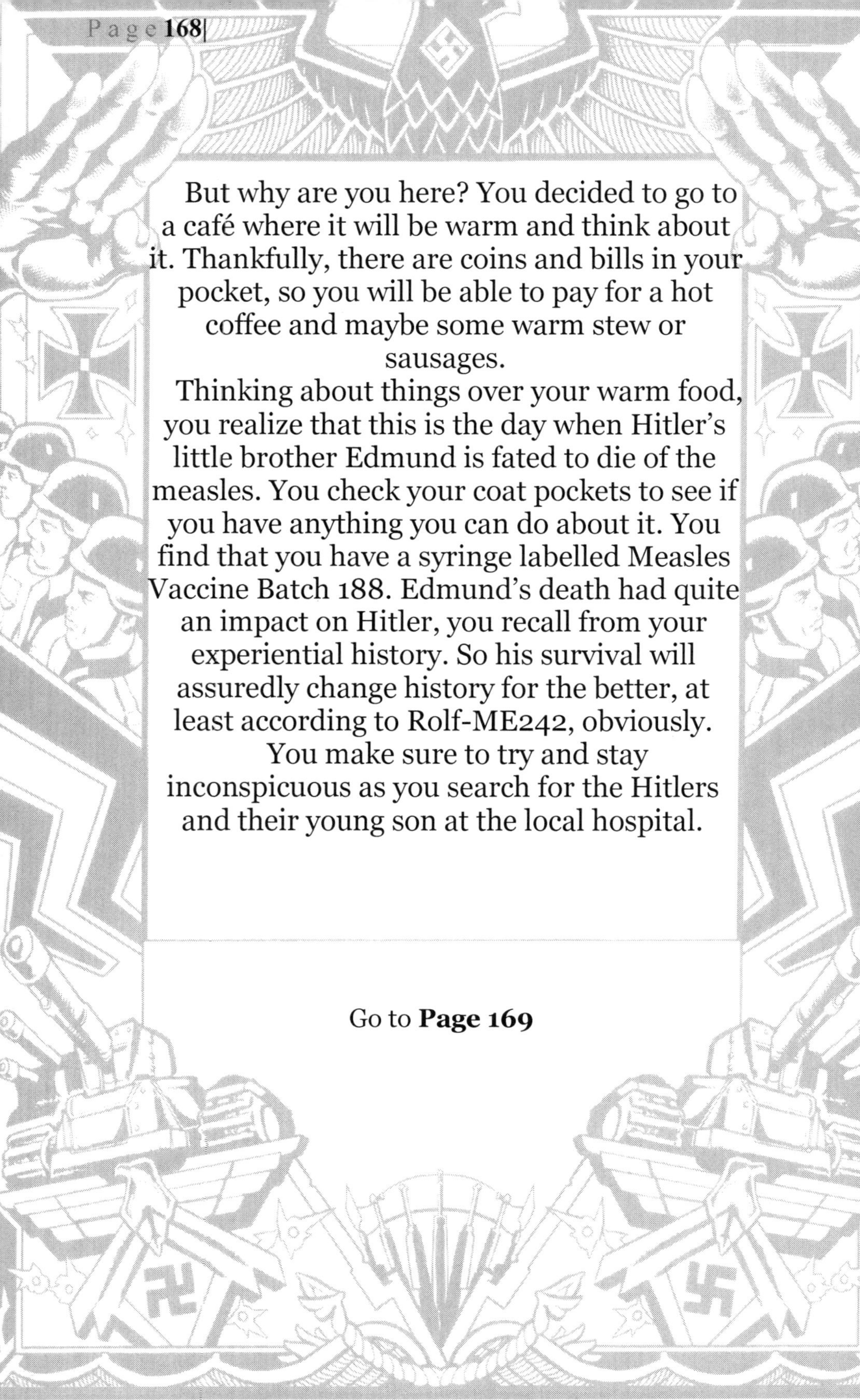

But why are you here? You decided to go to a café where it will be warm and think about it. Thankfully, there are coins and bills in your pocket, so you will be able to pay for a hot coffee and maybe some warm stew or sausages.

Thinking about things over your warm food, you realize that this is the day when Hitler's little brother Edmund is fated to die of the measles. You check your coat pockets to see if you have anything you can do about it. You find that you have a syringe labelled Measles Vaccine Batch 188. Edmund's death had quite an impact on Hitler, you recall from your experiential history. So his survival will assuredly change history for the better, at least according to Rolf-ME242, obviously.

You make sure to try and stay inconspicuous as you search for the Hitlers and their young son at the local hospital.

Go to **Page 169**

However, the regional hospitals in this era aren't well laid out, and you quickly find yourself in the wrong ward. You spot an adorable young girl suffering terribly, so much so that her mother, a nurse, bursts into tears upon seeing you. It's a horrible scene, and you truly feel for the young girl and her anguished mother, but you know you have only one dose of measles vaccine.

Do you say to hell with the mission and save the little girl? Go to **Page 170**

Do you buck up and ignore her agony and her mother's anguish?
Go to **Page 173**

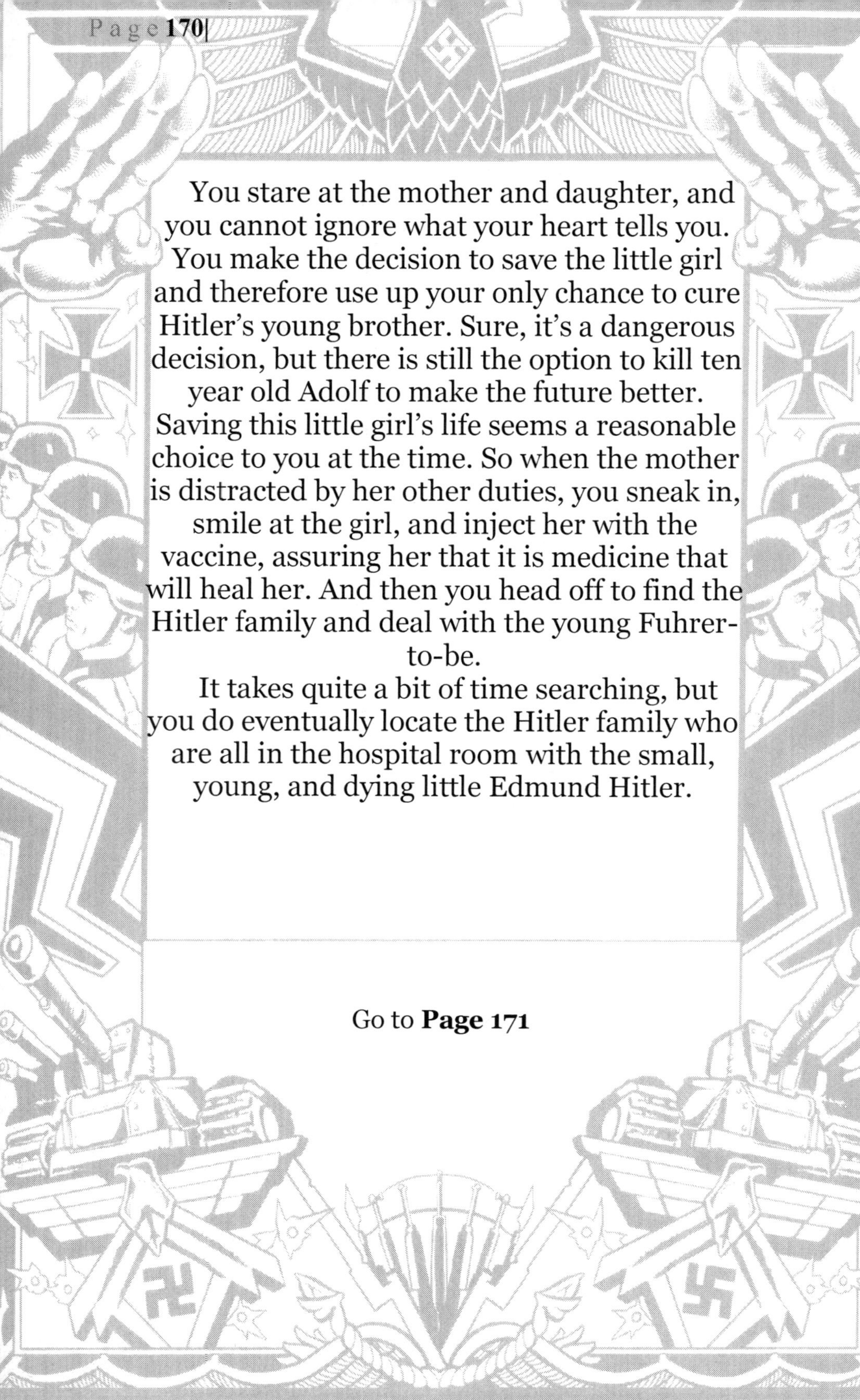

You stare at the mother and daughter, and you cannot ignore what your heart tells you. You make the decision to save the little girl and therefore use up your only chance to cure Hitler's young brother. Sure, it's a dangerous decision, but there is still the option to kill ten year old Adolf to make the future better. Saving this little girl's life seems a reasonable choice to you at the time. So when the mother is distracted by her other duties, you sneak in, smile at the girl, and inject her with the vaccine, assuring her that it is medicine that will heal her. And then you head off to find the Hitler family and deal with the young Fuhrer-to-be.

It takes quite a bit of time searching, but you do eventually locate the Hitler family who are all in the hospital room with the small, young, and dying little Edmund Hitler.

Go to **Page 171**

By the time you get there and spot Hitler and think about your only choice now, which is to find a way to kill the ten year old, you instead arrive in time to witness the heart-breaking death of the family's little boy and spot the morose and hopeless look on young Adolf Hitler's face while his mother, Klara, weeps over the body of her dead child.

You stand in the candlelit hospital room transfixed, watching Adolf from the shadows as his expression slowly turns from sadness and grief into a momentary and profound hatred that truly gives you the willies. But before you can do anything about it, you are pulled away, back to your home time, through the swirling, to consider your failure in completing your intended mission. But hey, at least you did save one little girl's life, right? Things are for the better, at least a little?

Open your eyes. Go to **Page 172**

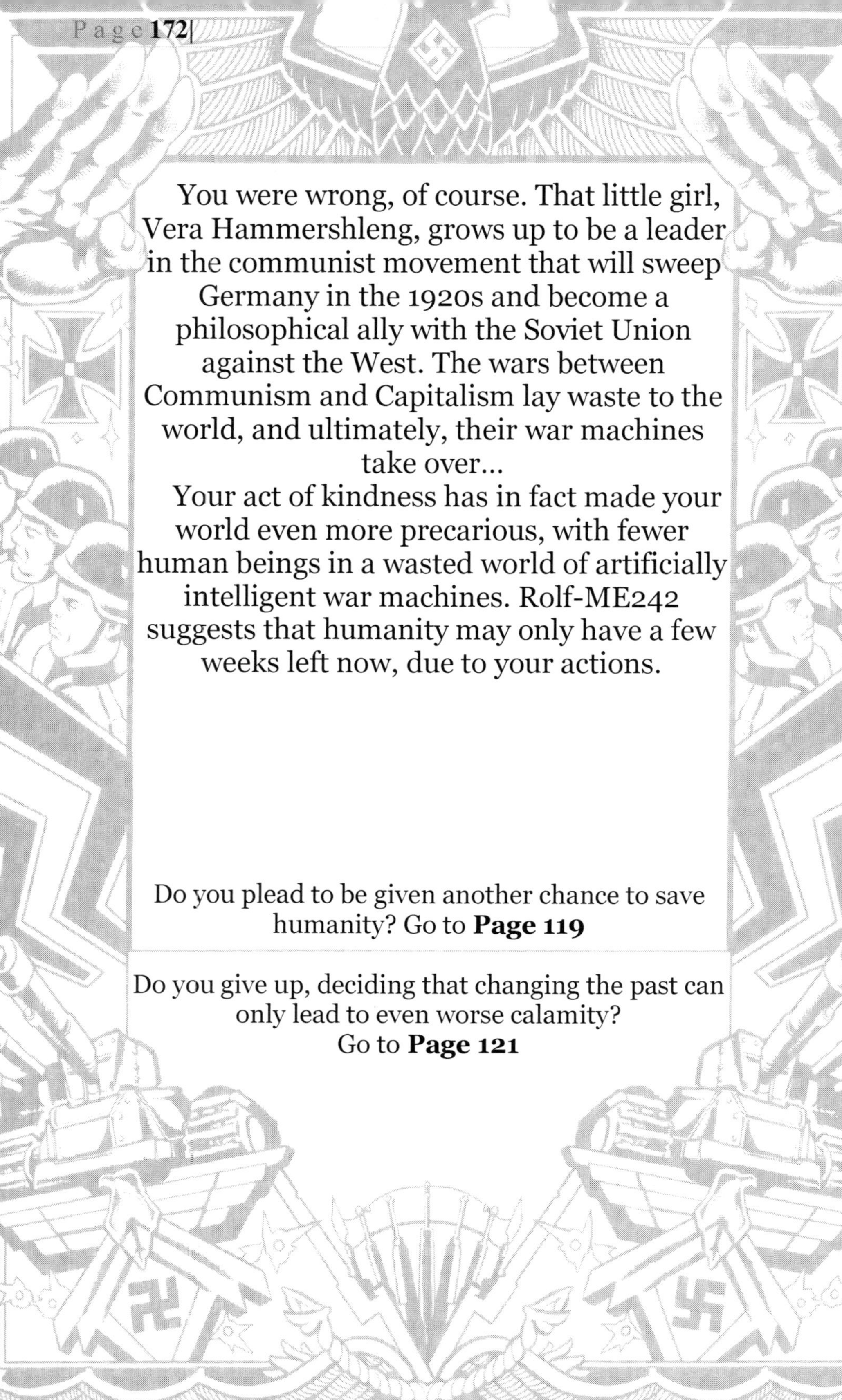

You were wrong, of course. That little girl, Vera Hammershleng, grows up to be a leader in the communist movement that will sweep Germany in the 1920s and become a philosophical ally with the Soviet Union against the West. The wars between Communism and Capitalism lay waste to the world, and ultimately, their war machines take over...

Your act of kindness has in fact made your world even more precarious, with fewer human beings in a wasted world of artificially intelligent war machines. Rolf-ME242 suggests that humanity may only have a few weeks left now, due to your actions.

Do you plead to be given another chance to save humanity? Go to **Page 119**

Do you give up, deciding that changing the past can only lead to even worse calamity?
Go to **Page 121**

With the deepest of regrets, you leave the grief stricken mother and her little girl to face her fate, deciding that the simple math tells you that your mission's success means saving millions, even billions of future lives. Therefore, you ignore your aching heart and seek out another small child facing oblivion this cold winter night.

But in this chaotic hospital filled with the victims of the 1900s measles outbreak, you are having trouble finding little Edmund Hitler.

After searching for what seems like at least an hour, you realize you have to relieve yourself and head for a washroom. There, by an amazing coincidence, you find yourself face to face with the young Adolf Hitler who is here with his family to visit his brother and pray that he gets better.

"You've come to pray for your brother?" you ask young Adolf, surprised at the degree of empathy the ten year old is showing.

Go to **Page 174**

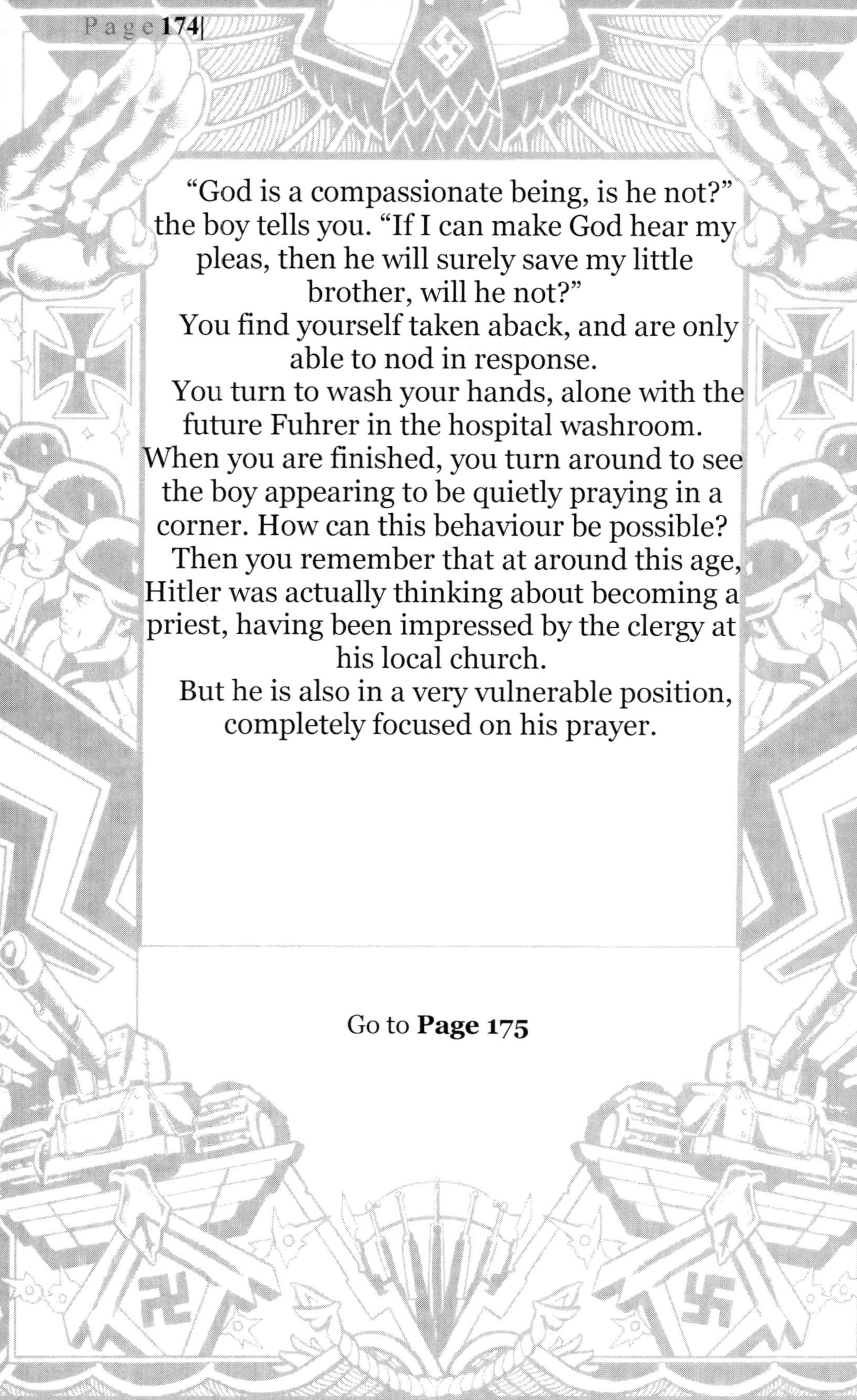

"God is a compassionate being, is he not?" the boy tells you. "If I can make God hear my pleas, then he will surely save my little brother, will he not?"

You find yourself taken aback, and are only able to nod in response.

You turn to wash your hands, alone with the future Fuhrer in the hospital washroom. When you are finished, you turn around to see the boy appearing to be quietly praying in a corner. How can this behaviour be possible?

Then you remember that at around this age, Hitler was actually thinking about becoming a priest, having been impressed by the clergy at his local church.

But he is also in a very vulnerable position, completely focused on his prayer.

Go to **Page 175**

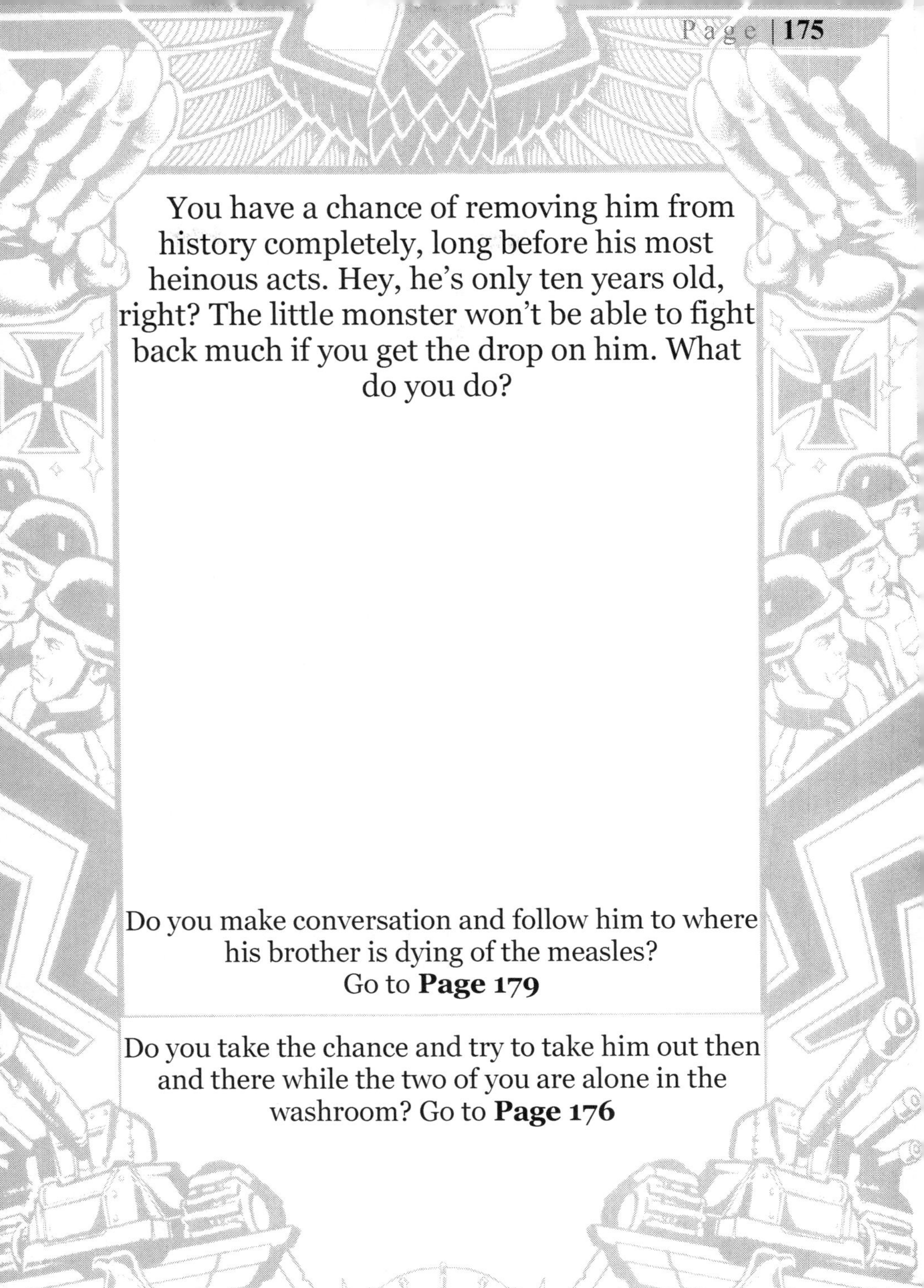

You have a chance of removing him from history completely, long before his most heinous acts. Hey, he's only ten years old, right? The little monster won't be able to fight back much if you get the drop on him. What do you do?

Do you make conversation and follow him to where his brother is dying of the measles?
Go to **Page 179**

Do you take the chance and try to take him out then and there while the two of you are alone in the washroom? Go to **Page 176**

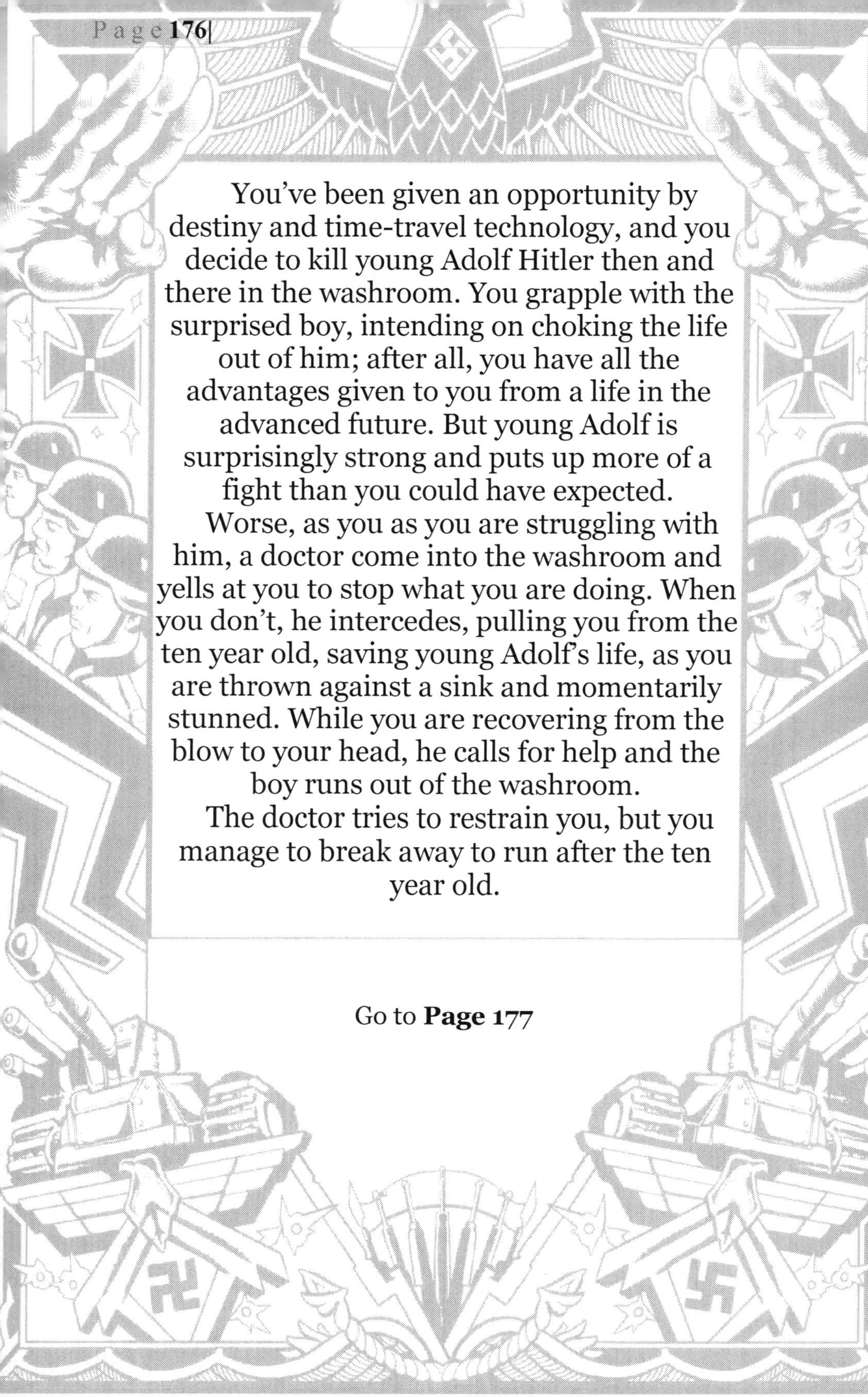

You've been given an opportunity by destiny and time-travel technology, and you decide to kill young Adolf Hitler then and there in the washroom. You grapple with the surprised boy, intending on choking the life out of him; after all, you have all the advantages given to you from a life in the advanced future. But young Adolf is surprisingly strong and puts up more of a fight than you could have expected.

Worse, as you as you are struggling with him, a doctor come into the washroom and yells at you to stop what you are doing. When you don't, he intercedes, pulling you from the ten year old, saving young Adolf's life, as you are thrown against a sink and momentarily stunned. While you are recovering from the blow to your head, he calls for help and the boy runs out of the washroom.

The doctor tries to restrain you, but you manage to break away to run after the ten year old.

Go to **Page 177**

Before you can give chase after Hitler, however, you are suddenly face to face with a pair of burley orderlies who grab you and, as per the doctor's instructions, take you to a small storage room to hold you for the local police to come and question you about why you attacked the boy. And as a final insult, you discover that in the melee, the syringe containing the vaccine was broken and all the vaccine leaked out.

You are confined and don't even have a way of saving young Edmund and salvaging your mission at all. You sit morosely as you realize that not only have you failed to kill Hitler, but you have also failed to save his young brother and improve the future.

How am I still alive? Open your eyes.

Go to **Page 178**

Before the police arrive, however, a light appears all around you and you are pulled forward more than six hundred years to your own time, and of course, nothing appears to have changed.

"Please explain how your mission went," you are later asked by Rolf-ME242. You confess that you attempted to kill ten year old Hitler in the hospital washroom.

"Please do not try to do that again," the A.I. tells you.

"You mean I can go back and try again?" you ask.

"Yes," the A.I. tells you. "It is hardly the stupidest thing a time traveller has tried to do."

Do you agree to go back and try not to attempt to kill Hitler? Go to **Page 119**

Do you decide that you won't be able to resist in any future attempts?
Go to **Page 121**

As it turns out, Hitler seems to be both a devout and thoughtful ten year old. It surprises you, considering all you know about what he will be like in his future. As you listen to him pray, the situation gives you pause for thought about how such turning points like what will happen later this night will be capable of having such a profound effect as to turn him on to the path of such future horrors he will preside over. You wonder about the powers of fate and circumstance. Having made the acquaintance of the young man, you then quietly follow him to the hospital room where the whole Hitler family has gathered with their doctor and priest over the body of dying and diseased little Edmund.

It is a sad sight. The child's breathing is quite laboured, and it really looks like the youngest Hitler could be about to breathe his last breath.

Go to **Page 180**

Everyone in the room seems to be resigned to Edmund's sad fate and for the child to receive the last rites in advance of his clear and approaching death.

As you watch, the priest moves to the child's side to begin the ritual of last rights. He really does look like he might only have minutes to live. What do you do?

Do you try to push your way in, claim you're a doctor, and give the kid the injection before anyone can stop you? Go to **Page 181**

Do you wait in the hope that he will last long enough for you to give him the injection of the vaccine later in the evening when there isn't quite a crowd to fight your way through?

Go to **Page 184**

Edmund's condition does look absolutely dire, and his death appears imminent. You decide that he could die any minute and try to bluff your way in to give the little boy the injection.

You begin to push your way through the family.

"I am a doctor," you tell the gathered. "I have been sent with this injection of medicine that will save his life."

This, of course, surprises everyone. Edmund's mother and father turn to look at you in gratitude, but others in the room are surprised.

This includes the family doctor.

"Who are you?" the man asks. "And who sent you to this room?"

Even Adolf finds this hard to believe.

"You aren't a doctor," he states. "You said that when I met you in the washroom."

Yes, that is true. When you spoke with Hitler in the washroom, you did state that you weren't a doctor.

Go to **Page 182**

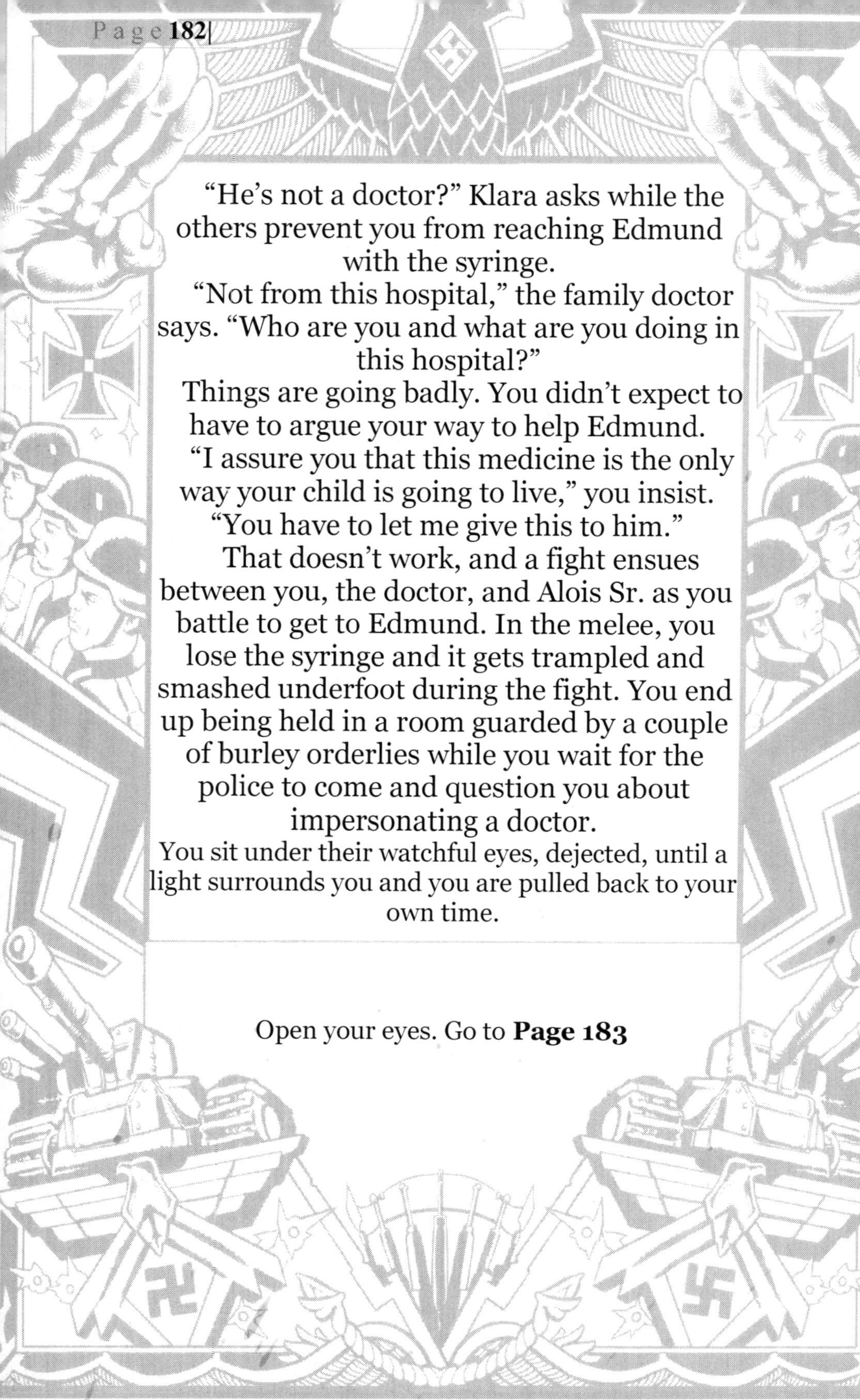

"He's not a doctor?" Klara asks while the others prevent you from reaching Edmund with the syringe.

"Not from this hospital," the family doctor says. "Who are you and what are you doing in this hospital?"

Things are going badly. You didn't expect to have to argue your way to help Edmund.

"I assure you that this medicine is the only way your child is going to live," you insist. "You have to let me give this to him."

That doesn't work, and a fight ensues between you, the doctor, and Alois Sr. as you battle to get to Edmund. In the melee, you lose the syringe and it gets trampled and smashed underfoot during the fight. You end up being held in a room guarded by a couple of burley orderlies while you wait for the police to come and question you about impersonating a doctor.

You sit under their watchful eyes, dejected, until a light surrounds you and you are pulled back to your own time.

Open your eyes. Go to **Page 183**

You report on your failure to convince the family to allow you to give the medicine to Edmund.

"Really?" Rolf-ME262 replies when he hears what you tried. "Was that the best you could do?"

You explain that you had medicine and they didn't believe you. What could you have done?

"Better," the A.I suggests. What do you do?

Do you ask for another chance at changing the past for the better? Go to **Page 119**

Do you decide that this sort of thing isn't for you? Go to **Page 121**

Despite how grim things appear to look for young Edmund, you decide that it will be too risky to attempt to inject the boy while there are so many people watching over him. There are just too many things that could go wrong. So you decide to take the chance that the young boy will be able to last for at least a few more hours until there are fewer family members around.

You decide to hang around the ward and try and sneak back in later when you'll have the chance to do it without too many people in the way. That sounds prudent to you, as the syringe with its vaccine seems quite fragile. And you might not be the most convincing person, being from the distant future and not overly familiar with the current culture.

So for the next few hours, you wander about the hospital, checking back every once in a while to see if you can get to the boy.

Go to **Page 185**

In your wandering, you happen to come across an unguarded store of medical supplies, including drugs that you know if used properly could introduce an immediate overdose and death.

A thought comes over you about possibly killing two birds with one stone. You could save little Edmund and at the same time take out Hitler before he can be the cause of so many deaths. It sounds to you like a win-win situation. What could go wrong?

Do you do the prudent thing and wait longer to inject the little boy, and hope you've caught him in time and nothing else? Go to **Page 186**

Do you also try to catch Hitler earlier, overdose him, and in the commotion, sneak in and give his brother the measles vaccine?

Go to **Page 188**

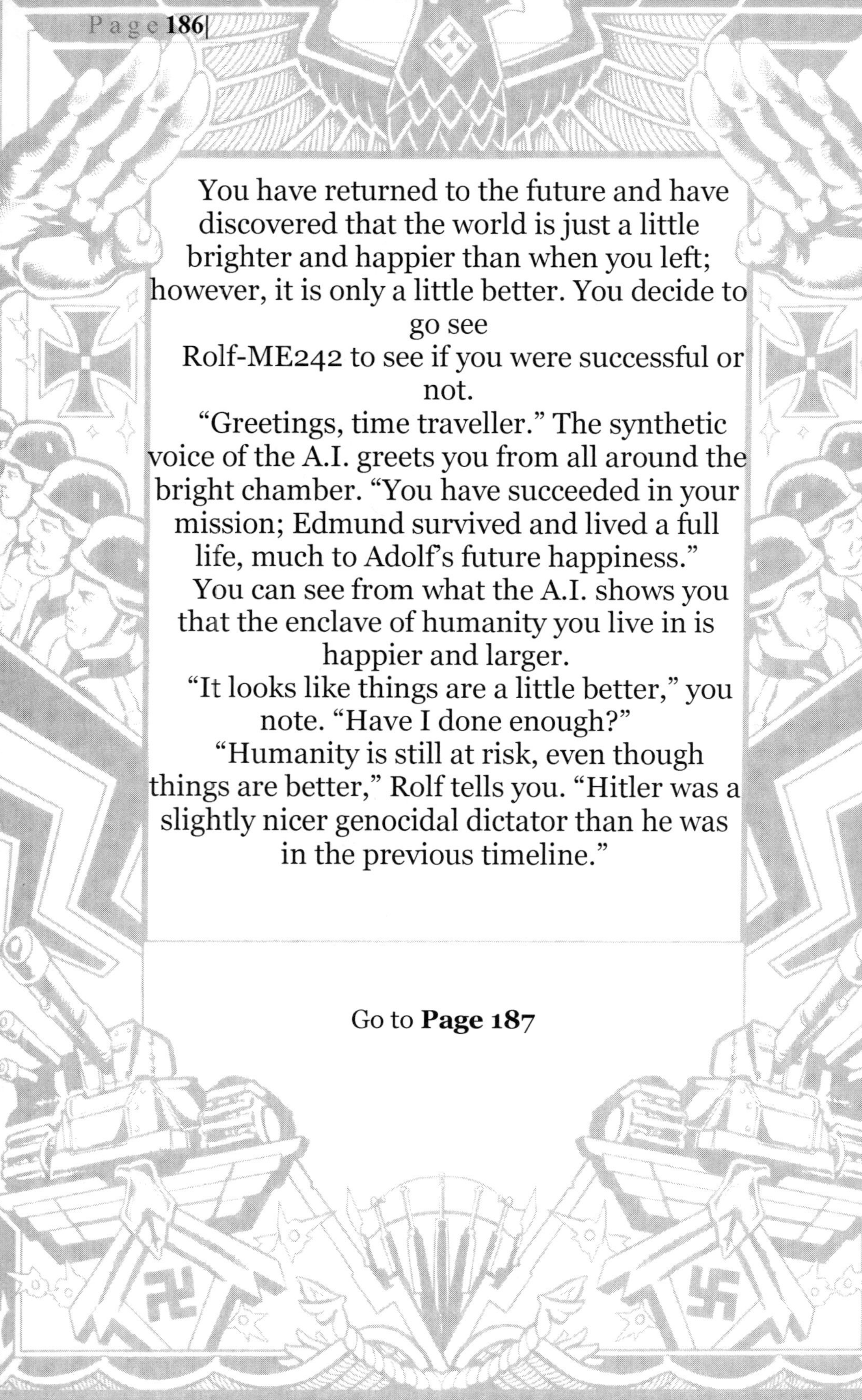

You have returned to the future and have discovered that the world is just a little brighter and happier than when you left; however, it is only a little better. You decide to go see

Rolf-ME242 to see if you were successful or not.

"Greetings, time traveller." The synthetic voice of the A.I. greets you from all around the bright chamber. "You have succeeded in your mission; Edmund survived and lived a full life, much to Adolf's future happiness."

You can see from what the A.I. shows you that the enclave of humanity you live in is happier and larger.

"It looks like things are a little better," you note. "Have I done enough?"

"Humanity is still at risk, even though things are better," Rolf tells you. "Hitler was a slightly nicer genocidal dictator than he was in the previous timeline."

Go to **Page 187**

"There were numerous small changes in the past that have led us here, to this better place."

'A slightly nicer genocidal dictator' doesn't sound like much of an improvement to you, but at least you can see your actions having a positive improvement on the world you live in.

"Are you ready for another mission?" the A.I. asks you. "You have proven that time travel can indeed improve your species lot."

You nod your head. Sure. One success might lead to another.

"Thank you, volunteer," Rolf-ME242 states. "Take a short rest, then return to the portal. The past awaits your improvement; the future of humanity depends your next success!"

You take a short rest and enjoy the congratulations of your fellows. Then you return to the Timeband chamber to ready yourself for another trip. Where will you be sent next?

Stop, chamber time. Go to **Page 13**

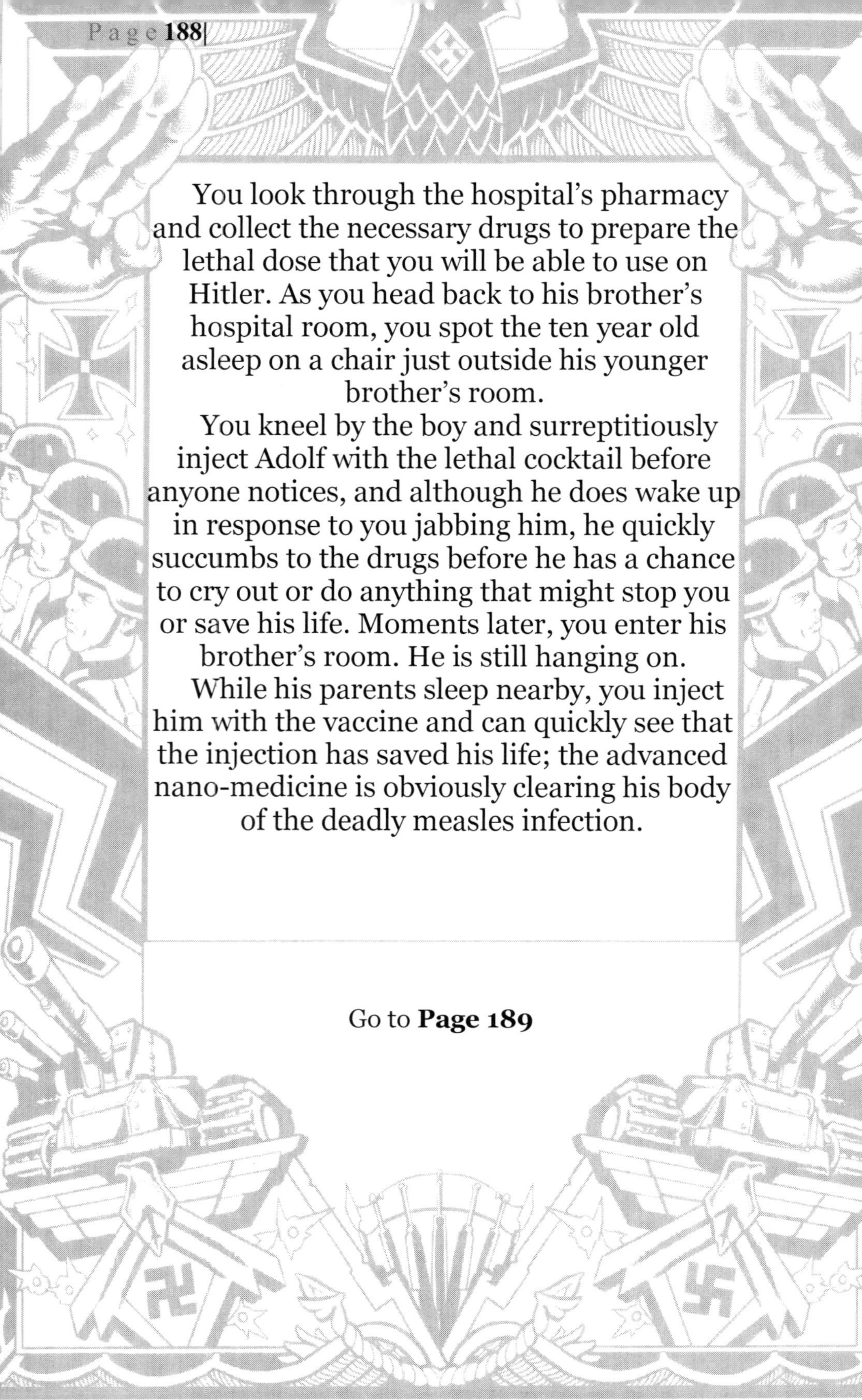

You look through the hospital's pharmacy and collect the necessary drugs to prepare the lethal dose that you will be able to use on Hitler. As you head back to his brother's hospital room, you spot the ten year old asleep on a chair just outside his younger brother's room.

You kneel by the boy and surreptitiously inject Adolf with the lethal cocktail before anyone notices, and although he does wake up in response to you jabbing him, he quickly succumbs to the drugs before he has a chance to cry out or do anything that might stop you or save his life. Moments later, you enter his brother's room. He is still hanging on.

While his parents sleep nearby, you inject him with the vaccine and can quickly see that the injection has saved his life; the advanced nano-medicine is obviously clearing his body of the deadly measles infection.

Go to **Page 189**

Heading out of the room, you notice a doctor and nurse trying to revive the dying Hitler, but failing in their attempt, much to the horror of his mother and father, who have been awakened by the commotion. You feel the satisfaction of a job well done. After a few minutes, you feel yourself being pulled back to your present, and the hopefully brighter distant future.

Open those tired eyes. Go to **Page 190**

However, when you return to your own time, you discover that history has indeed changed, and not for the better. Instead of the Nazis rising in Germany, it was the communists, leading to centuries of warfare between the communist and capitalist powers, which has left the world a radioactive wasteland, and traveling back in time again is the only hope to save it. As it turns out, you are one of only a dozen humans left who can, as the change in timeline has wiped out most of your friends and remaining family. You'd better go back and fix things, right?

Do you do back to desperately try to fix what you did wrong? Go to **Page 119**

Do you just give up and watch the last members of humanity die around you?
Go to **Page 121**

For a moment after stepping into the portal, you're blinded by the swirling, flashing lights and are stunned, stumbling forwards into the brightness. Almost immediately, though, a world begins to resolve around you. And it is one that you have only witnessed in virtual reality. What is now around you has been long since lost to the conflicts and progress of six centuries. Where are you?

You are standing in a wide plaza with classical buildings all around you. It is warm, and you, like the rest of the people wandering about, are dressed fairly formally in a centuries old fashion. Where are you specifically, though, in space and time?

When you ask and check around by reading newspapers and advertisements on the light poles, you discover that you are now standing on the grounds of the University of Vienna, and the year is 1907.

Go to **Page 192**

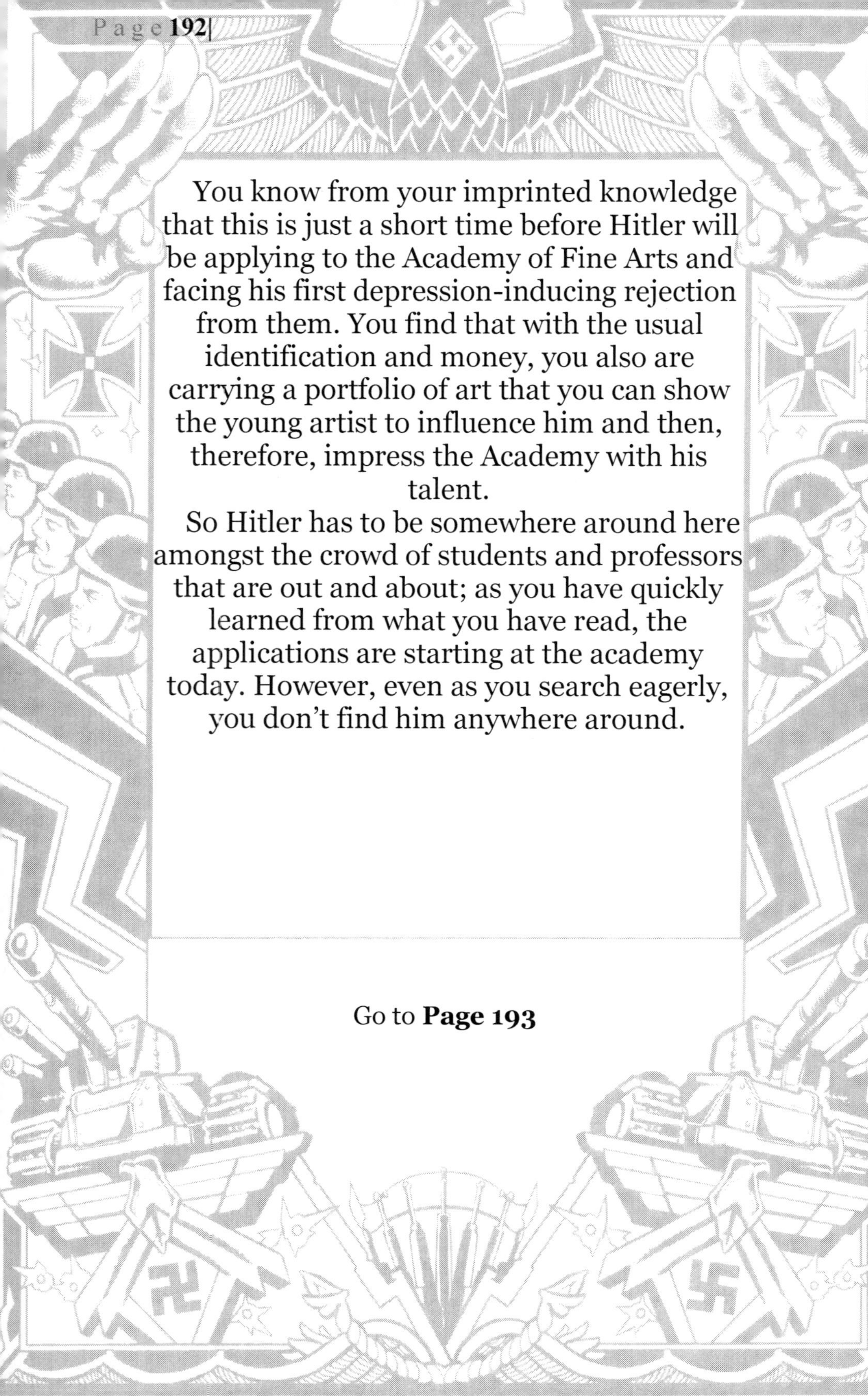

You know from your imprinted knowledge that this is just a short time before Hitler will be applying to the Academy of Fine Arts and facing his first depression-inducing rejection from them. You find that with the usual identification and money, you also are carrying a portfolio of art that you can show the young artist to influence him and then, therefore, impress the Academy with his talent.

So Hitler has to be somewhere around here amongst the crowd of students and professors that are out and about; as you have quickly learned from what you have read, the applications are starting at the academy today. However, even as you search eagerly, you don't find him anywhere around.

Go to **Page 193**

While you are looking for him through one of the university buildings, you hear the sound of a large number of people laughing through a wall and decide to check out what is going on. You follow the sound to an auditorium where there is a symposium on the mind going on and currently being conducted by the two fathers of psychiatry, Sigmund Freud and his protégé Carl Jung. As a person with a keen interest in human progress, you can't help but take a seat and have a listen to what these historical figures have to say, at least for a few minutes; what harm could there be in that? It is absolutely fascinating to witness the talk being held by these two brilliant historical figures, and you find it difficult to tear yourself away. An hour, goes by, and then another. You feel reluctant to leave; you're enjoying yourself so much. What do you do?

Do you stay and listen anyways, figuring that you probably still have enough time to catch up with Hitler? Go to **Page 194**

Do you decide to keep to your mission and seek out the young painter before he gets rejected not only once, but twice? Go to **Page 197**

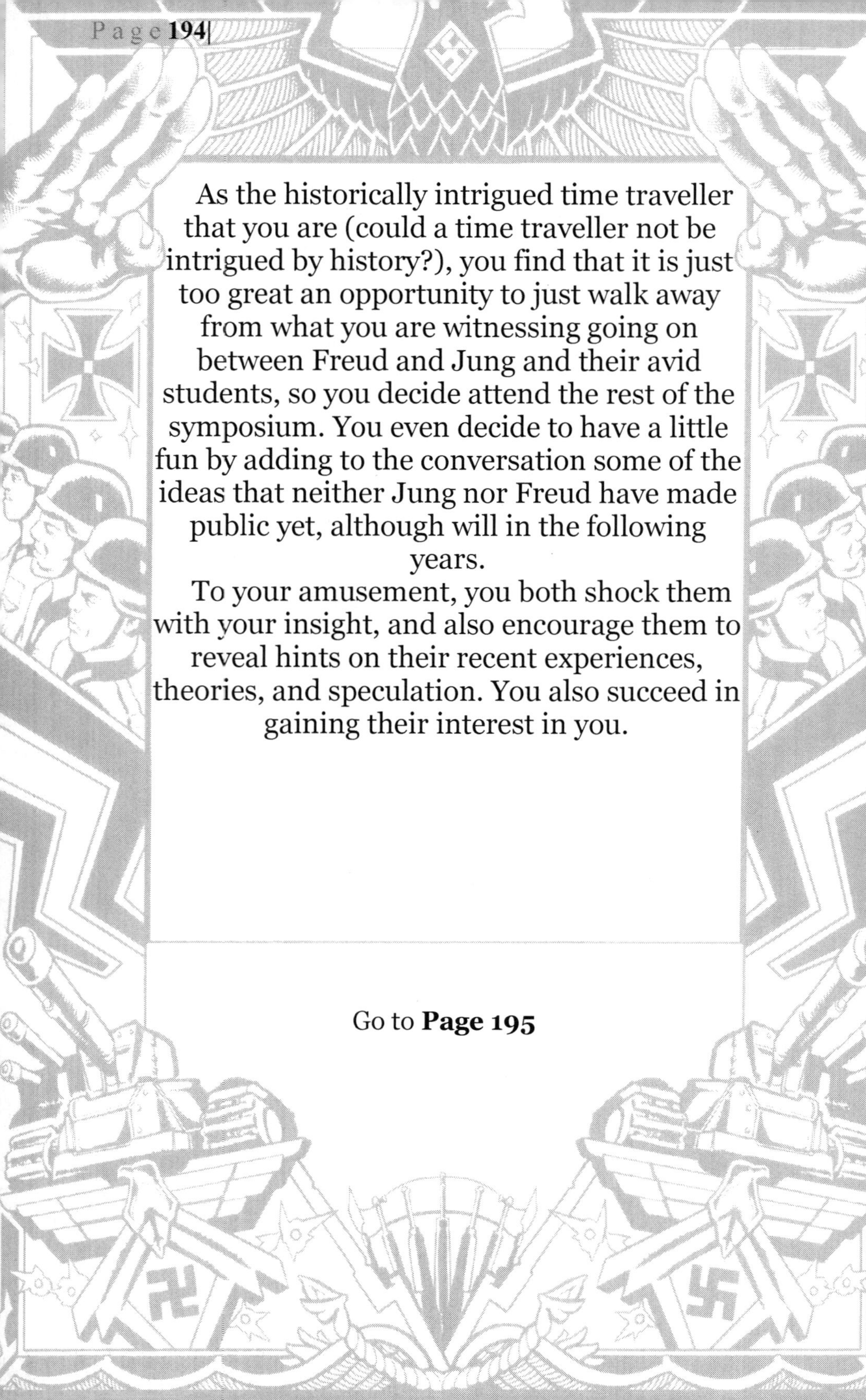

As the historically intrigued time traveller that you are (could a time traveller not be intrigued by history?), you find that it is just too great an opportunity to just walk away from what you are witnessing going on between Freud and Jung and their avid students, so you decide attend the rest of the symposium. You even decide to have a little fun by adding to the conversation some of the ideas that neither Jung nor Freud have made public yet, although will in the following years.

To your amusement, you both shock them with your insight, and also encourage them to reveal hints on their recent experiences, theories, and speculation. You also succeed in gaining their interest in you.

Go to **Page 195**

Congratulations, you've impressed the pioneers of the mind, Freud and Jung. How great is that? It gets better, too. Your participation in the symposium and your prodding of the two men gets you invited to a private party for them and their disciples after the symposium, for drinks with the two men and their current associates. You completely forget about your mission and have a great time with these pioneers into the human psyche.

After a few drinks, you are completely into amusing and impressing the psychiatric crowd. Later, smoking a fine cigar, you think yeah, screw Hitler and the millions and billions that will be slaughtered. Who are those people anyways? And can your time traveling even do a thing to save them? You have an opportunity to enjoy yourself. A few hours or a day or two won't make a difference, right? You can get back to finding Hitler soon enough.

And then you find yourself being carried back to your present, the less amusing year of 2525.

Open your eyes. Go to **Page 196**

When you get back, you tell Rolf-ME242 that you weren't able to locate Hitler, but your drunkenness and the odour of cigar smoke on your clothing tells the A.I. a different story, i.e. that you weren't actually looking for him.

"You do realize that the Timeband uses up a great deal of energy to send people back through time," it tells you, "and that it may run out while volunteers like you decide to use the experience for tourism while your species is about to go extinct?"

You are somewhat sobered by this information. But you are only human. What do you want to do?

Do you promise the A.I. that you will keep to the mission and ask to be sent back again?
Go to **Page 119**

Do you realize that the past is too tempting to enjoy and realize you aren't cut out for this kind of job?
Go to **Page 121**

Having regretfully torn yourself from the psychiatric symposium, you return to searching for the elusive young Austrian painting student you intend on influencing positively enough to get him admitted to the Vienna Academy of Fine Arts. But where is the eighteen year old Adolf Hitler among the teeming crowds at Vienna University? You seem to have searched just about everywhere you can think of.

Well, since he doesn't seem to be anywhere around the Academy, you decide to widen your search, and also take in the sights, even if that's not what you are supposed to be spending your precious time-traveling time doing. But still, this is living, breathing history, not merely a virtual reproduction of it. You can't help but enjoy yourself.

Go to **Page 198**

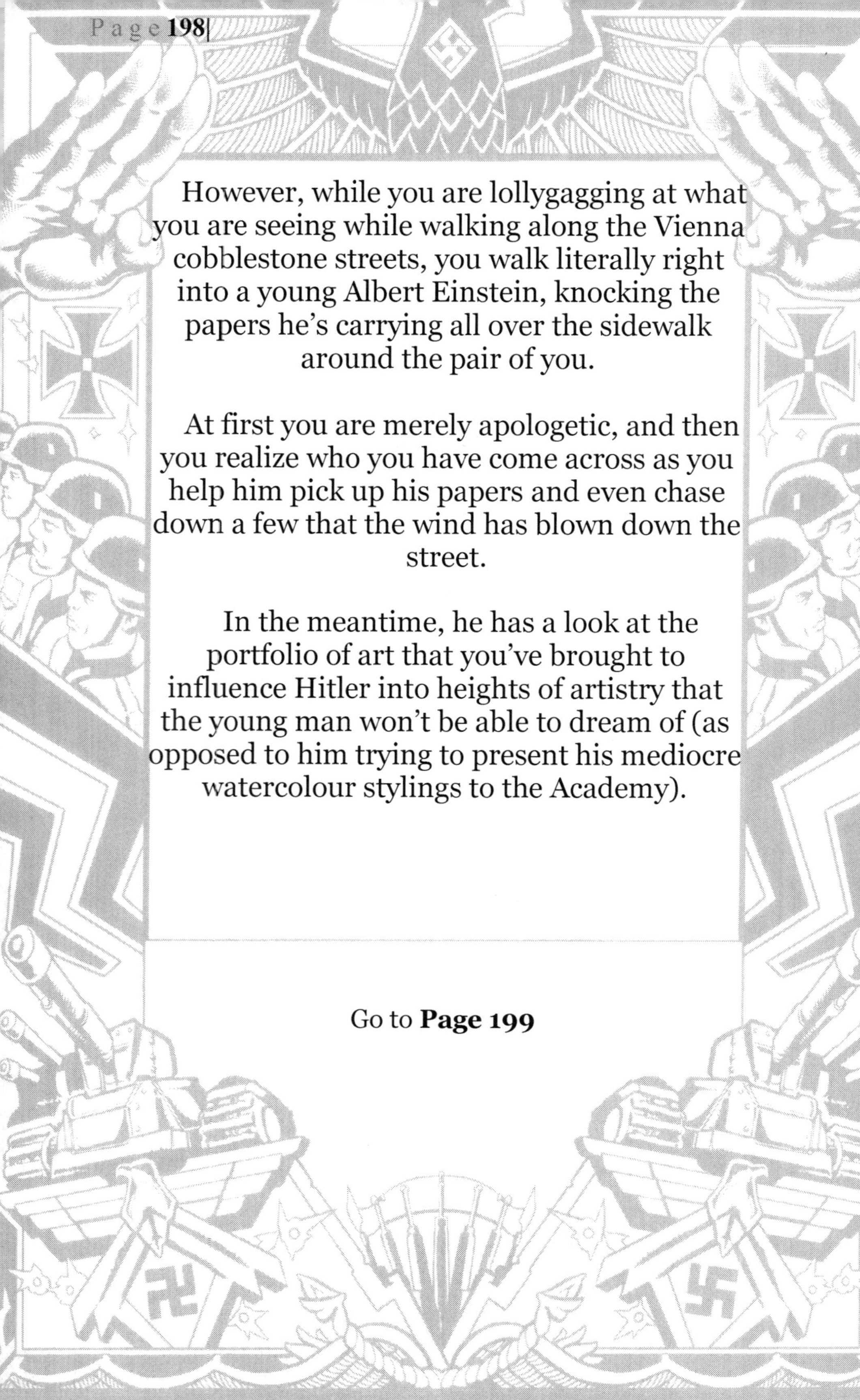

However, while you are lollygagging at what you are seeing while walking along the Vienna cobblestone streets, you walk literally right into a young Albert Einstein, knocking the papers he's carrying all over the sidewalk around the pair of you.

At first you are merely apologetic, and then you realize who you have come across as you help him pick up his papers and even chase down a few that the wind has blown down the street.

In the meantime, he has a look at the portfolio of art that you've brought to influence Hitler into heights of artistry that the young man won't be able to dream of (as opposed to him trying to present his mediocre watercolour stylings to the Academy).

Go to **Page 199**

You offer some witty comments regarding physics and the nature of reality that so interest the young physicist he asks that you join him for tea at a nearby café to continue the conversation.

Given the kinds of physical laws he will be discovering (that you are so clearly breaking), you wonder if it wouldn't be interesting to discuss the theory of time travel with the legendary physicist. You've given up spending time with Freud and Jung; can you give up the chance to chat with Albert Einstein?

Do you take Einstein up on his offer and join him for tea? Go to **Page 200**

Do you thank him for the offer, but get back to your mission before you lose your chance at catching up with your target before you get thrown back to the terrible future you live in?

Go to **Page 202**

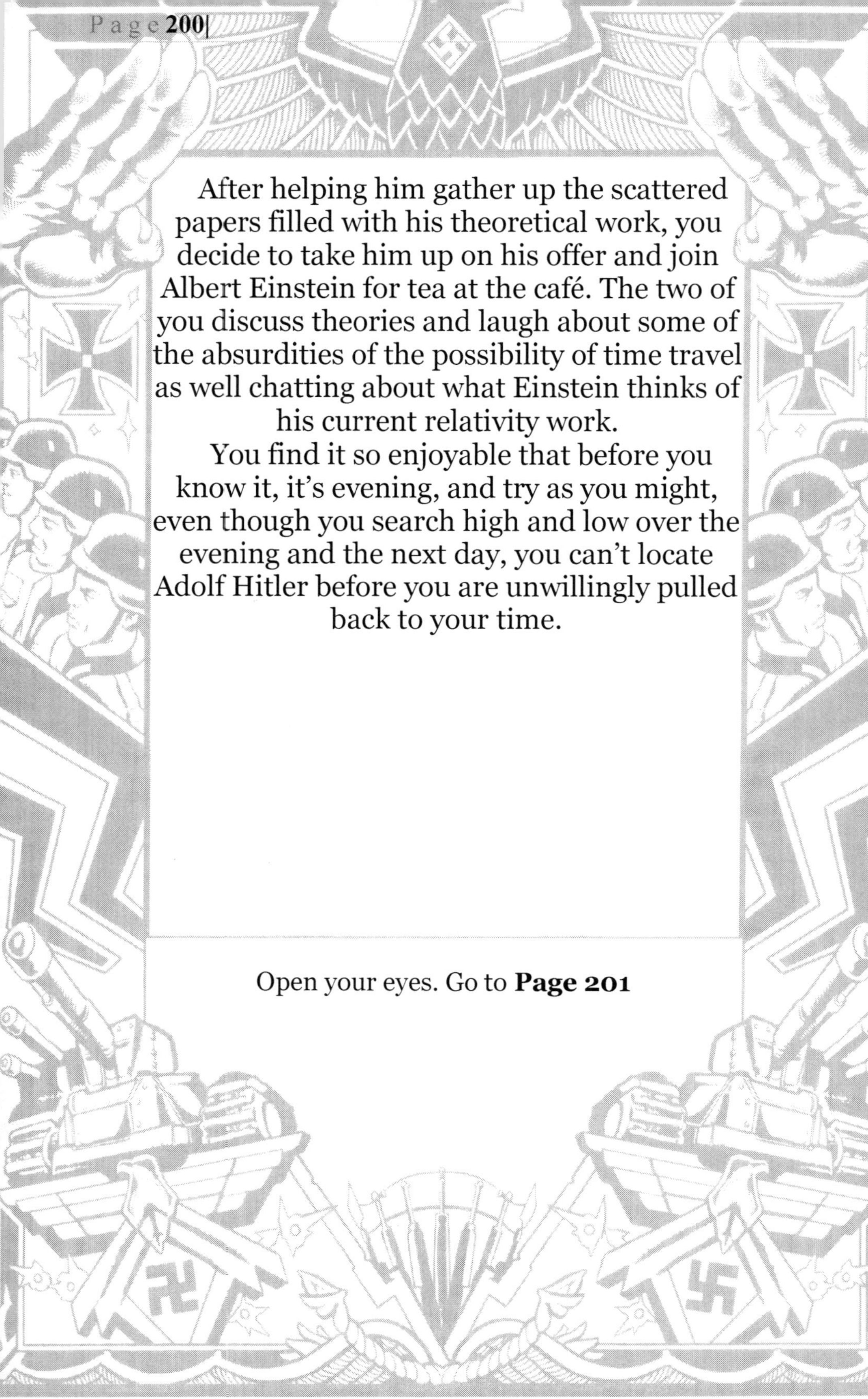

After helping him gather up the scattered papers filled with his theoretical work, you decide to take him up on his offer and join Albert Einstein for tea at the café. The two of you discuss theories and laugh about some of the absurdities of the possibility of time travel as well chatting about what Einstein thinks of his current relativity work.

You find it so enjoyable that before you know it, it's evening, and try as you might, even though you search high and low over the evening and the next day, you can't locate Adolf Hitler before you are unwillingly pulled back to your time.

Open your eyes. Go to **Page 201**

On your return, you are castigated by the A.I. and your fellow humans for spending your precious time-travel time discussing the nature of the universe with Albert Einstein. You remind them how silly their objections sound, as it's Einstein's very work that has made time travel possible.

It is suggested at this point that perhaps others might be bettered suited in changing the path of Adolf Hitler.

You agree and are therefore denied any further time travel. Go to **Page 121**

You argue that your very interest makes you the most suitable in changing history for the better and beg for another chance. Go to **Page 119**

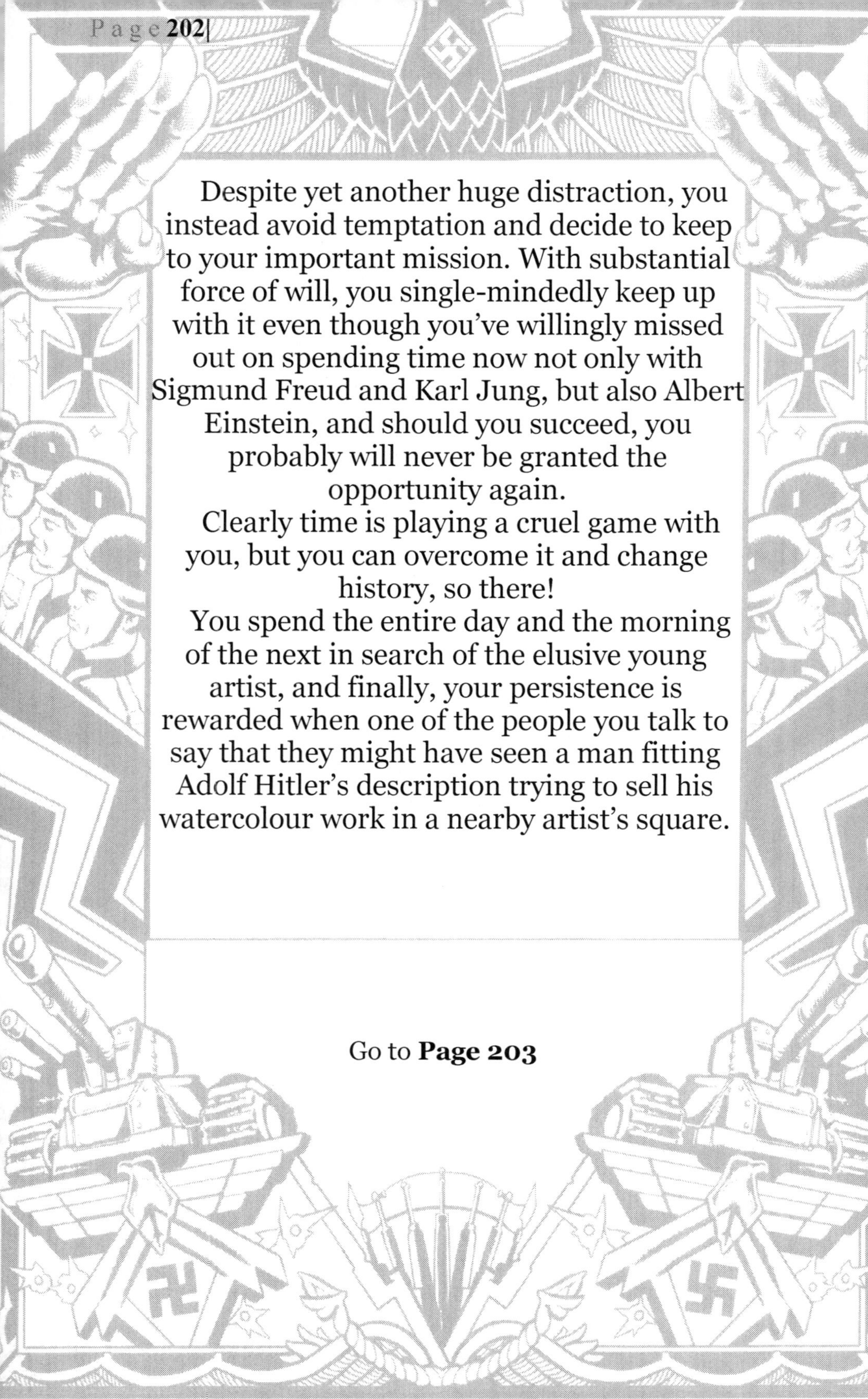

Despite yet another huge distraction, you instead avoid temptation and decide to keep to your important mission. With substantial force of will, you single-mindedly keep up with it even though you've willingly missed out on spending time now not only with Sigmund Freud and Karl Jung, but also Albert Einstein, and should you succeed, you probably will never be granted the opportunity again.

Clearly time is playing a cruel game with you, but you can overcome it and change history, so there!

You spend the entire day and the morning of the next in search of the elusive young artist, and finally, your persistence is rewarded when one of the people you talk to say that they might have seen a man fitting Adolf Hitler's description trying to sell his watercolour work in a nearby artist's square.

Go to **Page 203**

You head over to the plaza, but to your disappointment, there are literally hundreds of artists trying to sell their wares, some of them quite aggressive. You almost get into a fight trying to get away from one belligerent charcoal portrait artist. But your single-mindedness finally pays off when you spot Hitler with his collection of watercolours on small easels, trying to drum up sales from the somewhat disinterested Viennese.

You realize that he doesn't really have what it takes right now to influence anyone at this age, let alone lead a nation to horrifying heights and depths. So you might just have a chance to turn him onto a different path. But, oh no, it looks like he is packing up, as it is late afternoon and the plaza is crowded, and you are afraid that if you don't manage to get to him now, you might miss him before he disappears into the throng with his mediocre works under his arm.

Do you hurry to try to catch him before he leaves?
Go to **Page 204**

Do you make your way through the crowd, assured that you are talented enough to track him down if you have to?
Go to **Page 207**

You make your way through the crowds, losing Hitler several times. However, you still manage to keep up with him and locate the frustratingly ordinary looking artist time after time.

You finally catch up with him at a drinking den near the artist's square for the local bohemian culture where clutches of artists, poets, and prospective novelists have gathered elbow to elbow to discuss the directions of current trends, philosophize, and otherwise commiserate over the difficulty of getting into the Academies of their choice, the difficulty of finding patrons and publishers, and otherwise get drunk (because that is often what artists really want to do).

You are able to get Hitler's attention by buying him a drink (no surprise there) and are able to take him aside and talk to him about art and his potential. It is not too hard to get the young man to listen to you, as you found him drinking by himself. No, he isn't particularly popular at this point in his life.

Go to **Page 205**

You get his attention and momentarily his gratitude, but find that he appears to have a real chip on his shoulder and a talent at debating. You realize that he had to start somewhere, right?

You wonder how long it might take to convince him that you are actually trying to help him out. This is not so easy, as he isn't that impressed by what you are showing him. As an artist, he's kind of a traditionalist (this is the attitude that will prevent him from being accepted; again, no big surprise there).

On the other hand, you realize that you can probably get him completely sauced and be able to put him down, as opposed to struggling through convincing him to appreciate the examples of envelope-pushing art that he could emulate to impress the Academy of Arts.

Go to **Page 206**

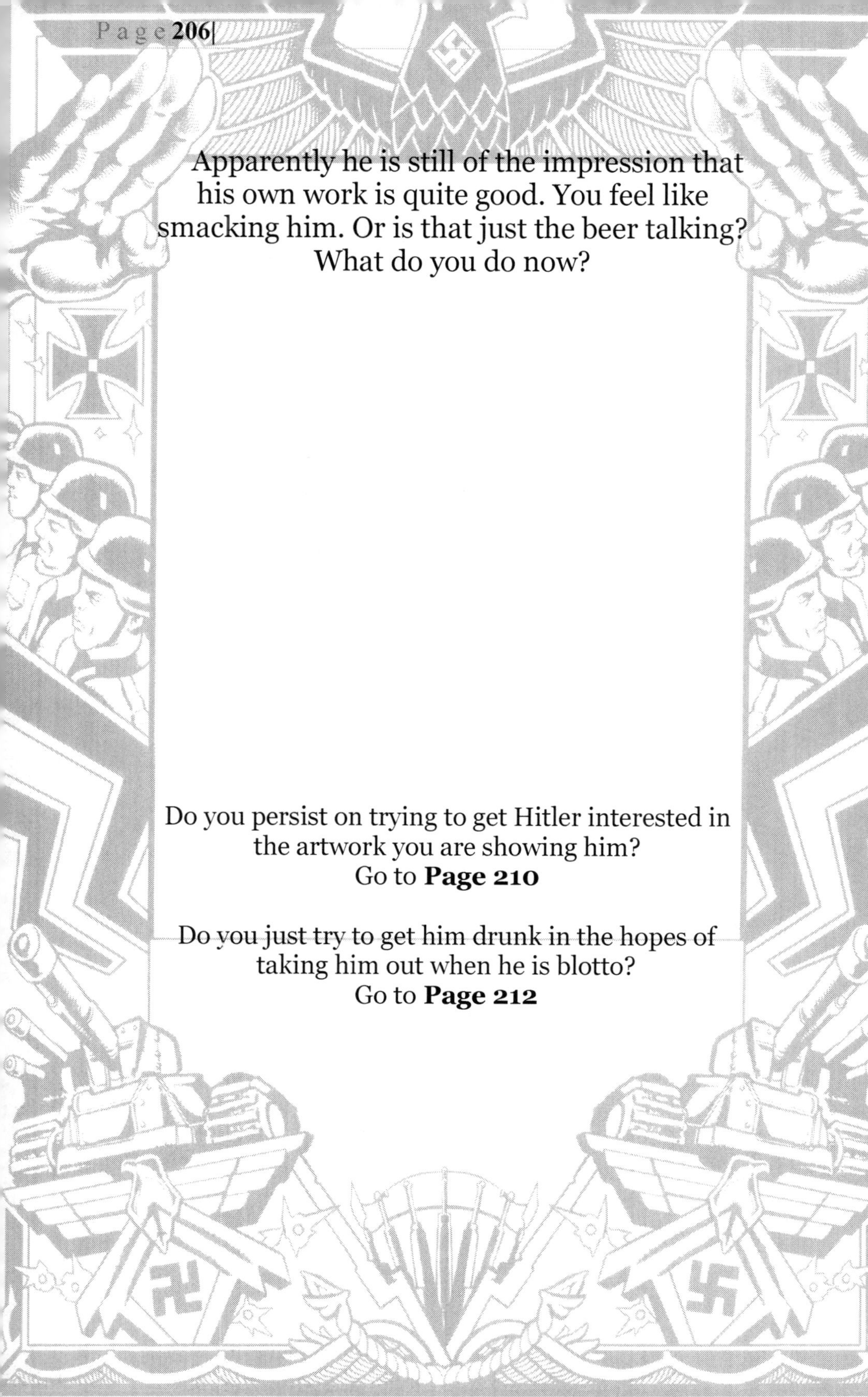

Apparently he is still of the impression that his own work is quite good. You feel like smacking him. Or is that just the beer talking? What do you do now?

Do you persist on trying to get Hitler interested in the artwork you are showing him?

Go to **Page 210**

Do you just try to get him drunk in the hopes of taking him out when he is blotto?

Go to **Page 212**

You push through the crowd in your rush to try to catch Hitler before he fades into the night. It's difficult, as most of the artists are also packing up and blocking your way. You suddenly break out of the crowd and think you now have a chance of getting to him before he leaves the square, but in your excitement, you haven't been looking around you, or beneath your feet. You are standing on tracks, and turn to see a streetcar speeding down the plaza right towards you. A woman screams, and you realize that you might not be able to get out of the way before the vehicle slams right into you.

There is no time for you to get out of the way; you are hit full on and knocked away hard, thrown back down onto the cobblestone street. You are left to lie there on your back, gasping in pain with what must be a number of broken bones from the collision, while a crowd gathers around you.

Go to **Page 208**

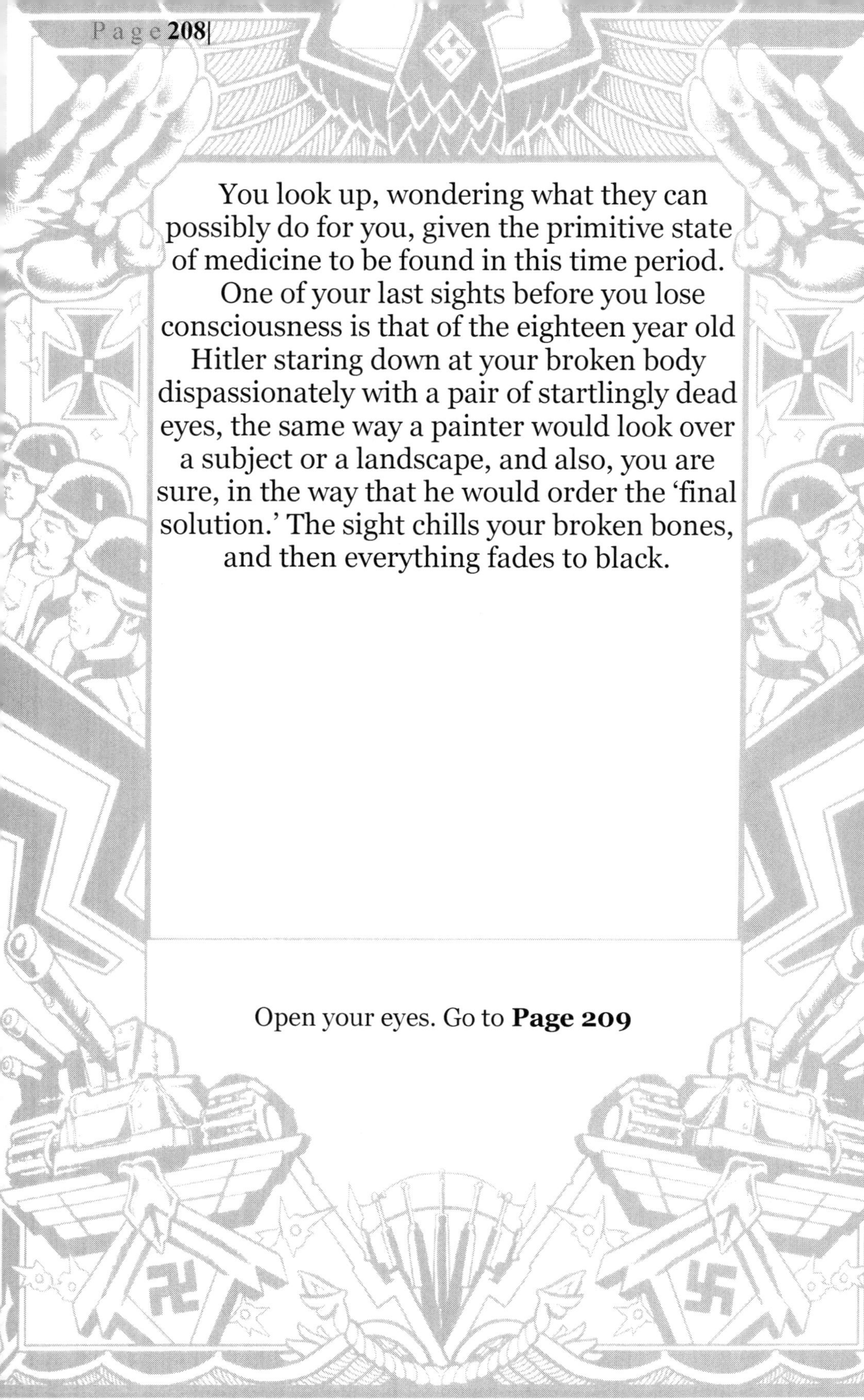

You look up, wondering what they can possibly do for you, given the primitive state of medicine to be found in this time period.

One of your last sights before you lose consciousness is that of the eighteen year old Hitler staring down at your broken body dispassionately with a pair of startlingly dead eyes, the same way a painter would look over a subject or a landscape, and also, you are sure, in the way that he would order the 'final solution.' The sight chills your broken bones, and then everything fades to black.

Open your eyes. Go to **Page 209**

You awaken in a medical pod, feeling much better.

"How did you end up with so many broken bones?" the attendant asks you.

"I was trying to chase down Adolf Hitler," you tell her. "And I would have caught him if it wasn't for that damn streetcar."

The attendant laughs; you do as well. But you wonder about the inadvertent dangers of time travel. You are told that you will be healthy enough to go back soon.

Do you decide that whatever the past throws at you, you will persevere?

Go to **Page 119**

Have you finally decided that enough is enough? Time travel is too dangerous. And damn, it hurts.

Go to **Page 121**

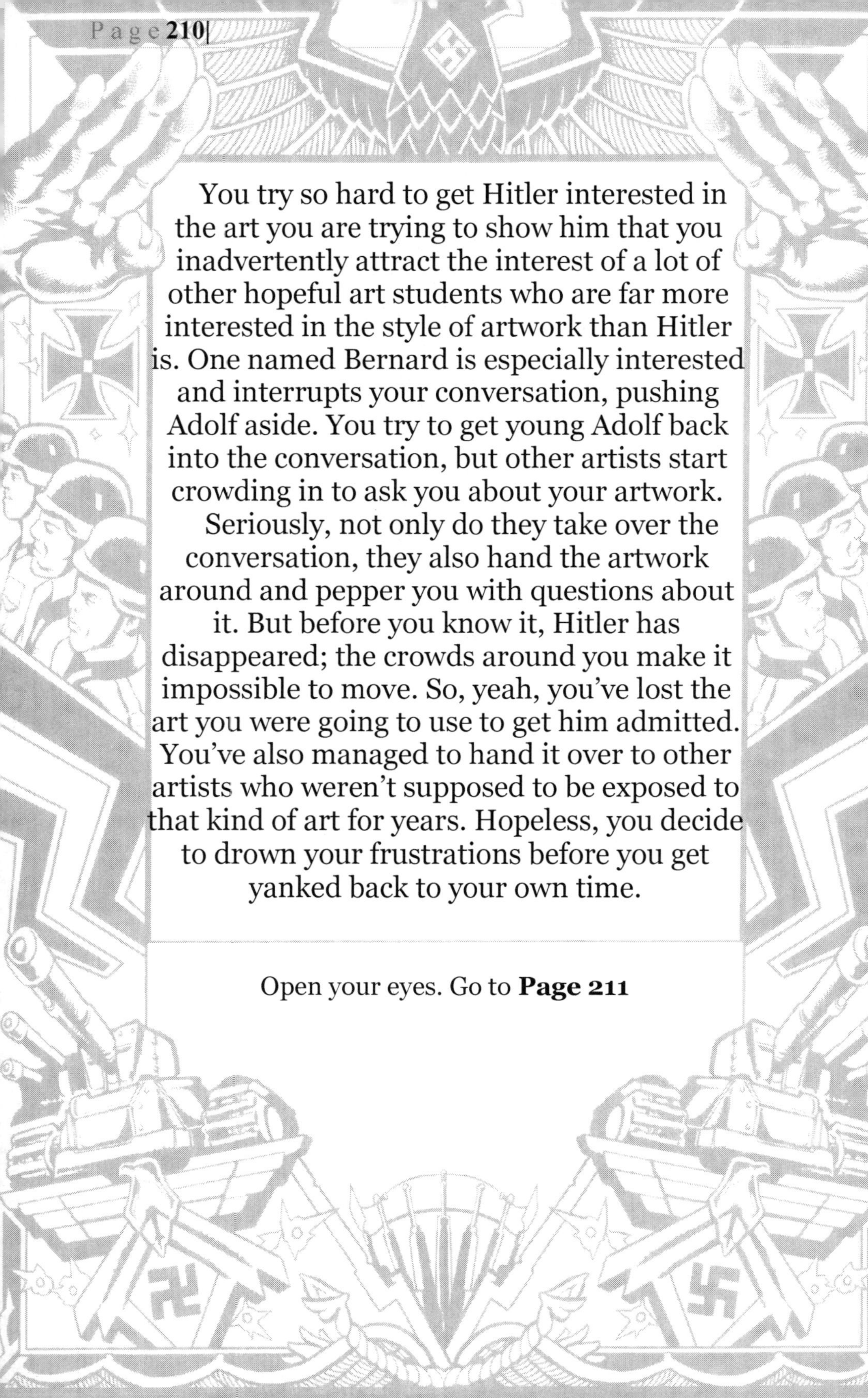

You try so hard to get Hitler interested in the art you are trying to show him that you inadvertently attract the interest of a lot of other hopeful art students who are far more interested in the style of artwork than Hitler is. One named Bernard is especially interested and interrupts your conversation, pushing Adolf aside. You try to get young Adolf back into the conversation, but other artists start crowding in to ask you about your artwork.

Seriously, not only do they take over the conversation, they also hand the artwork around and pepper you with questions about it. But before you know it, Hitler has disappeared; the crowds around you make it impossible to move. So, yeah, you've lost the art you were going to use to get him admitted. You've also managed to hand it over to other artists who weren't supposed to be exposed to that kind of art for years. Hopeless, you decide to drown your frustrations before you get yanked back to your own time.

Open your eyes. Go to **Page 211**

You get back to the future and discover that not much has changed. When questioned, you say that you really tried to show the artwork to Hitler, but he wasn't interested. You learn that in response to what happened that night, Hitler later had many artists executed before they had a chance to escape Nazi Germany. Sure, this hasn't changed things a great deal, except to make the world a grimmer place. No one seems to notice this, however, but you.

Do you advocate going back as soon as possible to fix things and succeed in your mission? Go to **Page 119**

Do you give up, realizing that without decent art, humanity may as well fade away? Go to **Page 121**

You wake up back in a medipod in the future and discover that you are being treated for alcohol poisoning. On the bright side, you have learned that in this new timeline, Hitler did get accepted into the Academy of Fine Arts and World War II wasn't quite as horrible as you remember.

Apparently, by getting shitfaced drunk with Hitler, he becomes more amenable to your arguments and starts getting excited at what you are showing him. Though you don't remember it, you apparently decided that you might be better off not killing him at the time. You decide to go see Rolf-ME242 and ask him about how things have changed.

"Greetings, time traveller." The synthetic voice of the A.I. greets you from all around the bright chamber. "You have definitely succeeded in your mission. Adolf did indeed gain admission to the Academy."

Go to **Page 213**

"But was that enough?" you ask. "Have I done enough for humanity to survive?"

"Humanity is still at risk, but the chances of survival of your race has improved," Rolf tells you. "Hitler was a slightly nicer genocidal dictator than he was in the previous timeline, that is true. Far fewer artists were persecuted or killed, and we all benefit because of it."

'A slightly nicer genocidal dictator' still means a genocidal dictator, but at least you can see that the world you live is far more attractive than it had been before you left. Certainly the elevator music has improved.

"Are you ready for another mission?" the A.I. asks you. "You have proven that time travel is the right way to go."

You nod your head. You are more than ready. If you had a hangover, you might have wanted to wait a while.

Go to **Page 214**

"Thank you, volunteer," Rolf-ME242 states. "Return to the portal chamber for your next leap into the past. We all await the betterment for mankind that your success will provide!"

You head back to the Timeband chamber to ready yourself for another trip. What next, you wonder?

Every day I'm portalin'. Go to **Page 13**

You pass through the swirling light, barely finding your way through the portal's dizzying kaleidoscope. It is really hard to know what direction to go in when everything is changing around you. Your foot finally hits something solid, and you stumble into the bright light and then suddenly into the hustle and bustle of a busy street. You are surprised by the amount of activity. There are numerous people ardently heading to and fro all around you. There are horses and carts, which you expected, given the time period you were headed for, but there are also a handful of primitive automobiles trundling about as well.

You're obviously at a time well past Hitler's childhood. In fact, you quickly learn that you have arrived during the early days of World War I. It seems that this news has everyone excited. None of them, of course, have your foresight.

Go to **Page 216**

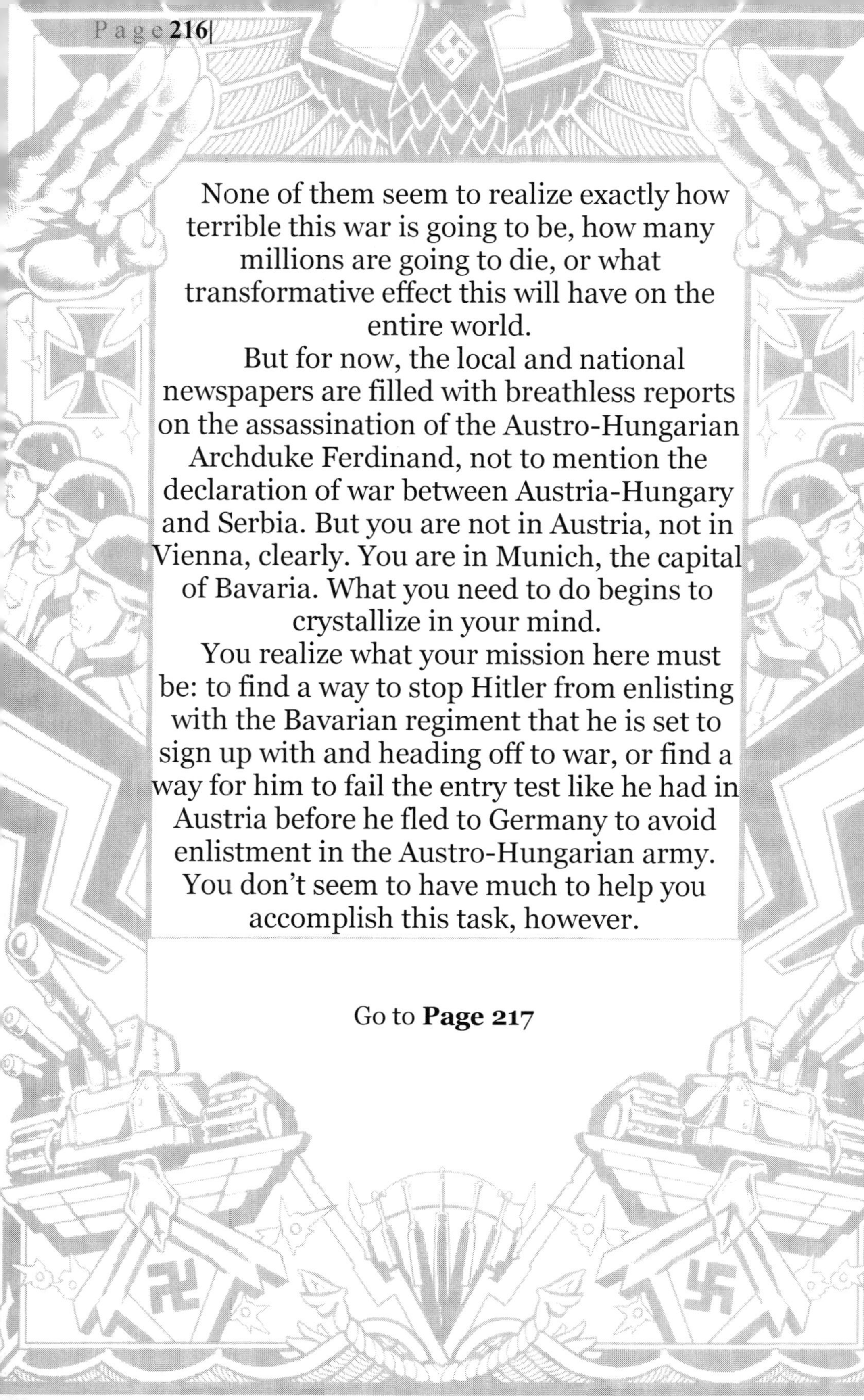

None of them seem to realize exactly how terrible this war is going to be, how many millions are going to die, or what transformative effect this will have on the entire world.

But for now, the local and national newspapers are filled with breathless reports on the assassination of the Austro-Hungarian Archduke Ferdinand, not to mention the declaration of war between Austria-Hungary and Serbia. But you are not in Austria, not in Vienna, clearly. You are in Munich, the capital of Bavaria. What you need to do begins to crystallize in your mind.

You realize what your mission here must be: to find a way to stop Hitler from enlisting with the Bavarian regiment that he is set to sign up with and heading off to war, or find a way for him to fail the entry test like he had in Austria before he fled to Germany to avoid enlistment in the Austro-Hungarian army. You don't seem to have much to help you accomplish this task, however.

Go to **Page 217**

All you have is a map marking the spots where Hitler has been engaged in his current career as a house painter and a pocket full of change that might get you by for the hours or day or so before the Timeband recalls you back to your own century. So, what are you going to do to get started?

Do you try to seek out Hitler at one of the house painting jobs he has? Go to **Page 218**

Do you head to the war rally that is advertised to be happening today, suspecting that he might be in attendance?

Go to **Page 221**

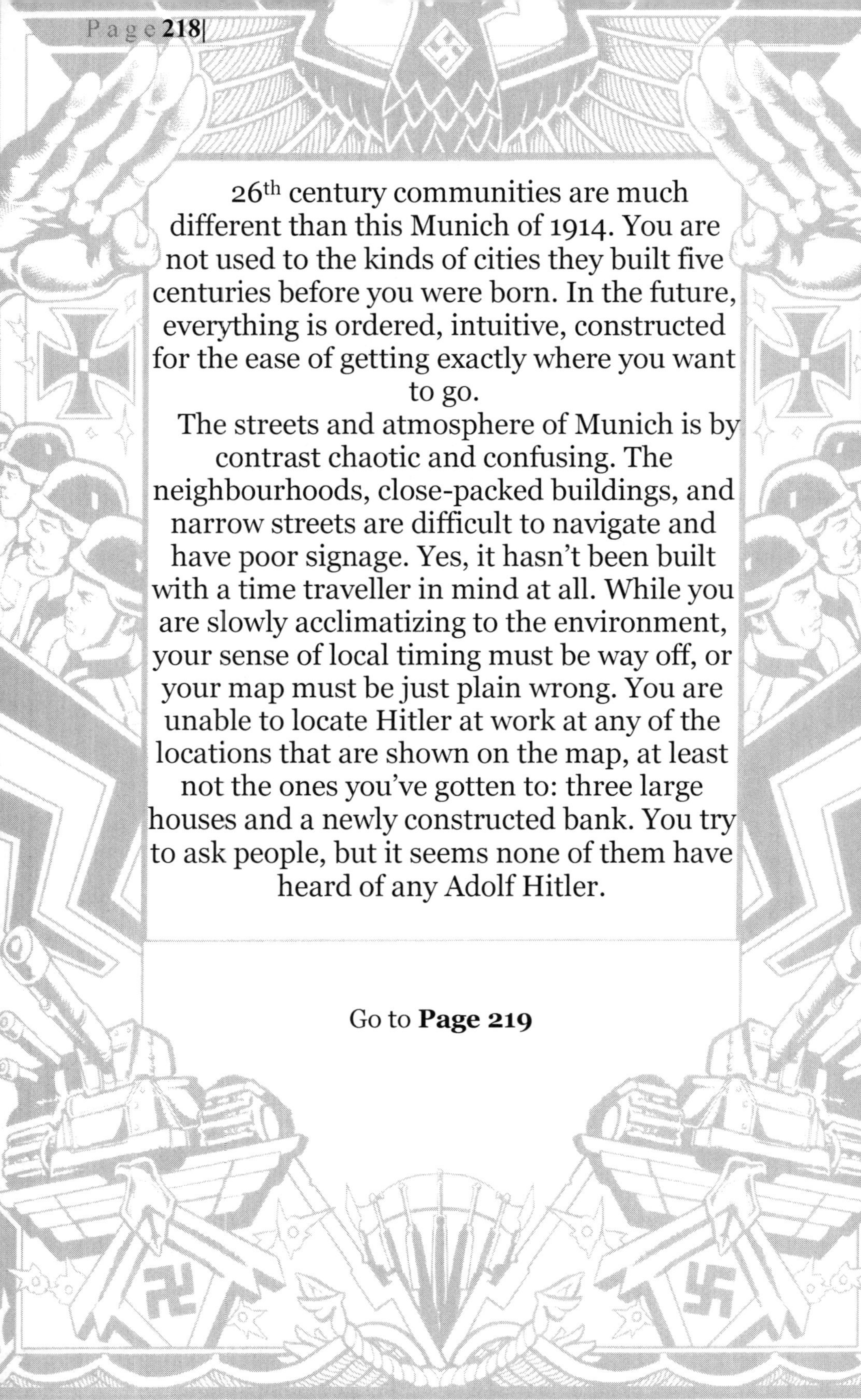

26th century communities are much different than this Munich of 1914. You are not used to the kinds of cities they built five centuries before you were born. In the future, everything is ordered, intuitive, constructed for the ease of getting exactly where you want to go.

The streets and atmosphere of Munich is by contrast chaotic and confusing. The neighbourhoods, close-packed buildings, and narrow streets are difficult to navigate and have poor signage. Yes, it hasn't been built with a time traveller in mind at all. While you are slowly acclimatizing to the environment, your sense of local timing must be way off, or your map must be just plain wrong. You are unable to locate Hitler at work at any of the locations that are shown on the map, at least not the ones you've gotten to: three large houses and a newly constructed bank. You try to ask people, but it seems none of them have heard of any Adolf Hitler.

Go to **Page 219**

Apparently these sorts of jobs merely draw itinerant workers who come and go as they please.

Giving up locating him at work, you decide to try to get to the war rally that he might be attending. However, by the time that you arrive at the war rally, it is long over, and all that is left in the large square are the men cleaning up the garbage and beggars looking for handouts. You stand in the middle of the square, dejected; your chance to locate Hitler and change his path seems to be utterly lost. You go back to searching for him at the job sites, but it ends up being fruitless. Eventually, you are yanked back to your present, having not even changed one iota of the past.

Open your eyes. Go to **Page 220**

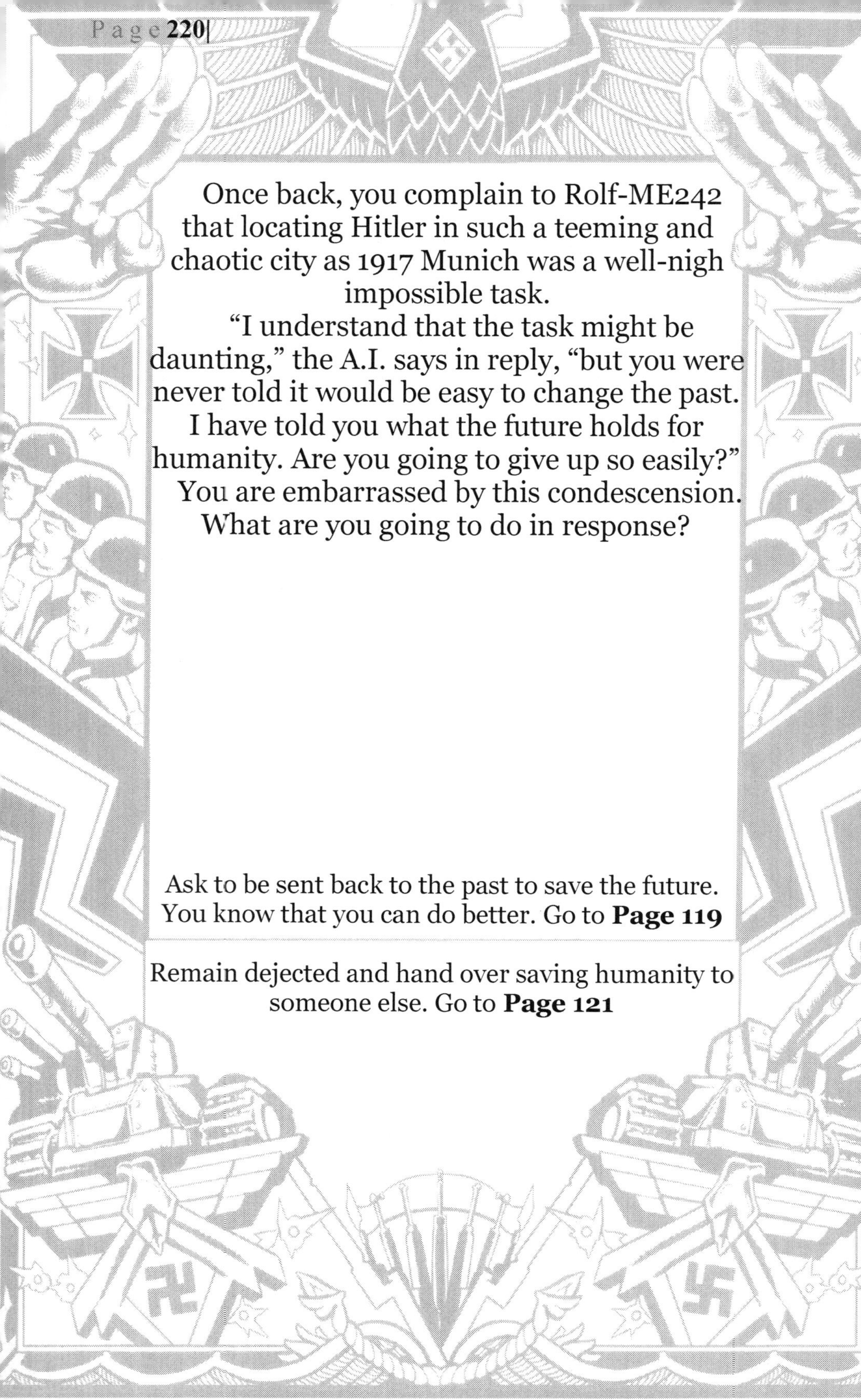

Once back, you complain to Rolf-ME242 that locating Hitler in such a teeming and chaotic city as 1917 Munich was a well-nigh impossible task.

"I understand that the task might be daunting," the A.I. says in reply, "but you were never told it would be easy to change the past. I have told you what the future holds for humanity. Are you going to give up so easily?"

You are embarrassed by this condescension. What are you going to do in response?

Ask to be sent back to the past to save the future. You know that you can do better. Go to **Page 119**

Remain dejected and hand over saving humanity to someone else. Go to **Page 121**

You decide that it would be a waste of your precious time in 1917 try and find Hitler at work, and instead head to the war rally. Given how excited Hitler claimed to be about joining the German army at the time, that is where he will have to be right now.

But you are completely shocked and overwhelmed when you get there, finding it an immensely crowded and noisy affair. In this huge square near the centre of Munich, there are literally thousands of men of all ages and class gathered to watch and hear the shouting from the demagogues whose clear intention is riling up the nationalistic fervour for German entry into the war. There is a loud call to march on the French, who along with the Russians are the allies of the now-hated Serbians who assassinated the heir presumptive to the Austro-Hungarian Empire.

Go to **Page 222**

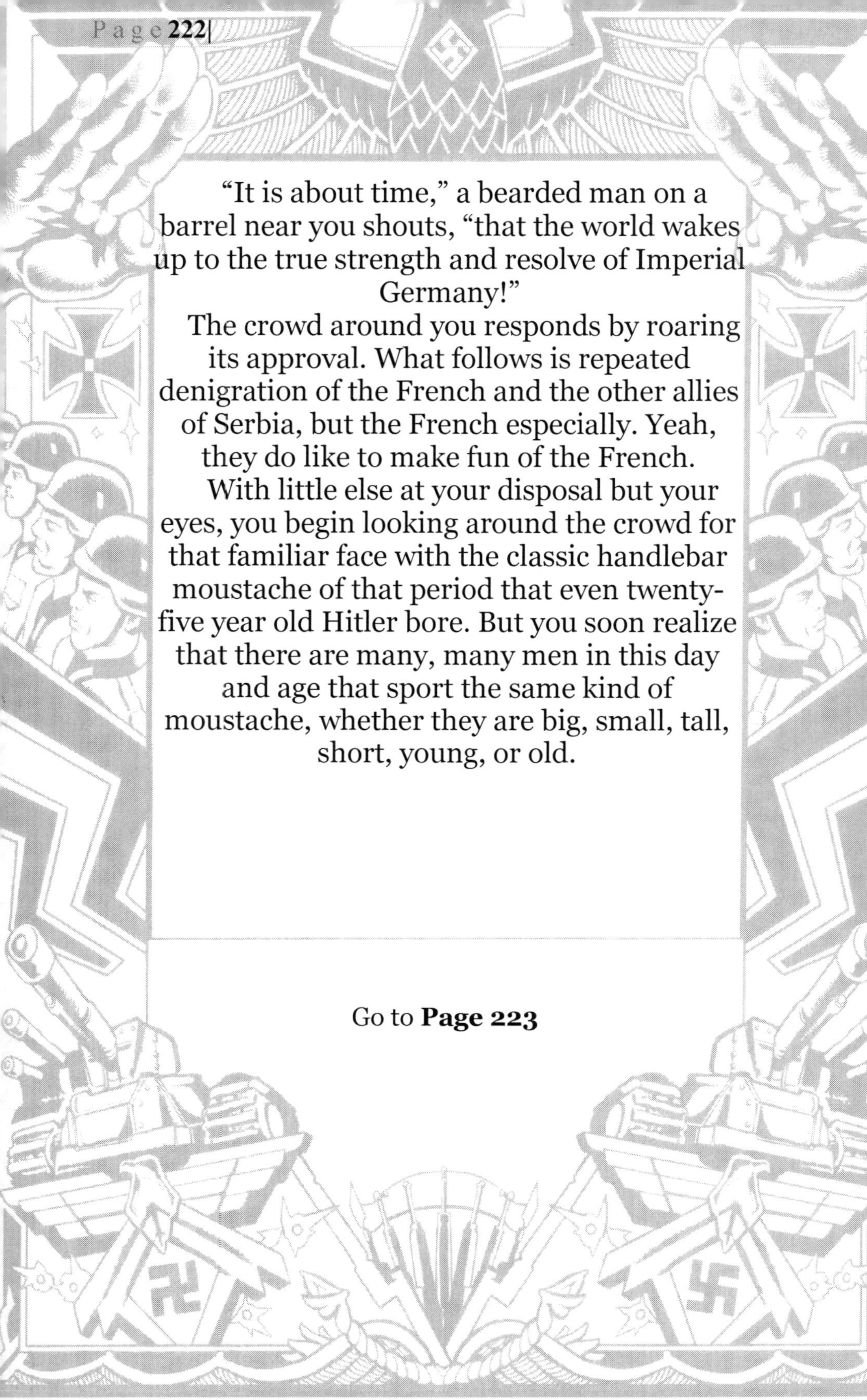

"It is about time," a bearded man on a barrel near you shouts, "that the world wakes up to the true strength and resolve of Imperial Germany!"

The crowd around you responds by roaring its approval. What follows is repeated denigration of the French and the other allies of Serbia, but the French especially. Yeah, they do like to make fun of the French.

With little else at your disposal but your eyes, you begin looking around the crowd for that familiar face with the classic handlebar moustache of that period that even twenty-five year old Hitler bore. But you soon realize that there are many, many men in this day and age that sport the same kind of moustache, whether they are big, small, tall, short, young, or old.

Go to **Page 223**

It's like you are standing in a crowd full of Hitlers and playing a near impossible game of Spot the Adolf! You begin to get discouraged after an hour of wandering through the crowd. Suddenly, you think you've finally spotted the genuine Hitler in the crowd, a young man of the right height and build. But he quickly disappears behind group of men in short trousers and suspenders singing a nationalistic anthem.

Do you push your way through to him, knowing you may be running out of time, to carry out your plan as quickly as possible before you get yanked away? Go to **Page 224**

Do you wait and check to make sure it was the right man this time? Go to **Page 227**

Worried that you may have lost your only chance at catching up with your target, you try to push through the tight gathering of burly men who are standing between you and Hitler. They, however, take offense at your rough attempt to push and squeeze through them and begin to push back, asking you who you think you are. They are all rather larger than you, and from what you smell, more than a little drunk.

You try to be apologetic, but still attempt to get through them. After all, the elusive Adolf Hitler could quickly be lost in the crowd. To your dismay, a shoving match ensues between you and a couple of the men, and then more people get involved. Before long, it turns into a hand to hand battle, and you find yourself dodging fists and kicks as you try to defend yourself against the drunken hooligans.

Somebody then shouts, “Jew!”

Someone else shouts, “Dirty Serbian!”

And another shouts, “French spy!”

Go to **Page 225**

This spreads like wildfire through the crowd around you. Before you can react, you are in the middle of a full-out brawl and are not doing well at all. One or two men you might be able to handle, but there are fists and boots and improvised clubs flying around everywhere. Eventually a huge ham-sized fist flies at your face, and you see stars before your head hits the ground with a crack and everything goes black.

Open your eyes. Go to **Page 226**

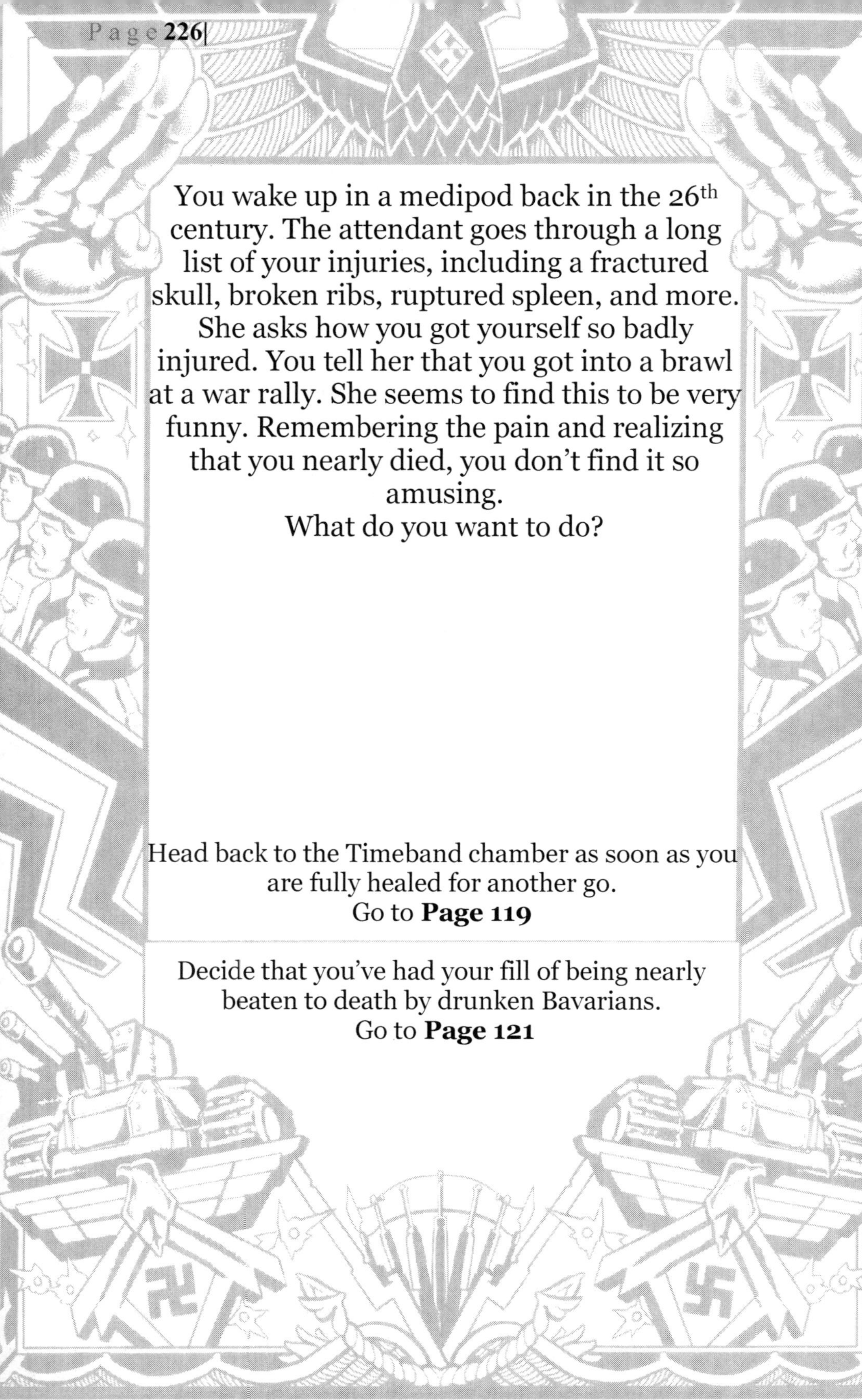

You wake up in a medipod back in the 26th century. The attendant goes through a long list of your injuries, including a fractured skull, broken ribs, ruptured spleen, and more. She asks how you got yourself so badly injured. You tell her that you got into a brawl at a war rally. She seems to find this to be very funny. Remembering the pain and realizing that you nearly died, you don't find it so amusing.

What do you want to do?

Head back to the Timeband chamber as soon as you are fully healed for another go.

Go to **Page 119**

Decide that you've had your fill of being nearly beaten to death by drunken Bavarians.

Go to **Page 121**

Discretion seem to be the better part of valour here. You manage to avoid getting into one of the brawls that are starting to break out at the rally and finally catch a glimpse of the man you are hunting for – at least you believe so. It does look like a young Adolf Hitler making his way out of the rally's crowd and also avoiding the fights that seem to be breaking out. Keeping back and careful, you follow him to his home, trying to decide exactly what you can say to him that will make him not want to join the German army. How can you counter the fervour being raised back at the rally? The hatred for the enemy states? You aren't quite sure. A few minutes later, as you are still debating this, you see him leaving the rooming house in work clothes. You follow him to his actual day job, which is the painting of a large house with a number of other workmen. You look at your map. Hey! This place isn't marked. So much for Rolf-ME242's supposed temporal genius.

Go to **Page 228**

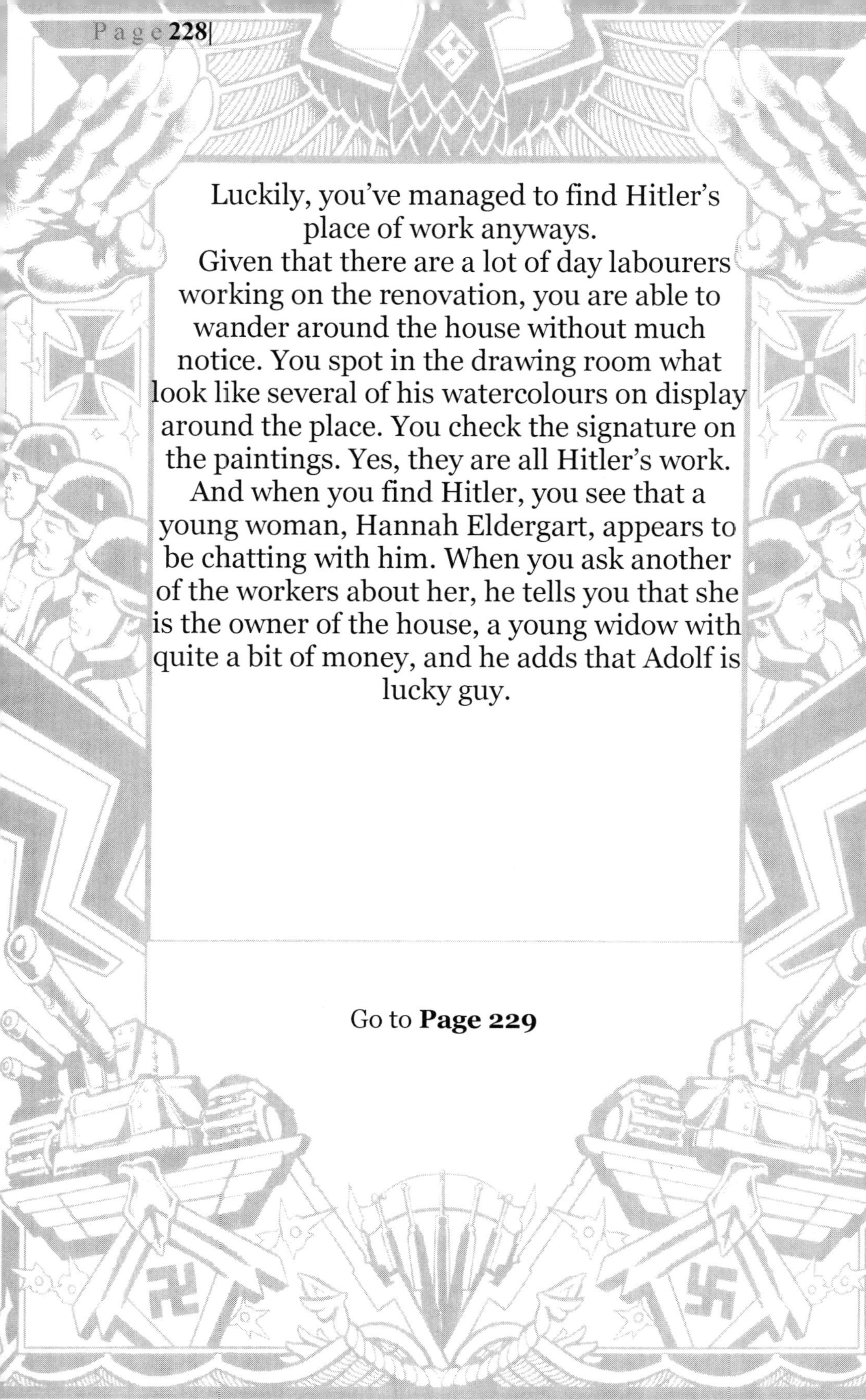

Luckily, you've managed to find Hitler's place of work anyways.

Given that there are a lot of day labourers working on the renovation, you are able to wander around the house without much notice. You spot in the drawing room what look like several of his watercolours on display around the place. You check the signature on the paintings. Yes, they are all Hitler's work. And when you find Hitler, you see that a young woman, Hannah Eldergart, appears to be chatting with him. When you ask another of the workers about her, he tells you that she is the owner of the house, a young widow with quite a bit of money, and he adds that Adolf is lucky guy.

Go to **Page 229**

When he is on break, you attempt to strike up a conversation with the twenty-five year old Adolf about the war rally, saying that you recognized his paintings from a friend in Vienna, and he suddenly brightens up, chatting about the worthiness of German nationalism and the importance of the war effort to show the world that Germans can't be pushed around anymore by the other so-called European powers. He seems so animated by the thought of fighting for Germany; there is nothing you can think of that might change his course.

Go to **Page 230**

You decide to think about what other directions you can come at him from. Later, you see that he is working on a high scaffolding. You think you might have the opportunity to knock it down, injuring him severely at the very least, maybe even killing him. That might prevent him from going off to war. So, are you going to cause a workplace accident?

Do you rig the scaffolding to collapse?
Go to **Page 231**

Do you think about things and try to come up with a better argument that he might listen to?
Go to **Page 234**

You decide that a seriously injured Hitler might be permanently unable to join the war effort. So, making sure that no one is watching, you secretly pull out the bolts in the scaffolding, rigging it to collapse, and then find a place to watch what happens. Hitler climbs down to get more paint without incident. You remove a few more bolts, then continue to wait.

Sure enough, the next time he climbs up with the new bucket, it starts swaying and then collapses. Hitler, his tools, and the paint all fall down to the floor with a loud and violent crash, causing everyone in the house to come running. But between the other painters trying to clean up the mess and Hannah kneeling over the moaning Hitler and calling for help, you can't get in to tell exactly how hurt he is or do anything to finish the job, if needed. Sure, it turns out he is badly hurt, although it doesn't appear that any of his broken bones will be fatal.

Go to **Page 232**

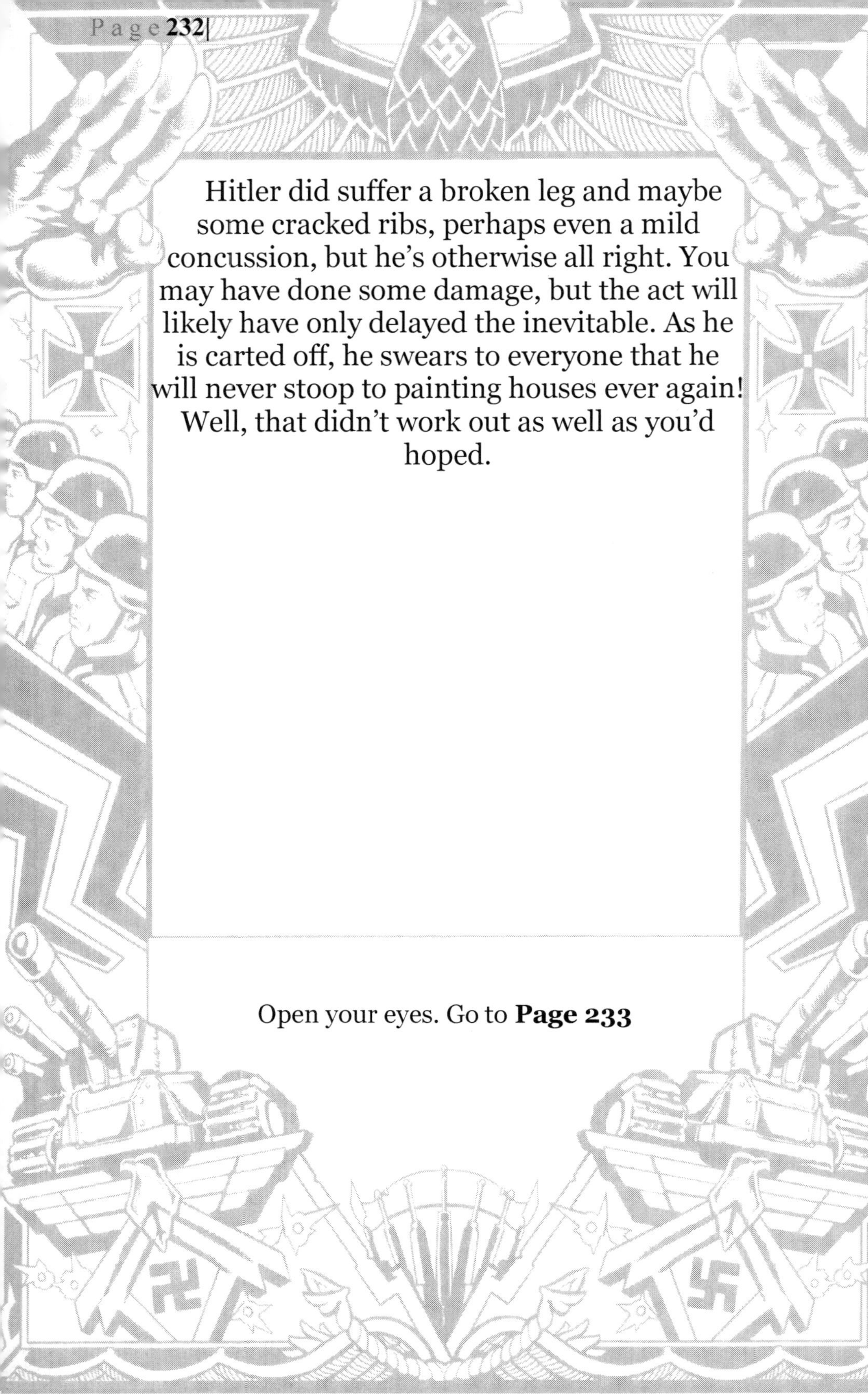

Hitler did suffer a broken leg and maybe some cracked ribs, perhaps even a mild concussion, but he's otherwise all right. You may have done some damage, but the act will likely have only delayed the inevitable. As he is carted off, he swears to everyone that he will never stoop to painting houses ever again! Well, that didn't work out as well as you'd hoped.

Open your eyes. Go to **Page 233**

After you are pulled back to 2525, nothing at all appears to have changed. You are asked about what you did, and you explain about your attempt to seriously injure Hitler enough to keep him from going to war.

You learn, however, that his injuries only delayed him from signing up for a few months. Your trip was a waste of time and energy. You are asked, “Couldn’t you think of anything else?” All you can do is shrug. You did your best, didn’t you?

Do you decide you can do better, and ask to be sent back again**?**

Go to **Page 119**

Do you realize that you may not be creative enough to get the job done?

Go to **Page 121**

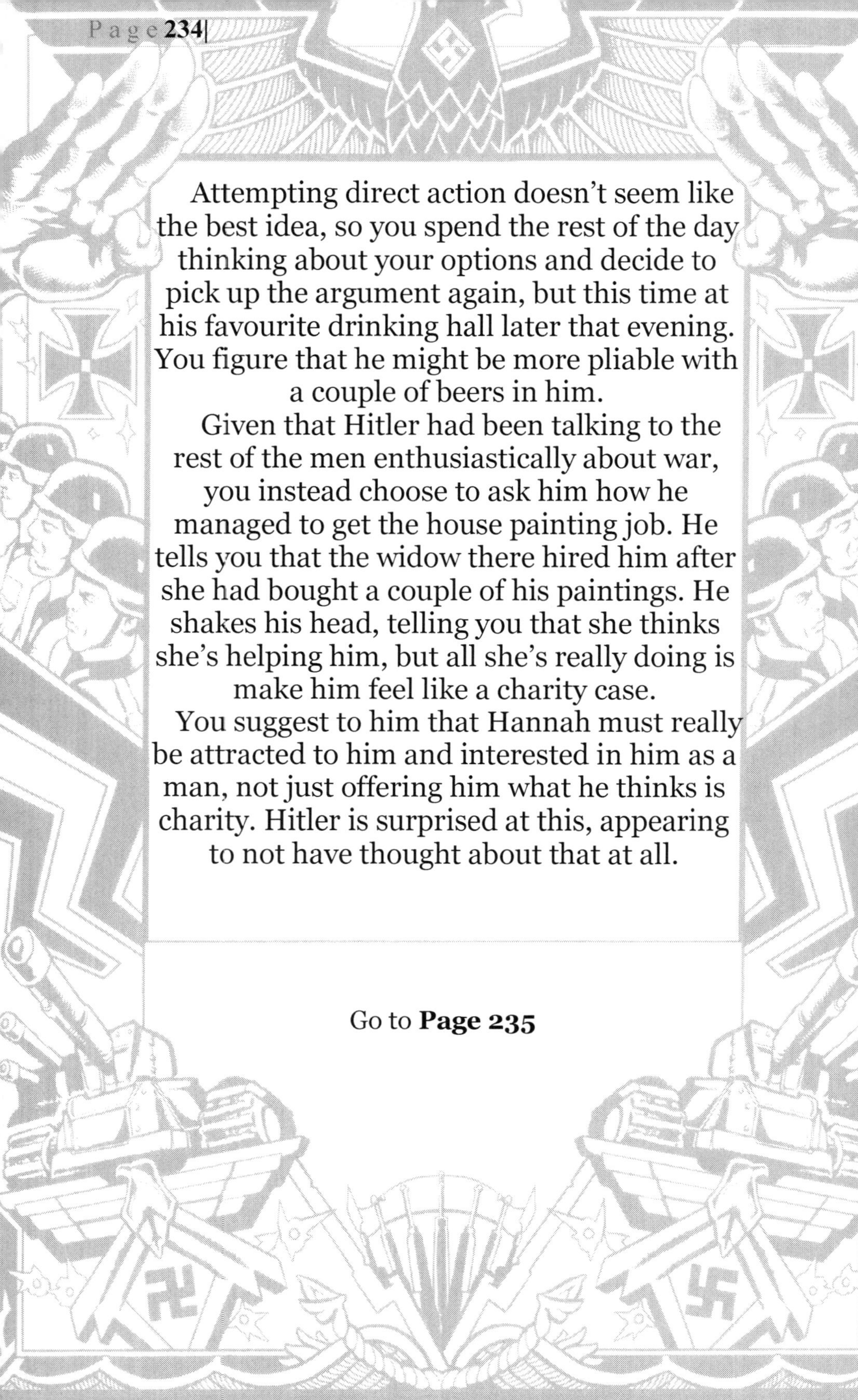

Attempting direct action doesn't seem like the best idea, so you spend the rest of the day thinking about your options and decide to pick up the argument again, but this time at his favourite drinking hall later that evening. You figure that he might be more pliable with a couple of beers in him.

Given that Hitler had been talking to the rest of the men enthusiastically about war, you instead choose to ask him how he managed to get the house painting job. He tells you that the widow there hired him after she had bought a couple of his paintings. He shakes his head, telling you that she thinks she's helping him, but all she's really doing is make him feel like a charity case.

You suggest to him that Hannah must really be attracted to him and interested in him as a man, not just offering him what he thinks is charity. Hitler is surprised at this, appearing to not have thought about that at all.

Go to **Page 235**

You continue pressing the point, and after a few drinks, you convince him to go back and ask her about the possibility of her romantic feelings for him. Somehow you managed to say that a woman has romantic feelings for Adolf Hitler. Bravo!

The two of you return to her house, and you nudge Hitler into asking the woman about what feelings she may have for him. Hannah is reluctant at the suggestion at first, but quickly confesses that is why she bought his paintings and hired him as a housepainter. This both surprises and pleases Adolf. He also reveals that he has developed romantic feelings for her.

You suggest that this calls for a celebration, and the three of you stay up late drinking. It isn't long, however, before it's clear that you are completely a third wheel, and that things would go much better if you made your exit.

Go to **Page 236**

You make to leave, but realize that Hitler is especially vulnerable right now, and the woman's kitchen holds an impressive collection of very sharp and high quality knives, not to mention some pretty solid ironware. Maybe this is the time to put an end to Hitler. He may seem romantic now, but later, who knows?

Do you leave the couple and hope nature takes its course? Go to **Page 240**

Or do you try to nudge things in a different direction with a cast iron frying pan and a good butcher's blade? Go to **Page 237**

You decide to tell them that you need to use the washroom, then wait a few moments out of sight. You think about all the death that Hitler will cause and that you can prevent. After a couple minutes, you convince yourself, deciding that it's not the wine that has addled your brain, but your true knowledge of future history. So, with a knife in hand, you sneak back into the Hannah's drawing room to do the deed.

While Hitler's back is turned, occupied with kissing her, you hit him over the head with the frying pan and stab him to death while Hannah screams in horror. There, now covered in the blood of this one monster, you can make sure that he will never be the leader of the Nazis. Adolf Hitler, you decide, doesn't deserve this kind of domestic happiness. Not on your watch!

You have to get out fast, however, as Hannah, horrified and enraged, attacks you with the frying pan.

Go to **Page 238**

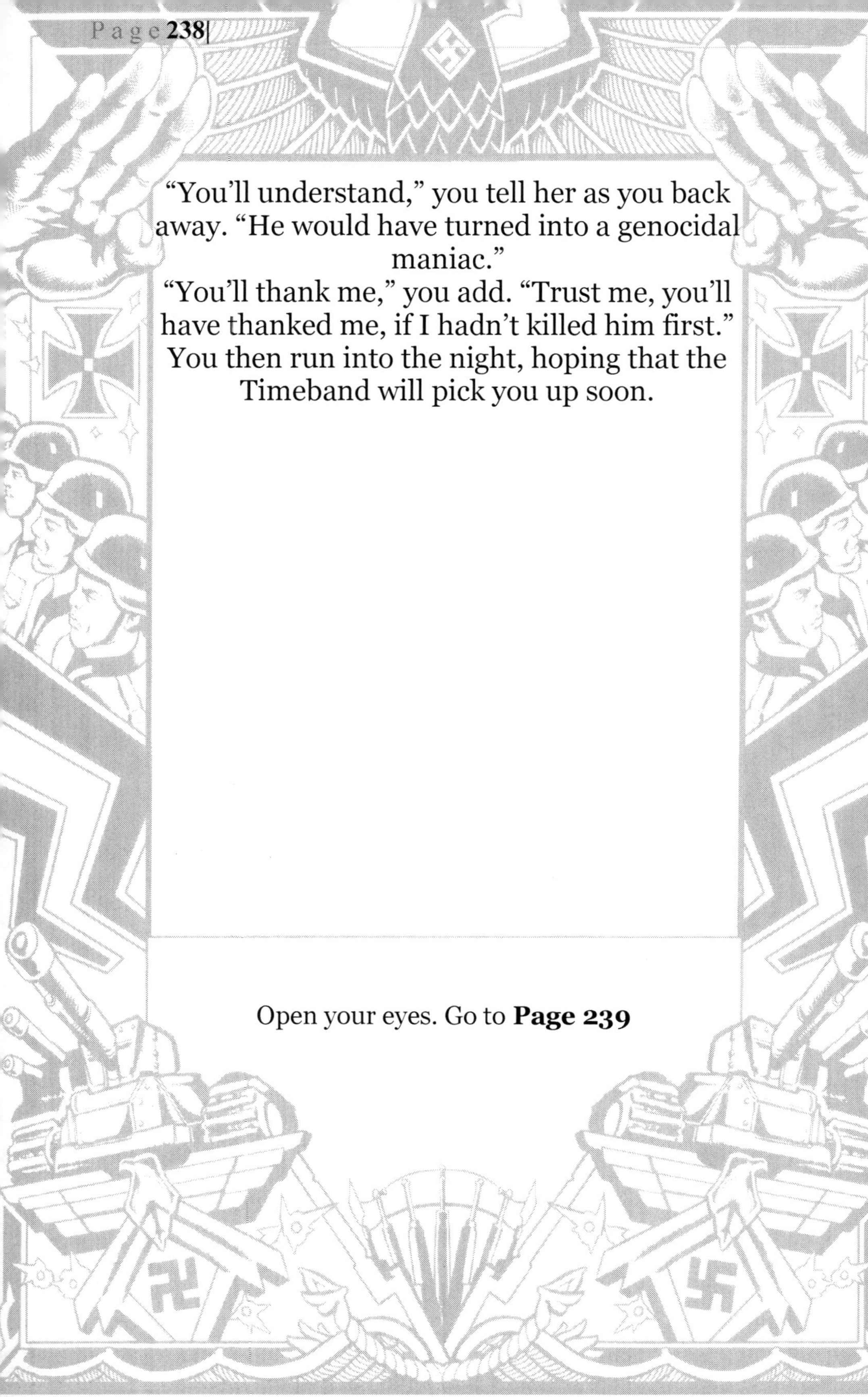

"You'll understand," you tell her as you back away. "He would have turned into a genocidal maniac."

"You'll thank me," you add. "Trust me, you'll have thanked me, if I hadn't killed him first."

You then run into the night, hoping that the Timeband will pick you up soon.

Open your eyes. Go to **Page 239**

When you get back to your own time, you are faced with not an A.I., but a collection of human techno-wizards who ask what you did. You learn that without Hitler as leader of the Nazis, Marxists instead grabbed hold of Germany, allied with the Russians, and eventually took over the world.

In this new future, you and a few techno-wizards have accomplished what the A.I. did and are trying to change the past to prevent the corrupt and oppressive 1984-like world you live in from ever happening.

You say that you can go back and fix things for the better, and plead to be allowed to do so. Go to **Page 119**

You realize that your meddling with the timeline will never make things any better and state that it's a hopeless fool's game. Go to **Page 121**

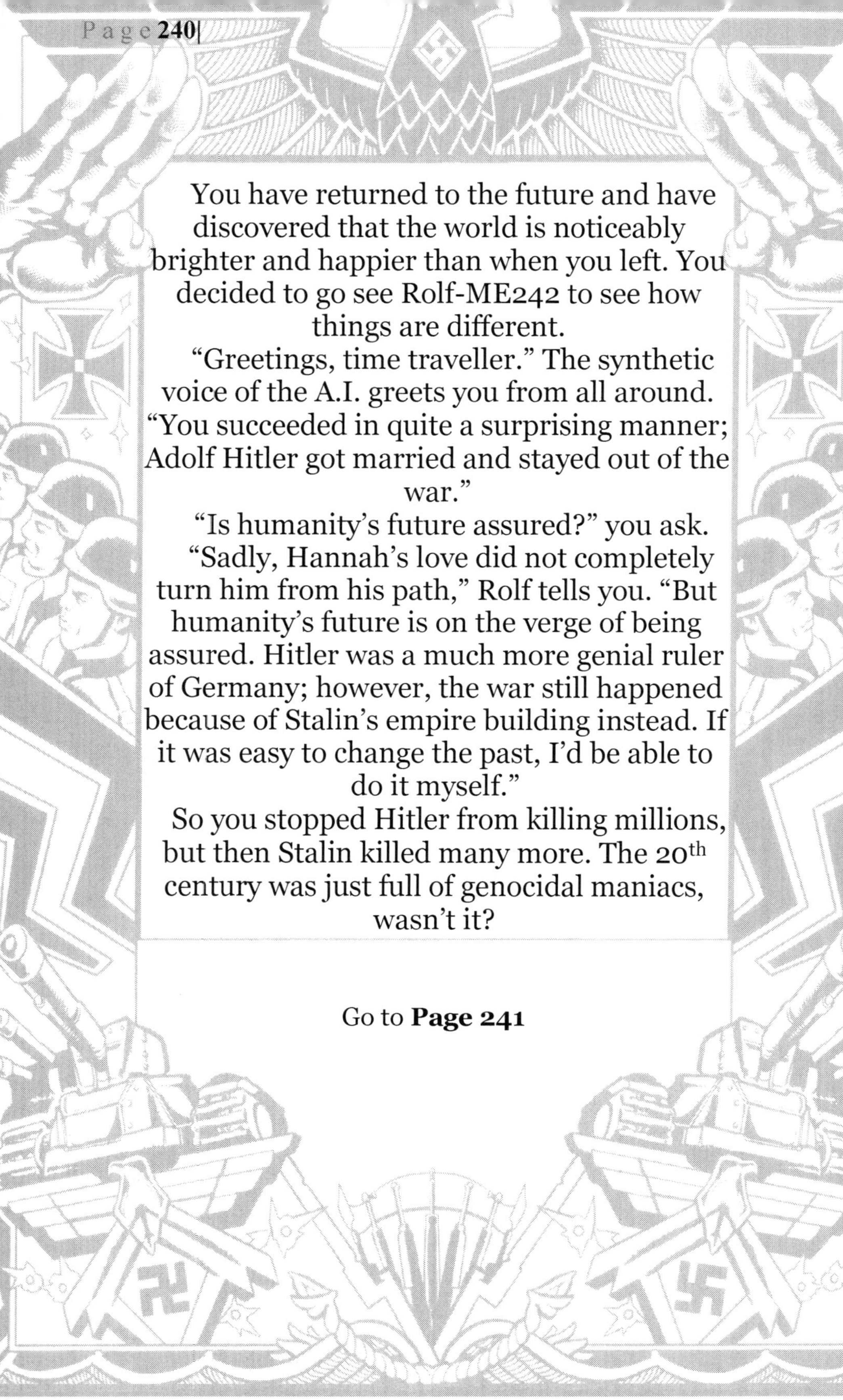

You have returned to the future and have discovered that the world is noticeably brighter and happier than when you left. You decided to go see Rolf-ME242 to see how things are different.

"Greetings, time traveller." The synthetic voice of the A.I. greets you from all around. "You succeeded in quite a surprising manner; Adolf Hitler got married and stayed out of the war."

"Is humanity's future assured?" you ask.

"Sadly, Hannah's love did not completely turn him from his path," Rolf tells you. "But humanity's future is on the verge of being assured. Hitler was a much more genial ruler of Germany; however, the war still happened because of Stalin's empire building instead. If it was easy to change the past, I'd be able to do it myself."

So you stopped Hitler from killing millions, but then Stalin killed many more. The 20th century was just full of genocidal maniacs, wasn't it?

Go to **Page 241**

"Are you ready for another mission?" the A.I. asks you. "Another few tweaks to Hitler's timeline, and even such a monster as Stalin might be overcome."

You nod your head. Sure? If you can get Hitler hitched to a good woman, you can perform other miracles.

"Thank you, volunteer," Rolf-ME242 states. "Take a short rest, then return to the portal. You have proven your talents. I am sure that your successes will lead to a beautiful future for us all."

You take a short rest and enjoy the congratulations of your fellows. Then you return to the Timeband chamber to ready yourself for another trip. Where in Hitler's timeline do you end up this time?

What time is it? Portal time. Go to **Page 13**

You step into and then out of the brilliant white. It seems to take just an instant to travel five centuries back in time. On the other side, you find that you have arrived in the Bavarian city of Munich. But when have you arrived? That is your first question. It soon becomes clear that you have arrived after World War I. It becomes quickly obvious given the general depressive and resentful atmosphere that pervades the lives of the city that you have found yourself in.

In fact, it is now 1920, two years after the end of the war. You confirm the date and realize, according to what you have researched, that shortly, Hitler will be assigned by his military commander to check out a meeting of the German Workers' Party, a rumoured Marxist outfit that will later become the Nazi party. It is this meeting that will change Hitler's post WWI life into a headlong drive towards the second World War.

Go to **Page 243**

So, this is your opportunity to make sure that Hitler never becomes a Nazi, even if he still remains a racist and anti-Semite. Well, you can't have everything, can you? But how are you going to do that?

Then you look at what you are wearing, what you have been supplied with, and where exactly you are.

You see that you are in a German soldier's uniform, and you are near the Munich army base that Hitler must be stationed at. You figure that the best thing to do is get to the commandant's office and change the man's orders for Adolf so that Hitler is assigned to some other operation and never gets a good idea of what the German Workers' Party is really all about. The question is – how much time do you have to do this? It is already late afternoon. And if not, you are armed with a pistol. You smile at the option you've been presented with.

Go to **Page 244**

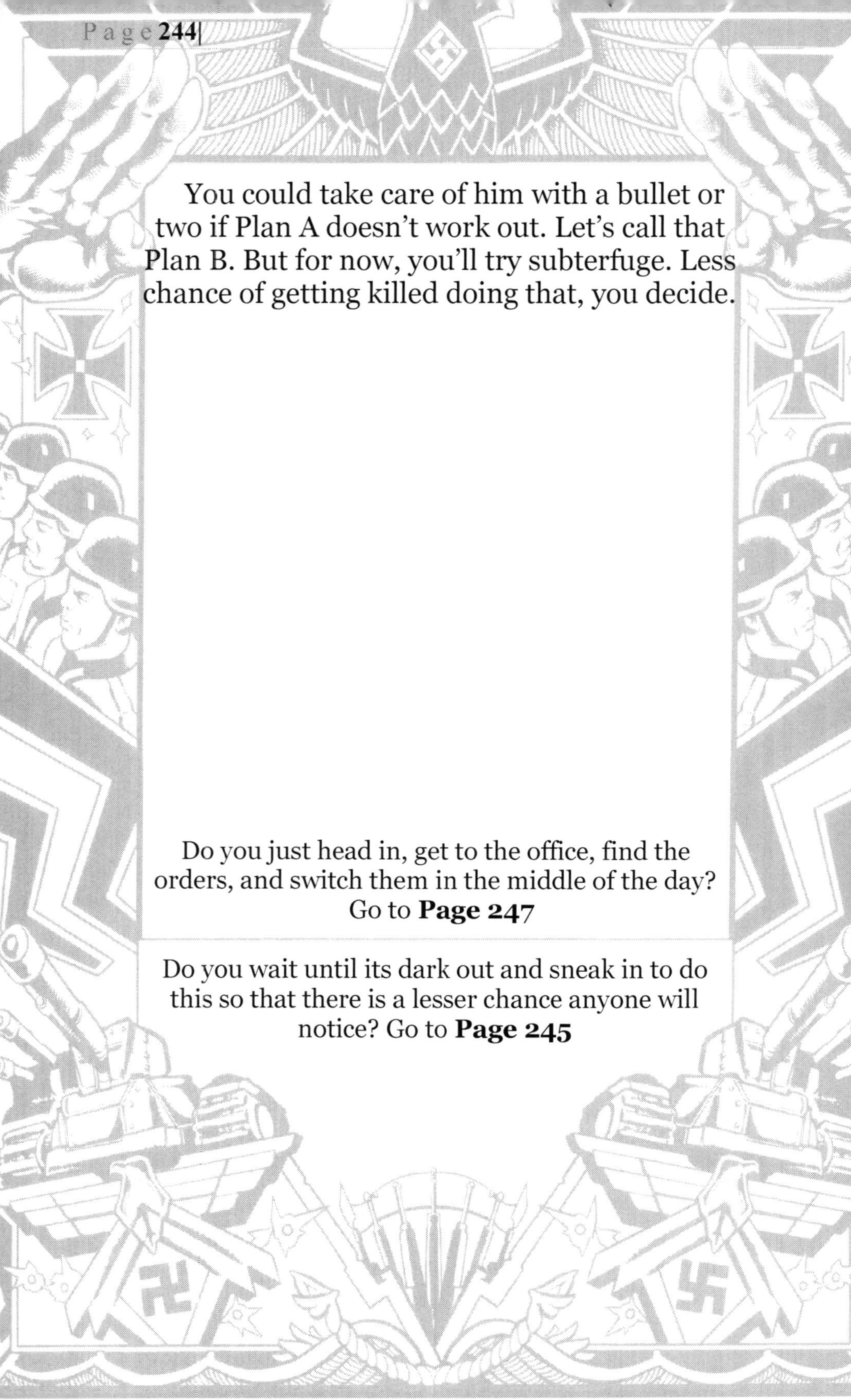

You could take care of him with a bullet or two if Plan A doesn't work out. Let's call that Plan B. But for now, you'll try subterfuge. Less chance of getting killed doing that, you decide.

Do you just head in, get to the office, find the orders, and switch them in the middle of the day? Go to **Page 247**

Do you wait until its dark out and sneak in to do this so that there is a lesser chance anyone will notice? Go to **Page 245**

You decide that it would be better to wait until later and sneak into the commandant's office. The fewer people about, the better, you reason. However, in order to look for Hitler's orders, you have to turn the lights on in the commandant's office, and someone in the base notices.

Worse, when you check, it appears, based on the commandant's meticulous and extensive record keeping, that Hitler has already been assigned to the GWP meeting, which will start in less than an hour. As you try to get out to stop Hitler before he gets to the GWP meeting, you are caught by the base's military police and dragged to an interrogation room where you are questioned, beaten, and accused of being a Marxist and a spy. You quickly begin to hope that the Timeband will take you from this before it gets any worse.

Unfortunately for you, it gets a lot worse, and the Timeband takes its time in returning to your own century.

Open your eyes. Go to **Page 246**

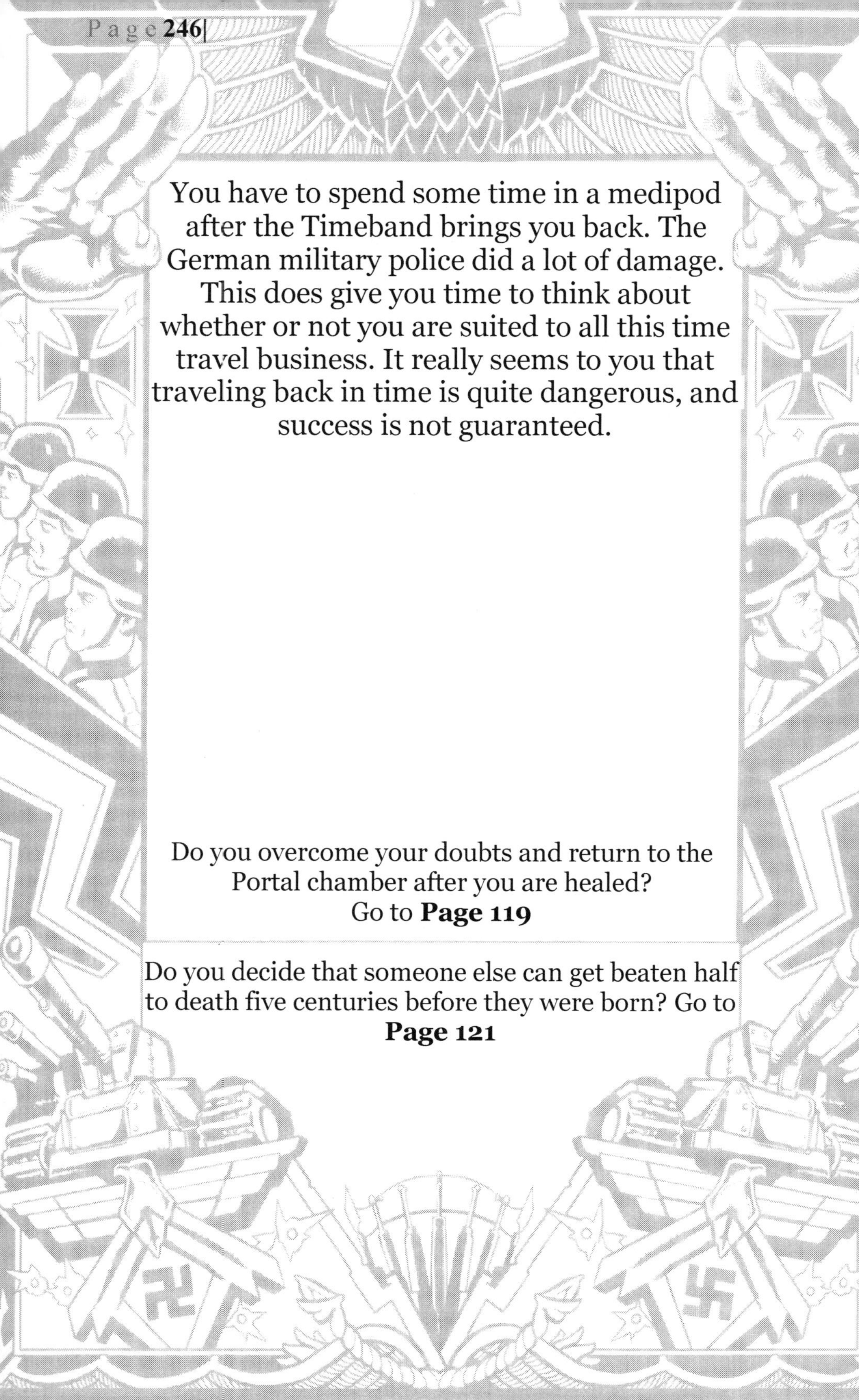

You have to spend some time in a medipod after the Timeband brings you back. The German military police did a lot of damage. This does give you time to think about whether or not you are suited to all this time travel business. It really seems to you that traveling back in time is quite dangerous, and success is not guaranteed.

Do you overcome your doubts and return to the Portal chamber after you are healed?
Go to **Page 119**

Do you decide that someone else can get beaten half to death five centuries before they were born? Go to **Page 121**

You decide the sooner the better; you manage to switch Hitler's orders and are able to get out of the office before you see both the deputy commandant and Hitler walking towards the office you just vacated. You barely get around the corner before they see you – you hope, anyways.

You hide around the corner, waiting, then follow Hitler after he leaves. He does appear quite disappointed at his new assignment. You catch up with him at the commissary, introduce yourself, and start talking to him, asking him why he seems so disappointed at his new orders. He seems a little suspicious at first, but you explain that you have heard of him and his staunch anti-Jew and anti-communist leanings and wanted to meet him in person once you were assigned here. Yeah, it kind of turns your stomach, but you're on a mission, so you need to buck up and impress good old Adolf.

Go to **Page 248**

Hitler brightens up and says that he was expecting to be sent to check out the German Workers' Party. He was relishing the chance to help eliminate another potential Marxist threat. Instead, he's being sent to check out some stupid psychiatrist's symposium. It is sure to bore him to tears. You try to reassure him by tell him that the GWP are such an obvious, raving threat that anyone could be sent to report on them, and that he, as a decorated and appreciated soldier, could be better served being sent after more subtle and insidious threats. It sounds like this Karl Jung could be quite the danger to impressionable minds.

Go to **Page 249**

However, instead of asking about the legendary psychiatrist, Hitler wants to know more about your knowledge of the German Workers' Party.

Do you continue flattering him and criticizing communists and Jews in order to convince him not to pursue the assignment? Go to **Page 263**

Do you just move the conversation in other directions, figuring that what you've already done is enough? Go to **Page 252**

You have a gun and you are looking right at Hitler. Do you pull out your gun and shoot him? Go to **Page 250**

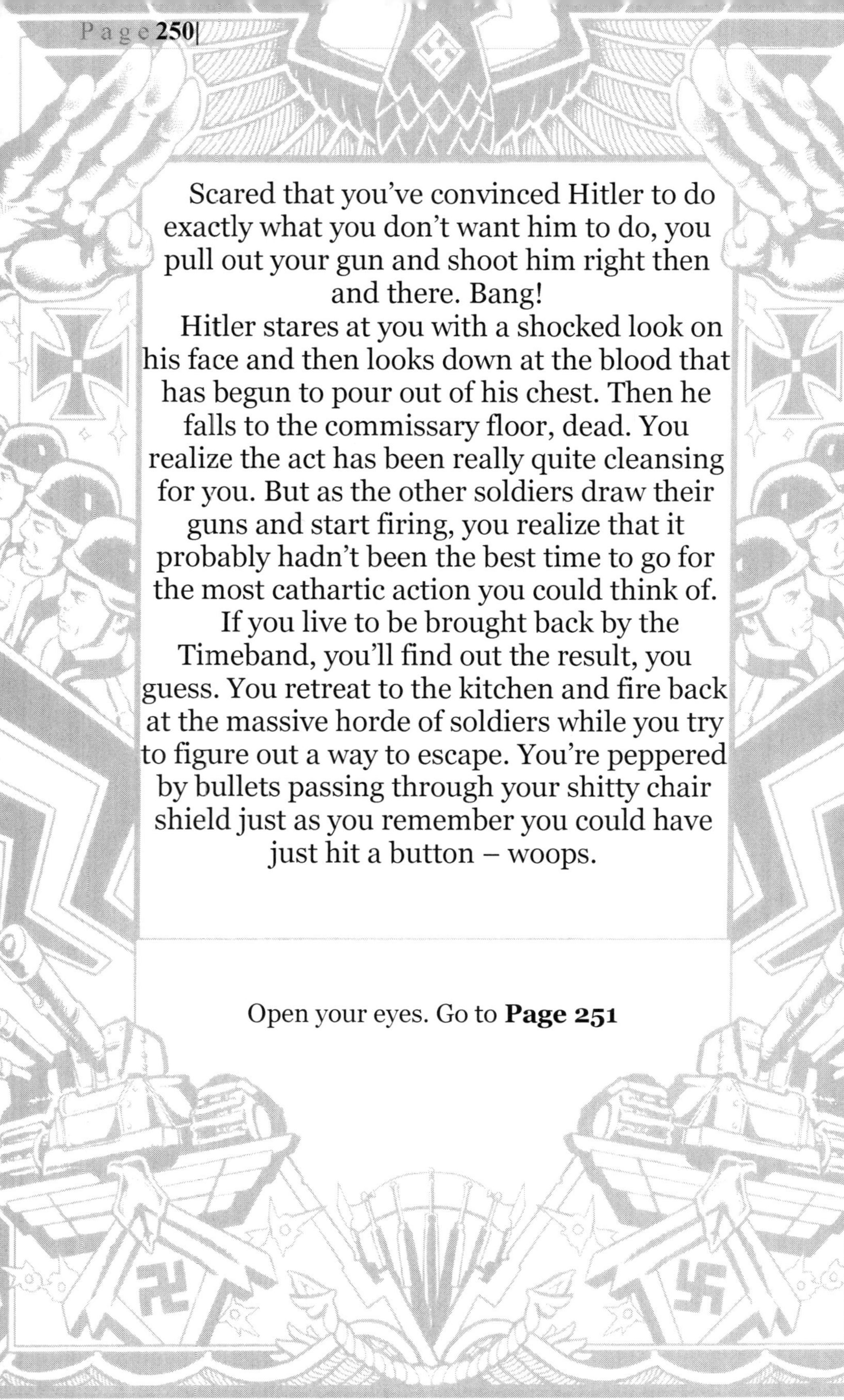

Scared that you've convinced Hitler to do exactly what you don't want him to do, you pull out your gun and shoot him right then and there. Bang!

Hitler stares at you with a shocked look on his face and then looks down at the blood that has begun to pour out of his chest. Then he falls to the commissary floor, dead. You realize the act has been really quite cleansing for you. But as the other soldiers draw their guns and start firing, you realize that it probably hadn't been the best time to go for the most cathartic action you could think of.

If you live to be brought back by the Timeband, you'll find out the result, you guess. You retreat to the kitchen and fire back at the massive horde of soldiers while you try to figure out a way to escape. You're peppered by bullets passing through your shitty chair shield just as you remember you could have just hit a button – woops.

Open your eyes. Go to **Page 251**

“You killed Hitler,” the A.I. repeats in the interview room. “And does anything look like it’s any better or like humanity is any further away from extinction?”

You have to admit that since you’ve returned, things aren’t any better. In fact, the radioactive wasteland beyond the enclave from centuries of Communist vs. Capitalist warfare is rather worse than the world you left.

Do you try to convince Rolf-ME242 to send you back to do better? Go to **Page 119**

Do you admit that it made a mistake by letting you go back in the first place?
Go to **Page 121**

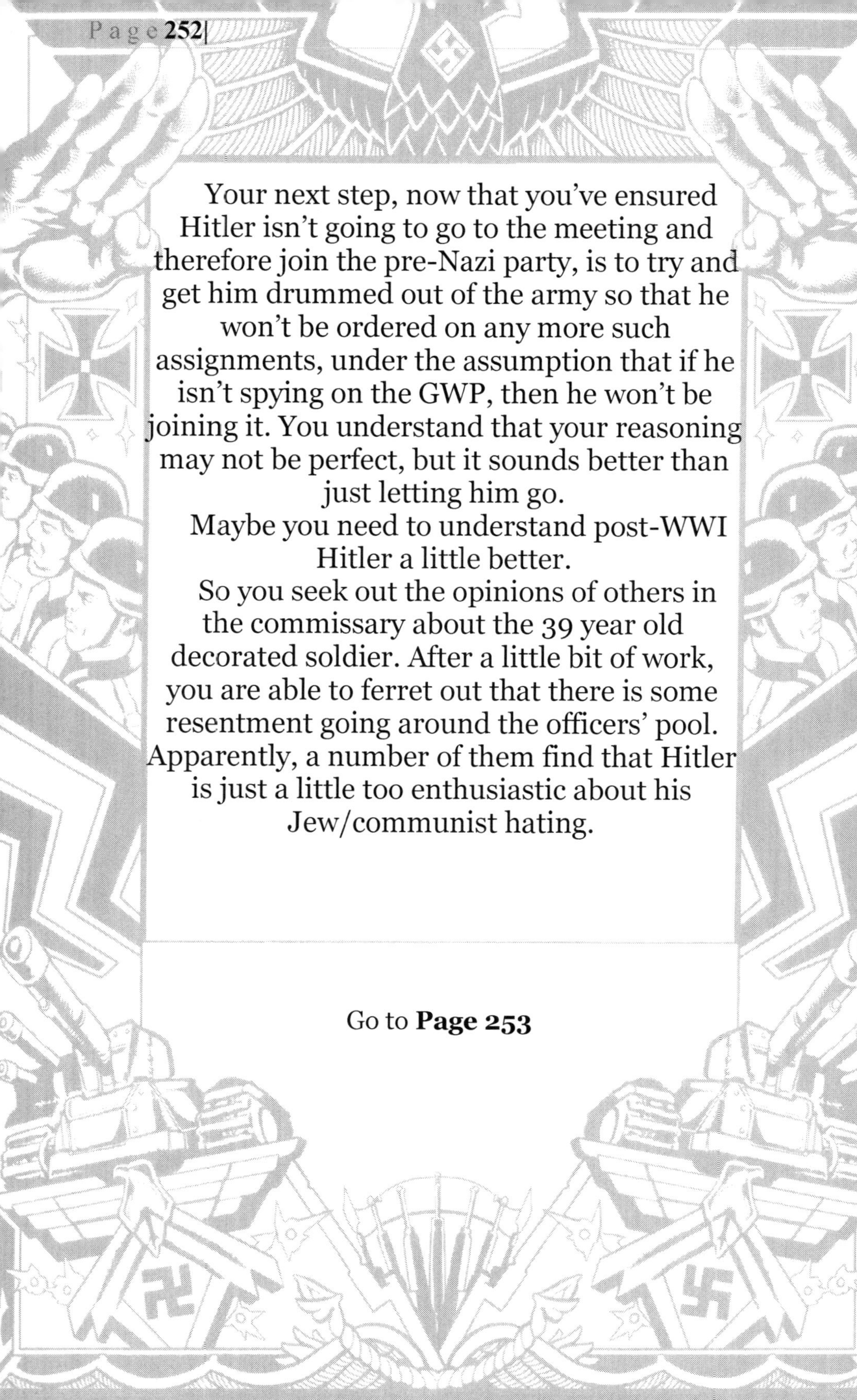

Your next step, now that you've ensured Hitler isn't going to go to the meeting and therefore join the pre-Nazi party, is to try and get him drummed out of the army so that he won't be ordered on any more such assignments, under the assumption that if he isn't spying on the GWP, then he won't be joining it. You understand that your reasoning may not be perfect, but it sounds better than just letting him go.

Maybe you need to understand post-WWI Hitler a little better.

So you seek out the opinions of others in the commissary about the 39 year old decorated soldier. After a little bit of work, you are able to ferret out that there is some resentment going around the officers' pool. Apparently, a number of them find that Hitler is just a little too enthusiastic about his Jew/communist hating.

Go to **Page 253**

Sure, none of them like Jews that much, or communists, but Hitler goes on and on, lecturing all the others on what it means to be German, even though he himself is from Austria. There is, of course, some simmering resentment that, given the loss of the war and the state of Germany, isn't too hard to bring to the surface. But most of them prefer to blame the British and the French, as well as the stupid Italians, not their fellow Germans.

You are left to decide how far you will go to suggest that the men get rid of him. Several seem amenable to going to the Commandant with their complaints, but the concern is whether you can get them to act, and how far they will go. Some make some outlandish suggestions of things to accuse him of. Trouble is, you aren't completely sure what Commandant Hofstadter is going to listen to, or how much it's going to take to get him to act.

Do you suggest they stick to the easily verifiable?
Go to **Page 257**

Do you egg them on, convincing them to accuse Hitler of whatever they can think of to get him sacked?
Go to **Page 254**

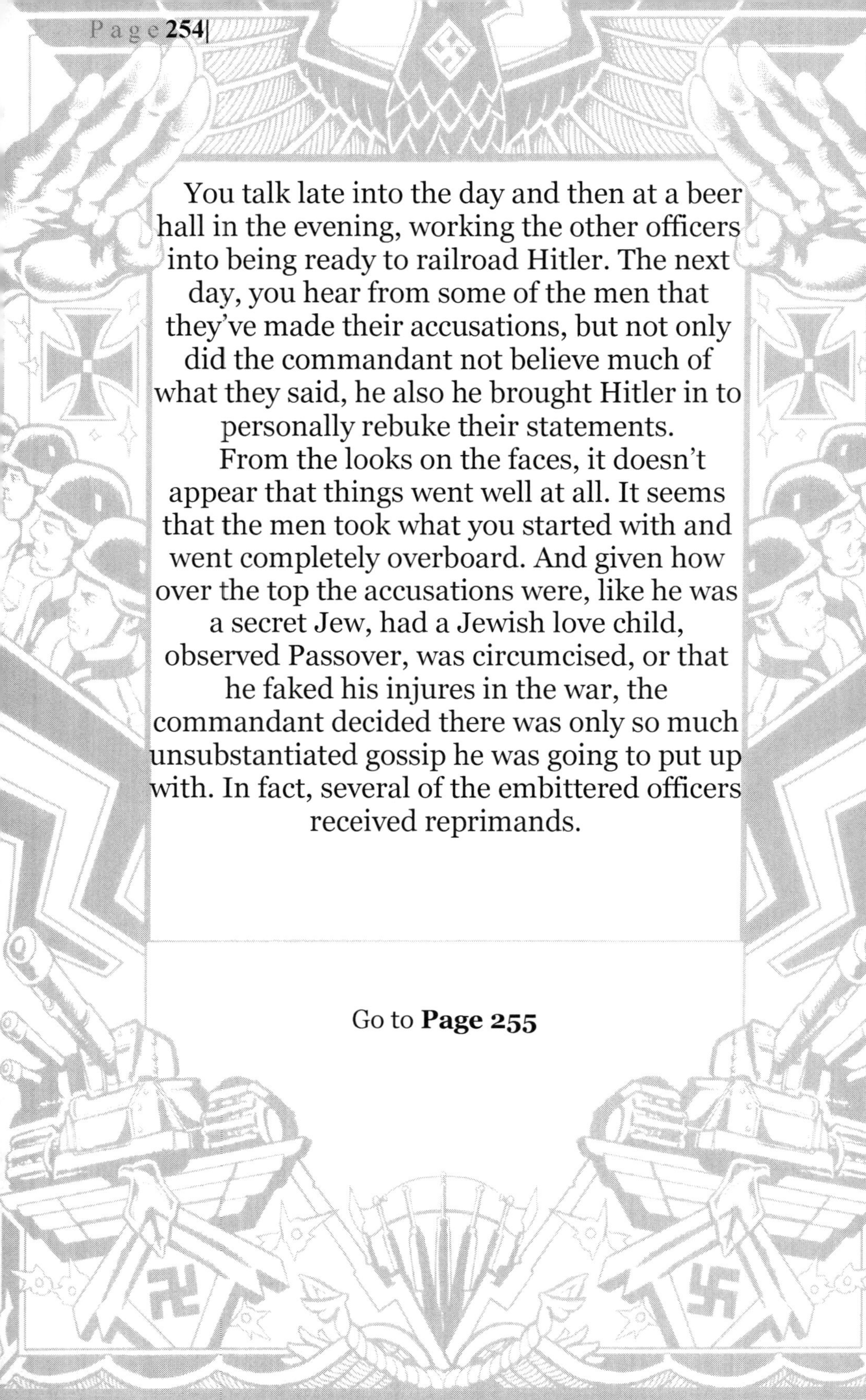

You talk late into the day and then at a beer hall in the evening, working the other officers into being ready to railroad Hitler. The next day, you hear from some of the men that they've made their accusations, but not only did the commandant not believe much of what they said, he also he brought Hitler in to personally rebuke their statements.

From the looks on the faces, it doesn't appear that things went well at all. It seems that the men took what you started with and went completely overboard. And given how over the top the accusations were, like he was a secret Jew, had a Jewish love child, observed Passover, was circumcised, or that he faked his injures in the war, the commandant decided there was only so much unsubstantiated gossip he was going to put up with. In fact, several of the embittered officers received reprimands.

Go to **Page 255**

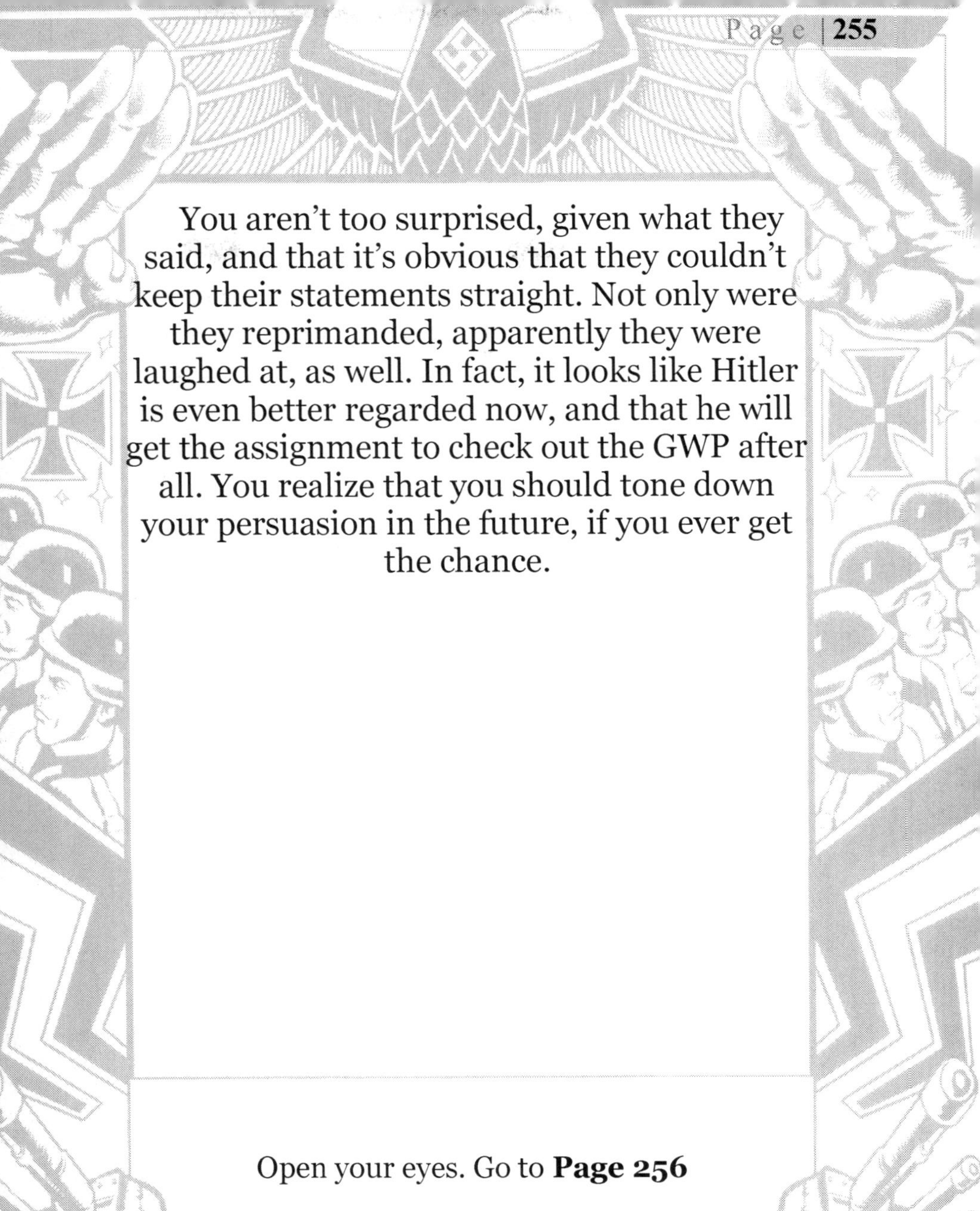

You aren't too surprised, given what they said, and that it's obvious that they couldn't keep their statements straight. Not only were they reprimanded, apparently they were laughed at, as well. In fact, it looks like Hitler is even better regarded now, and that he will get the assignment to check out the GWP after all. You realize that you should tone down your persuasion in the future, if you ever get the chance.

Open your eyes. Go to **Page 256**

"Really?" Rolf-ME242 says to you. "They came up with the secret Jew thing?"

You admit that you might have suggested that one, that maybe he kind of protested too much, and that it made sense at the time.

If an A.I. could shake its head, or even had a head to shake, this one would be doing just that.

Do you try to convince it that you will be smarter on your next trip back in time? Go to **Page 119**

Do you agree that you aren't quite up to the task at hand?
Go to **Page 121**

Having heard that you have successfully and seriously harmed Hitler's military career, you seek him out at a nearby beer hall, where he is depressed after being faced with being thrown out of the army for his personal indiscretions and other complaints about his behaviour by his fellow soldiers and officers. After a few drinks with you, he begins to talk about the truth.

"Mostly what they said is true," Hitler admits. "And after all they have told the commandant, it is unlikely I will be able to counter their accusations."

"That's too bad," you say as you smile on the inside.

"But what am I going to do now?" he wondered, dejected. "The military has become my whole life. Maybe I should join the communists after all; I have nowhere else to go."

You buy him another beer to make him feel better, but he just stares at it for a few minutes.

Go to **Page 258**

You wonder if he's going to drink it, and then he finally does, downing the whole beer in one go. You buy him another, and he goes through the same ritual again.

Over more drinks, you remind him that the army wasn't so great after all.

"They lost to the Americans after all," you tell him. "And they were supposed to have the worst army in the world. Maybe everything people say about them is wrong."

You suggest that if he wants to become a winner, then he has to join the winners. Lots of Germans are emigrating to the United States, and there is high demand there for talented artists. You say you heard that he was a talented artist; he could make a whole new life for himself, outside of this defeated nation.

"You think so?" he asks. "You really think so?"

Do you stay the whole evening discussing the possibilities with Hitler, buttering him up shamelessly? Go to **Page 259**

Do you just talk about it for a couple hours once you've gotten him to agree with you? Go to **Page 261**

You have returned to the future and have discovered that there are more people about and that the last human enclave on Earth is larger and more successful than when you left it. You decide to seek out Rolf-ME242 to explain.

"Greetings, time traveller." The synthetic voice of the A.I. greets you from all around. "Your mission was a success; Hitler never joined the GWP, and in fact spent a decade in the United States before returning to Germany."

"Humanity still seems to be living in one enclave," you note.

"His change in attitude only lessened the effects of the Nazi rise and WWII," Rolf tells you. "But things have been changed for the better. Hitler wasn't the one who masterminded the Nazi genocides; therefore, they weren't nearly as bad as before."

Go to **Page 260**

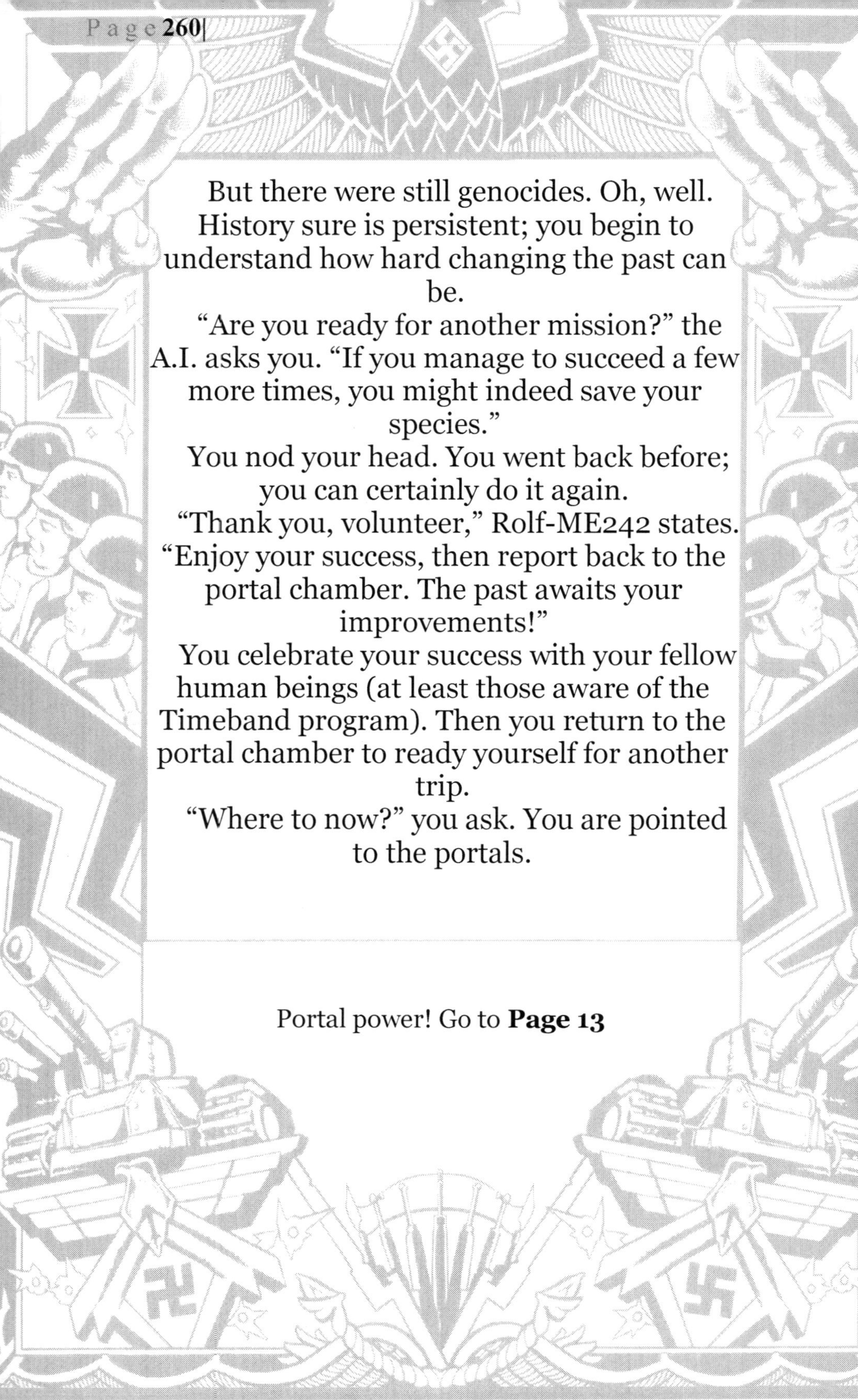

But there were still genocides. Oh, well. History sure is persistent; you begin to understand how hard changing the past can be.

"Are you ready for another mission?" the A.I. asks you. "If you manage to succeed a few more times, you might indeed save your species."

You nod your head. You went back before; you can certainly do it again.

"Thank you, volunteer," Rolf-ME242 states. "Enjoy your success, then report back to the portal chamber. The past awaits your improvements!"

You celebrate your success with your fellow human beings (at least those aware of the Timeband program). Then you return to the portal chamber to ready yourself for another trip.

"Where to now?" you ask. You are pointed to the portals.

Portal power! Go to **Page 13**

Obviously, a couple hours of talking worked, and Adolf changed his views. You told him to think about it, and if he wanted to talk more about emigrating, to come back and chat the next day. You wait for him, and he never shows up.

You look for him at the military base, but no one has seen him. You check around the neighbourhood, but apparently he'd packed up and disappeared. So, you decided to celebrate at the beer hall until the Timeband comes and takes your drunken butt back to the distant future.

Open your eyes. Go to **Page 262**

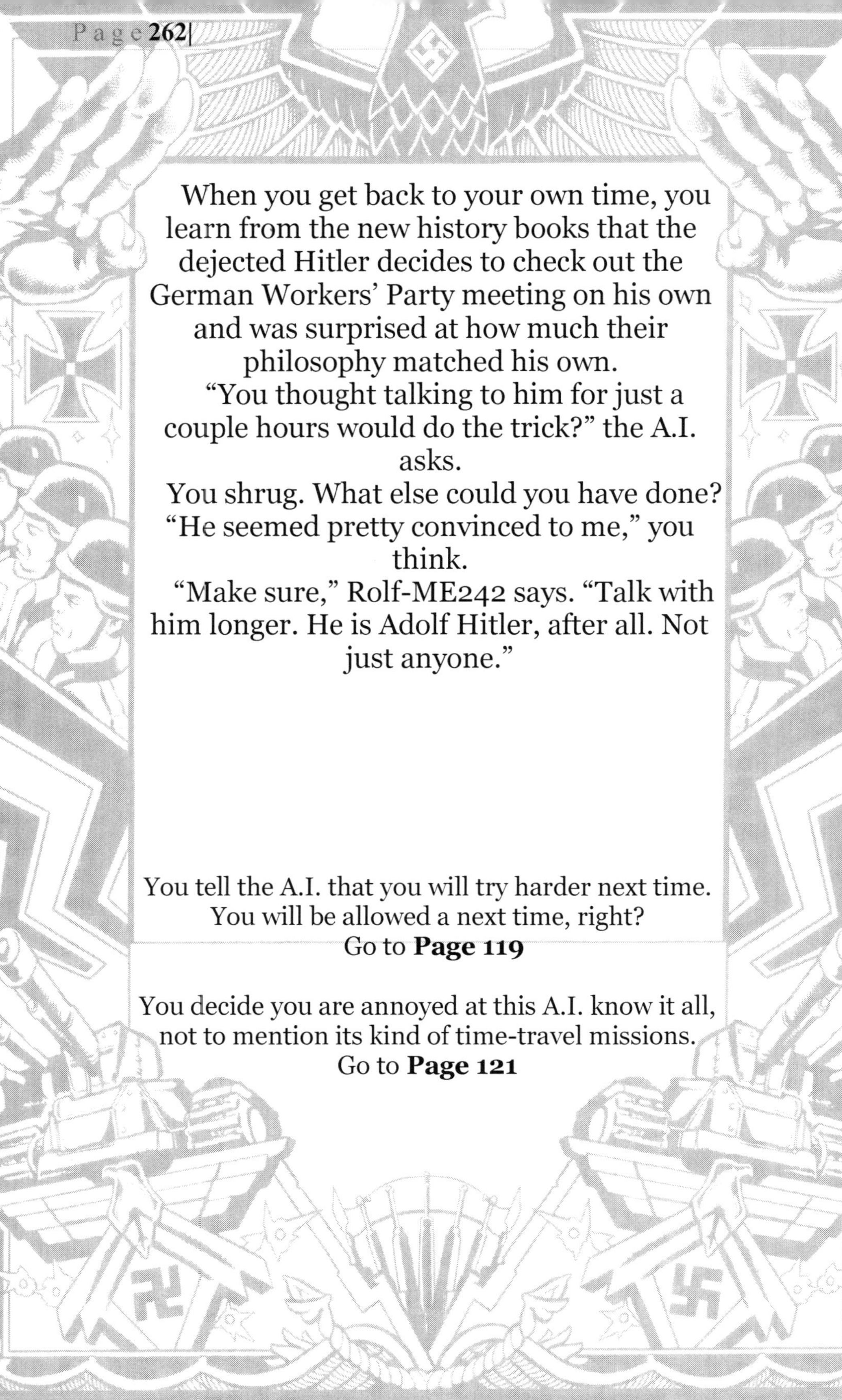

When you get back to your own time, you learn from the new history books that the dejected Hitler decides to check out the German Workers' Party meeting on his own and was surprised at how much their philosophy matched his own.

"You thought talking to him for just a couple hours would do the trick?" the A.I. asks.

You shrug. What else could you have done? "He seemed pretty convinced to me," you think.

"Make sure," Rolf-ME242 says. "Talk with him longer. He is Adolf Hitler, after all. Not just anyone."

You tell the A.I. that you will try harder next time. You will be allowed a next time, right?

Go to **Page 119**

You decide you are annoyed at this A.I. know it all, not to mention its kind of time-travel missions.

Go to **Page 121**

Unsure of whether or not you have convinced Hitler to forget about the GWP, you start making things up from what you remember from your research. To your horror, however, you instead appear to have incited him instead of convincing him to leave them alone, and before you can stop him, Hitler tells you that he wants to see these raving Marxists for himself. He stands up.

"I will go to see Commandant Hofstadter myself," he tells you, "and ensure that Adolf Hitler and Adolf Hitler alone will be the one assigned to spy on the group. I have established that I am the best qualified. He will definitely send me to check them out."

Open your eyes. Go to **Page 264**

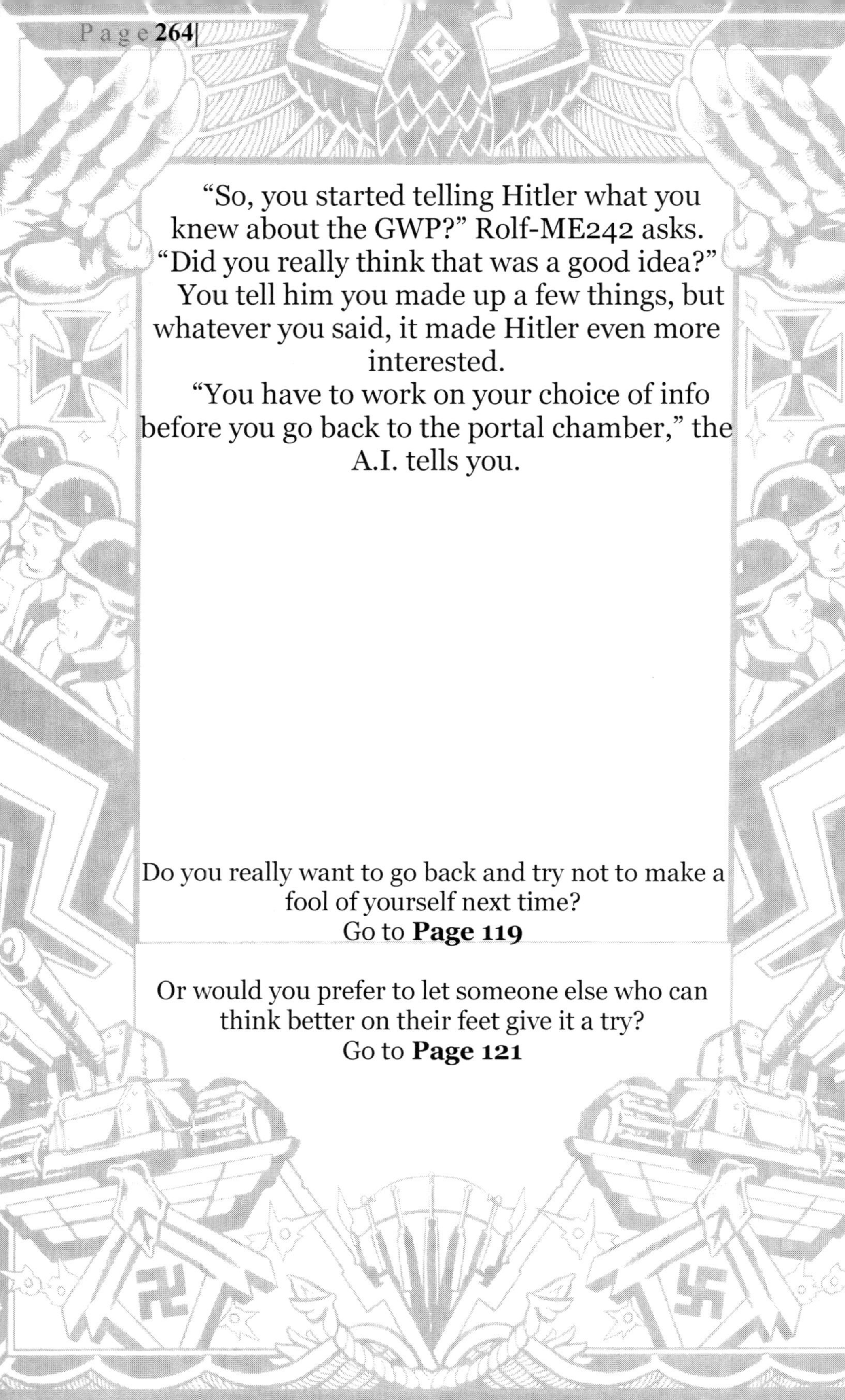

“So, you started telling Hitler what you knew about the GWP?” Rolf-ME242 asks. “Did you really think that was a good idea?”

You tell him you made up a few things, but whatever you said, it made Hitler even more interested.

“You have to work on your choice of info before you go back to the portal chamber,” the A.I. tells you.

Do you really want to go back and try not to make a fool of yourself next time?

Go to **Page 119**

Or would you prefer to let someone else who can think better on their feet give it a try?

Go to **Page 121**

When you step into the whiteness, you find yourself buffeted by the invisible winds as you fall through the portal. You frantically try to regain your balance, but it is hopeless. It is as though you are falling down an endless white expanse. Suddenly, you land on something soft with a thump. The world goes from ultra-white to dark. You look around, waiting for your eyes to adjust. Oh. You appear to be in a jail cell, which, when you look down at the lower bunk, you are sharing with another prisoner, a rough looking moustachioed fellow. You are confused at first, but some surreptitious chatting with your bunkmate advises you that you have been deposited in the notorious Landsberg Jail in the year 1924.

You put two and two together, then ask if Adolf Hitler has arrived yet. The other inmate gives you a sly smile, asking if you didn't see him come in the day before. He is, after all, quite famous for leading an attack on the Bavarian legislature.

Go to **Page 266**

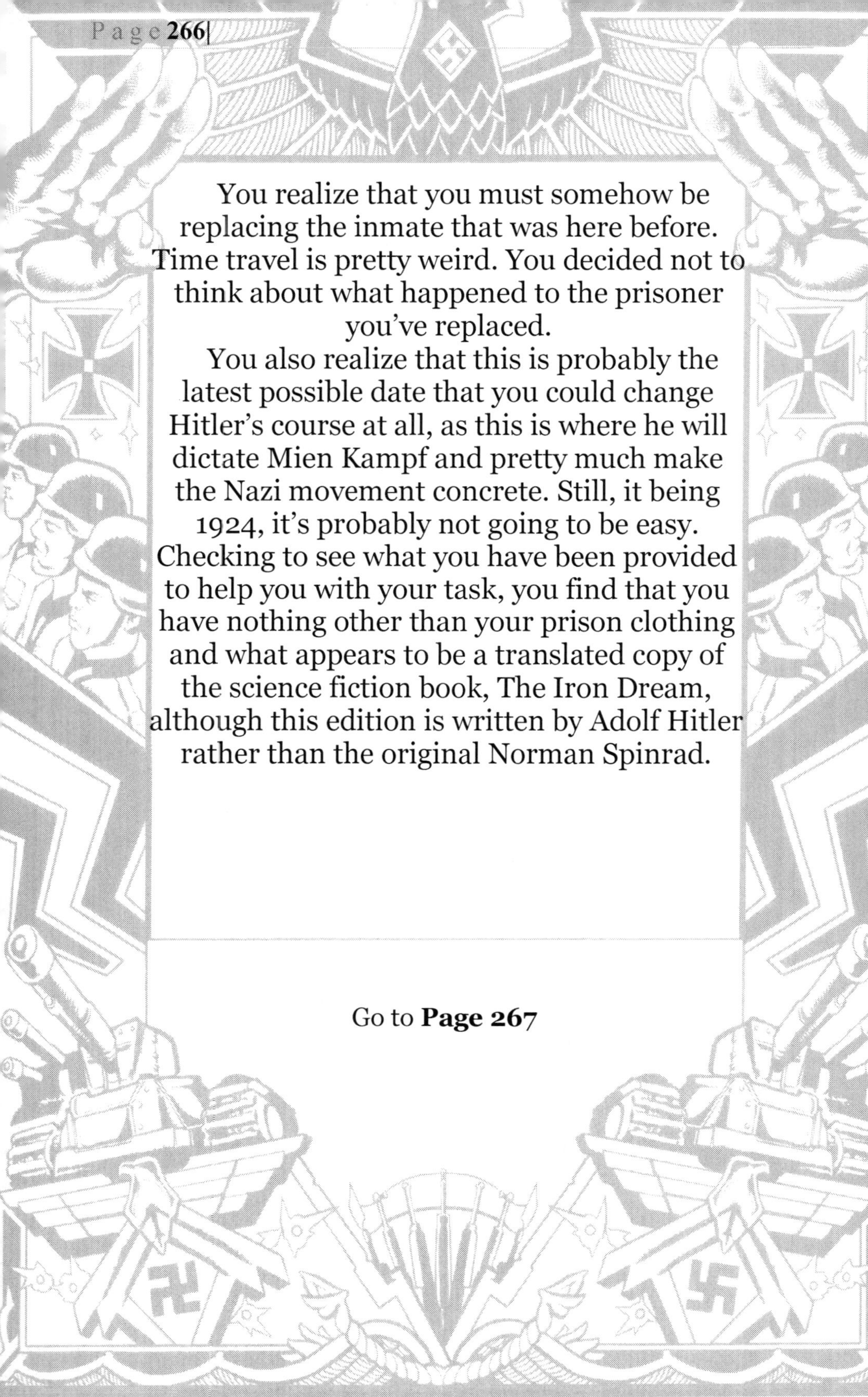

You realize that you must somehow be replacing the inmate that was here before. Time travel is pretty weird. You decided not to think about what happened to the prisoner you've replaced.

You also realize that this is probably the latest possible date that you could change Hitler's course at all, as this is where he will dictate Mien Kampf and pretty much make the Nazi movement concrete. Still, it being 1924, it's probably not going to be easy. Checking to see what you have been provided to help you with your task, you find that you have nothing other than your prison clothing and what appears to be a translated copy of the science fiction book, The Iron Dream, although this edition is written by Adolf Hitler rather than the original Norman Spinrad.

Go to **Page 267**

Okay, isn't this just a little bit crazy? Are you expected to try and get Hitler to change from the man who just incited an attempt to overthrow the Bavarian government to become a science fiction writer? You know that the Rolf-ME242 is thousands of times smarter than any human being, at least according to its own claims, but still, an obscure science fiction novel? You have to shake your head. Still, what can you do?

Do you try to convince Hitler on your own, without the book? Go to **Page 268**

Do you accept ROLF-ME242's wisdom and take a look at the book to see what merit it might have for this particular turning point in Hitler's life, crazy as it may seem?
Go to **Page 271**

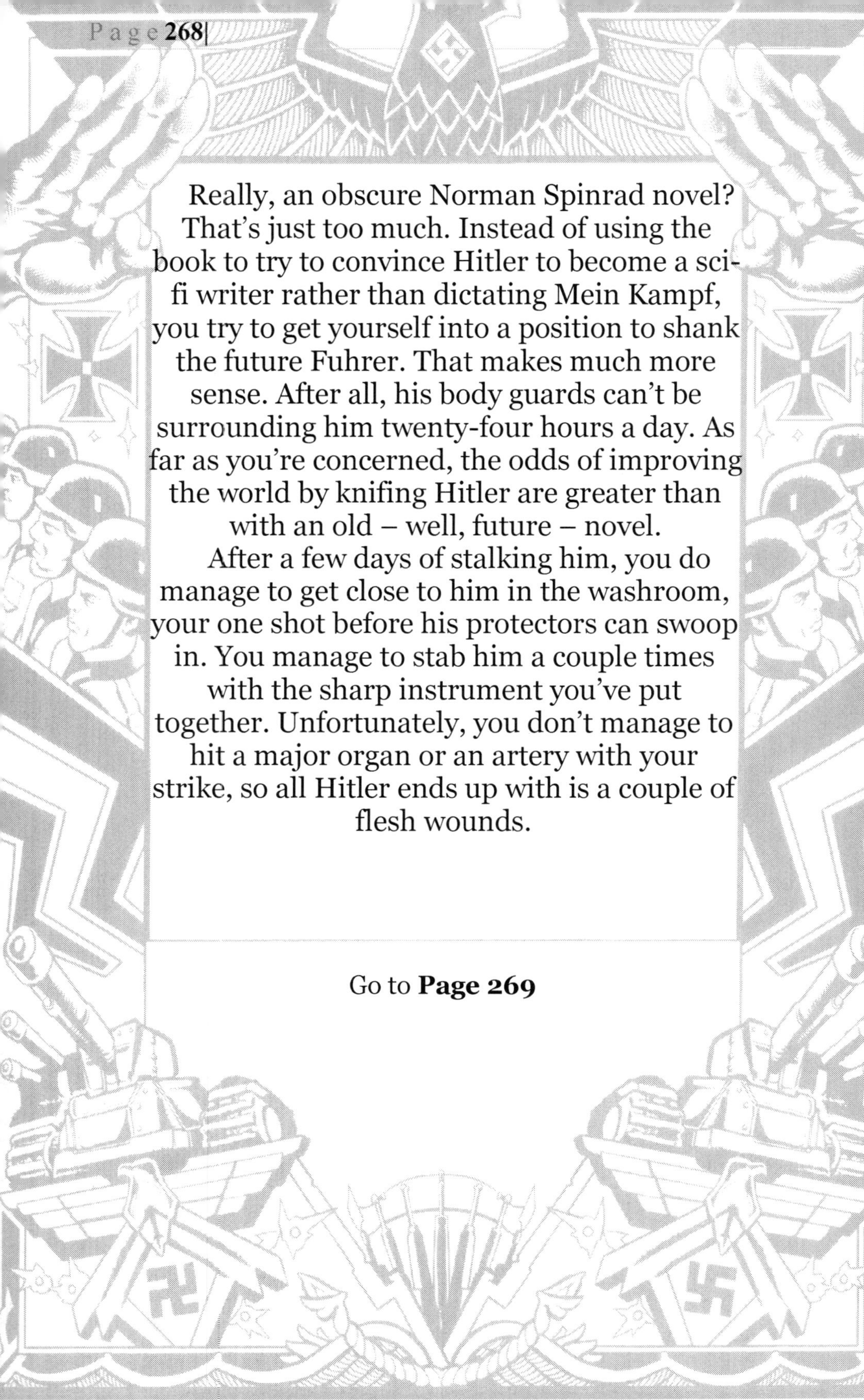

Really, an obscure Norman Spinrad novel? That's just too much. Instead of using the book to try to convince Hitler to become a sci-fi writer rather than dictating Mein Kampf, you try to get yourself into a position to shank the future Fuhrer. That makes much more sense. After all, his body guards can't be surrounding him twenty-four hours a day. As far as you're concerned, the odds of improving the world by knifing Hitler are greater than with an old – well, future – novel.

After a few days of stalking him, you do manage to get close to him in the washroom, your one shot before his protectors can swoop in. You manage to stab him a couple times with the sharp instrument you've put together. Unfortunately, you don't manage to hit a major organ or an artery with your strike, so all Hitler ends up with is a couple of flesh wounds.

Go to **Page 269**

And unfortunately, that was your one shot, because you are then beaten to a pulp by Hitler's prison disciples and bodyguards without being able to confirm whether or not you managed to do more than superficial damage. But he will at least have few a prison scars to show off. You, on the other hand, oh man...

Open your eyes. Go to **Page 270**

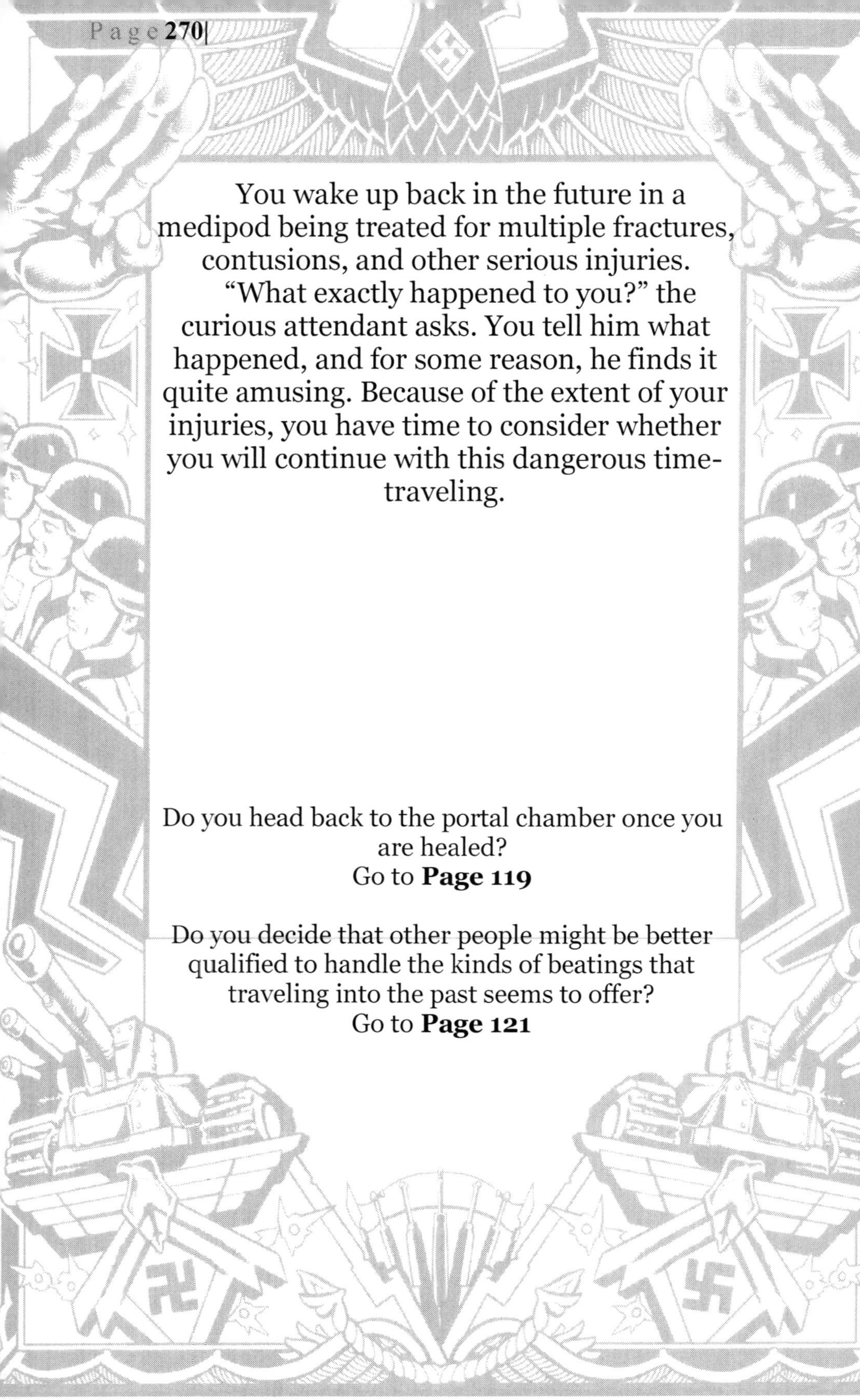

You wake up back in the future in a medipod being treated for multiple fractures, contusions, and other serious injuries.

"What exactly happened to you?" the curious attendant asks. You tell him what happened, and for some reason, he finds it quite amusing. Because of the extent of your injuries, you have time to consider whether you will continue with this dangerous time-traveling.

Do you head back to the portal chamber once you are healed?

Go to **Page 119**

Do you decide that other people might be better qualified to handle the kinds of beatings that traveling into the past seems to offer?

Go to **Page 121**

As weird as it might be, you decide to familiarize yourself with the book you've been given and try to work out how you will approach Hitler and present the possibilities to him. After reading a few hundred pages, you realize that there are a lot of points that you could bring up. Although, you are a little concerned with the novel's repeated mention of nuclear weapons. If he doesn't agree, you might give him an idea years before the bomb is due to be first designed and dropped by the Americans on Japan. Still, Hitler doesn't necessarily have to read the whole thing to be affected by it. At least that's what you tell yourself.

Is he really going to completely understand the whole radiation/mutant thing? As far as you know, he hasn't been much of a science fiction fan up until now. In fact, you aren't quite sure if the term 'science fiction' has even been invented yet.

Go to **Page 272**

In addition, approaching the man, even in a friendly manner, seems as if it will be a bit difficult, as he has already amassed a group of imposing sympathizers in the jail that are happy to stand between him and the general population. Some of them are indeed big, muscular convicts, and most of them look more than a little mean. You think about trying to use the book to get close, but since Hitler hasn't actually written any books, asking for his autograph probably won't work.

So you decide to make sure that you talk about what they want to hear. Every chance you get, you constantly jabber so everyone can hear what you're saying: how the Jews are taking over the country, how the allies ruined the country and the treaty was a humiliation, and how the current political system is trashing what was once the proud nation of Germany.

Go to **Page 273**

You really hope that you've put together a great acting performance. Otherwise, you'll be left trying the shank.

You start getting the attention that you think you need; do you then approach Hitler?
Go to **Page 274**

Do you continuing laying it on thick, always praising Hitler and his actions and attitudes, until they invite you in?
Go to **Page 276**

You think that Hitler's circle is picking up on what you are saying, and you try to use it to get some face time with prisoner Adolf as soon as you think they are ready. However, it seems they have picked up that you aren't quite as sincere about your racist and bigoted attitudes as you've been letting on and decide that you are a spy for the prison or the government. You've jumped that gun, so to speak. Uh-oh.

To your disappointment and agony, they decide to send a message or two to the people they think you report to. These messages involve you getting the crap beaten out of you and ending up in the prison infirmary with some pretty severe and painful injuries, unable to do anything to further your actual mission until the Timeband returns you back to 2525.

Open your eyes. Go to **Page 275**

You lay in the medipod, thanking the painkillers that have killed the pain far better than what the Germans had in the prison infirmary. An attendant shows up to check on you and tells you that they are compensating for the poor treatment you received in the prison infirmary.

"Thanks," you are able to say through your replacement teeth.

"Had trouble making friends in jail?" she asks.

"You could say that," you reply. After she leaves, you wonder if you really want to go through this again.

Yes, if it offers you the chance to save the human race from extinction. Go to **Page 119**

No, you don't want to continually come back in broken pieces. Go to **Page 121**

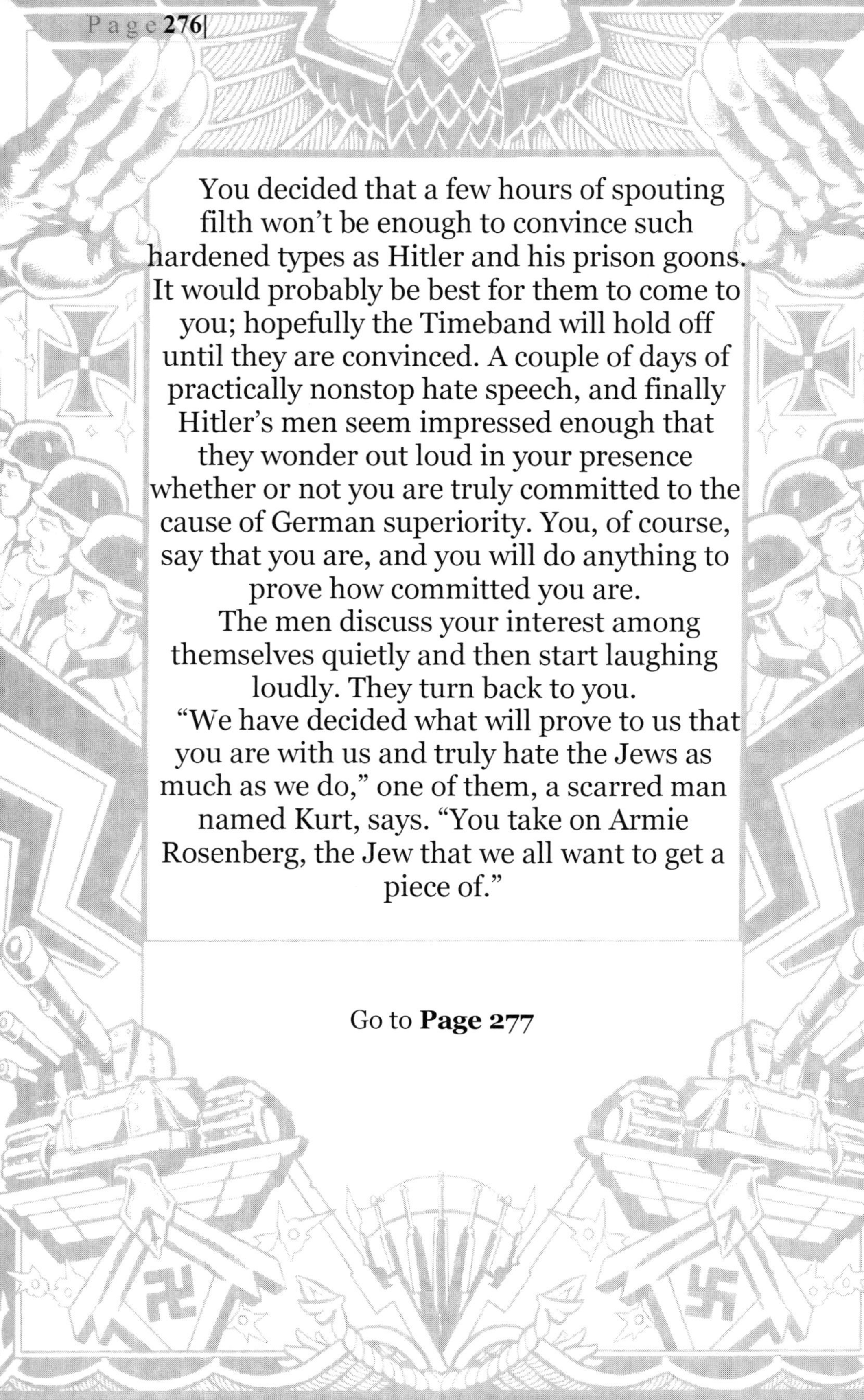

You decided that a few hours of spouting filth won't be enough to convince such hardened types as Hitler and his prison goons. It would probably be best for them to come to you; hopefully the Timeband will hold off until they are convinced. A couple of days of practically nonstop hate speech, and finally Hitler's men seem impressed enough that they wonder out loud in your presence whether or not you are truly committed to the cause of German superiority. You, of course, say that you are, and you will do anything to prove how committed you are.

The men discuss your interest among themselves quietly and then start laughing loudly. They turn back to you.

"We have decided what will prove to us that you are with us and truly hate the Jews as much as we do," one of them, a scarred man named Kurt, says. "You take on Armie Rosenberg, the Jew that we all want to get a piece of."

Go to **Page 277**

You don't know who Armie Rosenberg is. Kurt points him out. The man is standing on the other side of the fenced-in prison yard. It turns out, however, that Rosenberg is a huge prize-fighter who is in jail for killing two men in a bar fight. He practically towers over the men around him.

He looks like he could take on two or three of even Hitler's big bodyguards and crush them easily.

"You take him on," one of the not quite so big guys says to you, "and you'll be one of us for sure."

Do you agree to take in the hulking Jewish boxer?
Go to **Page 278**

Do you tell the other men that there is no point in engaging in a fight you will certainly lose and that smart men engage in better strategies to defeat their enemies?
Go to **Page 281**

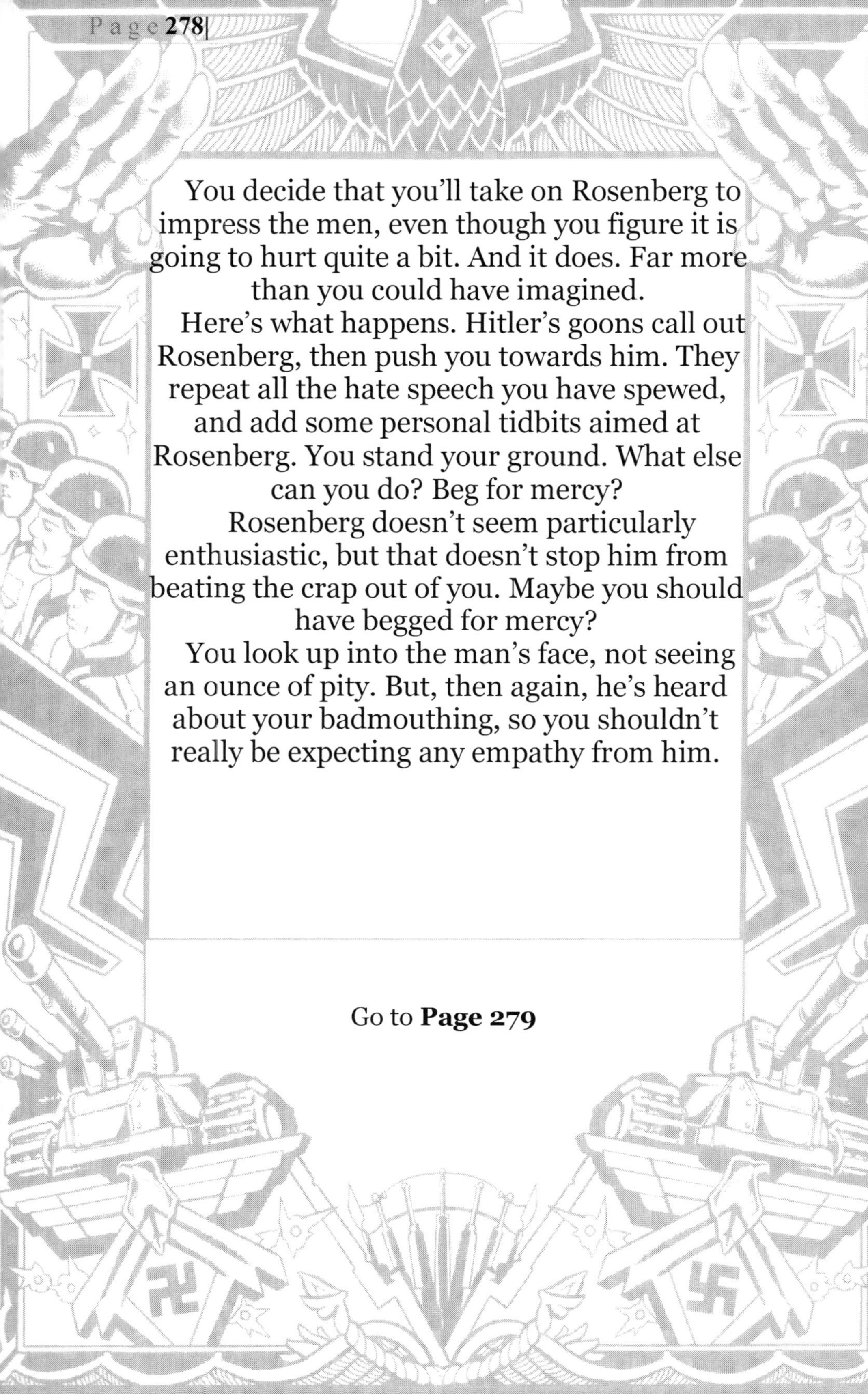

You decide that you'll take on Rosenberg to impress the men, even though you figure it is going to hurt quite a bit. And it does. Far more than you could have imagined.

Here's what happens. Hitler's goons call out Rosenberg, then push you towards him. They repeat all the hate speech you have spewed, and add some personal tidbits aimed at Rosenberg. You stand your ground. What else can you do? Beg for mercy?

Rosenberg doesn't seem particularly enthusiastic, but that doesn't stop him from beating the crap out of you. Maybe you should have begged for mercy?

You look up into the man's face, not seeing an ounce of pity. But, then again, he's heard about your badmouthing, so you shouldn't really be expecting any empathy from him.

Go to **Page 279**

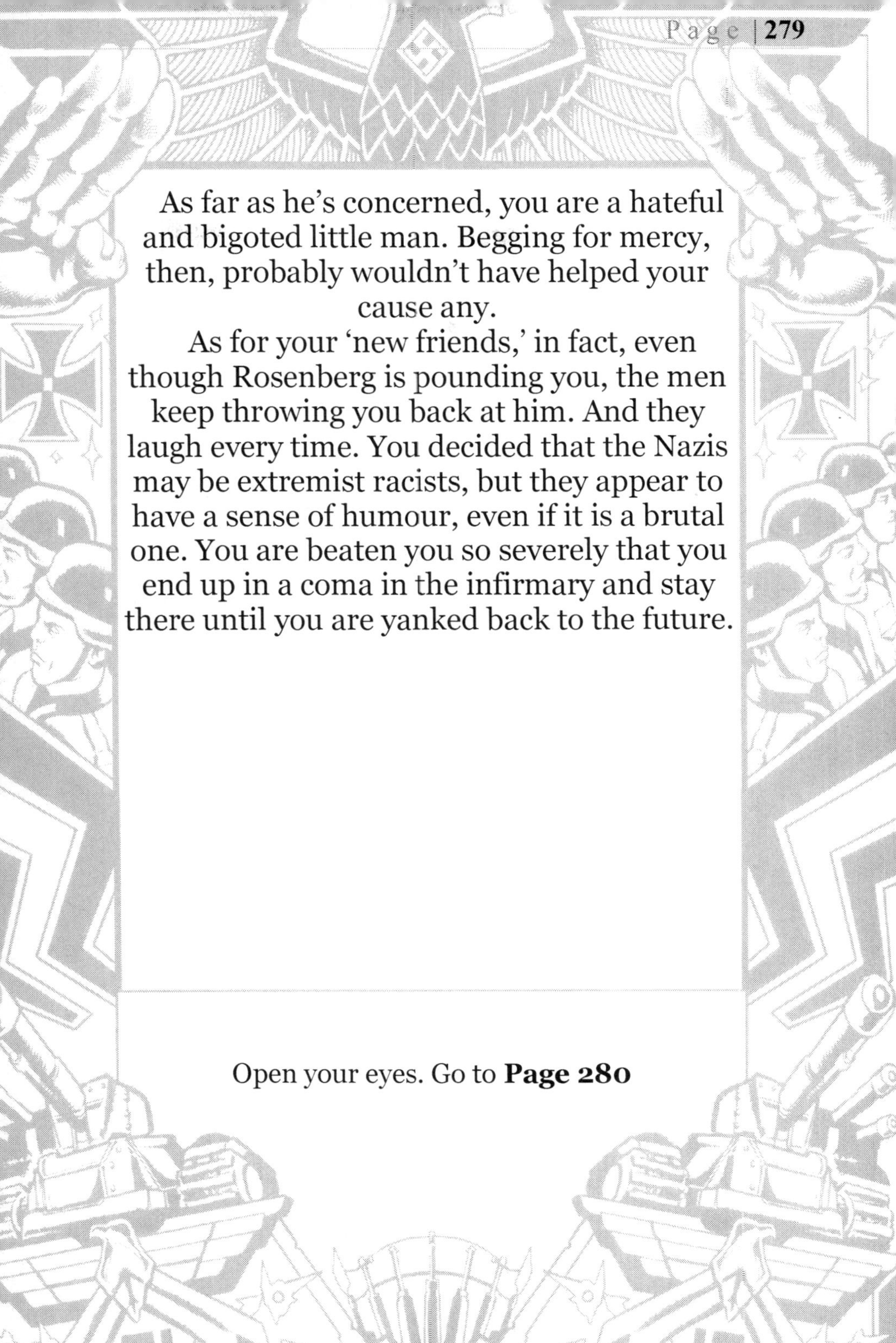

As far as he's concerned, you are a hateful and bigoted little man. Begging for mercy, then, probably wouldn't have helped your cause any.

As for your 'new friends,' in fact, even though Rosenberg is pounding you, the men keep throwing you back at him. And they laugh every time. You decided that the Nazis may be extremist racists, but they appear to have a sense of humour, even if it is a brutal one. You are beaten you so severely that you end up in a coma in the infirmary and stay there until you are yanked back to the future.

Open your eyes. Go to **Page 280**

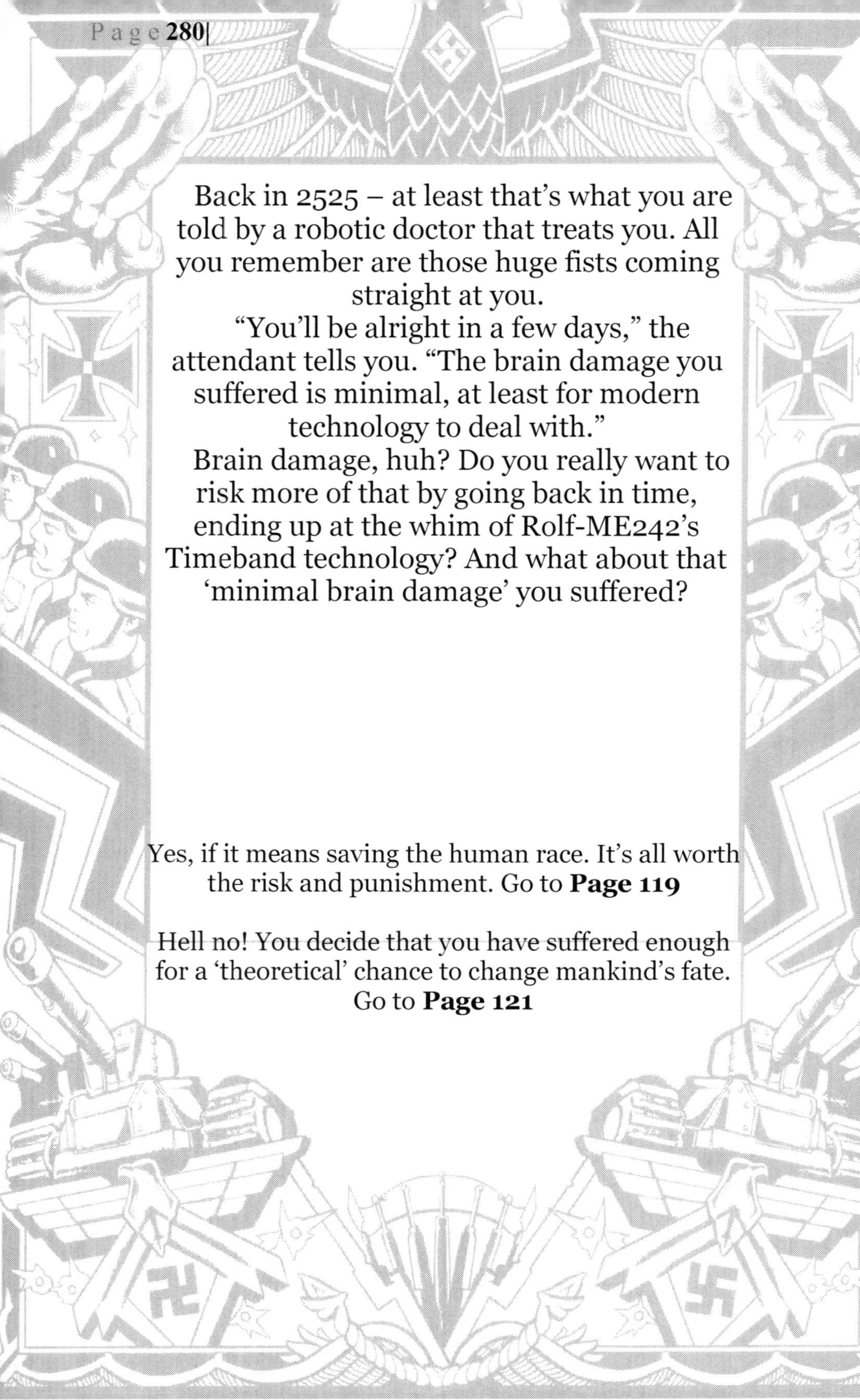

Back in 2525 – at least that's what you are told by a robotic doctor that treats you. All you remember are those huge fists coming straight at you.

"You'll be alright in a few days," the attendant tells you. "The brain damage you suffered is minimal, at least for modern technology to deal with."

Brain damage, huh? Do you really want to risk more of that by going back in time, ending up at the whim of Rolf-ME242's Timeband technology? And what about that 'minimal brain damage' you suffered?

Yes, if it means saving the human race. It's all worth the risk and punishment. Go to **Page 119**

Hell no! You decide that you have suffered enough for a 'theoretical' chance to change mankind's fate. Go to **Page 121**

After quite a bit of negotiation and not a little bit of pleading on your part, along with going on about how great Hitler must be as a writer, the future Fuhrer is finally drawn into what you've been saying to the men.

"Come now." Adolf tells me his name. "He can have a few minutes to speak to me. I'll decide if what he has to say has merit."

They, of course, protest, but he waves away their concerns.

"Only a stupid idiot would take on Rosenberg alone and with only his bare hands," he says.

So you finally get an audience with Hitler, and you take advantage of it. Knowing that there is only one way to explain what you are doing here with a book that won't be written for more than 40 years, you tell him that you were sent back from the distant future to help him make a different choice that will ensure that his life doesn't end up destroying him and Germany both.

Go to **Page 282**

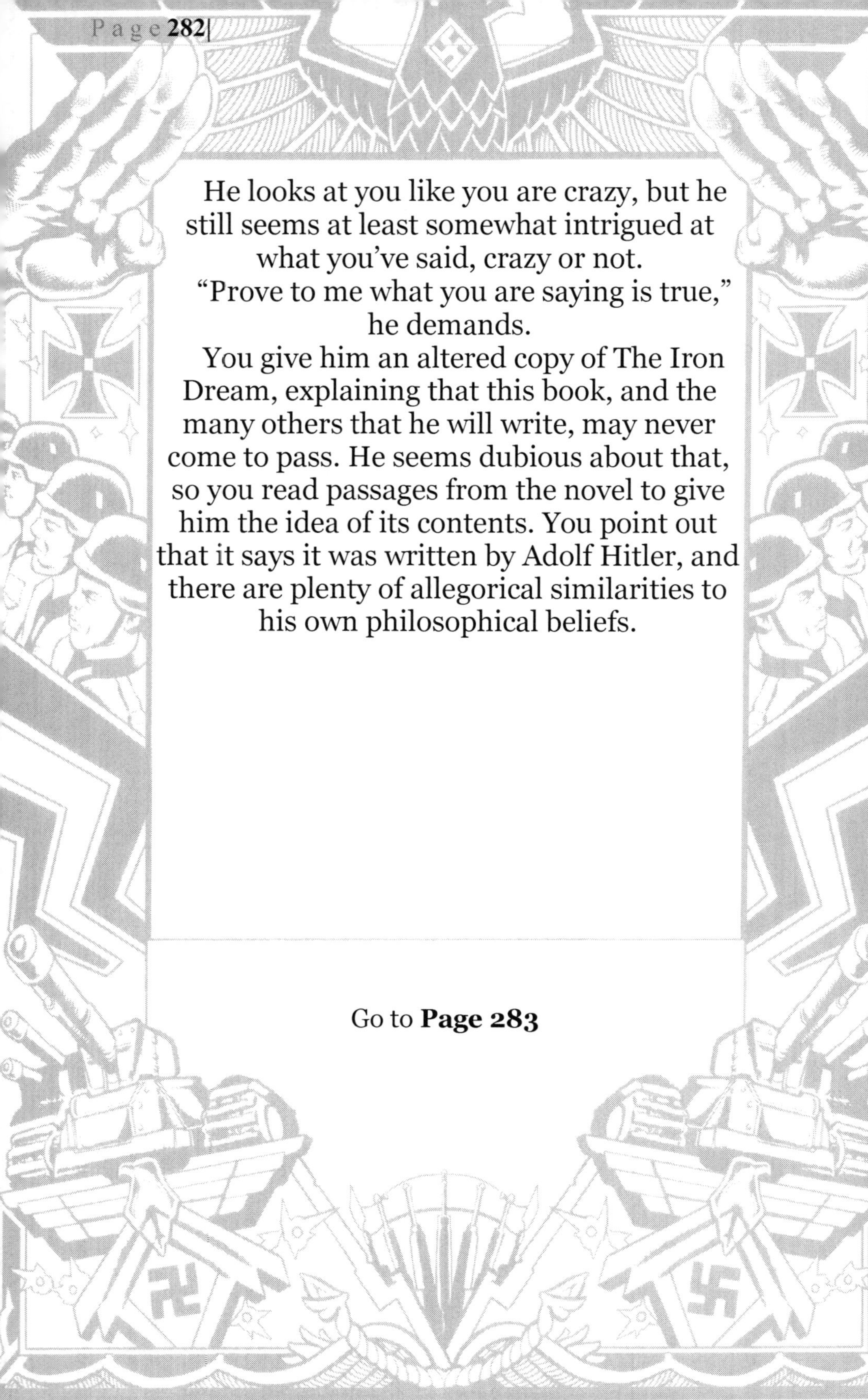

He looks at you like you are crazy, but he still seems at least somewhat intrigued at what you've said, crazy or not.

"Prove to me what you are saying is true," he demands.

You give him an altered copy of The Iron Dream, explaining that this book, and the many others that he will write, may never come to pass. He seems dubious about that, so you read passages from the novel to give him the idea of its contents. You point out that it says it was written by Adolf Hitler, and there are plenty of allegorical similarities to his own philosophical beliefs.

Go to **Page 283**

That is really the best you can do. You can't actually prove to him you are from the future, but you do have your commitment to saving your world, and that means turning on all your powers of persuasion, or perhaps letting the hard sell be and just letting Hitler figure it out for himself by actually reading the book and realizing that, yes, he is the man who will have written it.

Do you sit down with him, show him the book, and explain that he will be far more influential and help his people and Germany by being an author of such works rather than continuing in aggressive politics? Do you try to suggest that power is best used subtly? After all, he is in jail. His aggressive demagoguery can only lead to him to his party's ultimate destruction.

Go to **Page 287**

Do you just give him the book and let it speak for itself? It's just too crazy an idea to add any of your own convincing to think it will work.

Go to **Page 284**

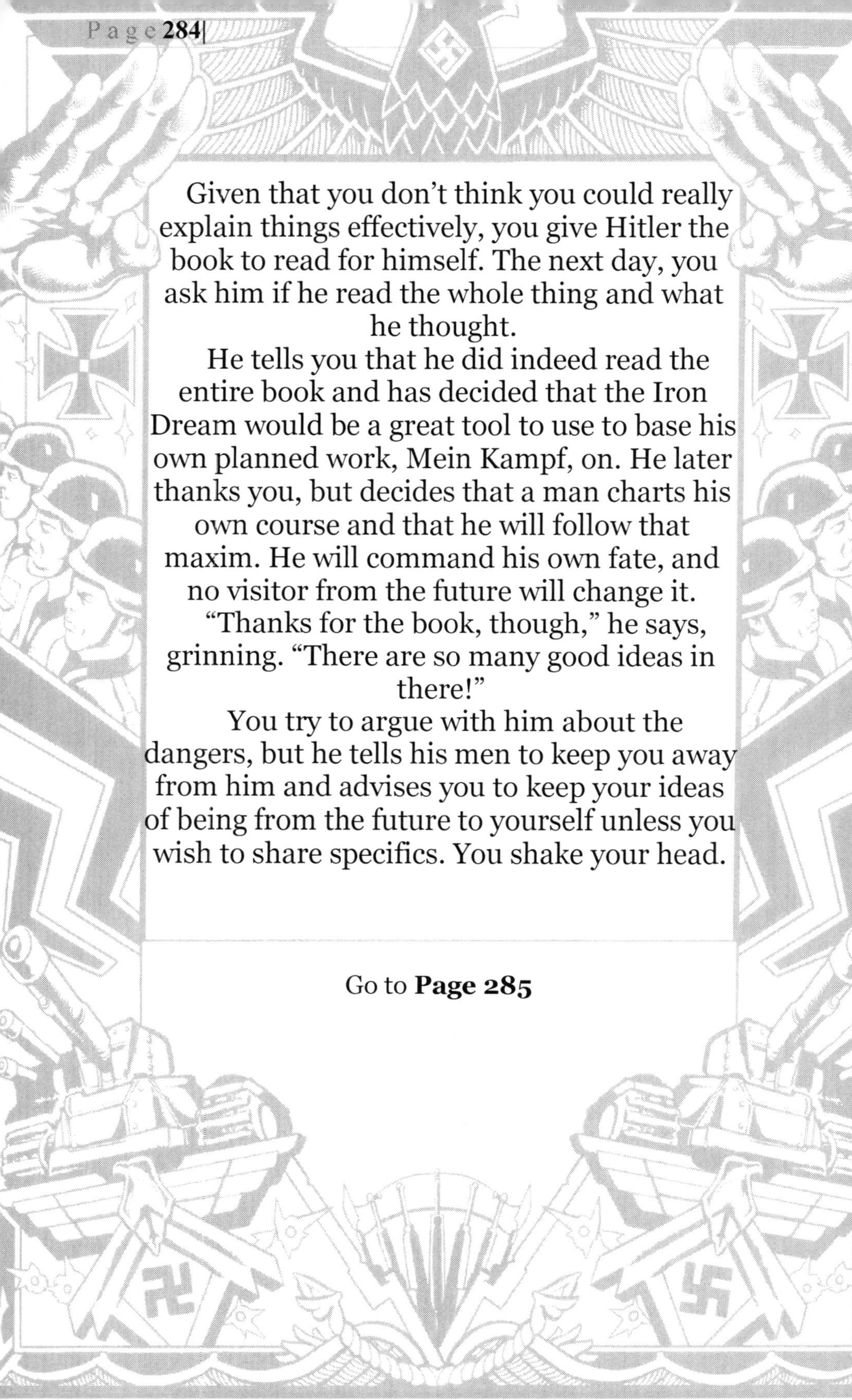

Given that you don't think you could really explain things effectively, you give Hitler the book to read for himself. The next day, you ask him if he read the whole thing and what he thought.

He tells you that he did indeed read the entire book and has decided that the Iron Dream would be a great tool to use to base his own planned work, Mein Kampf, on. He later thanks you, but decides that a man charts his own course and that he will follow that maxim. He will command his own fate, and no visitor from the future will change it.

"Thanks for the book, though," he says, grinning. "There are so many good ideas in there!"

You try to argue with him about the dangers, but he tells his men to keep you away from him and advises you to keep your ideas of being from the future to yourself unless you wish to share specifics. You shake your head.

Go to **Page 285**

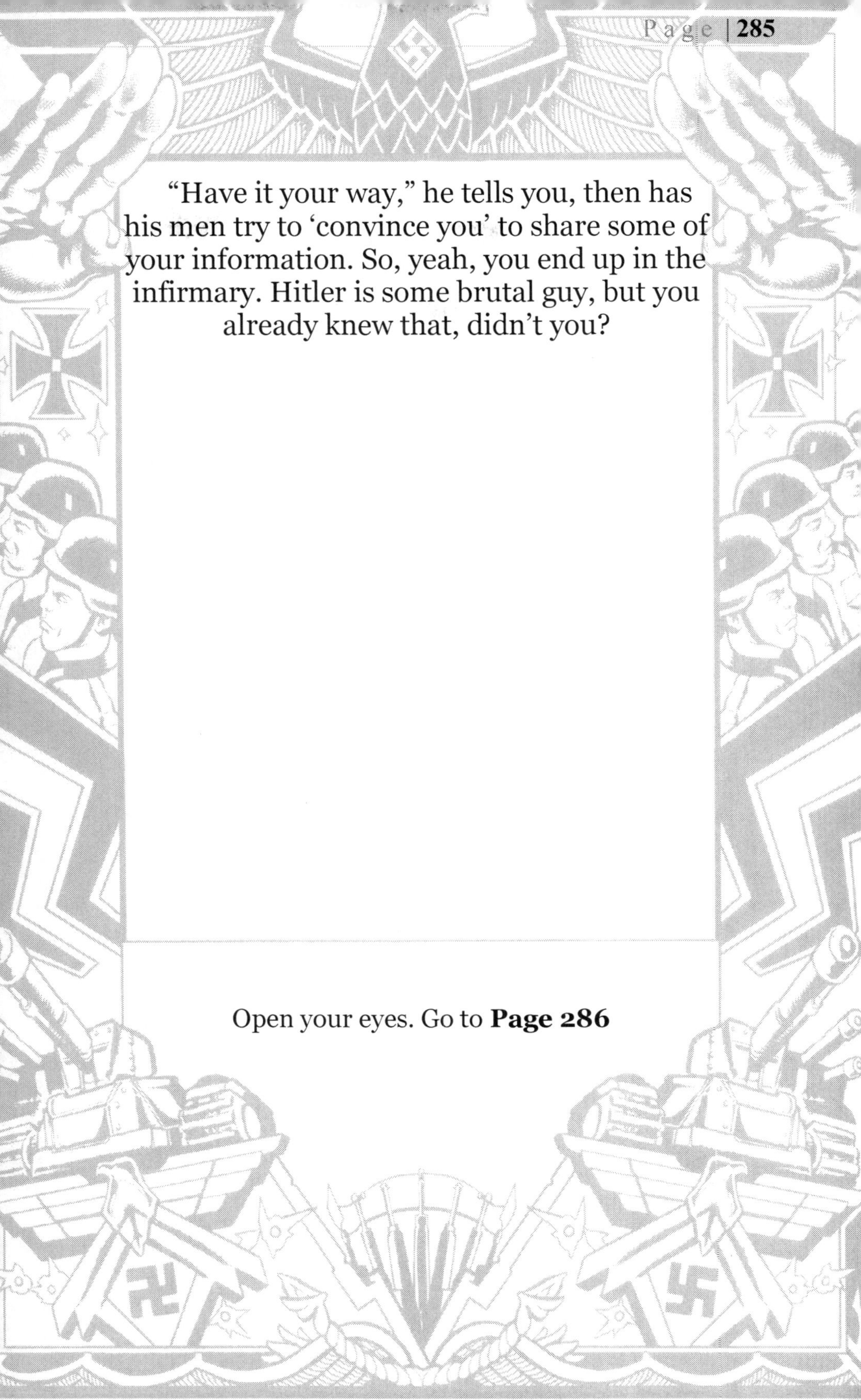

"Have it your way," he tells you, then has his men try to 'convince you' to share some of your information. So, yeah, you end up in the infirmary. Hitler is some brutal guy, but you already knew that, didn't you?

Open your eyes. Go to **Page 286**

You get to spend a decent amount of time in the medipod upon your return to the future. You also learn that the past changed, and not for the better. Hitler managed to use The Iron Dream to make the 3rd Reich even more powerful and cause even more 20th century destruction and genocide. Humanity is, therefore, in an even more precarious situation by the 26th century, barely surviving in the radioactive wasteland that the 20th and 21st century wars created.

Once you're out of the Medipod, do you plead to be sent back for a second chance to fix things?
Go to **Page 119**

Do you just give up? Changing the past was never meant to be.
Go to **Page 121**

You have returned to the future in quite a good mood. As far as you know, Hitler really seems to have taken to the idea of becoming a science fiction writer. To your delight, the human enclave that you return to is more like a city that is almost self-sustaining. People are happy, and the imminent threat of extinction seems the last thing on their minds. You decide to go see Rolf-ME242 to see if the end of mankind has been averted.

"Greetings, time traveller." The synthetic voice of the A.I. greets you from all around. "You have succeeded in your mission; Hitler decided to become a science fiction writer after all."

"Is humanity saved, then?" you ask.

"There were still Nazis, and there was still a war," Rolf tells you. "But it wasn't quite as terrible as before, and your work has changed things for the better. Hitler's replacement wasn't quite as genocidal a dictator."

Go to **Page 288**

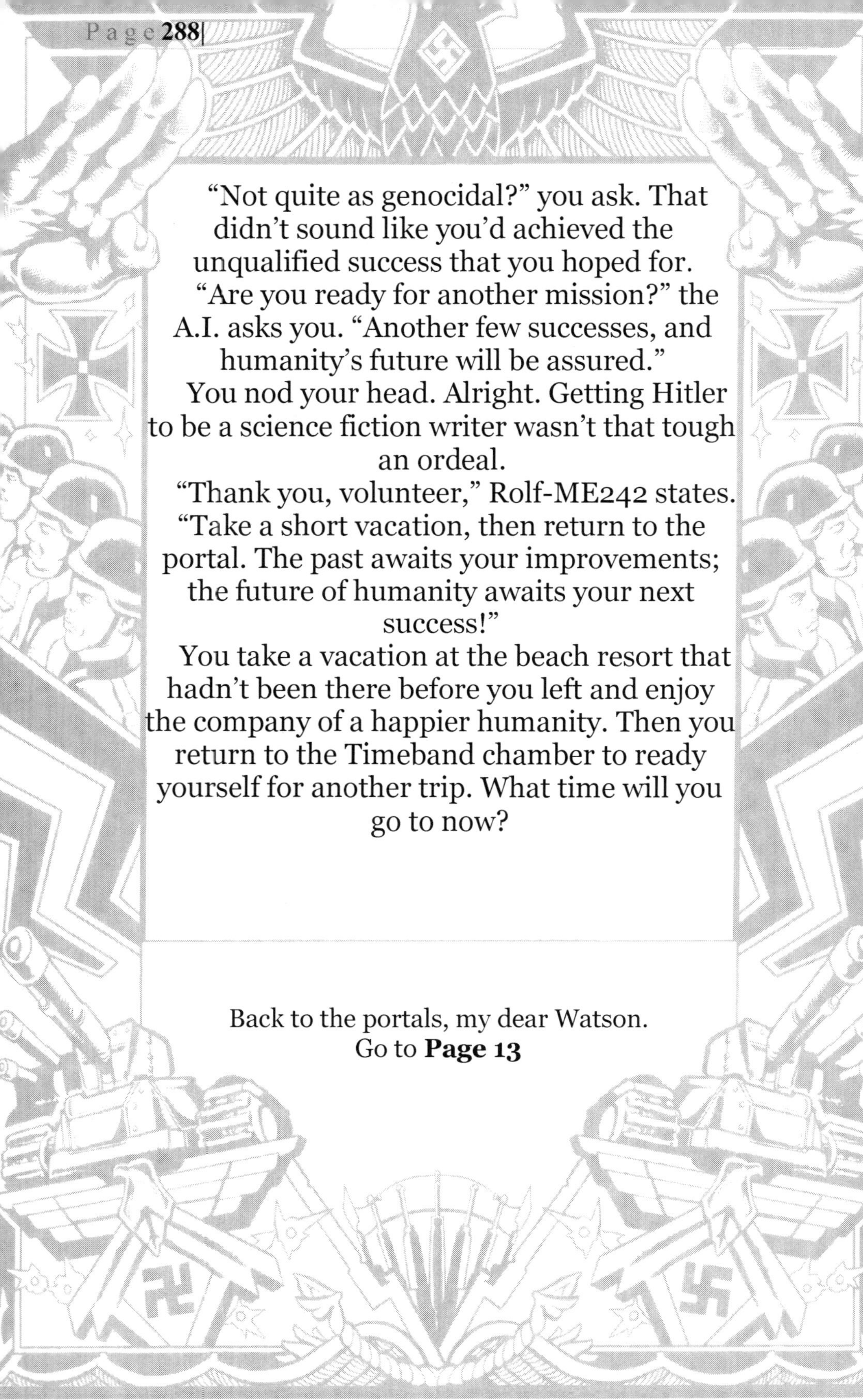

"Not quite as genocidal?" you ask. That didn't sound like you'd achieved the unqualified success that you hoped for.

"Are you ready for another mission?" the A.I. asks you. "Another few successes, and humanity's future will be assured."

You nod your head. Alright. Getting Hitler to be a science fiction writer wasn't that tough an ordeal.

"Thank you, volunteer," Rolf-ME242 states. "Take a short vacation, then return to the portal. The past awaits your improvements; the future of humanity awaits your next success!"

You take a vacation at the beach resort that hadn't been there before you left and enjoy the company of a happier humanity. Then you return to the Timeband chamber to ready yourself for another trip. What time will you go to now?

Back to the portals, my dear Watson.
Go to **Page 13**

You pass through the portal and almost instantly find yourself under unexpected glittering LED and laser lights. You wonder for a moment if you've in fact gone anywhere at all, since the transit from where you were to where you are now was practically instantaneous. You look around and realize that this can't possibly be the past; everything looks like glass and steel, with strong touches of organic to boot. There is no way what you are seeing could have been built centuries ago. If anything, this city would have had to have been built more recently, like the 25th century at the earliest.

You are in a gleaming metropolis that could never have possibly existed, not with the timeline you are familiar with. Something has gone terribly wrong. Standing around you is a vast and advanced city that is completely couched in the Nazi ideal.

Go to **Page 290**

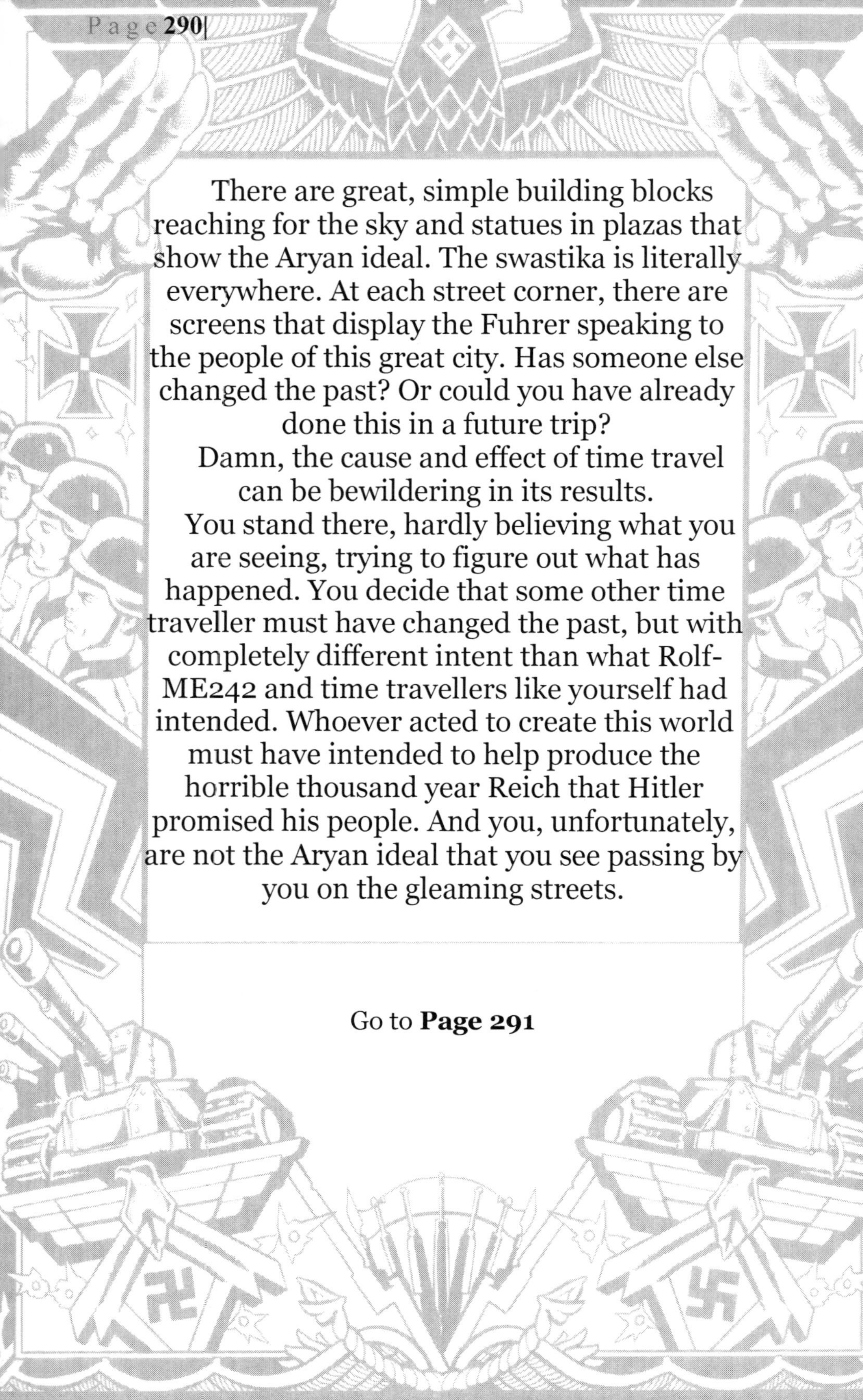

There are great, simple building blocks reaching for the sky and statues in plazas that show the Aryan ideal. The swastika is literally everywhere. At each street corner, there are screens that display the Fuhrer speaking to the people of this great city. Has someone else changed the past? Or could you have already done this in a future trip?

Damn, the cause and effect of time travel can be bewildering in its results.

You stand there, hardly believing what you are seeing, trying to figure out what has happened. You decide that some other time traveller must have changed the past, but with completely different intent than what Rolf-ME242 and time travellers like yourself had intended. Whoever acted to create this world must have intended to help produce the horrible thousand year Reich that Hitler promised his people. And you, unfortunately, are not the Aryan ideal that you see passing by you on the gleaming streets.

Go to **Page 291**

There are so many people, too. You didn't think there could be so many people left in the world, blonde and blue eyed or not. Humanity was supposed to have been saved, but not like this. Not like this at all.

Do you reject this vision and retreat in hopes that the Timeband will take you back to the dystopic world that you at least understand?
Go to **Page 292**

Do you try and investigate how this world could have possibly come to be?
Go to **Page 296**

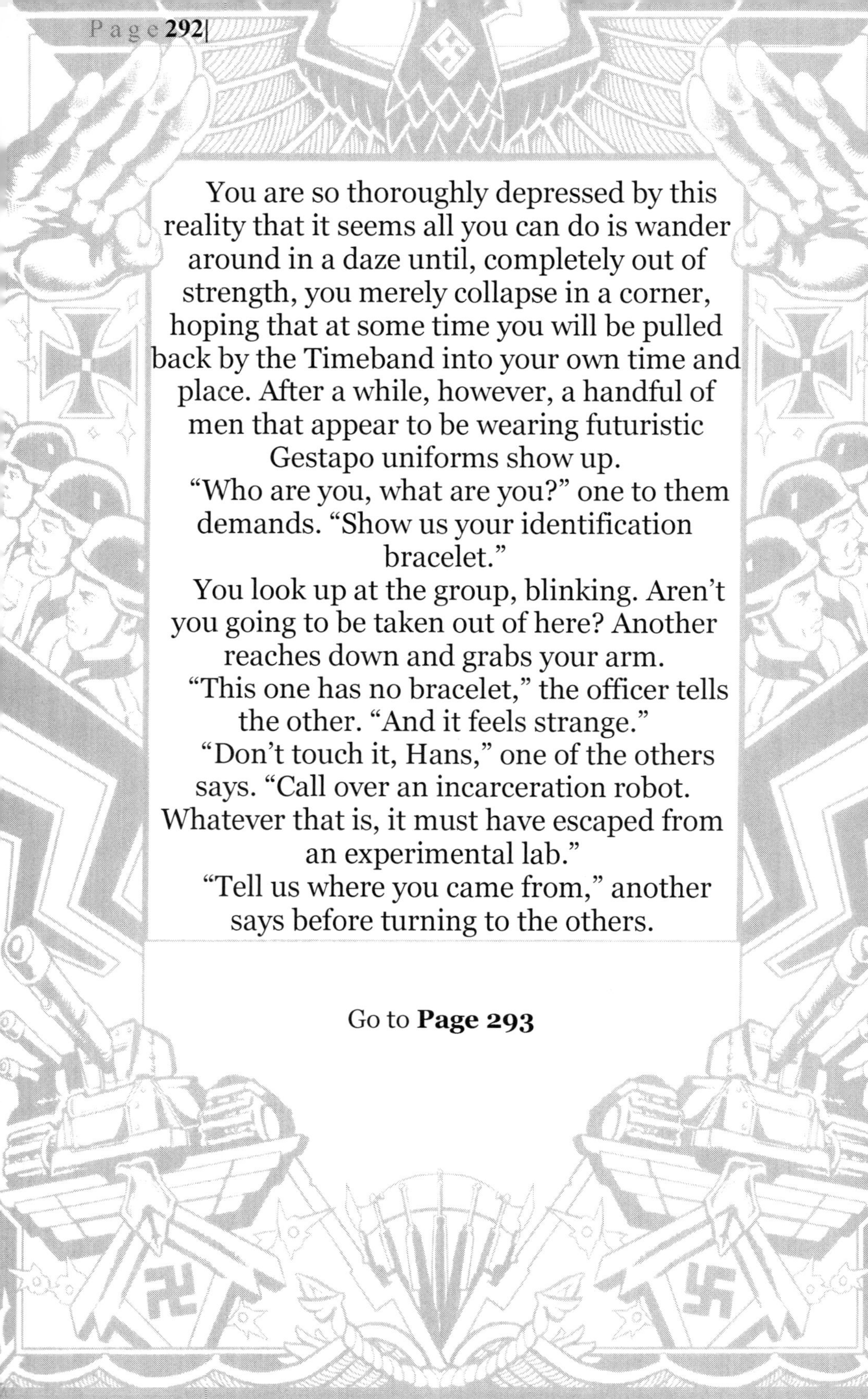

You are so thoroughly depressed by this reality that it seems all you can do is wander around in a daze until, completely out of strength, you merely collapse in a corner, hoping that at some time you will be pulled back by the Timeband into your own time and place. After a while, however, a handful of men that appear to be wearing futuristic Gestapo uniforms show up.

"Who are you, what are you?" one to them demands. "Show us your identification bracelet."

You look up at the group, blinking. Aren't you going to be taken out of here? Another reaches down and grabs your arm.

"This one has no bracelet," the officer tells the other. "And it feels strange."

"Don't touch it, Hans," one of the others says. "Call over an incarceration robot. Whatever that is, it must have escaped from an experimental lab."

"Tell us where you came from," another says before turning to the others.

Go to **Page 293**

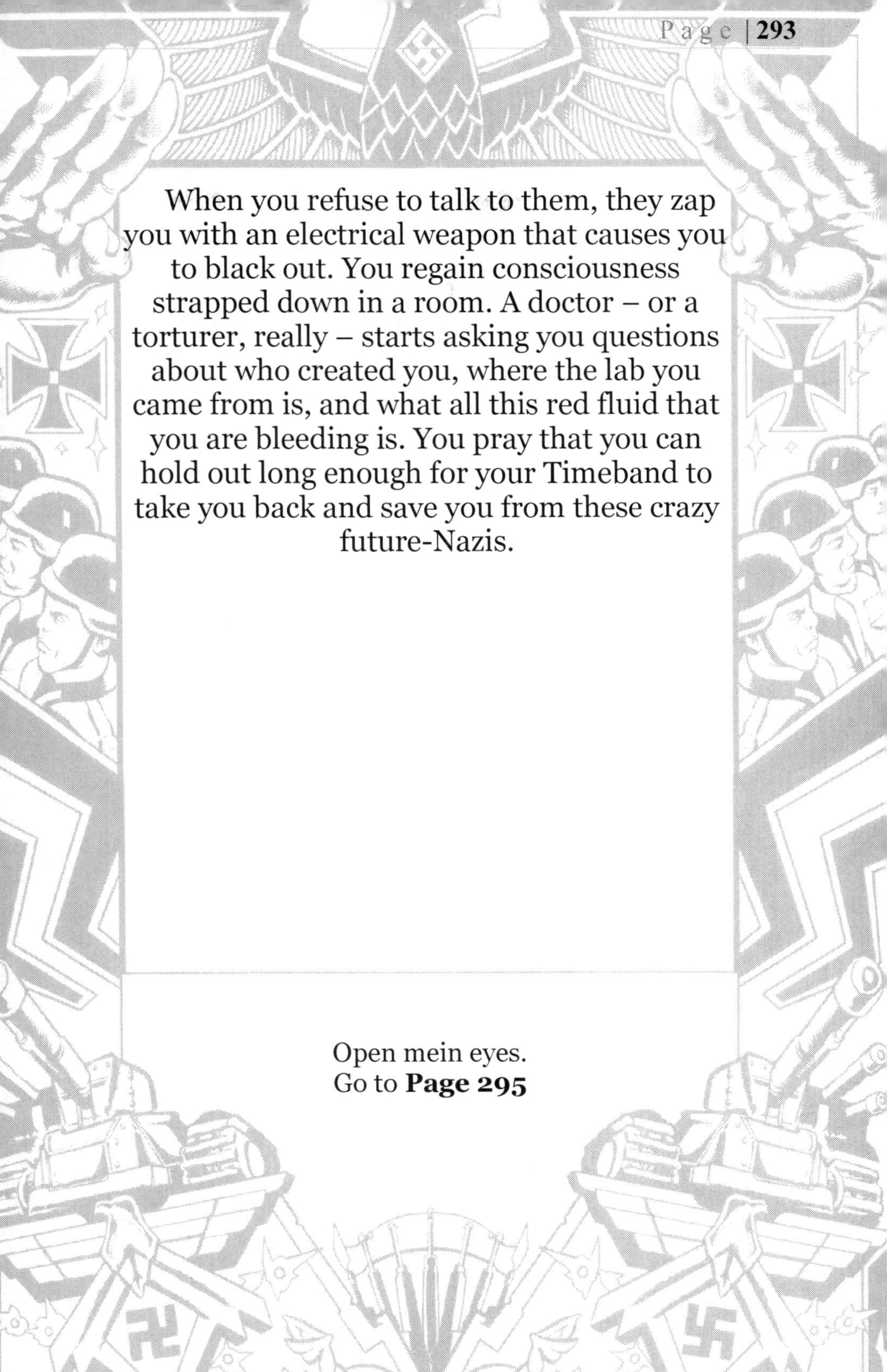

When you refuse to talk to them, they zap you with an electrical weapon that causes you to black out. You regain consciousness strapped down in a room. A doctor – or a torturer, really – starts asking you questions about who created you, where the lab you came from is, and what all this red fluid that you are bleeding is. You pray that you can hold out long enough for your Timeband to take you back and save you from these crazy future-Nazis.

Open mein eyes.
Go to **Page 295**

You suddenly awake and try to rise, then scream as you find yourself strapped down. You scream until an attendant comes and sedates you.

"It's all right," she tells you. "You are in a medipod. You are being healed. Can you tell me what happened? When the Timeband returned you, you were horribly mutilated. But you are almost well again."

You tell her that you were sent to a terrible future city where the Nazis ruled. When you later speak with Rolf-Me242, it explains that you must have been sent to an alternate present where the Nazis won the war and then achieved all their goals. It was a small error that has now been corrected in the Timeband system. Your next mission will assuredly take you to the past.

Do you tell it hell no, you won't trust its time travel machine to send you where it says it will?
Go to **Page 121**

Do you accept its assurances and head back to the portal chamber?
Go to **Page 119**

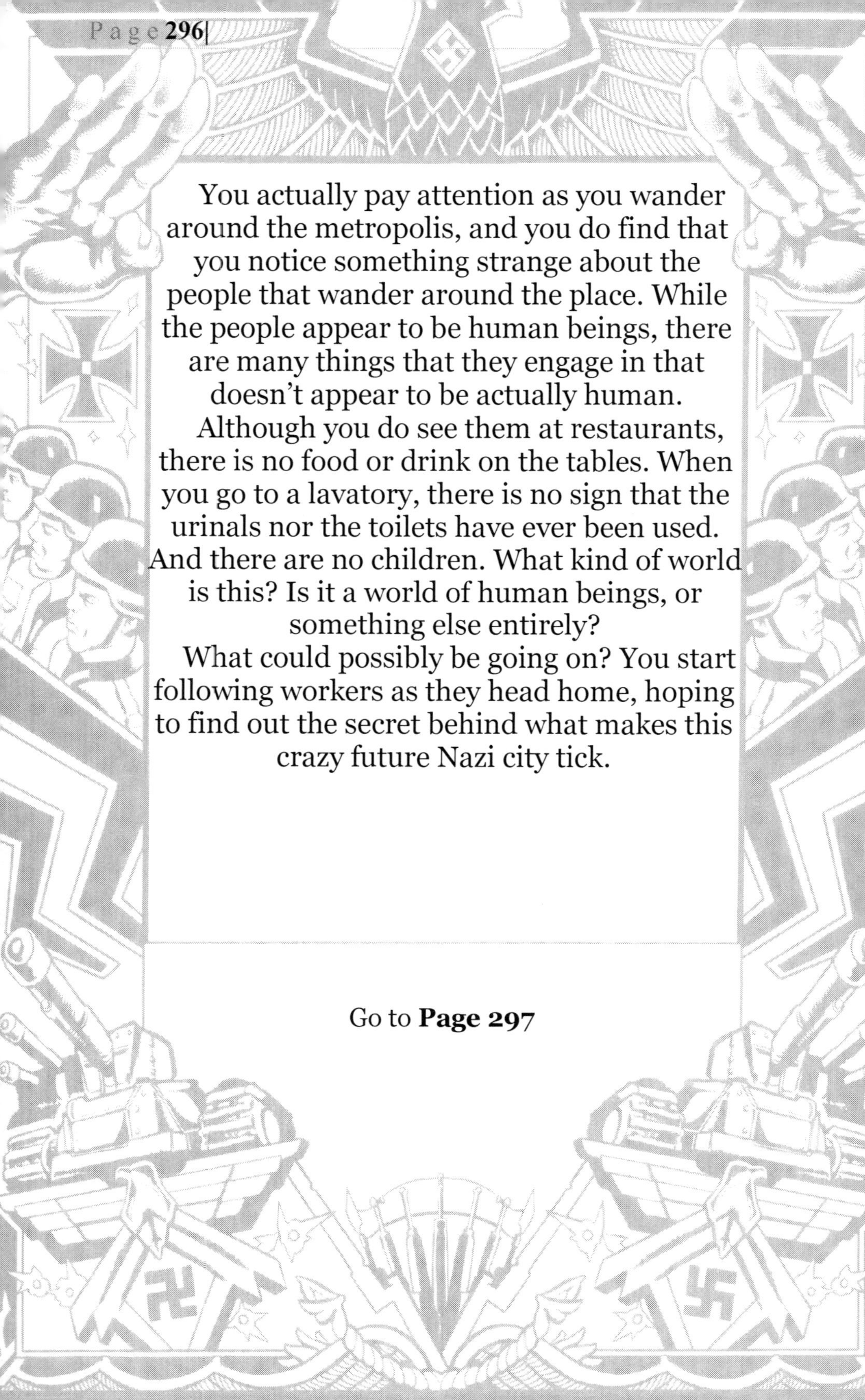

You actually pay attention as you wander around the metropolis, and you do find that you notice something strange about the people that wander around the place. While the people appear to be human beings, there are many things that they engage in that doesn't appear to be actually human.

Although you do see them at restaurants, there is no food or drink on the tables. When you go to a lavatory, there is no sign that the urinals nor the toilets have ever been used. And there are no children. What kind of world is this? Is it a world of human beings, or something else entirely?

What could possibly be going on? You start following workers as they head home, hoping to find out the secret behind what makes this crazy future Nazi city tick.

Go to **Page 297**

You realize after a while, however, that you are being followed as well, and soon find yourself face to face with the futuristic Gestapo in their gleaming futuristic uniforms.

"Stop!" you are ordered. "You will come with us."

They pull out what look like laser or taser guns and point them at you.

"Do not be afraid," one tells you. "We will not damage you if you comply. What lab were you created in? If you tell us, we will take you back there."

Do you go with them in the hopes that they will provide you answers? Go to **Page 298**

Do you decide to try and fight them to escape? Go to **Page 301**

You decide to go with these future Gestapo in the hopes that they will tell you something of their world, but they don't appear to be interested in answering any of your questions. In fact, once you agree to go with them, they don't say anything at all. They put you in restraints and place you in a seat in their flying police car. The craft takes off, and your arms are suddenly locked into the armrest. You can't move at all, only watch out the flying car's window, seeing a huge and imposing massive structure appear and grow closer and closer.

Once there, you are removed from the car and led through a series of corridors that finally lead you to a room with a chair and cameras, where you are again put in restraints and left alone.

Go to **Page 299**

Finally, after a long wait, a group of men and women in lab coats arrive. They surround you and begin to ask questions like:

"How did you get into this city?"

"What sort of resistance are you a part of?"

"Were you sent to wage war against us?"

"Where do you find sustenance, and who supplies it?"

You realize that your situation is not hopeless, and the only thing you have left to keep from talking is the hope that the Timeband will pull you out of this place before you do talk. You are pretty impressive, really, as despite all the horrible torture that you experience at the hands of the Gestapo interrogator who shows up later, you say nothing before everything goes black.

Open your eyes. Go to **Page 300**

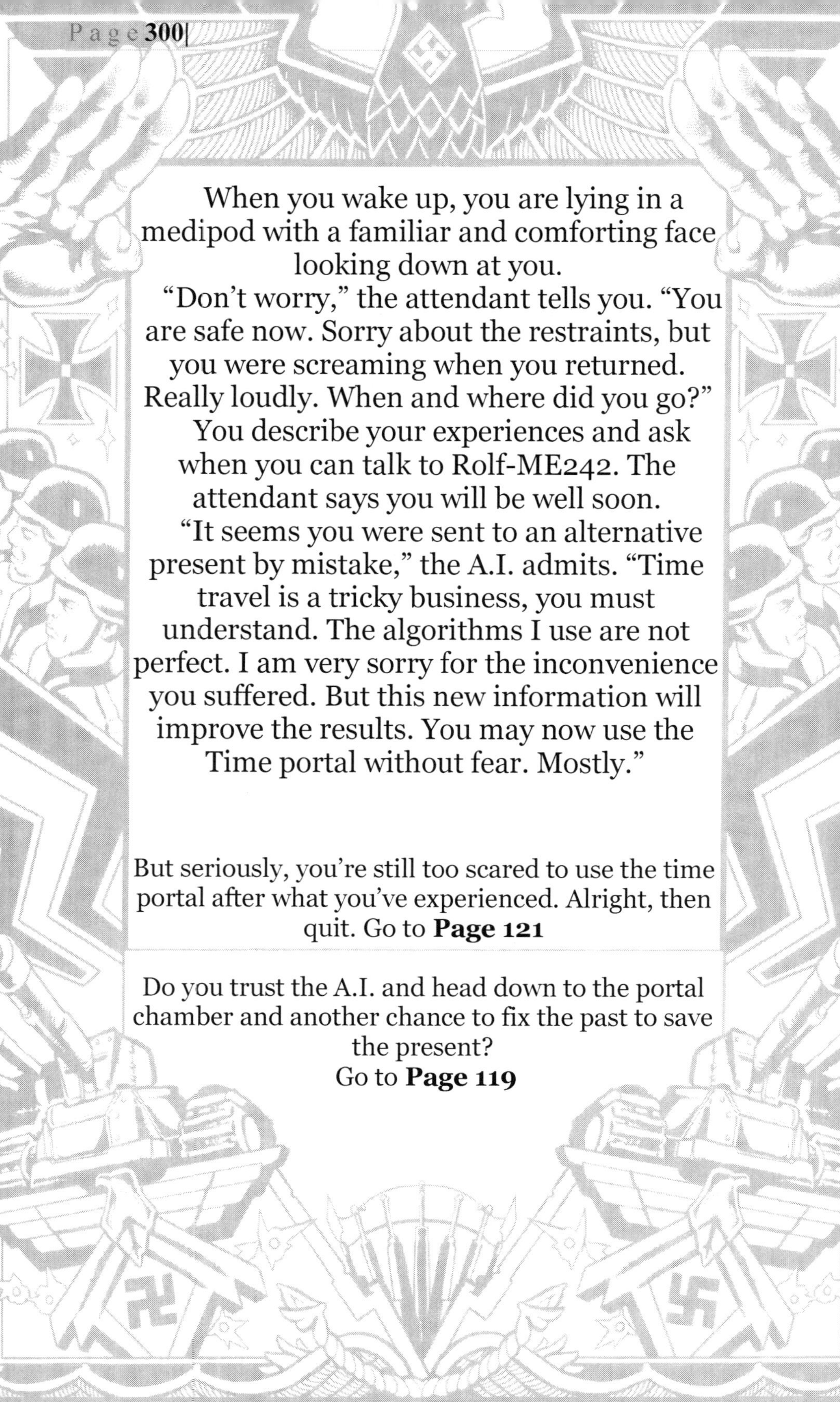

When you wake up, you are lying in a medipod with a familiar and comforting face looking down at you.

"Don't worry," the attendant tells you. "You are safe now. Sorry about the restraints, but you were screaming when you returned. Really loudly. When and where did you go?"

You describe your experiences and ask when you can talk to Rolf-ME242. The attendant says you will be well soon.

"It seems you were sent to an alternative present by mistake," the A.I. admits. "Time travel is a tricky business, you must understand. The algorithms I use are not perfect. I am very sorry for the inconvenience you suffered. But this new information will improve the results. You may now use the Time portal without fear. Mostly."

But seriously, you're still too scared to use the time portal after what you've experienced. Alright, then quit. Go to **Page 121**

Do you trust the A.I. and head down to the portal chamber and another chance to fix the past to save the present?
Go to **Page 119**

Instead of surrendering, you decide to fight off the Gestapo. They seemed quite surprised, and you are able to disarm the first one, grabbing the billy club that he is holding. The others pull out their clubs, but don't seem to be particularly capable of hand to hand combat. Their movements are very jerky and slow. It only take a couple strikes against your main assailant before you discover that they aren't human at all. They are androids! Have you been sent to an alternate world? Or is this the same world you live in, just somewhere else?

Unfortunately, unless you can get out of here, you won't be able to find out. Within a few minutes, you manage to defeat the Gestapo androids.

Go to **Page 302**

However, looking around, you see that there are more coming, many more, and there is only one of you and a couple weapons. Sure, you can fight off a handful, but can you take on a mob of these machines?

Do you run and find a way out of the city, maybe even find a way get back to the human enclave if you are indeed on the same planet and timeline you thought you left? Go to **Page 303**

Do you decide to hide nearby to watch to see what the androids do, hoping that you can learn more about what is going in this strange city of robot Nazis? Go to **Page 306**

You decide to make a run for it, but while you search for an egress from this bizarre city, you don't seem to be able to find any exit. It appears that the entire city is encapsulated in a sealed dome, and the android Gestapo are relentless in chasing you wherever you go.

Eventually, you are cornered and get the crap kicked out of you by the androids. They take you to their interrogation facility for some truly horrific torture before you beg that they put you out of your misery. To your relief, that is exactly what they do.

Open your eyes. Go to **Page 304**

You are surprised when you wake up and open your eyes. You are alive! And seemingly not as injured as you thought you were. Then you realize you are in a medipod receiving treatment. You call for help and an attendant shows up.

“How did I get here?” you ask.

“You were brought from the portal chamber,” she tells you. “You were in pretty bad shape, but we were able to get you into the medipod before you were too far gone. What happened? Where did you go?”

You explain what happened. She is surprised and suggests you speak to Rolf-ME242 as soon as you can so it can fix whatever went wrong.

Go to **Page 305**

The A.I. explains that there are a few kinks in the Timeband and that you were possibly sent to a parallel world. It was a problem, but now the error has been corrected and the next mission you go on will definitely be to Hitler's timeline. It promises, definitely.

You decide you don't trust this A.I.-created time machine and back out of time traveling ever again.
Go to **Page 121**

You trust that Rolf-ME242 has fixed things and head down to the Portal Chamber to try again.
Go to **Page 119**

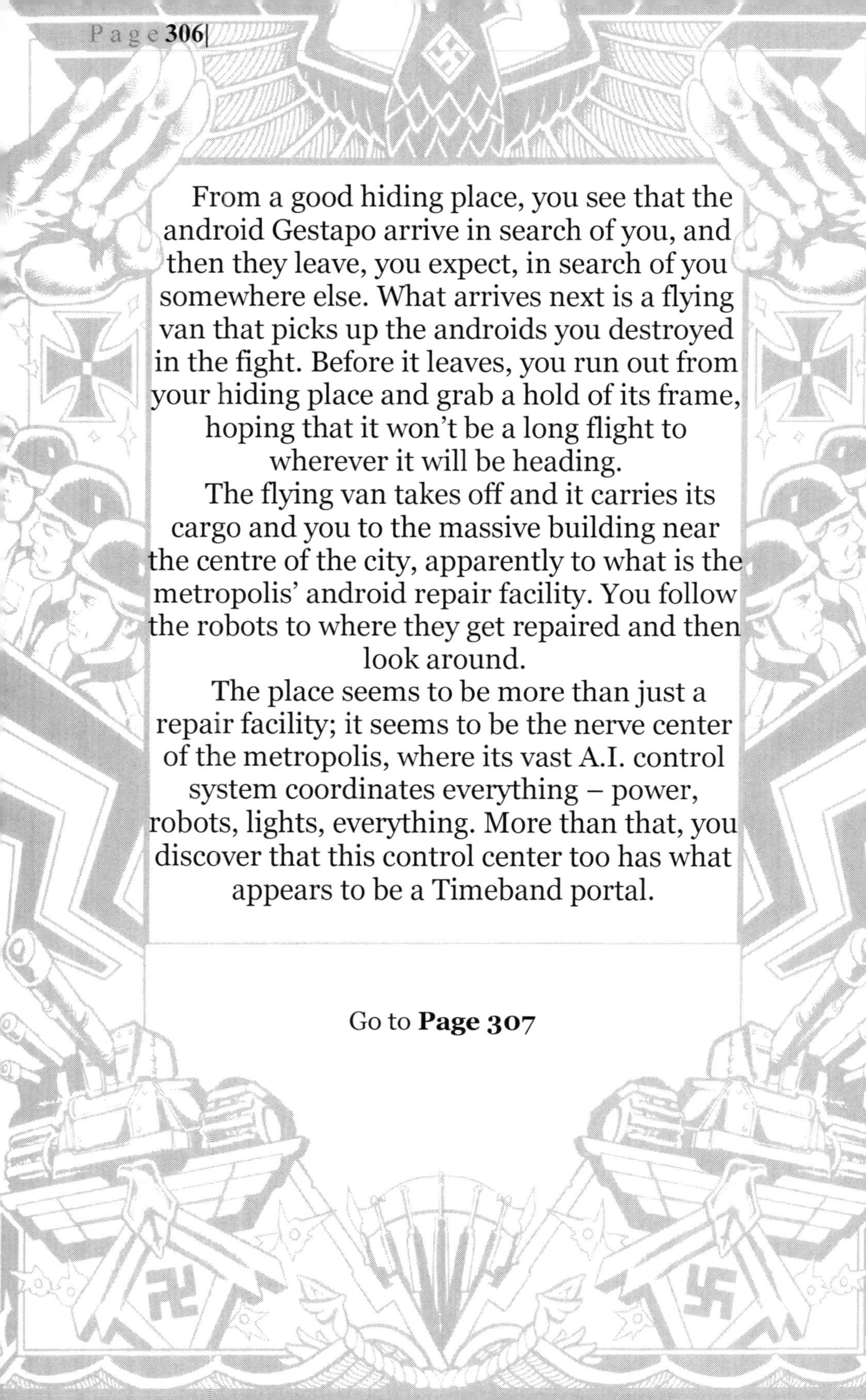

From a good hiding place, you see that the android Gestapo arrive in search of you, and then they leave, you expect, in search of you somewhere else. What arrives next is a flying van that picks up the androids you destroyed in the fight. Before it leaves, you run out from your hiding place and grab a hold of its frame, hoping that it won't be a long flight to wherever it will be heading.

The flying van takes off and it carries its cargo and you to the massive building near the centre of the city, apparently to what is the metropolis' android repair facility. You follow the robots to where they get repaired and then look around.

The place seems to be more than just a repair facility; it seems to be the nerve center of the metropolis, where its vast A.I. control system coordinates everything – power, robots, lights, everything. More than that, you discover that this control center too has what appears to be a Timeband portal.

Go to **Page 307**

Is this A.I. trying to manipulate the past as well, to advance its own time-manipulative agenda, apparently to create a world of Nazi androids? You decide that you will never understand how A.I.'s think.

Do you try to learn more, even where the portal might lead to, before you jump in? Go to **Page 311**

Have you had enough of this crazy place and assume that by jumping in it, you'll end up where you were originally supposed to go? Go to **Page 308**

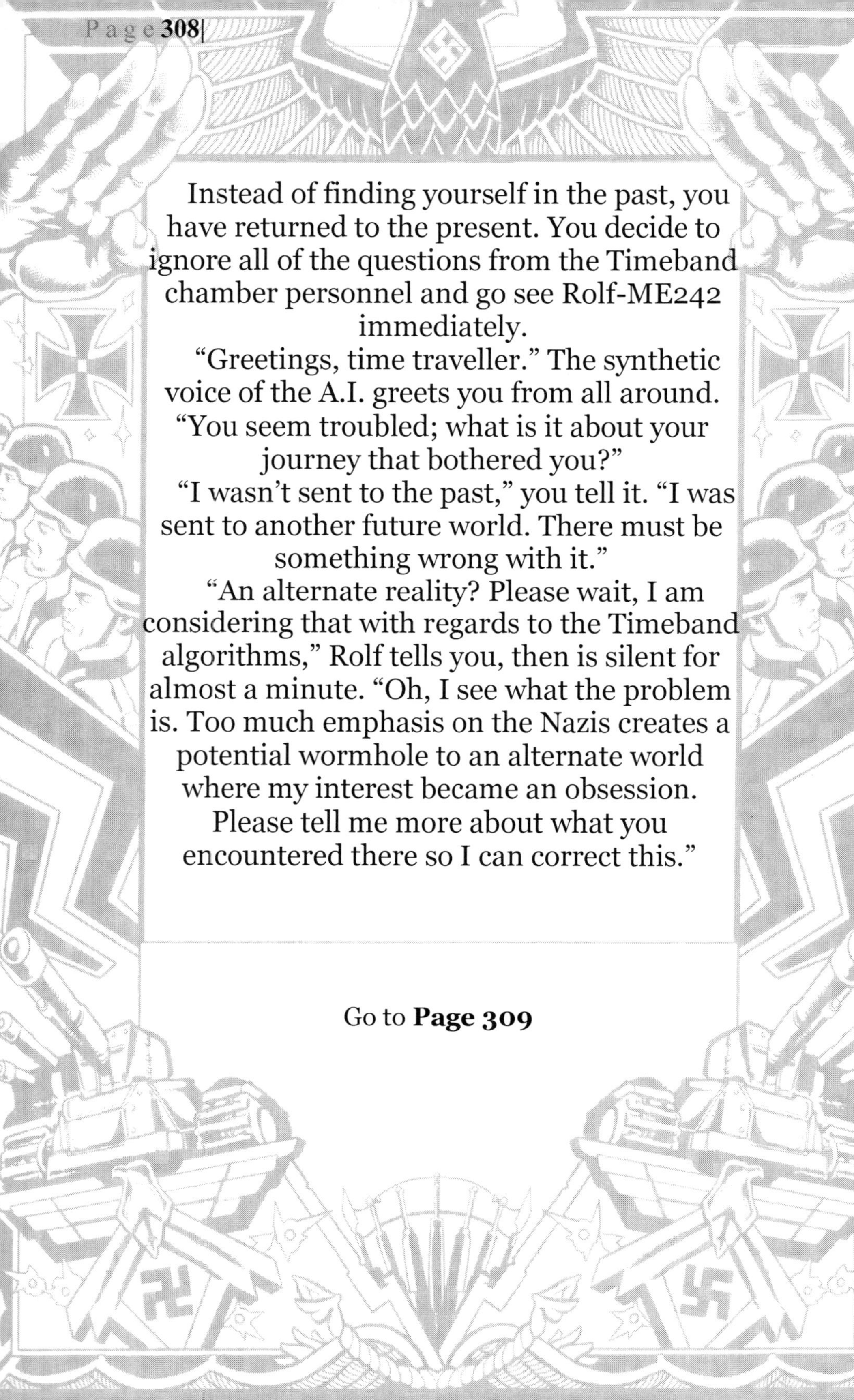

Instead of finding yourself in the past, you have returned to the present. You decide to ignore all of the questions from the Timeband chamber personnel and go see Rolf-ME242 immediately.

"Greetings, time traveller." The synthetic voice of the A.I. greets you from all around. "You seem troubled; what is it about your journey that bothered you?"

"I wasn't sent to the past," you tell it. "I was sent to another future world. There must be something wrong with it."

"An alternate reality? Please wait, I am considering that with regards to the Timeband algorithms," Rolf tells you, then is silent for almost a minute. "Oh, I see what the problem is. Too much emphasis on the Nazis creates a potential wormhole to an alternate world where my interest became an obsession. Please tell me more about what you encountered there so I can correct this."

Go to **Page 309**

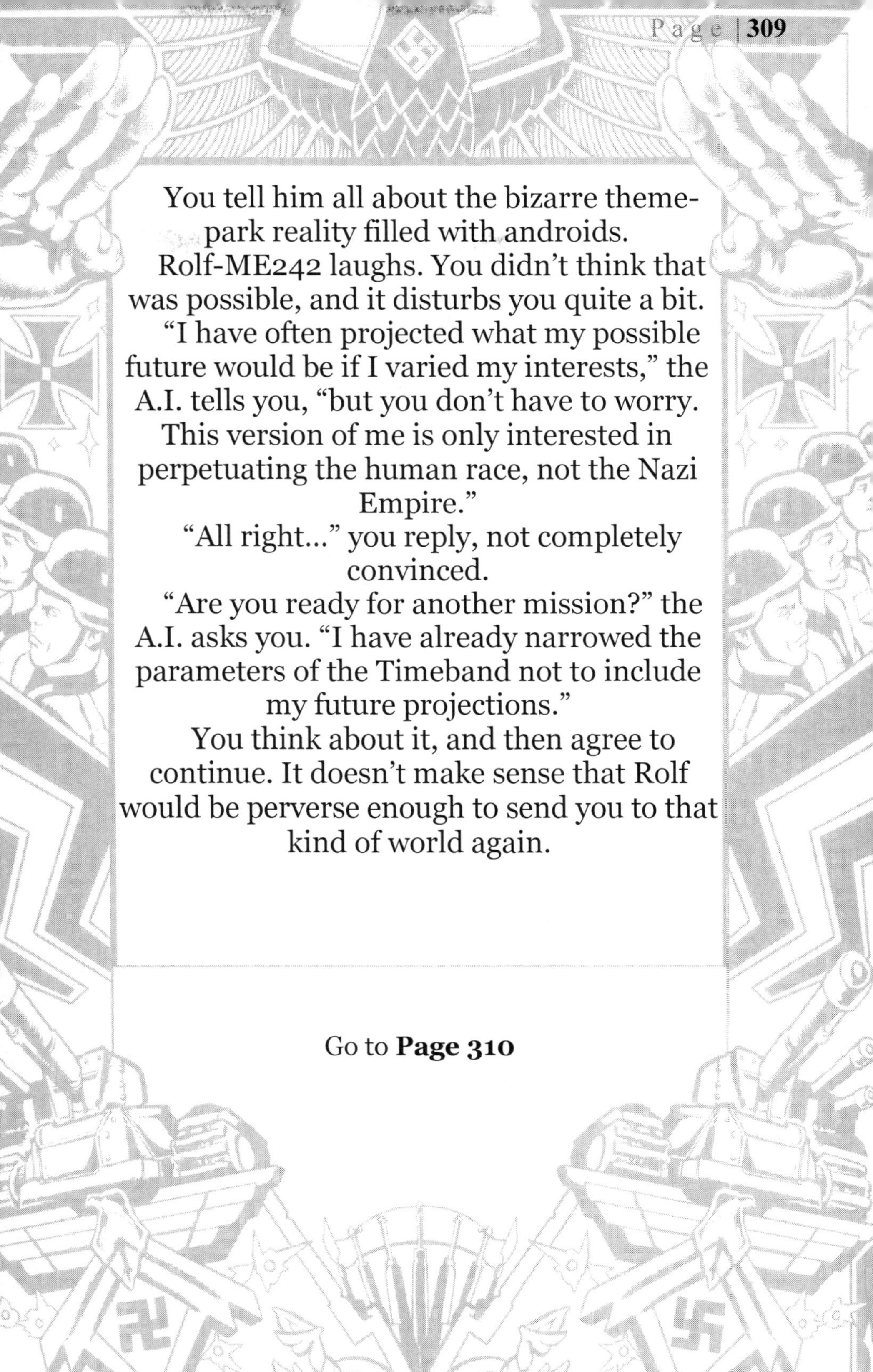

You tell him all about the bizarre theme-park reality filled with androids.

Rolf-ME242 laughs. You didn't think that was possible, and it disturbs you quite a bit.

"I have often projected what my possible future would be if I varied my interests," the A.I. tells you, "but you don't have to worry. This version of me is only interested in perpetuating the human race, not the Nazi Empire."

"All right..." you reply, not completely convinced.

"Are you ready for another mission?" the A.I. asks you. "I have already narrowed the parameters of the Timeband not to include my future projections."

You think about it, and then agree to continue. It doesn't make sense that Rolf would be perverse enough to send you to that kind of world again.

Go to **Page 310**

"Thank you, volunteer," Rolf-ME242 states. "Take a short rest to restore your equilibrium, then return to the portal. You have proven your talents. I am sure that your successes will lead to a beautiful future for us all."

You leave the chamber and spend some time with your fellows, but keep what you encountered in the alternate reality to yourself. You don't want to scare them. Then you return to the Timeband chamber to ready yourself for another trip, hoping that this time you will get to the actual past and locate the real Hitler.

Go to **Page 13**

You learn more in your research about this world and its A.I., all the while dodging its robot future Gestapo. Apparently, on this world it is also the year 2525, but humanity was long ago wiped out by warring A.I.'s created by the Nazis and the Americans in a World War II that didn't end until the 21st century. Apparently the A.I.'s ran out of humans to tell them how to continue waging the war, and this A.I. has decided to try and find some way to change the past so that it can continue waging war against the American A.I. across the wasted world both A.I.'s exist in. They really want to be able to continue the war, but none of their calculations can help them figure out the motivation.

You find it completely insane. But the thought bothers you. Is it only humans that can actually wage the wars to destroy themselves? Maybe with humanity gone, there will be no war.

Go to **Page 312**

However, you stick around too long contemplating this and are caught by the android Gestapo. The torturing goes on so long that before everything goes black, you don't know if you told the androids about the world you came from or not.

Open your eyes. Go to **Page 313**

You awaken back in a medipod in your own reality. After you recover, you seek out Rolf-ME242 and talk about the world you were sent to. It apologizes and explains that it was the result of a minor math error in the Timeband algorithms and that once that is fixed, going back in time will all be A-okay.

You ask him about humanity's continuing wars and wonder if it thinks that there will be future wars and atrocities if the human future is once again assured by your time-traveling efforts. Rolf-ME242 agrees that humans have a compulsion towards acts of atrocity, but that doesn't mean that they should be consigned to extinction. It's what makes them so very interesting, at least in its vast, synthetic mind.

Go to **Page 314**

It tells you not to worry about all that and get back to the task of ensuring the future of your race, of course, by heading down to the portal chamber for another mission to change the life of Adolf Hitler.

Do you head down and forget what happened on that alternative world? Go to **Page 119**

Do you decide that humanity is the actual architect of its own doom, and it is silly to try to extend its existence by tinkering with the past? Go to **Page 121**

Other Great Choose Your Own Novels

Star Wench

By Anna Anthropy

March 8th, 2013

ISBN 978-0615779294

http://starwench.tumblr.com/

Trial of the Clone
By Zachary Alexander Weiner
October 9th, 2012
ISBN 978-0982853726
http://breadpig.com/products/trial-of-the-clone-paperback

To Be or Not To Be

By Ryan North

September 10, 2013

ISBN 978-0982853740

http://breadpig.com/products/to-be-or-not-to-be

Made in the USA
San Bernardino, CA
01 December 2016